HUMAN PROGRESS

HOW OUR MODERN WAY OF LIFE
IN THE UNITED STATES
CAME TO BE

AND WHAT SUSTAINS IT

Brent Wahlquist

2024

For my grandchildren
And their children

TABLE OF CONTENTS

PREFACE

"Seek and Ye Shall Find". While the admonition in that quote comes to us in a spiritual context, it has universal application. It is what has led to virtually all inventions as well as scientific discoveries: our understanding of world and the universe. It is how knowledge, skills, understanding, and even wisdom are developed. It is how we find *Truth.*

In short, it is the key to Human Progress. It is how we humans got from clans of hunter/gatherers and subsistence farmers to modern life.

In the course of earning a PhD studying soil microbiology over 50 years ago, I learned to think analytically and look for cause and effect. While I have long been dismayed at the level of ignorance among policymakers and the general public about the critical roles of energy and materials in our lives, this effort really began after reading two books by Charles C. Mann, then adding that to all I was learning from many other sources (see *Acknowledgements*). All that broadened my concern to include our ignorance of human history – of how and why the way people live has changed so much – and the realization that there is a broader story here of how we humans got to our complex modern way of life that has apparently not been tied together in one place.

So, this is my attempt to, in a short but hopefully interesting and coherent way, tell that story. And that story is inextricably linked to the founding and development of the United States of America.

Since the historical facts presented here are not new or news to those historians and experts who have studied such things, I have not footnoted citations or provided an appendix. If you don't believe me, Google it, or check the sources in *Acknowledgments*. Any mistakes are my own.

This look at history is full of quotes. Those that are attributed to a named person are italicized and indented. Those in the body of the text without attribution to a named person are italicized and placed in quotation marks to make clear that these are things said by others, not me. My overriding goal is to tell the historical *Truth!* Worts and all. I then identify some issues I see facing society where choices yet to be made will impact a future that has yet to be written.

1: DOES HISTORY MATTER?

For most of us currently living in the United States of America (USA), we are living like no generation before us has ever lived. Yet, most of us understand little about how our modern way of life all fits together or even came to be. It just is. And somehow, all that enables our society to function just seems to happen quite smoothly (at least until COVID) without any centrally managed master plan as many of us contribute to, and are compensated for, some small part in all that is going on around us.

After work, we then go to our homes (most of which are larger, with fewer people living in each one than ever before) unless we already work from home via electronic connections. We get whatever we want to eat from the kitchen (which is larger, fancier, and used less), flip a switch or turn a dial (or tell Alexa) to make it warmer or cooler, lighter or darker, or entertain us with an endless variety of visual or audio options, or get other things we want. When the need arises, we go to one of our several bathrooms where hot and cold water is a touch away, and wastewater disappears down the drain without a thought about where the water comes from or where the wastewater goes. Whatever we need that is not at home, we just go to the store and buy it, with a charge or debit card, with no thought as to how all that endless variety of stuff (food, clothes, or whatever else we could possibly want) came to be or how it got to the store (most, maybe everything, even the wide variety of fresh fruits and vegetables, traveled over a thousand miles to get to that store). Or we order it online and have it delivered to our door. We set our garbage out, which is then hauled away to parts unknown. If we don't want to bother with fixing food, we can go out to eat at a wide range of options depending on our preferences and financial resources.

We interact with others through a wide variety of electronic media. In fact, virtually every aspect and minute of our lives is touched by electricity. We travel wherever we want by whatever means we can afford with little thought of all that needs to happen to provide and maintain the means of such travel and provide us with a wide selection of accommodations and services as we go. When we don't feel well, or something hurts, we can go to a wide variety of doctors, depending on our ailment, who can prescribe a zillion different kinds of pills or other medications for us. If we are suddenly very sick or injured, skilled EMTs will whisk us away to a hospital where a hundred different kinds of doctors and medical professionals will treat us or perform surgeries, depending on the need, and can even replace defunct organs with healthy ones from other people, or provide us with artificial joints or limbs if needed. When we get too old and feeble to take care of ourselves, we can go live somewhere that will provide us with all the assistance we need for daily life. With an endless amount of information just a click away, we live our lives with enormous freedoms and free time in a very open society full of opportunities and options in a human-constructed world with many of us having very little, if any, exposure to, or contact with, the natural environment. But how did all this happen? And at what cost? Is it sustainable? Should it be?

Since we now live like no generation before us has ever lived, let's look at how those British colonists in North America who declared their independence on July 4, 1776, lived, fed themselves, traveled, worked, communicated with each other, and died. It had far more in common with how the Greeks and Romans had lived two thousand years before than with how we live now. About 95% of those colonists were farmers, most living in small villages. There were no banks, nor was there a common currency. They had no electricity, cars, buses, trucks, trains, or paved roads. The only ways to travel (or move things and information) on land were to walk, ride a horse, or ride in something pulled by horses. Bridges were extremely rare. Thomas Jefferson complained that it took ten days to get from his home at Monticello to Philadelphia. Ships were powered by wind or men pulling oars. The only way to communicate with others was to talk face to face or write letters (using a feather quill pen).

Houses had no indoor plumbing or bathrooms. They had chamber pots and/or outhouses. Water was hauled in with buckets, and dirty water had to be hauled back out. Cooking was done bending over pots hung in the fireplace. There were no stoves, furnaces, or air conditioning. In most houses, windows were open spaces without glass that could be closed with solid shutters. Furniture, clothing, and everything else were all handmade, either at home or by local artisans in small shops using local materials, if possible, since anything that had to be hauled very far was quite expensive. There were no factories. Candles and oil lamps were the only light. Shoes and boots did not distinguish between left and right feet; they were interchangeable. Nearly every town and village had a blacksmith, cooper, wheelwright, cobbler, and tanner, along with a flourmill and sawmill. Public schools were rare. There were no EMTs, police, or any government social safety net. There were no dentists. Doctors often did more harm than good (still bled the sick), while hospitals were dangerous places, particularly to have a baby or for surgery, since doctors went from patient to patient with unwashed hands. Since a third of their children died before becoming adults and few reached old age, those colonists were constantly exposed to disease and death among family and friends. Their diet was limited and monotonous. They ate what they grew and sold any extra in the village.

There were no painkillers, supermarkets, drugstores, or refrigerators. Many were illiterate, while those who could afford it had private teachers if they could find one, usually a preacher or parson, who instructed them in Latin, math, natural science, and English grammar. Men consumed massive amounts of alcohol. Women's place was in the home, particularly the nursery. They were expected to be content with *"the tender and tranquil amusement of domestic life"* and were often married as young as fifteen. Yet few of those colonists would have been considered poor by the standards of the day. Single adults of either sex were rare and usually found themselves as servants or in service roles. And the list goes on. Nor was there any expectation that life would ever change. These conditions of their lives were no different than they had been for their parents or their grandparents. And they didn't expect conditions to be any different for their children or grandchildren. *"Experience forced on men's minds the conviction that what had ever been must ever be."* They believed that.

So, how did life end up changing so much in the last 200+ years? As one economics commentator put it: *"Modern humans first emerged about 100,000 years ago. For the next 99,800 years or so, nothing happened. Well not quite nothing. There were wars, political intrigue, the invention of agriculture – but none of that stuff had much effect on the quality of* *people's lives. Almost everyone lived on the modern equivalent of $400 to $600 a year, just above the subsistence level...Then – just a couple of hundred years ago – people started getting richer. And richer and richer still."* So, what enabled all that change and the increase in personal wealth and improved living conditions that we enjoy today?

How our modern way of life came to be is an incredible story. How the USA developed into what it is today is another incredible story. And these two stories, which are largely inextricably linked into a single story, full of highs and lows, strange twists, and common people doing uncommon things, both noble and ignoble, have given us an incredible gift. However, according to Pew research, there is an increasing level of ignorance of our history – about what happened to make life as we know it in the USA possible – as we now look toward an ever-changing future.

In a 2005 speech, the late historian, David McCullough, told of a college sophomore who came up to him after one of his campus speeches all excited because she had just learned from him that the original 13 colonies were only along the Atlantic Coast. How could a college sophomore not already know that? He has expressed his concern about our growing ignorance of history:

We have to get across the idea that we have to know who we were if we're to know who we are and where we're headed. This is essential. We have to value what our forebears...did for us, or we are not going to take it very seriously and it can slip away. If you don't care about it – if you've inherited some great work of art that is worth a fortune and you don't know that it's worth a fortune, you don't know it's a great work of art and you are not interested in it – you are going to lose it.

McCullough then said that our modern way of life:

that we take for granted – as we should never take for granted – are all the work of other people who went before us. And to be indifferent to that isn't just to be ignorant. It's to be rude. And ingratitude is a shabby failing. How can we not want to know about the people who have made it possible for us to live as we live, to have the freedoms we have?

He also pointed out that it is important for us to remember that nobody lived in the past. To be clear, Frederick Douglas, George Washington, Isaac Newton, or Queen Elizabeth – none of them went around thinking "T*his so exciting to get to walk around in these funny clothes while living in the past.*" Just like us, they lived in the present. In fact, everything that has ever happened happens in the present. But their present was vastly different from our present. And just as we don't know what is going to happen next, neither did they. Further, things didn't have to happen the way they happened. Actions have consequences. History could have gone off in any number of different directions, just as our own lives can. Had they done some things differently, we would be living in a drastically different world. They could not see into the future any better than we can and often did not understand how dramatically some of their actions would affect the world in which we now live.

It has been said that *"Planning for the future without an understanding of the past is like trying to plant cut flowers."* So, what is there in the history of the USA and of our modern way of life that we ought to know and understand if we are to avoid letting it all slip away? Accurate history is complicated and nuanced, like the people who lived it. Some important historical figures, like Columbus, can be easily viewed as heroes, villains, or both. The prevalent view of what is acceptable or unacceptable, or even right or wrong, good or evil, moral or immoral, can change over time and/or even between cultures living at the same time. Thus, the truth can only be understood if we understand the context in which historical events occurred. When we look at history, to be fair, we should keep in mind this caution expressed by Charles C. Mann:

It is always easy for those living in the present to feel superior to those who lived in the past.

The purpose of studying history is not so we can pass judgment and pat ourselves on the back about our superiority, technologically, morally, or otherwise. It is to learn what worked and what did not; what were the benefits and costs of what our predecessors did. The world we live in is the result of the decisions made and actions taken by them. It has also been said: *"We have all drawn from wells we did not dig and warmed ourselves by fires we did not light."* That is certainly true for all of us in our modern world, whatever race, continent, or culture our ancestors belonged to. If we are going to understand how we humans got to how we live today or pass judgment on the founding and founders of the USA, it should be done in the context of the larger world in which they lived, the issues they faced, and the result of their actions. *"By their fruits ye shall know them,"* whether those fruits are bitter or sweet, or sometimes both.

So, what are some questions that ought to be answered if we really want to understand how, in a challenging world, our modern way of life in the USA came to be?

Before 1800, other than a few traders, sailors, and nomadic tribes, very few people ever traveled more than 50 miles from the place where they were born. Of those who did, almost all never returned. Today, nearly everyone has traveled far more and moved far more. What changed?

In the 1400s, China was the wealthiest, most advanced, and most powerful nation on Earth economically, culturally, technologically, and militarily. China sent out large expeditions that sailed as far as Africa. Chinese ships had technical innovations like double hulls, airtight compartments, rustproof nails, and mechanical bilge pumps that Europe would not discover for another century or more. They had built the largest wooden ship that has ever been made (over 100 yards long). By comparison, the Spanish Armada had only about 130 ships, the largest being only about half as long as that large Chinese ship. China had built an enormous wall across its northern border and were even using paper money. Yet, by 1900, China was a backward nation economically, technologically, and militarily. What happened to them?

In the late 1400s, Europeans (Caucasians or whites) lived almost exclusively in Europe, which was a rather backward continent riddled by disease and famine among warring neighbor nations of diverse cultures and languages. After arriving a century before, the plague had killed over a third of its population. Societies were sharply stratified, with most countries having a small ruling elite that owned most land and resources. Most children were hard at work all day, every day, by the time they were eight years old. Few people were literate. Most rarely, if ever, took a bath. Nothing drew big crowds quite like public executions. Their diet was limited, while famine and malnutrition were common. In short, Europeans were a scraggly, smelly lot that were often hungry. Charles C. Mann posed a hypothetical question to seven experts (anthropologists, archeologists, historians) who were quite familiar with all that is known about both European culture in the late 1400s, and the Haudenosaunee (Iroquois) Indians (those then living in upstate New York) at that same time. He separately asked each of them, if they were living in 1492, which of these two groups would they rather be a part of? While some did not like the question, they all chose the Haudenosaunee Indians. Yet, by 1900, that Indian culture had all but disappeared while Europeans had spread themselves all over the world. In many areas outside Europe, Europeans were in control politically, militarily, technologically, and economically. In short, for better or worse, Europeans dominated the World by 1900. How did they do that?

In 1500, England had a total population of only about three million people, about half of what it had been when the plague arrived 150 years earlier. There were at least five different languages unique to the British Isles that were still spoken there. England was far behind most of Europe in science and technology. Following executions (which drew big crowds), heads were often cut off and put on spikes for public display in prominent spots (and would be for at least two more centuries). England had few ships and little sailing expertise. The future looked grim. Yet, by 1900, the sun never set on the British Empire, which included a third of the world's population. It was also the world's greatest economic and military force. How did that happen?

Slavery had been a part of human history for thousands of years within and among almost all cultures and races. In 1776, slavery was both legal and practiced throughout most of the world, including all of the Americas. By 1890, slavery was banned throughout the Americas (Brazil being the last in 1888), Europe, and much of the world (though government-sanctioned slavery still existed well into the twentieth century in some parts of Africa, Asia, and the Middle East). What happened? Had human nature suddenly changed, and mankind become much more moral? If so, why does human trafficking still exist worldwide, primarily related to the sex trade, across many races and ethnic groups? So, after being practiced for millennia worldwide in most cultures, why did legal slavery disappear so quickly across much of the world?

In 1798, a British economist, Thomas Robert Malthus, published a lengthy paper in which his main point was that mankind's ability to populate the Earth is greater than the Earth's ability to produce the food to sustain that population. Therefore, whatever mankind might do to increase the food supply will only lead to a population increase that will consume that food increase. So, humanity is doomed to always exist at the edge of starvation. This *Malthusian Trap* has been debated ever since. When he published that paper, there were less than a billion people living on Earth, while famine and malnutrition were quite common. The world population in 2022 hit eight billion, more than eight times larger than when Malthus first made his argument just 224 years before. As populations have soared, the percentage of malnourished has fallen. Hunger still exists, but only because of political and distribution problems. Current world food production is probably sufficient to feed ten billion people. Many of us now throw away or waste more food than ever before. How is that possible?

Today, it is hard to imagine Italy without tomatoes, Ireland, Germany, Russia, and much of the rest of Europe without potatoes, Belgium without chocolate, China and Southeast Asia without hot peppers and sweet potatoes, Africa without manioc (cassava), and sweet potatoes, or corn in Asia, Africa, and Europe. But they were not there in 1492. Where did they come from?

How did an isolated, brand-new, tiny nation of two and a half million British colonists scattered along the Atlantic Coast of North America even come to be? How, in just 200 years (by 1976), did that tiny new nation become the most powerful nation on Earth, militarily, economically, technologically, and culturally? Most new inventions occurred here. It led the world into building skyscrapers, building huge dams to harness floods and generate electricity, creating an electric grid and inventing new electronic communications systems and machines; building an atomic bomb then harnessing atomic energy to generate electricity; inventing flying, and then less than 66 years later, sending men to walk on the Moon and then bringing them safely home. It invented the modern home with all its conveniences. It invented telephones, then recorded music, radio, movies, and television, and the cultural industries that go with each. How could it do all that? And more? How did it become the most ethnically diverse nation on earth? Why does it continue to be the greatest draw for immigrants from all races and cultures the world has ever known? Almost all recent immigrants, particularly undocumented (illegal) immigrants risking life and all material possessions to try to get in, are non-white. In just the three years beginning with 2021, over seven million people from at least 145 countries illegally crossed our southern border. When Gallup asked people from around the world where they would immigrate to if they could go anywhere, most said the USA, three and half times more than the next most popular destination (Canada). Why are millions of people each year risking everything, including life itself, to try to get into the USA?

Wait, weren't there people already living here before immigrants started to arrive? The Americas were actually *full* of people before Europeans, Africans, and Asians started showing up. Who were they? What were they like? Why is there not a single country anywhere in the Americas that has indigenous Americans as its majority population? What happened to them?

Answering questions like these is important to understanding where we are and how we got here as we consider where we are going. History is generally presented in terms of nations, politics, and wars. Not so much here. After laying a tiny background on what I see as the forces that have shaped the development of civilizations, this look at history deals more with how people lived and with agents of change: the cause and effect of those people, events, ideas, materials, products, and forces, often unrecognized, that have played an outsized role, for better or worse, in reshaping the world over the last thousand years into what it is today, including the birth and development of the USA. Native Americans, or Indians (I generally use the term *Indians* since it is shorter and is used in

USA laws and structure), are also discussed, including a little on what they were like and what happened to them, since it is central to the rise of the USA. Ethnicity and bigotry based on ethnic differences, including race, are also discussed since racism is such a hot issue in the USA and the world today. Where facts are in dispute, I try to acknowledge that. I also draw some conclusions. However, I try to be clear when doing that.

2: EARLY CIVILIZATIONS

To begin to understand just how much the way people live has changed over time in the USA and throughout the world, we need to briefly consider just what we humans are like and then back up several thousand years to set a brief framework for just how civilizations occur and what the forces are that shape their development.

We humans are incredible creatures, both in body and mind. We are extremely bright and are capable of abstract thought, imagination, and planning. We are adept at forming and recognizing symbols, which, combined with our remarkable vocal skills, enable us to use specific sounds to represent various objects, activities, and abstractions, thus creating language. And language, any language, dramatically magnifies the ability of humans to communicate with each other, thus promoting group cohesion while facilitating the acquisition and sharing of experience and knowledge. We even create visible symbols to convert language into written form. Physically, we are upright when we walk and run. Our two eyes work together so we can see in 3-D. Our arms and hands are incredibly flexible. We have opposable thumbs so we can grip things. In short, the human body is a marvel. It is hard to imagine a better or more functional design.

We are also very social beings, naturally forming into groups. Parent-child and family bonds last a lifetime. We are capable of both tender love, care, and sacrifice for others and of vicious and brutal savagery against others. And we have free will to consciously choose how we will act and react: what we will *do* and *be*. Some of us believe we are created in the image of God and can choose between good and evil. Some do not, but recognize the need to choose acting for the common good over antisocial behavior. In any case, we humans have got to be among the most interesting critters, living on one of the most interesting planets, anywhere in the universe. I am grateful to exist here on this very beautiful planet at this very interesting time.

We humans are also extremely adaptable. Over millennia, we have spread out and covered most of the land on Earth from the tropics to the

Arctic, from deserts to jungles, and even some very remote islands across the Pacific Ocean.

ORIGINS OF HUMAN CIVILIZATIONS – It is commonly thought that humans began as clans of nomadic hunter/gatherers. In any case, early groups spent almost all their time on the four most basic needs for a group of humans to survive: 1) food, 2) water, 3) shelter, and 4) developing the next generation. There is also a spiritual need in us humans that has affected the development of civilizations. Meeting these basic needs required cooperation within, and loyalty to, the clan. The greatest threats to humans, individually and collectively in clans, were famine, disease, exposure to harsh weather, animal predators, and wars with other human groups. Shelters and fire played critical roles in protecting against these threats, particularly for their children. Fire gave light at night, warmed their shelters, and helped to protect them against predators and other threats.

As groups addressed their need for food, water, and shelter, they adjusted to what worked within their unique surroundings. More complex societies only developed where productivity increased: people, individually and/or as a group, getting more done in less time. Thus, they had time to do more than find food, water, and shelter so that society could become more complex. Increasing productivity and complexity depended on three things: **1) available materials, 2) energy, and 3) accumulated knowledge** passed from generation to generation and/or between groups.

To assist in their basic pursuits, all cultures developed various tools from the materials around them, like stone, clay, wood, and animal skins, fur, tissues, and bones. They made coverings, clubs, hammers, knives, containers, weapons, shelters, etc., to magnify the efficiency and productivity of the energy they expended in their labors. The better the tool, the more productive they could be with the same level of effort.

Their sources of energy were 1) the efforts of their muscles (individually and/or collectively – by cooperation or compulsion) and 2) fire. Fire did more than just provide warmth in their shelters and light at night. With fire, they could cook their food (making it easier to digest). Many also used fire to manage their landscape by clearing out vegetation and/or to assist in hunting game. While all cultures used fire, some also developed bellows and charcoal – partially burned wood that would then burn hotter and cleaner – that enabled other special uses requiring greater heat.

Any group's bank of accumulated knowledge included not only knowledge passed on from others but also those uniquely human but rare bursts of imagination, inspiration, or innovation that would suddenly expand the bank of accumulated knowledge available within the group. As cultures developed, some were far more open to innovation and change than others.

Then came the invention of farming (the Neolithic Revolution) with the development and refinement of domesticated crops. The one we know the most about began in the Middle East, where foraging societies grouped into permanent villages that learned to cultivate and breed the area's wild wheat and barley. Over the centuries, other food plants were added, along with hemp and flax for fabric. Animals were also domesticated and modified through breeding, beginning with sheep. Eventually, the wheel and metal tools were developed in this same area. Every European and Asian culture since, no matter how differently they turned out, sprang from these first farmers. As farming spread separately into Europe, Asia, and Africa, additional plants and animals, such as oats in Europe, rice and silkworms in Asia, and camels in the intervening deserts, were domesticated. There was also at least one Neolithic revolution in the Americas. More on that later.

Domesticated animals provided such things as meat, milk (and cheese and butter), eggs, leather, and wool. Some served as beasts of burden that eased peoples' workload and greatly increased their productivity (a new source of energy– the muscles of their domestic animals). However, providing for these animals required additional space and effort. But they were worth it. With the increase in productivity, not everyone needed to spend most of their time on food and shelter. Specialized skills and crafts developed. And with that came *economic activity*.

Economic Activity is the exchange of goods and services (commodities) between two or more parties for their mutual benefit. It enables various individuals to make different contributions to benefit themselves while also benefiting the group. Thus, economic activity is the engine that enables the development of any society more complex than Stone Age nomadic hunter/gatherer clans, resulting in urbanization and stationary civilizations. As societies got more complex, it usually led to stratified castes and classes and a ruling elite minority. With large stationary civilizations came public works projects, from roads to large buildings to pyramids. These projects required a large labor force (paid labor or slaves) fed by those more productive farmers.

A big challenge to urbanization and developing more complex societies was the increased need to move things, be it food, building materials, people, or other things. Thus, transportation costs were a major impediment to urbanization. Access to water was critical to life. Therefore, larger developments were near a water source. Somewhere, early on, people realized that putting things on rafts or boats that would float on water and then moving that raft or boat around was a whole lot easier than carrying things and/or people on land. Thus, people generally settled along rivers, lakes, or the ocean, while boat and ship development were part of early civilizations. Sails were also developed, in varying degrees of complexity, to use wind (a new source of energy) to move their boats and ships, further increasing productivity. Water could also be used for irrigation, greatly increasing the productivity and security of a food supply.

With the invention of the wheel and axle came the development of machines with movable parts, beginning with carts and wagons. These greatly lightened their workload by increasing the productivity achieved from the same amount of energy expended. Productivity was further increased when they used animals to power these machines, which enabled them to get much more done for their efforts. This gave them time to specialize further and then exchange the products of their labors with other specialists. The use of waterwheels (another new source of energy) to power machines dates back at least to the Romans. As specialists and artisans developed, some cultures, in addition to manipulating and shaping the materials around them like wood, leather, stone, clay, and bone, also developed new materials from their surrounding raw materials like ceramics, brick, linen, silk, cotton, wool, and metal (bronze, brass, iron, and even steel). Developing some of these new materials, like ceramics and metals, required hotter fires. Thus, they were only developed where bellows were used. While that required more effort in gathering and preparing fuel and then developing and maintaining hotter fires, an iron ax is 100 times more efficient at chopping down a tree than a stone ax.

The more sophisticated cultures developed some fixed form of exchange, such as metal coins, wampum, or other precious materials, to facilitate the exchange of commodities (materials, land, animals, products, services) among individuals and groups. This is what we now call money. John Steele Gordon provides an explanation of how money functions:

Money is a commodity, no different from pork bellies, legal services, or computer keyboards, except in one vital respect. Money, by definition, is a commodity universally acceptable in exchange for every other commodity. It is one of the seminal inventions of human economics. In a barter economy, someone wanting, say, to sell oranges and buy apples needs to find another trader who has apples and wants oranges. In an economy that uses money, the first trader can sell his oranges for money to anyone who wants oranges and use the money to buy apples from anyone who has apples for sale. This enormously increases the number of transactions that can take place in an economy. Thus, money functions economically in much the same way that a catalyst does in chemistry: it speeds up the reactions while remaining itself unchanged. Further, the value of all other commodities is expressed in terms of money.

Thus, the more effective a society's monetary system, the larger and more sophisticated its culture could become because an effective form of money greatly facilitates economic activity. Defining money in terms that would be generally accepted, whether through shells, stamped coins that authenticated its value, or paper currency, has been an essential element for any political body wanting recognition and respect internally or with outside groups. Islam was particularly quick to grasp this advantage, which aided its spread significantly.

A few large cultures developed a written language through visible marks, including symbols for counting things (numbers), that facilitated passing on an ever-expanding knowledge base to the next generation. However, written language requires something to write on and something to write with. Hmmm, whole new problems. Thus, written languages only developed where materials to write on and to write with were developed. However, a written language greatly facilitated passing on sufficient accumulated knowledge for complex civilizations to develop.

From that basic framework, it is amazing how dramatically different civilizations turned out after farming began and spread to other hunter/gather groups in Asia, the Middle East, Africa, Europe, the Americas, and around the world, as various peoples accumulated knowledge and made decisions in utilizing the materials and energy available to them.

Inevitably, conflicts arose between groups as they competed for space and materials. These conflicts led to a diversion of materials and energy into means for aggression and defense as groups fought and parleyed with each other. Wars, alliances, uneasy truces, domination, and subjugation resulted. The history of the world is often told in the context of human conflict between different groups, with ethnocentrism at the heart of many of those conflicts.

ETHNICITY, ETHNOCENTRISM, AND BIGOTRY – Humans are very social beings with a basic need to feel connected to others as part of a group. In fact, human survival depends on people functioning as groups. As groups of humans slowly spread across the earth, they encountered and successfully adapted to a wide variety of environments and habitats as they went. And as they adapted, they changed. Because travel was slow and limited, these changes became characteristics that distinguished one geographical group from the one in the next valley over the hill, as well as from other groups so far removed from them that there was no longer any contact. Thus, the further removed (in geographic space and/or in generational time), the greater the differences. These differences are what we now call ethnicity or ethnic differences. Ethnocentrism – having ethnicity as a central concern and/or the belief that one's own ethnic group is superior – is a very natural and universal human trait. It was important in group cohesion as various groups clashed with neighboring groups over land and resources. Thus, ethnocentrism includes bigotry and prejudice based on any ethnic factor. Historically, loyalty to one's own ethnic group (and resultant bigotry toward other groups) was seen as natural, expected, and as socially acceptable as family loyalty. And that remained true long after transportation improved and there began to be greater intermingling of different ethnic groups.

There is a tendency, apparently growing in the USA and the West, to look at bigotry based on various ethnic differences and call it all racism. But that is not only misleading; it is dangerous to societal cohesion in a modern multiethnic society. At least in English (the only language I know), ethnic characteristics or differences are now defined as race, religion, language, culture, tribe, and/or nationality. As we look at each of these differences, the smallest is tribe or clan. Then, if the tribe over the hill shapes their pots or cooks their food differently, that is culture. The more complexity and technical expertise found within a culture, the more apt its adherents are to see themselves as superior. Language is a noticeable difference that then extends to larger language groups with common roots. Cultures with a written language have always viewed themselves as far superior to those without a written language. Religion, how spiritual needs are addressed within a group, can be a huge ethnic difference, particularly when adherents to a religion see it as the divine *Truth* and all others as false. Nationality is a concept that has developed over the past few centuries as geographic boundaries began to be defined as nations.

Race is unique. Our current concepts of race didn't even exist 500 years ago. For over a thousand years, Europeans generally thought of Jews as a different race. The English thought of coal miners and the Irish as different races 500 years ago. Today, our understanding of race, unlike the rest of the ethnic differences discussed above that are all human constructs, is that it is genetically based – inherited traits that make us look different. Since racial differences, unlike other ethnic differences, are what we are born with and are unchangeable, feelings of racial superiority are vastly more destructive than feeling our food is better than yours. Racial bigotry has sometimes been incredibly intense, vicious, and destructive, as has religious bigotry. Within this framework, there will be more discussion of ethnicity and ethnocentrism (ethnic bigotry, including racism) as we go along.

THE GREEKS – The Greeks have had an enormous impact in the development of our modern world. There are a few things about the Greeks beyond the writings of their philosophers and their construction expertise that are instructive. Around 430 BC, the 27-year Peloponnesian War between Athens and Sparta was beginning. By that time, other conquered groups on the Greek peninsula west of Corinth provided all the needs of daily life for Spartans, the ruling minority, who devoted themselves to military power in support of their autocratic rulers who exercised enormous control over their citizens and conquered subjects. Among Spartans, only physically perfect infants were allowed to live. At age seven, Spartan boys were taken from their families and trained in military school until age 20. For the next ten years, they would live in military barracks as soldiers. While they could marry, they could only sneak out occasionally to visit their families. At age 30, they became full citizens but remained in military service until age 60.

On the other side, Athens had unified the eastern end of the peninsula east and north of Corinth and was the world's first recorded democracy. As such, it did not have to contend with an oppressed and discontented underclass. A citizen assembly governed it. All adult males (about 40,000) could attend, make proposals, debate, and vote in the assembly, which would meet at least 40 times a year. However, attendance rarely exceeded 6,000. These assemblies would make all policy decisions, foreign and domestic, military and civil. Thus, detailed decisions were debated before thousands of people before votes were taken on each proposal. It was majority rule. Athens had the world's most powerful navy and controlled the Aegean Sea. They had also established trade routes throughout the Mediterranean and onto the Black Sea.

In varying degrees, virtually every settlement on the Greek mainland and across its numerous islands was aligned with either Sparta or Athens. It was somewhat like a protection racket on both sides. Either you align with us and pay tribute for the privilege, or we will destroy you and take all you have. The only moral authority needed for conquering any weaker group was having the power to do it. Might made right, which is pretty much the same standard almost universally applied around the world throughout history. This has become known as the *Right of Conquest* and was a recognized principle of international order around the world until the creation of the *United Nations* after World War II. Thus, it has only been within my lifetime that this *Right of Conquest,* which was the foundation upon which empires throughout the world had always been built, has fallen completely into disrepute. While the longstanding practice of powerful nations or peoples moving in on weaker ones without an expectation of mass condemnation from other nations or peoples is at long last over, to now act as if it never existed, or was the creation of European colonialism since Columbus, is to rewrite history.

Shortly after the war began, the autocratic leaders of a settlement on the isle of Lesbos (across the Aegean Sea near the Turkish mainland) decided to switch allegiance from Athens to Sparta. Athens put down the rebellion, killed its leaders, and brought 1,000 prisoners of war back to Athens. There followed a lively debate before the citizens of Athens over what to do with the rest of the Settlement. The military leader who put down the revolt wanted to kill every adult male and sell all the women and children into slavery. Then, a counterproposal was put forward by a prominent citizen. His argument went like this. We should not let any feelings of compassion or charity affect our decision. Whatever punishment we inflict on them, even killing them all, they deserve no less. The key issue here is not what punishment they deserve but what is in our own best self-interest. Since it was their leaders and not the people who directed this revolt, would we not be better off letting them live aligned with us and paying heavy tribute? It means we will still receive continued tribute from them while letting our other allies see that, should any other ally waver in their commitment to us, they could reconsider and return without an expectation that they would be utterly destroyed and without us having to expend so much effort destroying them. His argument prevailed. Athens only killed their 1,000 prisoners of war and let the rest of the settlement remain an ally. Self-interest prevailed over vengeance.

The battles between Sparta and Athens had some remarkable rules of engagement. After each day's battle, whichever side felt it had won would put up a banner signifying victory. Then, the following day, there would be a truce during which each side would gather up their dead from the previous day's battle. Developing rules of engagement between warring groups was not unique to the Greeks. In fact, it has been a common practice worldwide and still is. However, when vastly different cultures, used to relying on vastly different rules and/or encountering vastly different and unimaginable weapons, went to war, the results could be unimaginably catastrophic for one side, while the prevailing side thought it was a fair fight.

THE ROMANS – As the Roman Empire expanded over several centuries, it was accomplished entirely through military conquest. Again, the only moral justification needed was that they could prevail. Conquest was usually followed by some level of plundering and then varying levels of occupation to collect regular tributes. Although the details varied considerably from place to place, that was the general pattern. Through conquests, generals gained status in Rome. The Roman Empire thus expanded into cultures, ethnic groups, and races far beyond Rome.

Rome's conquest and centuries of occupation of Gaul (France plus) and much of England had world-changing consequences. Why? They brought with them not only a written language and an alphabet to Western Europe but also the very concept of a written language that, along with that alphabet, then slowly spread to Europe's own languages. Later, they also brought Christianity, which eventually spread Judeo-Christian values across Europe, as its priests and monks became the keepers of written languages after the Roman occupation collapsed. If Rome had never occupied Gaul and England, it is impossible to know if or when any form of written language would have come to Western Europe. Without Christianity, neither the Crusades nor what we now think of as the *West* would have ever happened. Thus, these two things brought by the Romans have dramatically altered the history of Europe and the entire world. Without Rome's colonization of Western Europe, today's world would be vastly different. In retrospect, while being conquered and then subjugated for a few centuries by Rome was a terrible time for those who endured it, the permanent benefits to their descendants were dramatic.

Roman government was more complex than in Athens. For centuries it was a republic with a representative Senate, an executive, and a tribunal system that adjudicated compliance with Roman law. In short, Rome was governed by the rule of law – sort of. Then, it was ruled by Emperors. For much of the time, a person did not need to be Italian to be a Roman citizen. Anyone freeborn within the Empire was a citizen. Citizenship could also be earned or bought.

Among the most remarkable technical advances of the Romans were their structural engineering abilities and their development and use of cement to make concrete structures. They created colosseums, huge unsupported domes (the Pantheon), elevated aqueducts, and other structures that have stood for two thousand years. However, the use of cement then lapsed for over a thousand years.

In the last decade, reports have come out on research into how the Romans made such enduring concrete structures without using any reinforcement steel (rebar) as is used now in virtually all concrete construction. It turns out that the Romans poured their concrete while hot with a mixture that left granules of lime scattered throughout as it cooled and hardened. Then, as any cracks would start to form in the future, water would seep into those cracks, dissolve some of the lime granules along those cracks, and, within a few days, the cracks would self-heal so that the structure was again solid concrete.

As with the Greeks, slavery was common throughout the Roman Empire. It was an equal opportunity practice in that there were slaves of all ages, sexes, cultures, and races. Slaves played a major role in the construction of Rome's many public works projects, from large buildings and public baths to highways and aqueducts. Slave servants were also crucial to the lifestyle of the upper classes. The general aspiration of slaves was not the elimination of slavery, an unimaginable goal at that time, but to gain their individual freedom and someday maybe even have slaves of their own. And this happened often enough to help keep slaves compliant.

3: THE IMPACT OF THE CRUSADES

It is hard for us to grasp what life was like a thousand years ago. How we humans lived in 1024 anywhere in the world was dramatically different from how we live today, even in today's least developed countries. By then, Constantinople (now Istanbul) was the capital of what remained of the Roman Empire (Rome had fallen centuries before) and was the largest city in Europe (and still is). By then, there were also other intellectual and cultural centers in the world, including China, India, Islam, Inka, and the Aztecs.

Life was challenging for everyone everywhere, including the ruling elites. Compared to life in 1776, as described above, it was more primitive and less structured in 1024 (the invention and spread of the chimney in Europe in the intervening years was a major difference in daily life there).

World population was probably about 300 million (about 4% of what it is today). Only about half, maybe less, lived in cultures with a written language. Even there, almost all were illiterate. Food didn't travel far, so diets were limited, while many were often hungry. Malnutrition and famines were common. Women had many children. But child mortality was high (a third died before their first birthday and another third before reaching adulthood), and old age was rare. Death was constantly at the door among family and friends. Slavery was a common part of most societies across the world. Life was hard.

The Crusades were a series of military campaigns by European Christians to retake control of Jerusalem from Islam and then maintain that control. They began in 1096 and lasted for almost 200 years.

The significance here is not the battles but that the Europeans, who sometimes stayed for years, were exposed to ideas and things they did not have back home that altered the course of world history. The Moors' colonization of Spain and their recapture by Christians late in the Crusades also played a role in this exchange. Here, we will address six items that have proved critical to how and why the world has changed so much over the last thousand years.

THE CONCEPT OF ZERO – For millennia, people had been counting things. Different cultures developed different counting systems as part of their language. In doing so, all systems began with their word or symbol for one or 1, then two or 2, etc.

Roman numerals were the most prevalent form of numbers in Europe when the Crusades began. It is a system based on five, with a different alphabetical letter used for 5, 10, 50, 100, 500, and 1,000. It is a cumbersome system just to write a number. Try to add or subtract two Roman Numerals. Or try to multiply or divide them. It is impossible. And there is no zero. Nor are there any fractions or decimal points.

Around 650 A.D., a mathematician in India came up with the idea of zero. That is, to count apples, the first number is not one, but zero, for no apples: then one for the first apple, and so on. The discovery of zero has been called *"one of the greatest single accomplishments of the human race."* It was a *"turning point in mathematics, science, and technology."*

About a century later, as Islam was spreading east, Arabs came across this concept and incorporated it into their symbols for numbers, which gave them ten number symbols, zero through nine, similar to the symbols we use today. The system then started over with a one and a zero to make ten, etc. Just adding a zero to the right of any number increased its size tenfold. Adding and subtracting numbers was suddenly simple. Even a child could learn to multiply and divide, which also produced decimal points and fractions. Our modern system of numbers and arithmetic was born.

By the time of the Crusades, Islam was at its heights concerning intellectual and scientific pursuits and was far ahead of Europe. However, during the thirteenth century, for reasons unrelated to the Crusades, education within Islam shifted to much more emphasis on religious training and less on secular knowledge. Although they had already invented algebra by then, scientific and technological progress within Islam largely came to a halt.

From interaction with Muslims during the Crusades, this new method of counting, using Arabic symbols, began to show up in Europe around 1200 A.D. Merchants loved this new simple system because it not only greatly simplified their record keeping but the concept of zero revolutionized how to balance their account books.

This new numbering system, including zero, enabled the invention of double-entry bookkeeping in Italy in the fourteenth century. That new method of bookkeeping is still a bedrock principle of accounting today and is the foundation for the free-market capitalism that would follow.

Still, nations and the Catholic Church initially hated this new numbering system, probably because it came from Islam. Some nations even banned its use. However, the advantages were so overwhelming that this new numbering system was in broad use across Europe by 1400.

While some mathematical concepts, such as geometry, had been used by the Greeks, Romans, and Chinese for over a thousand years, this new numbering system greatly facilitated all branches of mathematics. Around 1600, Galileo insisted that the Book of Nature was written in the language of mathematics. That changed natural philosophy from a verbal qualitative account to one based on mathematics. With Galileo, experimentation became a recognized method for discovering facts about nature.

However, the Catholic Inquisition broke his spirit and forced him to recant one of his strongest convictions: that the earth revolves around the sun, not the other way around. With that, scientific and technical progress ended in Italy and moved north into protestant Europe, where it flourished.

Isaac Newton later brought the new field of calculus. None of that, or the whole fields of engineering, structural design, nautical navigation, statistics, accounting, economics, and much of science as we know them today, would have been possible without zero. In short, Europe borrowed zero and the Arabic number system, then ran with it such that their level of accumulated knowledge began to expand almost exponentially.

I would note here that since mathematics, as now taught around the world, is based on an arithmetic system that comes from India and Islam, expecting kids to learn how to get the one right answer is not racist, nor is it promoting a white supremacy culture. Instead, it has been critical in the development of the modern world and is essential to its maintenance and progress. I would not want to ride in a plane or in a car across a bridge if any of those were designed by someone who was taught that there is not just one right answer when doing math.

PAPER – If a civilization is going to develop a written language, it needs something to write on. Going back a few thousand years, various groups were using stone, metal, and ceramics. Papyrus, made from the stems of the *Papyrus* plant, a reedy plant found in Egypt, goes back at least as far as the pyramids. It could be made into long sheets that could be rolled up in scrolls, as in the Dead Sea Scrolls. Parchment, made by treating animal skins, usually sheepskin, also goes back at least 3,000 years. It was the most common writing material used in Europe at the time of the Crusades (vellum, made from calf skin, was also used).

Paper, made from plant pulp (usually rice) and fabric rags, was invented in China about 2,000 years ago. It was picked up by Arabs during the spread of Islam so that they were producing their own paper by the time of the Crusades.

Paper began to show up in Europe as the Crusades progressed. This production and use of paper, which was much cheaper and less susceptible to humidity fluctuations than parchment, foreshadowed the invention of the printing press in Germany around 1440 by Johannes Gutenberg. But for the availability of paper, something inexpensive and durable to print on, no printing press would have been invented since it takes a lot of sheep to provide enough parchment for a single book.

The invention of the printing press by Gutenberg is considered by many to be the single most important invention of the last thousand years. It is the invention that made possible the reformation, the enlightenment, and everything else that has followed. And it was a monumental task with numerous problems to solve.

Gutenberg had to develop a movable mirror image typeset that would retain a sharp edge (used a low melting point metal alloy of lead, tin, and antimony), ink that would remain on the typeset for sharp lines (oil based), paper that was properly prepared to accept that ink, and a process for pressing the inked typeset to the paper without smearing. It took resources that were always in short supply.

He was constantly in debt. His first commercially successful printing job was indulgence forms for the Catholic Church. He printed the Gutenberg Bible in 1455, the first Bible (and the first book) ever published.

For us in today's world, it is difficult to imagine a world in which literally every piece of written material was written by hand. The only way to duplicate any document was to rewrite it by hand. Even though paper was in broad use by then, there were only about 50,000 books in all of Europe in 1440 (almost all owned by the Catholic Church and its universities and schools). By 1500, there were more than ten million books on an endless variety of subjects in Europe.

Europe had crossed a threshold that humans had never crossed before. And the world was forever changed. *"The Church's monopoly on knowledge was broken and, soon, so was its monopoly on religion."* And with that end of its monopoly on religion came the Enlightenment as long-held beliefs on a wide range of fields and endeavors were challenged and questioned as never before.

Gutenberg's printing press had introduced publishing to the world. Further, up to that point, Latin had been the primary language of record across Europe, the language often used for written materials. The printing press brought about the stabilization and standardization of other European languages as they began to be used more in written materials. The printing press enabled the rapid dissemination of new knowledge and, along with zero and Arabic numbers, fostered continued innovation that led to an ever-expanding base of Accumulated Knowledge throughout Europe when compared to the rest of the world.

A shining example of that is Nicolaus Copernicus, a Polish mathematician and Church cleric. Near the end of his life, in 1543, he published a compilation of his life's work on astronomy. He had spent decades studying the night sky without a telescope.

At that time, the conviction across Europe, the Catholic Church, and probably most of the world was that the sun revolved around the earth. No less than Aristotle had so declared almost 2,000 years before. Copernicus carefully observed the night sky with its vast field of stars that rotated in fixed positions relative to each other from dusk to dawn and noted that there were five that gradually changed positions relative to the rest over the course of many nights. These five changed positions, in relation to the rest of the stars, independently of each other, with each in its own fixed pattern.

One of these five took only a few months to get back to where it started, and one took several years, while the other three were in between, with one of them also taking less than a year. He also noted the moon's changing phases in its 28-day cycle and the changing length of daylight during the seasons of the year. Then, he put his math skills to work to try to come up with a rational explanation for all this. And he found a framework that explained it all. Every detail. The framework he came up with was this: The Sun does not revolve around the Earth. The Earth moves around the Sun in a 365-day orbit, giving us the year. The Earth also rotates on an axis, giving us the 24-hour day. But the axis is slightly tipped, giving us the seasons with varying lengths of daylight as it orbits around the Sun. The Moon orbits around the Earth in a 28-day cycle, giving us the phases of the Moon. Those five stars that move independently of the rest are, like Earth, planets that revolve around the Sun. The shorter the length of their cycle in the night sky, the closer they are to the Sun.

Thus, two are closer to the Sun than Earth (Mercury and Venus), while three are farther away (Mars, Saturn, and Jupiter). The length of their cycle determines how far from the Sun they are. The rest of the stars in that fixed night sky are other suns far beyond the influence of our own sun. They rotate in the night sky from dusk to dawn as the earth rotates on its axis.

He didn't expressly claim that this framework is the way things are, which would go against his Catholic faith; he just said that this framework was the only one that could explain, mathematically, all he had observed.

Copernicus was not the first to track the planets or raise the idea that the Earth goes around the sun. However, it had been almost 2,000 years since Aristotle squashed the idea. And Copernicus' ideas went far beyond that. Thanks to the printing press being invented a century before, his whole framework was published, making it widely available so that others could build on it rather than starting from scratch again as he had largely done. And that published work certainly influenced Galileo 50 years later. What difference has paper and the printing press that followed made to the world? Everything!

However, I must note that Copernicus also studied monetary systems. He was the first to lay out the principle that the price of goods is correlated to the amount of money in circulation. That is, the more money in circulation, the more things will cost. That has proven to be a bedrock economic principle exemplified again when Europe was flooded with American silver around 1600.

Yet, four hundred years after that, the powers that be in the USA apparently forgot that principle when, in response to the 2020 COVID outbreak and corresponding lockdowns, they handed out all kinds of relief payments that increased the amount of money in circulation by 40%, and then were surprised when prices started going up, giving us the worst inflation in 40 years. Then, in August 2022, Congress passed another bill to hand out half a trillion dollars more and, get this, named it the *Inflation Reduction Act!* The wisdom of the ages is of no value, even when readily available and with a proven track record if we choose to be blissfully ignorant of it. This is a classic example of why understanding history can be of value and that there is a price to be paid for ignoring the lessons of history. Now, back to the past.

It is not my intention here to diminish the significance of the Renaissance philosophers and artists, beginning with Dante in Florence, who first wrote in the people's language in 1317, or the Church reformers' contributions to Europe's *Enlightenment.* My point is that paper and the printing press were critical to initiating and enabling that influence to spread and effect change. Then, in the 1700s, Europeans developed the process for using wood pulp to make paper, as well as its mass production in pulp mills. This enabled the beginning of widespread literacy and the continued rapid expansion of accumulated knowledge, which enabled Europe to change the world.

The world we live in today would never have come into existence without paper to facilitate the development, collection, and dissemination of accumulated knowledge.

SUGAR – Although Sugarcane was first domesticated in New Guinea, the process for extracting sugar and getting it into a crystalline or granular form was developed in India. Sugar production found its way to the Middle East during the spread of Islam. By the time of the Crusades, Arabs were growing sugarcane and producing sugar in the Middle East. When the Crusaders first tasted it, they thought it was the most wonderful thing they had ever tasted. Some expressed the idea that tasting sugar alone *"was compensation for the sufferings they had endured."* They took some home. Europe suddenly had a sweet tooth. However, initially, only nobles could afford it.

Because sugarcane is a semi-tropical plant, about the only places Europeans could grow it that Islam did not control were islands in the Mediterranean. In that period, most farmers, in Europe, and around the world, would try to meet their own needs first. Then, if they had any extra, they would sell it. However, sugarcane is cumbersome and soon rots, so it is not easy to sell or transport. It also takes a lot of labor to grow and harvest. Sugar, on the other hand, is durable and easy to ship.

However, converting sugarcane into sugar was a labor-intensive process that was more economical when processing lots of sugarcane into sugar for shipment far and wide. It was impractical as a backyard process for a small farmer. So, the production of sugar for shipment to the far-away markets in Europe required large areas of land devoted to growing sugarcane, with an adjacent sugar mill and lots of laborers close to a shipping port. Thus, the plantation was born. And sugarcane was the perfect plantation crop.

Initially, the Europeans paid well enough that people migrated to Sicily and other Mediterranean islands to work the plantations. However, as demand grew, Europeans looked to islands in the Atlantic off the African coast, most of which were uninhabited, for new places to produce more sugar: Portugal went first to Madeira, then the Azores, the Cape Verde islands, Sao Tome and Principe. Spain to the Canary Islands.

This was the first time Europe had gone outside its own natural borders to produce something in high demand to ship back home: extracting wealth from foreign lands on a large scale for shipment back to Europe.

Slavery had existed continuously on the Iberian Peninsula (modern s existed continuously on the Iberian Peninsula (modern-day Spain and Portugal) since Roman times.

At first, many were taken from the Slavic communities along the northeast coast of the Adriatic Sea (hence the word "slave"). Then, the main source shifted to captured Muslim soldiers. Having slave servants was very much a status symbol. However, on Madeira, slavery was transformed. Here, the sugar plantation was joined to African slavery for the first time in about 1450. Madeira was where the world of plantation chattel slavery of black Africans serving European (white) masters, with all its terrible consequences, came into existence: its *"social, political, and economic starting point."* By 1493, sugar production was so successful on Madeira that it had become a major source of sugar for Europe. In 1502, Spain began shipping black African slaves to the newly discovered Americas to work on the newly established sugar plantations there. Over the next 350 years of the transatlantic slave trade, almost 85% of the millions of black slaves shipped from Africa to the Americas would go to sugar plantations.

THE MAGNETIC COMPASS – The magnetic compass was invented in China. The Arabs had picked it up before the Crusades. By the end of the Crusades, the compass was in use by European seamen. It would prove crucial to ships sailing on the open Atlantic Ocean as Portugal and Spain began exploring islands off the African coast – and beyond.

BLACK POWDER – The Chinese were also the first to develop and use black powder (gunpowder), which would burn instantaneously with explosive force. They used it in a variety of ways. It first showed up in Europe around the end of the Crusades. Although it was also found within Islam by then, some claim that the Mongols brought it into Europe as they invaded Eastern and Central Europe rather it than coming back with the Crusaders.

In any case, I have included it here because of its importance in enabling Europe to spread its influence around the world in the ensuing centuries. The first use of black powder to shoot a projectile (bullet) occurred in Europe in the fifteenth century. The first *gun*. The development of muskets, pistols, and cannons soon followed with continuous improvements in the ensuing centuries.

THE SPINNING WHEEL – The spinning wheel was apparently invented within Islam over a thousand years ago, after cotton had been brought back from India and was being grown throughout Islam. Spinning wheels first appeared in Europe as the Crusades concluded near the end of the thirteenth century. By then, they could also be found in China and India. These wheels greatly facilitated the production (both in efficiency and quality) of yarn or thread from fibers (wool, hemp, flax, cotton, or silk). By 1400, spinning wheels had enabled textiles to become the mainstay of England's economy and would be an essential precursor for the textile revolution that would occur in Britain four centuries later.

For us today, surrounded by affordable fabric of all kinds, colors, and patterns, in a huge range of uses from clothes to home furnishings and more, it is almost impossible to grasp what a treasure a piece of fabric still was by 1776, or the human cost it took to make it. The sails of the Mayflower were canvas made from weaving together hemp and linen. It has been estimated that it required a million yards of yarn to make them. Even with spinning wheels, that would require several thousand hours. Today, with a 40-hour work week, a person works about 2,000 hours a year. In 1600, European workers were expected to work at least 72 hours each week (12 hours for six days), so they worked over 3,600 hours a year. It would still have taken one worker a few years just to make the yarn for the Mayflower's sails.

Then, add in the time needed to weave that yarn into canvas with hand looms, plus the time it would take to grow that much flax and hemp and prepare the fibers for the spinning wheel. To reproduce the Mayflower's inferior sails today in the same way they had been made 400 years ago would cost several million dollars. Even after the arrival of the spinning wheel, the only fabrics produced in Europe were linen (from flax fibers), wool, and hemp, while royalty and wealthy nobles imported limited amounts of silk and cotton.

And it took up to twenty spinners to keep one weaver with a handloom busy making fabric. *"The spinners never stand still for want of work; they always have it if they please' but the weavers sometimes are idle for want of yarn."* In 1656, Massachusetts even enacted a law requiring every family with *"idle hands"* – women and children who weren't otherwise employed – to spin a minimum amount of yarn or be fined. Yarn was precious. Unmarried adult women had few options to provide for themselves in that era, so many took to the spinning wheel to make a living. Thus, the term *spinster* for unmarried adult women.

COMPULSORY SERVITUDE IN EUROPE – Various levels of slavery continued for centuries in Europe after the fall of the Roman Empire. A thousand years ago, about ten percent of the population in England were slaves. However, the Catholic Church had begun advocating against Christians enslaving Christians. By 1200, the middle of the Crusades, the Scandinavian countries (Vikings) in Northern Europe had been largely converted to Christianity, while European Christians had largely stopped enslaving each other. After the Crusades, they only enslaved Muslims, while Muslims continued to enslave Christians.

It was religious bigotry, not racial bigotry. Still, by the fifteenth century, Europeans, like the rest of the world, saw one's station in life, whether royalty, noble, peasant, or slave, as God's will. *"Slavery was a personal misfortune, not a societal abomination."* In fact, for centuries, in many European countries, most rural peasants were serfs. That is, they were bound by law to the land where they worked and could not leave. Most coal miners in Scotland were legally bound (until 1799) to the coal mines, where they began working as children. If serfs or such miners tried to run away, they were subject to capture and return just as slaves would be. However, they were not bought and sold like chattel slaves, which enabled the establishment of stable family units and communities.

Societies across Europe continued to be very stratified, with virtually no potential for escaping upward from the class one was born into. However, in 1215, the King of England signed the *Magna Carta*, which gave nobles there some shared power with the King. Efforts to express their new power soon evolved into Parliament. As explained by Daniel Roman:

For centuries, political thought in Europe had been defined not in terms of the "rights" of individuals as people, but rather through the privileges of classes and offices. The Magna Carta of 1215 might have been progressive in that it restricted the power of the English King, but it restricted the power of the King over a class, his nobles. The right of nobles to govern their estates as they saw fit, to avoid taxation without their consent, and to be guaranteed a jury of their peers in any legal proceeding, meant the peasants unlucky enough to live on their estates, or Jews living in their towns, lost the ability to appeal to the King for protection.

A century later, there would be two chambers, with nobles and clergy sitting in the upper chamber, the House of Lords, and knights and burgesses sitting in the lower chamber, the House of Commons. Each of these two chambers' composition and comparative power would vary over time. The power of Parliament in relation to the Crown has also varied considerably during the almost seven centuries since the two separate chambers first began to function.

4: THE OLD WORLD MEETS THE AMERICAS

The arrival in the Americas of Christopher Columbus (or Cristobal Colon, as he was known in Spain at that time) on October 12, 1492, is viewed by many as the most significant and important world event in the last 2,000 years. Some biologists view it as the most significant event since the extinction of the dinosaurs. One American politician has said of the event: *"Columbus didn't discover America. America was here all the time. Columbus was lost."* Hmmm. Still, whether viewed as a hero or a villain, as a discoverer or an intruder, his arrival led to a whole new world through all the resultant dramatic worldwide changes that followed, some of them marvelous and some absolutely tragic. The whole world is a vastly different place because of that event and all that flowed from it. All the intercontinental movement of people, animals, plants, products, and diseases, sometimes intentional but much of it accidental, is sometimes referred to as the *Columbian Exchange* that began the era of Globalization. So, whether you honor Columbus or despise him, October 12, 1492, is a critically important date in world history.

The arrival of Columbus also demonstrated the tremendous advantage of being able to draw on the Accumulated Knowledge of many cultures. As explained by Thomas Sowell, economist, fellow at Stanford's Hoover Institute, and prolific author on economic and racial issues:

The technology that the Europeans brought to the Western Hemisphere was not simply the technology of Europe...Europeans were able to bring to bear in the Western Hemisphere the cultural features of lands extending far beyond Europe but incorporated into their civilization. Europeans were able to cross the Atlantic Ocean in the first place because they could steer with rudders invented in China, calculate their positions on the open sea through trigonometry invented in Egypt, using numbers created in India. The knowledge they had accumulated from around the world was preserved in letters invented in China. The military power they brought with them increasingly depended on weapons using gunpowder, also invented in Asia. The cultural confrontation in the Western Hemisphere was, in effect, a one-sided struggle between cultures acquired from vast regions of the earth against cultures from much more narrowly circumscribed regions of the New World. Never have the advantages of a wider cultural universe been more dramatically or devastatingly demonstrated than in the conquests that followed.

In short, Columbus had access to vastly more Accumulated Knowledge gathered from across Europe, the Middle East, and Asia when compared to the island natives in the Caribbean.

As this clash of civilizations began at the end of the fifteenth century, Europe was already divided into various ethnic groups by language and culture. And they were astonishingly diverse. These adjacent but diverse groups, who all looked much the same (they were all Caucasian or white), had interacted and fought over land, resources, religion, and power for centuries with changing alliances and enemies. The same was true just within the British Isles. And throughout Asia, the Americas, and Africa. Wars with neighboring groups were the way of the world.

With Columbus reaching the Americas, there began to be increasing interaction and intermingling of various ethnic groups around the world. Still, ethnocentrism (including racism) largely remained common and socially acceptable. There were stark observable ethnic differences between the natives of the Americas, the Europeans who started showing up on their shores, the Africans they would bring with them, and the Asians they would bring the other way.

Charles C. Mann explains that with this new contact between the peoples of different continents, people who looked quite different, each group viewed the others as curious strangers who did not fit within their known frameworks of enemies and allies. In these new contacts, each side tried to benefit. In most cases, each side considered itself superior (ethnocentrism) and was thus convinced that it could control the encounter to its advantage. Initially, this was as true for Indian groups in the Americas as it was for the Europeans who showed up on their shores bringing unimaginable goods like iron tools and weapons. It was also as true for the black African leaders capturing, transporting, and selling black slaves to European slave traders along the African coast for rum, textiles, and manufactured goods as it was for the European slave traders buying them. Both sides felt they were getting a good deal. As one historian put it: *"Africans themselves controlled the supply of African slaves, selling them to Europeans in the numbers they chose at prices they negotiated as equals."* However, those black slaves being captured, sold, and shipped had a very different story to tell that will be discussed later.

Sometimes, the cause of ethnic bigotry has been mislabeled. As contact between Europeans and American natives began, the stark ethnic differences between the two groups, beyond race, were evident as they saw each other for the first time. For Columbus, the Pilgrims, and many other Europeans encountering Native Americans for the first time, they spoke in glowing terms of the stature and appearance of the natives they encountered with little, if any, mention of skin color. Instead, it was the Europeans' culture (including technology) and religion that made Europeans feel vastly superior. Yet, many have mislabeled this racism. Instead, it was toxic ethnocentrism. They didn't feel genetically superior. They didn't even understand the concept. They could see the natives were larger, stronger, and better formed than themselves. Nor did they think the natives were stupid. Europeans felt vastly superior in culture and religion (they felt God was on their side). And with that feeling of superiority, they felt justified in killing, subjugating, or displacing the original inhabitants, things they had already done to other Europeans. Their bigotry toward Indians was based far more on religion and culture than race.

Expressing views that had prevailed for at least a hundred years, in 1934, one of the founders of American anthropology stated that the Indians of eastern North America had lived changeless lives of constant *"warfare that was insane, unending, and continuously attritional. Ninety-nine percent or more of what land might have been developed remained virgin."* As one Harvard expert wrote in 1937, *"the open, park-like woods have been from time immemorial, characteristic of vast areas of North America."* He considered the idea that they were a result of Indian fires as *"inconceivable."* Just sixty years ago (when I was in college), most historians considered the pre-Columbian Americas as two continents of wilderness populated by scattered bands whose way of life had changed little since the Ice Age. The only exceptions were Mexico and Peru, where the Aztecs and Inca were somewhat civilized. The 1964 Wilderness Act, one of the initial laws of the worldwide environmental movement, uses the phrase *"untrammeled by man"* in seeking to protect *"wilderness."* I remember that after the first Earth Day in 1970, billboards went up all across the country showing an Indian weeping over polluted land, implying that Indians never changed their environment from its wild state. In 1971, Samuel Eliot Morrison, a two-time Pulitzer Prize winner, stated in his two volume *European Discovery of America* that Indians had created no lasting monuments or institutions. Instead, stuck in a changeless wilderness, they were:

pagans expecting short and brutish lives, void of any hopes for the future.

A 1973 forestry college textbook stated, *"It is at least a fair assumption that no habitual or systematic burning was carried out by Indians.* As late as 2002, one geographer wrote that the *"modest"* Indian population *"modified only a tiny fraction of the total landscape for their everyday living needs.* In short, the expert and general perception of Indians before Columbus, which was then promoted as part of the environmental movement, was that of the timeless noble savage living harmoniously within a pristine wilderness.

As we have learned during the COVID pandemic, expert consensus sometimes changes. That is certainly true for the assessment of pre-Columbian Indians. The views above were based on questionable science and were inconsistent with contemporary accounts written by early European explorers and settlers who encountered them.

Thus, as explained by Charles C. Mann, it is now widely thought that when Columbus arrived, the Americas were immeasurably busier, more diverse, and more populous than previously imagined. It was a thriving, stunningly diverse place teeming with a multitude of empires, languages, trade, and cultures. In fact, languages and cultures were as diverse and varying in complexity as those of Europe, Asia, and Africa. And they were not timeless. Many had a very complex history. However, many histories were not written down, and most of what was written has been destroyed. Most were not nomadic. While many lived in some of the world's biggest and most opulent cities, most Indians were farmers. Also, they modified their environment far more than previously thought. It was far from pristine wilderness *"untrammeled by man."*

Particularly in North America, most ecosystems had been dominated by fire; and for centuries, most of those fires had been deliberately set by humans. In 1523, an Italian sailing up the coast from the Carolinas to Maine commented on the many large smoky fires that could be smelled from over a hundred miles away. A Dutchman living around Albany in the 1640s (then New Netherlands) spent a great deal of time with Indians. In describing the Indians' annual burns, he said they set fire to *"the woods, plains, and meadows to thin out and clear the woods of dead substances and grass, which grow better the ensuing spring."* He further stated, *"such a fire is a splendid sight when one sails on the rivers at night while the forest is ablaze on both banks. Fire and flames are everywhere, and on all sides...a delightful scene to look upon from afar."* In 1792, among the first European to explore southern Alberta, while traveling with Indians, described vast areas day after day of burning or burnt prairie. He also described the benefits of such burning, which *"In the ensuing Spring & Summer makes excellent fine sweet feed for the Horse & Buffalo, &."* With fire, the great plains tall grass prairie was extended, and maintained, through otherwise natural woodlands, across parts of Illinois and Indiana, and on into Ohio. These retooled ecosystems encouraged not only more deer, elk, and bear, but even buffalo, which could be found from New York to Louisiana in the 1600s. As one historian has observed, when the Indians hunted elk, deer, and buffalo, they *"were harvesting a foodstuff which they had consciously been instrumental in creating. The English...accustomed to keeping domesticated animals, lacked the conceptual tools to recognize that the Indians were practicing a more distant kind of husbandry of their own."* Another scientist stated that *"when Lewis and Clark headed west from St. Louis, they were exploring not a wilderness, but a vast pasture managed by and for Native Americans."* While Indians in North America were living in a sustainable balance with nature, they had their thumb heavily on the scales. They shaped and continually managed the landscape for their comfort and convenience.

In short, the Americas *"was a region where tens of millions of people loved, hated, fought, and worshiped as people do everywhere. Much of this world vanished after Columbus, swept away by disease and subjugation."* This wipeout was so thorough in many areas that, within a few generations, not only the invading Europeans and the Africans they brought with them, but even the few Indians still left behind, did not know that such a world had ever existed.

THE VOYAGES OF CHRISTOPHER COLUMBUS – The fall of Constantinople to Muslim forces in 1453 (so it became Istanbul), seriously impacted Europe's ability to satisfy its increasing appetite for Asian products like silk and porcelain from China (Ah! So that is why fine dinnerware is called *china!*), spices from Southeast Asia, and cotton from India. With the loss of Constantinople, anything from Asia had to come across a vast area controlled by Islam. Merchants from Venice and Genoa then linked up with Islamic caravans to lock up the market of Asian goods in Europe. Thus, there was a strong desire in Europe to find another way to access Asian goods. By then, the Portuguese were refining their new three mast ship design, greatly facilitating their move to produce sugar on islands off the African coast. These new three masted ships were capable of taking on the open Atlantic Ocean as Portugal continued to push down Africa's west coast to see if there was a southern end that would enable them to sail around the tip of Africa and reach Asia by ship (they would reach that tip in 1488 but would not reach India going that way until 1498, six years after Columbus reached America). Other European countries also soon began using three masted ships that facilitated sailing on the open ocean.

By that time, most educated Europeans understood that the earth was a sphere rather than a tabletop. Further, estimates made 1,500 years earlier were remarkably accurate as to its size. However, Columbus believed Earth was much smaller. He thought Asia was less than 3,000 miles to the west of Spain rather than the actual 11,000 miles. After failed attempts to find support from Portugal, Venice, or Genoa, Columbus pressed hard on the king and queen of Spain to support a voyage heading due west to find Asia. They refused to back him until they saw he was going to take his proposal to France. Even then, they only agreed to cover three fourths of the cost of a small expedition of three small ships with combined crews totaling about 90 men.

Five weeks after resupplying on the Canary Islands, Columbus arrived in the Bahamas on October 12, 1492. He then visited a couple of other islands before running his flagship, the Santa Maria, aground on the Island of Hispaniola, probably in what is now Haiti. He found each island full of natives that he called *Indios* (Indians) since he was convinced that he was just off the coast of Asia. He described the population on Hispaniola as:

innumerable, for I believe there to be millions upon millions of them.

His various journal entries during that first voyage included the following descriptions of the natives on the islands he visited:

They brought us parrots and balls of cotton and spears and many other things, which they exchanged for glass beads and hawks' bells. They willingly traded everything they owned...They are well-built with good bodies and handsome features... They do not bear arms, for I showed them a sword, they took it by the edge and cut themselves out of ignorance. They have no iron... They would make fine servants. With 50 men, we could subjugate them all and make them do whatever we want.

The fact that the natives had cotton probably contributed to Columbus's conviction that they had reached Asia. By then, Europeans knew about cotton, which Arabs had brought from India. By the time of the Crusades, it was being grown in Egypt. However, other than royalty or rich merchants (who might wear linen or imported silk or cotton), most Europeans still dressed in leather, wool, or hemp. They also produced linen, which was not used much for clothes.

Because Columbus was now down to two ships, he left 38 men behind to establish a settlement and sailed for home bearing golden ornaments, brilliantly colored parrots, peppers, and about ten captive Indians. The king and queen were so enthusiastic about his voyage that they sent him back just six months later with 17 ships and a combined crew of about 1,500, including about a dozen priests to convert the natives. It was the second of his four trips to America. When he returned to Spain 18 months later, having failed to establish a viable settlement, he brought 500 Indian slaves as a gift for the queen. She was appalled and ordered him to take them back. She considered all the lands Columbus had visited as now being part of Spain and that, therefore, its inhabitants were her subjects and immune from being enslaved. Instead, they were to be converted.

On the other hand, it was fine to enslave Africans because they were part of Islam, heretics who had rejected the true faith. This was reciprocal: North Africans continued to enslave captured Europeans, usually sailors, for another three centuries (totaling over two million Europeans enslaved). Initially, it was Christian vs. Islam rather than race.

Although Columbus' initial efforts to establish settlements were disastrous for both sides, the waves of invading Europeans, often bringing Africans with them, had begun. And they brought cattle, sheep, horses, sugarcane, wheat, bananas, coffee, etc. Equally important were others who, unknown to the colonists, snuck aboard their ships, including earthworms, mosquitoes, cockroaches, dandelions, various grasses, rats, and infectious diseases. They then jumped ship like eager immigrants into new lands totally unprepared to deal with them. For example, on the island of Hispaniola, not only had the human population been almost entirely replaced by those arriving on ships, but also much of its vegetation and animal life.

INFECTIOUS DISEASES – Infectious diseases have been a major force in shaping the world. Even as late as 1900, over 37% of deaths in the United States were caused by infectious diseases (now less than 2%), while 20% of babies died before their first birthday. Those numbers were probably the lowest they had ever been around the world throughout history. In fact, infectious diseases were a powerful force in natural selection. Those who survived a disease were the ones left to produce the next generation. Within a few generations, the people left were those with the greatest genetic (natural) resistance to the disease. In a few cases, immunity developed. Europe and Asia had been living with many infectious diseases for centuries. Epidemics were common. While some diseases might show up in an epidemic wave with devastating consequences and then disappear for decades, others were endemic. However, people understood almost nothing about the causes of diseases or how to prevent them. Around the world, disease, including epidemics, was generally seen through a spiritual lens (divine intervention or retribution?) rather than a secular perspective. Europeans' close contact with animals: sheep, cattle, cats, dogs, horses, chickens, swine, and rodents, who shared and helped transmit some diseases, contributed significantly to the problem, as did urbanization. Over centuries, it had become well-engrained throughout much of Europe that diseases were caused by bathing and breezes. And these convictions don't die easily. While living in Romania in 2011, we sometimes saw old ladies riding the trams who would go into absolute panic when someone opened a window on a 100-degree day because they were sure the wind coming in that window would kill them.

Many of these diseases simply did not exist in the Americas because of its geographic isolation. So, along with all the animals and plants that Europeans brought to America, both intentionally and unintentionally, came new diseases: viral diseases, including smallpox, influenza, hepatitis, measles, encephalitis, and viral pneumonia, along with bacterial diseases, including tuberculosis, diphtheria, cholera, typhus, scarlet fever, and meningitis. And they came into populations of natives that had no genetic predisposition, through prior exposure, to survive them. While there is still some debate about its origin, syphilis seems to be the only disease that went the other way, first showing up in Europe following Columbus' first voyage.

The worst (and most easily distinguishable) of these new diseases for Indians was smallpox. In Europe, the mortality rate for smallpox was as high as 30%. As Europe was expanding into the Americas after 1492, most adult Europeans were smallpox survivors who bore pox scars around the face and neck. The first smallpox outbreak in the New World started on Hispaniola in 1518. The mortality rate for smallpox among Native Americans was much higher. It quickly killed a third of the population of Hispaniola before jumping to Puerto Rico, Cuba, and then on to the mainland. Then, it would come back again interspersed with other diseases for which the natives had no inherent defenses. For example, smallpox epidemics swept through Peru in 1525, 1533, 1535, 1558, and 1565 along with typhus in 1546, influenza in 1558, diphtheria in 1614, and measles in 1618. With that, the native population in Peru had been reduced by at least 90%. *"Disease turned whole societies to ash."* Often, the areas hardest hit were those with the highest population densities since most infections were spread from person to person. It is impossible to know how many died. Credible academic estimates show a native population of about 25 million in Central Mexico declining by 97% within 100 years of the first Smallpox outbreak. The native Taino Indians of Hispaniola became extinct. While the brutality of the invading Europeans certainly contributed to some declines, infectious diseases were the biggest killers by far, with current estimates reaching as high as 95% of the native population of the Americas. Many groups were essentially wiped out before they even saw Europeans as diseases raced ahead among native peoples. Therefore, the first whites to explore many parts of the Americas encountered places that were already largely depopulated. From New England to Puget Sound, initial settlers and explorers encountered deserted villages, and human remains promiscuously scattered that were evidence of recent epidemics. Europeans understood the brutal logic of quarantines. For centuries, when an epidemic broke out, people had boarded up their houses and headed for the countryside. However, Indians tended to gather at the sufferer's bedside to help and comfort them. One Blackfoot Indian explained, *"We had no belief that one man could give a disease to another any more than a wounded man could give his wound to another."* And this only aided in spreading disease.

We recently experienced the worldwide COVID-19 pandemic response that exploded in the USA in March 2020. In its first three years, the mortality rate for confirmed cases (while many cases went unconfirmed) in the USA was about 1.1%. Yet, we initiated various measures that crippled some segments of our economy and altered our behaviors. Some areas closed schools for a year or more even though the mortality rate for children was less than 0.01%. In the first three years, it killed about 0.35% of the population of the USA, with the majority of those being over seventy and/or having co-morbidities, particularly diabetes and obesity. It is almost impossible to grasp the psychological or sociological impact on a community or its survivors of an epidemic with mortality rates of 30% to 90%, particularly when they had no understanding of what caused it or how it spread. The devastation had to have been indescribable. As stated by Charles C. Mann:

Languages, prayers, dreams, habits, and hopes – all gone. And not just once but over and over again. In our antibiotic era, how can we imagine what it means to have entire ways of life hiss away like steam? How can one assay the total impact of the unprecedented calamity that gave rise to the world we live in?

Africa had its own tropical diseases, particularly malaria and yellow fever, to which Europeans were as susceptible as Native Americans. Both of these diseases are transmitted only by particular species of mosquitoes. In 1486, the Portuguese moved sugar plantations onto the island of Sao Tome, along the Equator, in the Gulf of Guinea off the African coast. However, unlike Madeira, this island was heavily infested with mosquitoes that bore malaria and yellow fever. For Africans, yellow fever was a common childhood disease that was relatively minor in children but rendered them immune for life. However, it had a mortality rate of about 50% in adult Europeans and Indians. Malaria is much more complicated. Suffice it to say here that, between yellow fever and malaria, Europeans died by the thousands on Sao Tome. The first two efforts totally collapsed. The third brought in a mass of slaves, mostly Jewish children, but few survived. Then, they brought in black African slaves. While the island was soon producing more sugar than Madeira, the ratio of black slaves to white masters was more than 100 to one. Even then, many of the overseers were of mixed race, while the white owners never went near their operations. The story was much the same for the nearby island of Principe. *"With their tiny fever-ridden European populations brutally overseeing thousands of enchained workers, Sao Tome and Principe were the progenitors of the extractive state."* This set the pattern for extractive operations that were broadly followed in the Caribbean and South America. Sugar production from the islands off the coast of Africa peaked around 1550. By 1600, the big new sugar plantations in Brazil and the Caribbean had largely knocked them out of the sugar market.

As sugar plantations were being established in the Americas (Spain in the Caribbean and Portugal in Brazil), they initially used native Indians for slave labor. However, enslaving Indians was opposed by the Spanish crown. Further, those Indian slaves died at an alarming rate. So, they soon began to import slaves from Africa. And with those African slaves, malaria and yellow fever came along for the ride with devastating consequences for their European masters (as well as Indians). This will be further discussed later.

THE CONQUIESTADORS – In the 16th century, Europeans, representing a handful of countries, made their way into the Americas with one or more of three goals in mind: 1) find treasure to plunder and take home (or places they could create it, such as new sugar plantations), 2) convert the natives, and 3) find a water passage across the landmass to the Pacific Ocean. This discussion will focus on four Spanish conquistadors covered by Mann and others. The first two destroyed two of the world's great civilizations: civilizations standing on the same soil where their predecessors developed the crops that now feed and clothe much of the world. The world we live in would simply be unable to support its current population without those crops. The last two discussed here reached into what is now the United States with significant consequences.

Hernan Cortes, in 1518, disobeyed recall orders and took about 500 soldiers, 13 horses, and a few cannons on 11 ships to the Yucatan Peninsula, where he defeated the natives, found a Catholic priest who could speak the language and translate for him, and took 20 young native women, some capable of speaking the language of the Aztecs. He then, in 1519, sailed on to Vera Cruz, where he famously scuttled his ships so there could be no retreat before taking his army on to invade the Aztec Empire (Historians now commonly use the term "Triple Alliance" rather than Aztec. I will stick with Aztec since it is shorter).

The Aztec empire was massive and impressive. Its population in central Mexico at the time has been credibly estimated at about 25 million people. After spending two years battling and then building alliances with the Tlaxcala Indians, who had been struggling to remain independent from the Aztecs, Cortes then marched, along with about 20,000 Tlaxcalans, on the Aztec capital, Tenochtitlan (which Cortes later renamed Mexico City). The city, built on an island in a lake, *"dazzled its invaders – it was bigger than Paris, Europe's greatest metropolis. The Spaniards gawped like yokels at the wide streets, ornately carved buildings, and markets filled with goods from hundreds of miles away. Boats flitted like butterflies around three grand causeways that linked it to the mainland. Long aqueducts conveyed water from distant mountains across the lake and into the city. Even more astounding than the great temples and immense banners and colorful promenades were the botanical gardens – none existed in Europe. The same novelty attended the force of a thousand men that kept the crowded streets immaculate. (Streets that weren't ankle-deep in sewage? The conquistadors had never conceived of such a thing.)"*

After conquering the city (through brutal treachery, the help of Tlaxcala Indians, and thanks to a raging smallpox epidemic), Cortes wrote about its ruler in a letter to the king of Spain:

> *Can there be anything more magnificent than that this barbarian lord should have all the things to be found under the heavens in his domain, fashioned in gold and silver and jewel and feathers? And so realistic in gold and silver that no smith in the world could have done better? And in jewels so fine that it is impossible to imagine with what instruments they were cut so perfectly? In Spain there is nothing to compare with it.*

The Aztecs had inherited a rich cultural and philosophical heritage from their Mesoamerican predecessors, including the Olmec and Maya, who were also pioneers in mathematics and astronomy. They had a remarkable intellectual tradition that, like the Greeks and Chinese, included the past writings of lyric poets. They had achieved remarkable engineering feats and developed a mathematical system that included the concept of zero. They had invented several different writing systems, established trade networks, tracked the orbits of planets, created a 365-day calendar, and recorded their histories in books made of fig tree bark paper. However, their only use of the wheel was on children's toys. They also practiced extensive human sacrifice. A group of Franciscan monks who were sent to convert the natives met with a delegation of Aztec priests in 1524. *"Having expected childlike natives, empty vessels waiting to be filled by the Word, the Franciscans instead found themselves fencing with skilled rhetoricians, proud of their intellectual traditions."*

Over previous millennia, Mesoamerica had been the site of another Neolithic revolution. These early farmers developed corn (maize), most beans we now see on our dinner tables (including green beans), squash, and avocados. They also developed cocoa (chocolate) and raised tomatoes and some other food crops that originated in the Andes. They were well fed with a balanced diet, augmented by fish and wild game. Because they had developed crops that provided much more food on less land with less effort than could be achieved growing wheat and barley (or even rice), this increase in food productivity gave them a substantial advantage over European and Asian farmers. However, they had no domesticated animals, which more or less offset that advantage. Metallurgy was limited to ornamental use, primarily gold and silver. They had no metal tools or weapons. Corn, beans, and squash were usually grown together in group plantings called *mulpas* so that the beans, a nitrogen-fixing legume, helped fertilize them all as the beans climbed the corn stalks. This practice had spread across North America to the Atlantic Coast centuries before the English arrived. Indian farmers in Virginia and New England were growing corn, beans, and squash in combined plantings when they first encountered Europeans.

Francisco Pizarro had heard stories of a golden empire along South America's Pacific Coast. On his third effort, he finally the Inca city of Cajamarca in November 1532, with 168 armed men, 62 horses, and a few cannons.

At the time, the Inca Empire was the largest empire on earth, even bigger than Ming Dynasty China. It stretched for over 3,000 miles along the Pacific coast from southern Columbia in the north, past Concepcion, Chile in the south. It extended east over the Andes Mountains, with its peaks over 20,000 feet high, and on into the Amazon rainforests of Brazil and Bolivia, as well as into northwest Argentina. However, the empire had only been in existence for about 100 years and was still in growth mode. The Inca had taken over numerous different cultures, speaking different languages. They were melding them together into one culture by shipping them far from their homeland and forcing them to intermingle with other groups and speak only the Inka language. Their methods were brutal, audacious, and efficient enough to make Stalin and Hitler proud. They had established a road system of paved stone walking paths that was 25,000 miles long.

The Inca's home territory was high in the Andes Mountains in very steep terrain, with Cuzco as its capital (a fairly new city at an elevation above 11,000 feet). However, Lake Titicaca, at 12,500 feet, had been a cultural center for at least 2,000 years and was where the Inca originated. Because of the short distance from this seaside to mountaintop, there is an enormous range of environmental conditions. Communities could interact with those living up and down the Andes western desert slopes, exchanging everything from fish and shellfish from the ocean to wool and meat from high in the mountains, with various crops grown in between. The same was true on the mountains' eastern slopes extending down into the Amazon rainforest's upper reaches.

There is still some debate over whether a third Neolithic revolution took place in the area of the Inca. In any case, an astounding number of important crops originated in the area in the millennia before the Inca arose. These include potatoes, sweet potatoes, tomatoes, all kinds of peppers, peanuts, pineapple, manioc (cassava), quinoa, tobacco, peach palm, and a species of cotton (the species that now provides over 90% of the world's cotton). They also grew corn, which originated in Mesoamerica. They were well-fed by very productive farmers. Their predecessors had also developed two closely related domesticated animals they used in the mountains: llamas and much smaller alpacas, both cousins of camels. Llamas served as pack animals but were not large enough to ride. Both animals provided meat and fleece, but the alpaca fleece was higher quality, sort of like cashmere. The Inca had no wheels. They had considerable expertise in metallurgy but made no metal weapons, tools, or containers. Their only use of metals was ornamental. They refined iron and then pounded it while hot into the desired shapes for plating with silver or gold since iron was much harder and would retain its shape better than solid gold or silver objects. They used cotton fiber for a variety of things. They made suspension bridges across mountain gorges that terrified the Spaniards because they had never seen bridges without supports under them. They made armor with cotton so tightly woven and quilted that it was as effective as the Spanish armor but much lighter. They made boats and ships by weaving reeds together. The Europeans first encountered the Inca on a ship made of reeds 300 miles from its home port under sails of finely woven cotton. It had a crew of 20, plus cargo. The Inca developed a form of writing that consisted of sequences of knots on strings that formed a binary code.

Pizarro was fortunate that a smallpox epidemic had swept through the Inca Empire a few years before he got there. It had killed about 200,000 Indians, including the emperor, his brother, his wife, his son and designated heir to the throne, his uncle, most of his military leaders, and the two regents running the empire in Cusco. Civil war then followed in the resultant power vacuum, led by two other sons of the now-dead emperor, Atawallpa and Washker, each claiming the throne. After a few years of back-and-forth battles, Atawallpa prevailed in a horrendous battle that left about 35,000 dead and Washker captured. Washker was sent back to Cusco, where his wives and children were executed in front of him before he was killed. Meanwhile, Atawallpa led a triumphant cavalcade of about 80,000 slowly toward Cusco. While passing near Cajamarca, he learned that a bunch of hairy, pale men, who sat on enormous animals, had arrived there and were in the city. So, carried in his gilded and feather-decked livery, he went to meet them, accompanied by about 5,000 troops.

After hiding all but a few of his men, Pizarro met the Inca in the town plaza, where a Christian book was presented to Atawallpa. He quickly tossed it aside. That was all the excuse needed for an attack. With cannons roaring and smoke billowing, armored cavalry charged into the Inca with swords swinging. They essentially scared the Inca to death. What these battle-hardened troops saw and heard was so beyond anything they could have ever imagined: the deafening roar of a cannon never heard before as men, who seemed to be made of iron, sitting on the backs of enormous animals never before seen, charged out of the smoke into and over them. These iron men had long, sharp extensions of iron on the ends of their arms (swords) that cut right through them. The Inca were so terrified they trampled each other to death, trying to get out of the way. Pizarro's troops obliterated the entire Inca force escorting the emperor, then imprisoned him without losing a single man. Pizarro agreed to free the emperor in exchange for a room full of gold and two rooms full of silver. After the ransom was paid and had been shipped to Spain, he killed the emperor anyway and went to war. In November 1533, he captured Cusco. He then established the new city of Lima, on the coast, as the new capital of Peru.

Hernando De Soto, who had been with Pizarro in Peru, landed nine ships near Tampa Bay in Florida with an army of 600 soldiers, 220 horses, and 300 pigs, in May 1539. For four years, his force wandered through what is now Florida, Georgia, North Carolina, South Carolina, Tennessee, Alabama, Mississippi, Arkansas, Louisiana, and Texas, looking for gold and wrecking pretty much everything along the way. He found natives everywhere. Most were mound builders living in permanent settlements. He made enemies of almost all of them. They often fought back but were totally unprepared to understand his motives or the sight and sound of horses, muskets, and swords. By the time the expedition reached the Mississippi River, he had lost almost half his men and most of his horses in wars with Indians. However, the number of pigs had doubled. They crossed the river somewhere south of Memphis. As they were building the barges for the crossing, several thousand Indians approached *"within a stone's throw"* to mock them, sometimes shooting arrows. They found both sides of the river *"thickly set with great towns"* such that *"two or three of them could be seen from one."* After going west until they reached the dry open areas of Texas, they turned east again and then floated down the Mississippi out to sea. When De Soto died, his men sunk his body in the Mississippi River. They were attacked by Indians all along the way out to sea, where the survivors eventually were picked up and made their way to Mexico City.

Europeans did not visit this area of the Mississippi River again until 1682, 140 years later. This time by Frenchmen in canoes. They didn't see an Indian village for 200 miles. The area was deserted. What happened? Along with the diseases De Soto's men probably brought, like smallpox, he brought pigs as a walking meat locker. Pigs transmit anthrax, brucellosis, leptospirosis, trichinosis, and tuberculosis. A few wandering off into the forest could contaminate deer and turkey, which can infect people. Disease-ridden pigs apparently spread across the southeast and into Arkansas and East Texas, where wild boar are still a problem. So, Indians who had never seen or heard of De Soto still died from the disease. The Caddo, along the Texas-Arkansas border, and the Coosa, in western Georgia, both disintegrated shortly after De Soto passed through. Credible estimates show the Caddo population dropping over 95%. As one anthropologist put it, *"That's one reason whites think of Indians as nomadic hunters, everything else – all the heavily populated urbanized societies – was wiped out."* The calamity of De Soto extended across much of the southeast.

Francisco Vazquez de Coronado, in 1540, led an expedition of 400 armed and armored Spaniards, about 1,500 natives, several black slaves, 1,000 horses, 500 cattle, and 5,000 sheep that went northeast out of Mexico into part of what would become the United States searching for cities rich in gold. Their journey passed through parts of Arizona, New Mexico, Oklahoma, Texas, Colorado, and Kansas. He sent smaller parties out to search in various directions. One of them became the first Europeans to look into the Grand Canyon. The expedition terrorized various Indian groups along the way (seeing men in armor riding on strange huge animals) as they would confiscate food and supplies as they went. They were particularly hard on the Zuni. As they moved further north, the expedition began to fragment.

With a smaller part of his original group, Coronado reached as far north and east as the area where Salina, Kansas, is now located. They saw buffalo by the thousands. They met two Indian groups in that general area. They spent almost a month with the Quivira. He described them as: *"well settled...along good river bottoms, although without much water, and good streams which flow into another."* He believed there were about 25 settlements of Quivira, each consisting of up to 200 straw-thatched houses. They had fields growing corn, beans, and squash. He found the Indians to be: *"large people of very good build"* who were naked. A single copper pendant was the only evidence of wealth. He then went to meet the Harahey. They were: *"all naked – with bows and some sort of things on their heads, and their privy parts slightly covered."*

He found no evidence of wealth. He then finally decided it was time to turn back. He had been gone two years and found no gold. So, his expedition dribbled home.

What do we learn from this? Smack in the middle of the Great Plains, in 1542, there was a sizable group (25 villages of up to 200 homes each would probably mean 10,000 to 25,000 people) of well-fed, robust Indian farmers living in stationary settlements. The Harahey seemed to be as numerous. And there were many others throughout the Great Plains. I have passed through Salina many times. While the higher ground is prairie, without human intervention, the stream and river channels would be heavily wooded. They must have cleared these for fields and villages with controlled fires. Farmers living in permanent villages growing corn, beans, and squash is simply not the image of Great Plains Indians that I have heard about all my life.

Coronado's expedition was the first time cattle and horses reached the American Southwest and Great Plains. Undoubtedly, some escaped. More were just left behind. The Spanish constantly brought more horses and cattle up from Mexico over the next two centuries. These Spanish cattle, whose ancestors were brought from India to Spain by the Moors, were the ancestors of the Texas longhorns that, by the thousands, roamed wild over the plains on both sides of the Rio Grande River by the mid-1800s. In 1607, Spanish priests established Santa Fe, which became a main center of trade with Indians. Beginning with the Comanche and Apache, the plains Indians were well on the way to transforming to a horse culture by 1650 as bands of wild horses were spreading across the southern Great Plains. By the time of the American Revolution, due to disease and horses, Indian life on the Great Plains had been totally transformed. There were far fewer Indians in wide-roaming cultures, with some becoming nomadic hunters, even though there had not yet been contact with English immigrants. And they developed a state of constant warfare with one another through raids to steal slaves and horses. Thus, the fierce nomadic plains Indians riding horses that Lewis and Clark encountered along the Missouri River in 1804 were dramatically different from those encountered by Coronado 260 years earlier.

CHINA AND THE SILVER TRADE – Books have been written about why China, easily the most advanced nation on earth at the time, basically closed itself off from the world beginning over 500 years ago, including prohibiting foreigners from entering China's ports, just as Europe was beginning to spread its influence across the globe. Some have claimed *"China lacked range, focus, and above all, curiosity."* Others have pointed to China's *"empty cultural superiority and self-engrossment."* However, there is also a more straightforward explanation. During its seafaring adventures in the 1400s, China simply found there was nothing out there they didn't already have that they were interested in. China stopped *"for the same reason the United States stopped sending men to the moon – there was nothing there to justify the costs of such voyages."*

China had already been struggling for a couple of centuries to maintain a stable currency, including periodic efforts at using paper money. The preferred currency for merchants was silver since it had intrinsic value independent of the whims of the latest emperor. However, the silver supply was limited. Then, in the 1560s, Spain began sending shiploads of silver from South America to the Philippines. China was soon addicted to Spanish silver.

As described by Mann, in April 1545, a man was out walking along a barren, windswept ridge high in the Andes Mountains (above 13,000 feet) at what is now the southern tip of Bolivia. As he stumbled, he grabbed a shrub. As it pulled loose from the shallow soil, he saw a metallic sparkle in the hole where the roots had been. Good silver ore is, at most, 2-3% silver, usually less, often much less. This ledge was as much as 50% silver. It was so rich the Spaniards had no idea how to smelt it without boiling the silver away. However, the local Indians, who were better metallurgists than the Spaniards, showed them how using low-temperature smelters burning dried grass and llama dung as fuel. The boomtown of Potosi soon sprang up with thousands of these little smelters. In 1549 (just four years after the initial discovery), one account of a single shipment describes how 7,771 stamped bars (each 60-pound bar was 99% silver – 230 tons of silver) were hauled down from the new mountain town of Potosi to the coast by a llama pack train of over 2,000 llamas while being guarded by over a thousand Indians, who over 100 Spanish guards watched.

By 1565, Potosi had a population of 50,000. By 1610, the population was 160,000, as large as Paris and Amsterdam, despite Spain's efforts to keep people out. It was the highest and richest city on earth. Its opulence, depravity, and lawlessness were unmatched anywhere in the world. For one celebration, a street was paved with bars of silver. The city's coat of arms proclaimed, *"I am rich Potosi – the treasure of the world, the king of the mountains, the envy of kings."* And they loved to cheat the Spanish crown on taxes. By 1600, two-thirds of the mines and the municipal council of Potosi were controlled by Basques, who had no love for Spanish royalty.

In the 1550s, large mercury deposits were discovered at an Andean peak, Huancavelica, 800 miles to the northwest of Potosi. About the same time, miners discovered how to use mercury to extract and purify silver.

By essentially marrying the two mines together, the Spanish Viceroy was able to eliminate the small Indian smelters and shift the Indians into a conscripted labor force to work both mines. Some African slaves were also brought in, but they were a minor part of the workforce. Miners, working in deplorable conditions, died by the thousands. Because mercury is so toxic, the conditions at that mine were the worst. Foremen and supervisors died, too. Natives became so determined to keep their children from working the mercury pits that they would maim their children so they would be unable to serve. Decomposed bodies of dead workers would leave puddles of mercury. Even at Potosi, where conditions were much better, one priest complained to the Spanish royal secretary, "*If twenty healthy Indians enter on Monday, half come out on Saturday as cripples.*" Potosi continued to produce silver for over 300 years.

Some of that Potosi silver was minted into Spanish silver pesos (*pieces of eight*) and shipped to Europe. It became the primary currency of exchange not only in Spain but also across much of Europe. However, by 1640, there was so much silver in Europe that its value began to plummet, so a peso was worth only a third of what it had been 100 years before. So Spain was suddenly poorer. However, most of the Potosi silver went west across the Pacific to China.

Since no outsiders were allowed in China, Spanish merchants established the city of Manila in the Philippines in 1571 as its port for handling trade in Asia. Chinese merchants from Yuegang then established a nearby community from which to trade for Spanish silver. They brought everything from the mainland, not only silk and porcelain, but also tea, spices, cotton, iron, sugar, chestnuts, ivory, and more. They brought anything they thought the Spanish might be interested in. They soon learned not only to send silk fabric but also to sew knockoffs of the latest European fashions in clothes and accessories. And they could produce them far cheaper than European Artisans. It was like Walmart had arrived four centuries early. Basically, China had outsourced its money supply, and was ramping up production of almost everything and trading it all away just to maintain that money supply. That was not a good deal. "*For hundreds of years China produced silk, porcelain and tea to acquire a commodity, silver, which was needed to replace the paper notes the government had made valueless*", while picking up none of the new technology and scientific knowledge that was accumulating in Europe.

The Spanish traders were also still busy cheating the Crown by vastly understating how much silver they were shipping to China (and thus had to pay taxes on). Mexican officials, in 1602, found that the ships that year had exported 400 tons of silver to China, eight times the declared amount. In 1654, a Spanish ship sank shortly before arriving in Manila. Its manifest claimed it was carrying 418,323 silver pesos. Over three centuries later, salvagers found the ship. They brought up 1,180,865 pesos, over 2.8 times the declared amount. That is a lot of contraband.

TOBACCO – The first product from America to sweep around the world was tobacco. Members of Columbus' voyages reported the Indians smoking and chewing it and its effect on them. By 1510, it was in common use throughout Spain. It rapidly spread throughout Europe and the world. By 1550, seeds had been introduced in France, and the Portuguese had taken them to Japan. Claims of its medicinal value were widespread. By 1600, smoking houses and nicotine addiction were common in Delhi, Nagasaki, Beijing (it even somehow got into China, where it was grown extensively), Istanbul, and any other large city around the world. A traveler in Sierra Leon reported that tobacco could be found in *"about every man's house, which seemeth half their food."* Within just one century, the whole world had a serious nicotine addiction.

THE POTATO – It has been said that any history of Europe that doesn't discuss the potato should be ignored since its introduction there was a key factor, not only in Europe's history but in the history of the entire world. This is Charles C. Mann's characterization of the standard of living in Europe prior to the introduction of the potato:

European living standards were roughly the equivalent of those today in Cameroon and Bangladesh; they were below Bolivia or Zimbabwe. On average, European peasants ate less per day than the hunting-and-gathering societies in Africa or the Amazon.

Pizzaro's troops in Peru were the first Europeans to see and eat potatoes, which had been developed in the Andes. They sent a few home to Spain. By the time of the American Revolution, potatoes were being grown all over Europe. The impact of the potato on Northern Europe (including the British Isles) was enormous. Far more food could be produced on an acre of ground by growing potatoes than with wheat or barley. Even after adjusting for the higher moisture content, potatoes would produce at least four times as much food as wheat from the same plot (corn produces about twice as much while rice produces about one and a half times as much compared to wheat). Thus, potatoes became *"an ever-dependable staple, something eaten at every meal."* Further, *"their widespread consumption largely corresponded with the end of famine in Northern Europe."* As one Belgian historian put it: *"For the first time in the history of Western Europe, a definitive solution had been found to the food problem."*

Potatoes are uniquely nutritious. Thanks to the science of nutrition, it is now understood that *"the potato can better sustain life than any other food when eaten as the sole item of diet. It has all the essential nutrients except vitamins A and D, which can be supplied by milk."* While everyone in Europe was eating potatoes, *"roughly 40 percent of the Irish ate no solid food other than potatoes; the figure was between 10 and 30 percent in the Netherlands, Belgium, Prussia, and perhaps Poland. Routine famine almost disappeared in potato country, a two-thousand-mile band that stretched from Ireland in the west to Russia's Ural Mountains in the east. At long last, the continent could, with the arrival of the potato, produce its own dinner."*

And populations soared. Not because people were having more children but because more of their children survived. In fact, they thrived, not only because famines were prevented but also because being better nourished, they were less likely to die of infectious diseases, the primary killer of children in that era. This was most apparent in Ireland, where the most potatoes were eaten and where the population increased four-fold in the century after potatoes became the primary food. *"Ireland's sharecroppers were among Europe's most impoverished people. Yet, they were also among its most well nourished, because they ate potatoes."* These dramatic increases in populations in Europe resulted in crowding and the interest in migrating to new open lands. The magnitude of Europe's colonization of the rest of the world, particularly the Americas, simply would not have happened, but for the potato feeding the burgeoning population there that then needed new areas to expand into. As one scholar put it; *"Potatoes, by feeding rapidly growing populations, permitted a handful of European nations to assert dominion over most of the world."* As another historian put it: *"The potato fueled the rise of the West."*

CORN, SWEET POTATOES, AND OTHER AMERICAN CROPS- Europeans were not the only people to adopt new crops from the Americas to feed themselves. Despite its ban on foreign visitors, China managed to adopt American crops quicker than any other place in the Old World, particularly corn and sweet potatoes. *"The nation's agriculture, based on* *rice, had long been concentrated in river valleys. Sweet potatoes and maize could be grown in the dry uplands. Farmers moved in numbers to these areas, which had previously been lightly settled. The result was a wave of deforestation."* As described by Alfred W. Crosby:

> *While the men who stormed Tenochtitlan with Cortez still lived, peanuts were swelling in the sandy loams near Shanghai; maize was turning fields green in south China, and the sweet potato was on its way to becoming the poor man's staple in Fujian.*

In addition, other American crops, tobacco, hot peppers, pineapple, cashew, and manioc (cassava), were all being grown in China within a century. Today, China grows three-fourths of the World's sweet potatoes and is the world's second-largest corn producer. Corn is now the number one crop in the world. Its current importance in feeding the world's burgeoning population cannot be overstated. Enough about corn (maize).

Sweet potatoes, which are not botanically related to potatoes, were also developed in the Andes. They are quite distinct from yams, which come from Africa. However, all the canned or fresh *yams* that we see in the grocery store are really sweet potatoes from the Andes, not African yams. Sweet potatoes and corn, along with some help from potatoes, did for China (and, to a lesser extent Southeast Asia and Africa) what potatoes did for Europe. They fueled a population explosion. These crops could be grown on slopes and in soils where rice could not. One Chinese historian commenting on the population boom that took place during the Qing dynasty noted: *"Most of the increase took place in the areas with American crops. The families that Qing policies encouraged to move west needed to eat, and what they ate, day in and day out, was maize, potatoes, and sweet potatoes."* Another Chinese historian called the arrival of American crops *"One of the most revolutionary events"* in imperial China's history. Vast areas of forested hillsides, particularly in western China, were stripped of trees in order to grow sweet potatoes. The size of China's cultivated areas almost tripled between 1700 and 1850. This practice, spurred again by Chairman Mao, exploded in the 1960s in order to grow more sweet potatoes. However, it has led to serious wind and water erosion problems on unstable slopes, particularly in those areas recently deforested under Chairman Mao.

Unfortunately, this Chinese population boom brought on by American crops occurred almost exclusively among the peasants, China's poorest, while providing no new opportunities to expand the population's

Accumulated Knowledge. In short, China had walled itself off from the rest of the world and stood still while Europe moved on, encircling the globe in the process.

New American foods, which slave traders brought in, primarily manioc (cassava), sweet potatoes, and corn, enabled Africa to maintain a fairly stable population during the centuries of the transatlantic slave trade despite millions of slaves being shipped abroad. Manioc is now the primary food for 700 million people in central Africa. Sweet potatoes and corn are also staples.

Additional new foods from America, like tomatoes, squash, pumpkins, most beans, all kinds of peppers, peanuts, pineapple, avocados, and chocolate, have also made their way around the world. While they have not had the population-shifting impacts that corn, potatoes, sweet potatoes, and manioc have had, they have certainly brought greater variety to dinner tables around the world. Some, like tomatoes in Italy and hot peppers in China and Southeast Asia, have become an integral part of the culture's cuisine.

RUBBER – After Cortez toppled the Aztec Empire in Mexico, Spain was still debating whether the local natives should be enslaved or converted and made Spanish citizens. As explained by Charles C. Mann, the anti-slavery faction of the Catholic church, in 1526, brought a group of Aztec Indians to Seville so they could demonstrate their intelligence, skill, and other noble qualities. The Indians were divided into teams and played an Aztec game that was a little like soccer before a Spanish crowd. There were no team games or sports of any kind in Europe at that time, so this was quite novel. Each team tried to drive a ball about the size of a softball through hoops at opposite ends of the playing field. The ball was never to touch the ground; players could only hit it with their hips, chest, or thighs. They wore pads and played with *"so much dexterity that it was marvelous to see, sometimes throwing themselves completely on the ground to return the ball and all this done with great speed."* As fascinating as the players were to their Spanish spectators, those spectators were just as fascinated by the ball used in the game. They wrote whole paragraphs trying to describe what the ball could do. They had to write all that because the Spanish language had no word for *bounce*. After all, none of them had ever seen anything *bounce* before because there was nothing in all of Spain that *bounced*. The ball was made of what we now call rubber, extracted from a particular type of tree unique to the Amazon Basin.

It is impossible to overstate the importance of rubber in our modern world or to try to imagine just what our world would be like today if there was no rubber. Although it would be another two and a half centuries after that game in Seville before rubber would be put to any significant economic use (an early use in Britain was to rub off, or erase, unwanted marks on paper or walls – thus the name *rubber*), today it is used in thousands of products ranging from raingear, medical gloves and equipment, engine belts, and O-rings, to tires for bicycles, cars, trucks, and airplanes. The essential role of rubber in the industrial revolution is covered later. Suffice it to say here that all our lives would be unimaginably different without it, while rubber tree plantations, from a few stock trees stolen from Brazil more than a century ago, have now transformed both the landscape and the economy in sections of the Philippines, Indonesia, Malaysia, Thailand, Laos, Vietnam, and China. And farmers there are thankful for the opportunities it provides. Just as the potato played a critical part in the rise of the West, growing rubber is now revolutionizing the economies in many areas of rural southeast Asia.

GUANO – Really? Did guano from America contribute to our modern way of life? *Yup!* How? Okay, here's how!

The Chincha Islands are a small cluster of islands more than ten miles off the coast of southern Peru. For reasons we won't go into here, the ocean around these islands and along the coast there are among the richest ocean fisheries on the planet. For millennia these waters have been fished by large shore birds; pelican, cormorant, and booby. And these birds – by the thousands – nested, rested, and did their business on these barren islands. Almost anywhere else on Earth, rain would have washed much of that guano (a mixture of bird doo and urine – bird urine is a semi-solid) away, or at least leached it. However, the coast there is part of the driest desert on Earth. These islands receive less than an inch of rain a year. They can go years without a raindrop. So, the guano accumulated, reaching thicknesses of as much as 150 feet deep. For centuries, the Andean Indians had known the value of guano as fertilizer and had hauled it to distant farms with llama pack trains. The Inca had even parceled out guano rights and had rules restricting when guano could be taken to protect the birds' nesting season. The Spanish showed no interest in what the Indians were doing with guano or why they were doing it. Over the next three centuries, Indians continued to come from long distances to take guano home.

Around 1800, an extremely curious German scientist, Friedrich Wilhelm Alexander von Humboldt, who helped pioneer botany, geography, astronomy, geology, and anthropology, spent five years traveling through the Americas. He was fascinated by the many Indian guano boats he saw along the Peruvian coast.

One could smell them a quarter of a mile away. The sailors, accustomed to the ammonia smell, aren't bothered by it; but we couldn't stop sneezing as they approached.

So, he took a little guano home for testing by two French chemists. The chemists found it to be high in nitrogen and recommended it as fertilizer. Initially, there was little interest.

Farmers in Europe and throughout the world had come to understand that continually raising crops on the same piece of land depleted the soil, and crop yields went down. Several things had been tried to alleviate this: leaving fields fallow for a year or two, rotating crops, spreading manure, etc., with varying levels of success. The most sought-after soil supplement in Britain, France, and Germany by 1800 was bone meal made by pulverizing bones from slaughterhouses. The demand for bone meal was so high they even used human bones from the battlefields of Waterloo and other battles. In 1822, a London newspaper noted: *"It is now ascertained beyond a doubt, by actual experiment upon an extensive scale, that a dead soldier is a most valuable article of commerce."* The value of bones also became a primary cause of grave robbing. So, when a few bags of guano showed up in European ports in the 1830s, they found a market.

Then, in 1840, a pioneering organic chemist, Justus von Liebig, who had built a strong reputation with the public by promoting potatoes and corn, published *Organic Chemistry in Its Application to Agriculture and Physiology.* In it he criticized the use of bone meal as a soil supplement (because it lacked nitrogen) while praising the use of guano.

It is sufficient to add a small quantity of guano to a soil consisting only of sand and clay, in order to procure the richest crop of maize.

Large landowners were suddenly rushing to buy guano. In 1841, Britain imported almost 2,000 tons of guano from the Chincha islands. Just four years later, in 1845, Britain imported over 220,000 tons of guano. *"Yields doubled, even tripled. Fertility in a bag! Prosperity that could be bought in a store!"* In just 40 years, Peru exported 13 million tons of guano, primarily from these islands. Sometimes, there would be as many as 150 ships from Europe lined up at the islands' docks, waiting to be loaded with guano. This all marked the beginning of today's fertilizer-driven agriculture, dictated by scientific research, that now feeds eight billion people.

The USA wanted in on the guano boom. In 1856, Congress passed the *Guano Islands Act,* authorizing US citizens to seize any guano islands they saw. Under that act, merchants claimed title to 94 islands and atolls between 1856 and 1903. The State Department made 66 of those US possessions. Most had little guano and were soon abandoned. The USA still controls nine of them. The most successful as a supply of guano was Navassa, 50 miles west of Haiti.

However, the guano boom came with two terrible consequences. First, the stinky stuff needed to be dug out of the mountains of guano and loaded into ships. An atrocious job that no one undertook willingly. So, the job was almost entirely done by illiterate Chinese peasants who were tricked into signing on as indentured servants at ports in China with the understanding that they would be shipped to other jobs in America. Once aboard ship, they were captives treated no better than African slaves taken across the Atlantic, while their mortality rates were about the same. They were taken to these islands, from which there was no escape, and forced to work in deplorable conditions. They were often overseen by African slaves, who were just glad not to be doing the guano digging themselves. Because death rates were high, more had to be constantly brought over. At least 100,000 Chinese were brought into Peru during the decades of the guano boom. However, not all dug guano. Some of them worked on the mainland building railroads and other infrastructure paid for with the profits from guano.

The other terrible consequence was that, somewhere in those guano shipments to Europe, the potato blight, *Phytophthora infestans,* came along for the ride. The blight first showed up in Belgium in July 1845. It spreads via airborne spores and had reached Ireland by September. Over a fourth of the season's crop had been lost by October. The next few years were worse. Since 40% of the Irish ate nothing but potatoes and the rest ate a lot of potatoes, Ireland was in total crisis. Civil order completely broke down. At least a million died of starvation, and millions more fled, mostly to America. Even as late as the 1960s, Ireland's population was still only half of what it had been in 1840. The potato famine also hit other European countries hard, but nowhere was the impact on a country so severe as Ireland because they ate more potatoes.

5: ENGLISH COLONIZATION OF NORTH AMERICA

Spain had gotten rich from its exploitation of the Americas, while Portugal had also done very well. Spain settled St, Augustine, Florida, in 1565. They also came up from Mexico and established Santa Fe in 1607. Other countries began showing interest and making claims for settlements in North America. France established Quebec in 1608. The Dutch established a fort at Albany, New York (and claimed all of the Hudson River valley as New Netherlands) in 1614.

England was also interested. As one Englishman put it *"those wreched people of America cry out unto us to bring unto them the gladd tidings of the gospell."* He stated that Spain, *"formally a poore and barren nation"* had converted *"many millions of infidels"* such that God had *"opened the bottomless treasures of his riches"* to them. However, the English Crown simply lacked the financial resources to launch such adventures.

Even its defeat of the Spanish Armada in 1588 was done largely with private ships. Queen Elizabeth had also authorized privateers, such as Francis Drake, to raid Spanish ships. Then, in 1606 – three years after assuming the throne upon the death of Queen Elizabeth, King James created the Virginia Company, a private joint stock company (ancestor to the modern corporation) consisting of several wealthy nobles mostly based in London. Its express purposes were to build up England's merchant fleet, broaden trade, increase the number of able mariners, find precious metals, found a protestant colony, and convert the heathen. However, overriding all that, its primary purpose was to make a profit for its investors.

And it was to do all that by organizing and financing colonization along the Atlantic coast of North America. The next year 1607, Jamestown was launched as a private profit-seeking venture. The problem was *"The commercially savvy and often very wealthy London merchants who dominated the Virginia Company simply had no idea what it took to establish a successful colony on the edge of the American wilderness, three thousand miles and three months from home."*

JAMESTOWN – On April 26, 1607, three small ships with about 105 colonists arrived in Chesapeake Bay. What they found was not uninhabited, pristine wilderness. Thousands of Indian farm families were scattered around in permanent villages amid their fields.

However, these *farms* were utterly unrecognizable to the English settlers. They simply could not comprehend what they were seeing. There were no fences, plowed fields, crops planted in rows, or domestic animals grazing in green pastures; all the things that made a farm a farm to the English. Open areas seemed to be a mass of disorganized green stuff. Old tree stumps were common, even in large open areas. And much of the land was largely treeless for miles back from rivers and large streams.

The forest consisted of large trees, trunks up to six feet in diameter, supporting a high closed canopy and virtually no understory. One could ride a horse or drive a carriage almost anywhere in the forest without encountering undergrowth or needing to duck under branches. Streams weren't the free-flowing brooks bubbling over rocky stream channels they were used to in England, but wide, slow-moving ponds between beaver dams. Why the difference? The Indians had no oxen, horses, or mules (or any other domesticated animals) to pull plows or pull up stumps. Since they had no animals and property was communal, they needed no fences.

They had no metal to make plows, shovels, or saws to cut wood. Stumps were useful as protection and trellises when planting their mixtures of corn, beans, squash, and occasional melons, gourds, and tobacco, such that vines ran helter-skelter everywhere. Fallow fields were full of other useful plants but just looked like overgrown weed patches to the English.

The Indian's primary means of maintaining this landscape was fire. And they used it annually. It cleared and maintained the open fields and, in the forest, kept the canopy high and the undergrowth out.

The colonists had been directed to settle back from the Ocean in order to avoid detection by the Spanish. However, all the good upland areas were already occupied by Indians. On May 14, they finally docked at the tidewater's limits, near a bend in the James River where it was deep enough that they could tie their ships to trees. It was not a good spot, which is why there were no Indians there. The saltwater boundary tends to trap sediments and organic waste from upstream. They were drinking the foulest water on the James River.

They were also starving. Most of them had been far more interested in looking for riches or a passage to the Pacific Ocean (which they believed to be within 200 miles) than planting and tending crops for winter food. Further, the Virginia Company retained title to all land, which limited interest in developing farm fields. By January, eight months later, there were only 38 still alive.

At that point, Powhatan, the Indian leader in the area, agreed to trade food for things that were new to the Indians: fabric, axes, swords, knives, iron pots, mirrors, glass beads, copper sheets, and guns. They figured they could expel the settlers anytime they wanted. As one historian put it, *"confidence born of ignorance"* was the attitude of both the English and the Indians toward each other.

The next summer, another 190 immigrants arrived. And they decided to fight with the Indians, a serious mistake. There were several skirmishes, with serious losses on both sides. Also, despite living in the middle of one of the world's richest fisheries (both fish and shellfish), they were starving. They simply didn't know how to catch them or even realize all that abundance was there.

Another problem was that many of the colonists simply did not work. Of these first 295 colonists at Jamestown, 92 were *gentlemen:* men who, because of their social status, had never done any work nor had the slighted inclination to start now. Another third were *"the personal attendants that gentlemen thought necessary to make life bearable even in England."* These personal servants were also defined as doing no manual labor. In the spring of 1610, another convoy arrived with 250 new colonists and a year's supply of food. Within months, 150 of them had died. By 1616, the investors had spent a fortune and shipped 1700 men to Jamestown. But all they had to show for it was a rickety fort at a lousy spot on the James River housing 350 sick and hungry survivors. Why so many died will be discussed later.

Jamestown survived despite the ghastly death rate for three reasons. First, initially, the overconfident Indians not only let them survive but also helped them because of the unique trade goods they brought, particularly metal tools, weapons, and containers. The Indians finally went against Jamestown in a serious way in 1622 and killed a third of the settlers. But it was too late to wipe out the colony.

Second, economic conditions in England were so poor that there was no shortage of desperate people willing to take on the adventure, despite health risks, even as indentured servants.

Third, tobacco. But not the nasty local stuff the Indians around them smoked. Instead, John Rolfe had brought the good stuff, a separate species, up from Trinidad, where the Spanish were cultivating it. With the help of local Indians (in 1614, he married the Indian princess Pocahontas), he learned the exacting process of growing and curing tobacco. In 1616, he took his first shipment of tobacco to England. It was an immediate hit.

That prompted the Virginia company to immediately begin allowing colonists to own their own land. It also began giving 50 acres of land to each person who paid their own way or whose way was paid by a fellow traveler. Any indentured servant who survived long enough to complete their years of indentured service obligation would also get 50 acres.

By that time, because Jamestown was continuing to drain resources, the Virginia Company lacked sufficient financing to launch any other ventures. Therefore, they decided to offer franchises for any future settlements elsewhere along the Atlantic Coast by issuing subsidiary patents to those interested in settling.

In 1618, 20,000 pounds of tobacco were shipped. In 1620, the Virginia company shipped 90 women to Jamestown as mail-order brides for bachelor settlers (at a price of 125 pounds of tobacco for each bride). Prior to that, only a handful of women (wives or servants) had gone. And most of them had died. More contract brides followed, which began a slow shift in the social fabric of Jamestown from the masculine atmosphere typical of a mining camp to that of a normal English settlement. In 1622, 60,000 pounds of tobacco were shipped despite the loss of life to Indian attacks.

However, it was not enough to save the Virginia Company, which was bankrupt by 1624, having shipped about 7,000 colonists to Jamestown, of which 80% had died, most within their first year. So, King James revoked their charter and made Jamestown a Crown colony from that point on. In 1627, 500,000 pounds of tobacco were shipped. In 1638, three million pounds of tobacco were shipped.

By then, Jamestown had become the major source of tobacco for Western Europe. For over three centuries, tobacco remained the principal agricultural crop and economic force of the coastal plain and piedmont of Virginia and North Carolina.

VOYAGE OF THE MAYFLOWER – While the USA became a nation on July 4, 1776, its political and philosophical roots were planted much more at Plymouth, Massachusetts, in 1620, than at Jamestown in 1607. Why? Because the purpose of the Jamestown settlement was, like all other European ventures into the Americas, to extract wealth and to establish a route to Asia. Few women came to Jamestown in the first 12 years.

However, the Pilgrims on the Mayflower came for a very different reason. They were families: men, women (three were pregnant), and children, looking to start a new life in a new place where they would be free to worship God in the way they felt He should be. That made them distinctly different from all previous European settlements in the Americas. Rather than looking for wealth to take home, they were looking for a permanent new life. Many were religious refugees, some of whom had already sought refuge in Holland for a dozen years.

Some of them were part of a sect called Puritans that rejected many aspects of the Church of England and sought to separate themselves (so sometimes called Separatists) from it, an illegal act during the reign of King James. As other groups of Separatists had done, a few hundred went to Holland in 1608, where they settled in Leiden.

However, after ten years, their economic and persecution problems were such that the group began planning to go to America, where they hoped to recreate an English village while worshiping God as they saw fit.

Two prominent patrons still in England managed to get a subsidiary patent in 1619 from the Virginia Company for a settlement at the mouth of the Hudson River. They were now ready to go but needed to figure out how to get there. "*We are well weaned from the delicate milk of our mother country and inured to the difficulties of a strange hard land, which yet in a great part we have overcome. We are knit together in a body in a most strict and sacred bond. It is not with us as with other men whom small things can discourage, or small discontentments cause to wish themselves home again."* However, only about 125 (a third of the group) wanted to be part of the first venture. The rest said they would follow later.

Their patrons in England were working to secure financing and transportation. Although they had hoped to already be underway by June 1620, they had not yet found a ship. Without the Leiden group's knowledge, their financier committed them to six days a week as indentured servants for the first seven years instead of the original idea of four days a week. Further, he insisted that others from London, unknown to them, whom we will refer to as the *others*, be part of the first group in order to obtain a ship.

Concerned about delays, those in Leiden pooled their meager resources and bought a small ship, the Speedwell, they planned to keep in America and use for fishing to pay their debts. At the end of July, with a new mast installed, the Speedwell sailed from Holland packed with Puritans.

By then, the Mayflower and crew had been secured in London for the voyage. It was a larger and older ship. It was soon loaded with some supplies, a few Puritans already in England, and the others. It then sailed to South Hampton, where it met up with the Speedwell. As they were balancing the passenger load between the two ships and loading up a year's supply of food, those from Leiden learned of the new indentured service requirement and refused to honor it. The financier then walked away without providing the funds needed to pay for the food supply. Thus, they set sail woefully short of food.

When they got under full sail, the Speedwell began to leak. *"She is open and leaky as a sieve."* So they sailed back to Dartmouth, 75 miles west of South Hampton, for repairs. At that point, several of the Puritans were ready to bail out. However, the appointed governor of the passengers, one of the others, refused to let anyone off the ships. After quick repairs, they set sail again. And again, the Speedwell began to leak. It turned out the new mast was too large for the ship, so that with full sails, it put so much strain on the hull that the boards slid and spread enough to cause leaks. So both ships sailed back to Plymouth, a little further west, knowing they would have to abandon the Speedwell and take as many as possible in just one ship, the Mayflower.

The Mayflower finally left Plymouth on September 6, 1620, extremely late in the season, with a crew of 20 – 30 sailors and 102 passengers, just half of whom were Puritans. All, whom we will call Pilgrims, had already been aboard the ship for 30 days.

As they traveled west, the captain knew he was too far north but pushed hard as fast as he possibly could because of the condition of his passengers. They finally saw land on Thursday, November 9, after 64 days at sea. By then, the Pilgrims had been aboard ship for almost 100 days, their supplies, particularly anything to drink, were depleted, and almost all showed serious scurvy symptoms.

In short, they were in desperate shape. The captain knew from his maps that he was looking at the Cape Cod peninsula. He turned south, very concerned that he desperately needed to get the passengers off the ship as soon as possible and that they still had a long way to go through largely uncharted treacherous waters that were known to have already wrecked a few ships to reach the mouth of the Hudson River. As they sailed south, the crew constantly measured the depth as many Pilgrims happily watched the shoreline from the deck.

Initially, things went well. However, as they neared the gap between the mainland and Nantucket Island in mid-afternoon, the wind shifted, the depth suddenly became dangerously shallow, clouds darkened the sky, and the currents began to swirl. The captain had had enough. He made the momentous decision to disregard his contract to take them to the Hudson River and turned north to take them into Cape Cod Bay.

That put the Pilgrims in an absolute uproar. Some were glad because of the excellent fishing there. It had already been named Cape Cod (in 1602 by an Englishman) for a reason.

Disputes erupted, particularly with the more belligerent and profane of the others. One insisted that *"when they came ashore they would use their own liberty, for none had power to command them."* Yet, the Pilgrims' governor, one of the others, had finally learned to respect the discipline of the Leideners and recognized that for the colony to have any chance of survival in this harsh new land with winter approaching, they needed to stick together. So, on Friday, as they sailed north, they hammered out an agreement that all men would need to sign before leaving the ship. It became known as the Mayflower Compact and said in part:

...These present solemnly and mutually in the presence of God and one another, covenant and combine ourselves together into a civil body politic, for our better ordering and preservation...and by virtue hereof to enact, constitute and frame such just and equal laws, ordinances, acts, constitutions and offices, from time to time for the general good of the colony, unto which we promise all due submission and obedience.

Considering all the disparate views and feelings among the pilgrims and the enormous challenges ahead, it *"represented a remarkable act of coolheaded and pragmatic resolve."*

About sunrise Saturday morning, November 11, 1620, the captain steered the Mayflower into Provincetown Harbor, inside the western side of the tip of the Cape Cod Peninsula. They had arrived in America. As one Pilgrim later described it: *"Here I cannot but stay and make pause and stand half amazed at this poor people's present condition. They had no friends to welcome them nor inns to entertain or refresh their weather beaten bodies; no houses or much less towns to repair to, to seek for succor. What would sustain them but the spirit of God and His Grace? "*

THE PILGRIMS SETTLEMENT AT PLYMOUTH – The Pilgrims finally all went ashore on Monday, November 13, 1620, after having spent Sunday onboard the ship to observe the Sabbath despite their wretched condition. The captain was anxious to get the Pilgrims and all their equipment off his ship as soon as possible so he could sail back to England. However, they needed to find a site for a permanent settlement before unloading the ship. The next few weeks were spent exploring south and then west along the peninsula, both on land and using the smaller boat they had reassembled during their first couple of days on shore.

Along the disappointingly rather barren landscape, they found two cashes of corn totaling about 14 bushels. They raided both totally since they were short on food supplies. They found a grave, opened it up, and found some artifacts, then decided it probably was not a good idea to be raiding Indian graves since they would be living among them. They found another grave covered with sawed boards with carvings on them. They looked like they were probably from a wrecked ship. In the grave, they found a skull with yellow hair. That made them nervous. Had the Indians killed him or taken care of him? They saw a couple of groups of Indians, but the Indians ran away, and they could not catch them. They found a small Indian settlement with a few wigwams in it that had been very quickly and recently abandoned. They found clay pots, wooden bowls, and reed baskets. They took the best of them. One morning, a group of Indians attacked with arrows and harrowing war cries as their shore party was breaking camp. They returned fire with their muskets. No one was hit. After the Indians fled, they gathered up 18 arrows, *some headed with brass, others with harts' horn, others with eagles' claws.* From the beginning, they were genuinely concerned about relations with the Indians. Yet, everything they had done so far could only have negative impacts on such relationships. It wasn't looking good.

They had not yet found a suitable settlement site. They needed a site at the mouth of a stream large enough to supply ample fresh water. Yet it did not seem to dawn on them that the peninsula they were exploring was way too narrow to ever generate a stream that large. The advance party finally sailed west across Cape Cod Bay in the smaller boat. After a harrowing journey in which they nearly crashed on the rocks, they finally settled into a large protected harbor with an island in it, along with a few significant streams. On Monday, December 11, 1620, they began to explore what would be their new home. They then went back for the Mayflower and the rest of their party. The Mayflower sailed into the harbor of their new home on Saturday, December 16. Because the harbor was shallow, they had to leave the Mayflower a mile offshore. After a few more days of exploration on shore, they finally decided where they would build their new settlement on December 20, 1620, and went to work. They would name it Plymouth.

The selected site had several excellent features, including the fact that it had already been cleared and settled. Although no structures remained, it had obviously been the site of a substantial Indian village. *Their skulls and bones were found in many places lying still above ground..., a very sad spectacle to behold."*

Much like the area around Jamestown, there were large deforested areas, while the forested areas were incredibly open and park-like (a person could ride a horse around in it) with large trees, including white pine five feet in diameter and 100-200 feet tall. As one pilgrim put it: *"Thousands of men have lived here, which died in a great plague not long since: and pity it was and is to see, so many goodly fields, and so well seated, without men to dress and manure the same."* They came across one treeless area over five miles wide that had recently been burned.

As they began to try building a settlement, storms raged, fevers spread, scurvy symptoms continued, and people began to die. It took over two weeks to get the first structure up, a twenty-foot square log building with no foundation and a roof of thatched reeds and cattails. Because the ship's crew also got sick, with some dying, the captain realized he was stuck here for the winter. While the Pilgrims tended to their sick, the crew showed little interest in looking after the sailors who were ill. When one, the boatswain, who had often cursed and scoffed at the Pilgrims, fell ill, the Pilgrims looked after him. In his final hours, he said, *"Oh, you, I now see, show your love like Christians indeed one to another, but we let one another die like dogs."* Sometimes, there were two or three deaths on the same day. By spring, 52 of the 102 Pilgrims were dead, along with some sailors. Only four families, including two families of the others, remained intact. The rest lost family members, resulting in several widows, widowers, and even orphans.

They lived in constant fear of an Indian attack. They frequently saw Indians, but they would disappear if they tried to approach them. They all appeared tall, strong, and healthy. As one Pilgrim put it, they were *"as proper men and women for feature and limbes as fine as can be found."* They had none of the smallpox scars or rickety limbs caused by malnutrition that were common to Europeans of that era. It was apparent they were being constantly watched. A few times, the Indians shouted and yelled, but the attacks never came. They established military drills and alarms. In mid-February, they positioned their half-dozen cannon on a nearby knoll. What had started just two months before as a ramshackle little group of highly combustible houses was on its way to becoming a well-defended little fortress. They did their best to hide the fact that so many of them had died. Then, on March 16, 1621, after over four months with no direct contact, a single Indian strode *"very boldly"* right into their little settlement and up to where they were all gathered for a meeting. He towered over them, *"a tall straight man",* with black hair and a hairless face. He was *"stark naked"* with just a fringed strap of leather around his waist (a loin cloth?). The Pilgrims made no mention of his skin color. He was armed with a bow and just two arrows, one with a head and one without (if the intent was to signal the options of war or peace, the Pilgrims apparently missed it). He then enthusiastically said with a loud voice:

Welcome Englishmen!

What a remarkable statement! And what a surprise! He spoke English! So, what could the Pilgrims learn from this? First, there may be the potential to avoid armed conflict. What a relief! Second, they would be able to communicate, at least to some extent (his English was quite limited). Third, since he called them Englishmen, it demonstrated that the Indians already knew there were different groups of these pale little men, with hair all over their faces, who came around from time to time in ships. After all, they spoke several different languages. And they had observed the Pilgrims enough to know that their language identified them as Englishmen.

In fact, European ships had been showing up off the coast of New England for well over a century by the time the Pilgrims arrived in 1620. In 1501, a Portuguese explorer abducted 50 Indians along the coast of Maine. To his surprise, two of them had items from Venice, a broken sword, and two silver rings. So even he was obviously not the first European in the area. Since then, fishermen had been increasingly working the waters along the coast from Cape Cod to Quebec. In 1523, an Italian sailed up the coast from the Carolinas to Maine. He observed that the coastline everywhere was *"densely populated."* At what is now Providence, an Indian chief came out to his ship, with twenty canoes and leaped aboard. He was a tall, long-haired man *"as beautiful of stature and build as I can describe"* with colorful jewelry about his neck and ears. By the time the ship got to Maine, it was apparent the Indians there had already had many previous encounters with Europeans. By 1610, England alone had about 200 fishing ships operating from Cape Cod to Quebec. Other countries were there as well. The fishermen all agreed the shores were thickly settled and well-defended by Indians.

The Indians along the coast generally viewed Europeans with as much disdain as the Europeans viewed the Indians. As one disgruntled missionary put it, the Indians thought Europeans possessed *"little intelligence in comparison to themselves."* They considered these pale, hairy little men as weak, gabby without much to say, disingenuous, often treacherous, sexually untrustworthy, shockingly ugly and dirty, and just plain smelly (the European sailors, who never bathed, were amazed at the Indians' interest in personal cleanliness). The Indians were disgusted by handkerchiefs. One priest reported, *"They say we place what is unclean in a fine white piece of linen and put it away in our pockets as something very precious, while they throw it on the ground."* But the Europeans had great stuff! Their ships were like grungy floating shops that came by from time to time willing to trade marvelous and unheard-of stuff like steel knives and hatchets, iron pots, copper kettles, and fabrics just for furs, something they had plenty of. They were intrigued by fabrics since they had nothing but animal skins to wrap themselves in. While they were happy to trade with Europeans, they would not let them settle. Anyone who stayed for more than a month or so was harassed until they left.

By mid-March, the Pilgrims had been at Plymouth for almost three months and were clearly settling in. What to do about it? The Indian who had walked into their midst identified himself as Samoset. He was not local but from an area along the Maine coast frequently visited by English fishermen, so he had learned some English. He gave them the names of Englishmen he knew. He told them he was just visiting the area and that where they had settled had been called Patuxet, but most of the residents had died in a recent terrible plague (Patuxet had been there for centuries with well over a thousand residents. In fact, in 1605, a Frenchman, Samuel Champlain, explored the area and drew a detailed map of some harbors, including Plymouth Harbor, showing locations of fields, houses, and woods). Samoset said he was visiting Massasoit, who lived to the west in the village of Pokanoket (where Providence now is). Massasoit was the *sachem* (both spiritual and temporal leader) of the local people who were called the *Pokanoket* (who were a subset of a larger group called the *Wampanoag*) that had included the village of Patuxet. There were four groups of Indians in the area that were significant to the pilgrims' arrival and survival. In addition to the Pokanoket, those to the south and east on Cape Cod, where they had stolen the corn, were the *Nauset,* which Samoset said were ill-disposed toward the English. To the north, around Boston Harbor, were the *Massachusett*. These two groups were also part of the Wampanoag alliance. The group west of Providence and on into Connecticut were the *Narragansett*, who were the chief antagonists of the Pokanoket. There was a fifth group on Martha's Vineyard. Their languages were part of the Algonquin language group.

Although there had been many European visitors to Patuxet before, the most consequential for the pilgrims was that of Captain John Smith from Jamestown, who visited the area with two ships in 1614. After a very successful and cordial trading visit, Smith sailed away, leaving the other ship behind to finish loading supplies and trade goods. Captain Hunt invited a large group of Indians to tour the ship as they were finishing up. Among them was a young man named Tisquantum (or Squanto – from here on, I will use Squanto because it is shorter). Hunt then ordered the Indians thrown in the hold. A fight broke out in which several Indians were killed, while the remaining 20 were kidnapped, including Squanto. The ship then stopped out on Cape Cod, where another seven Indians were kidnapped while more were killed. Hunt then sailed to Spain, where he intended to sell them all as slaves. However, the Catholic Church intervened in the sale since it strongly opposed enslaving Indians. Squanto somehow made his way to England, where he lived in London for a few years with a shipbuilder with investments in Newfoundland.

He taught Squanto English and liked to show him off as his Indian. It seemed to be far easier for the Indians to learn English than the other way around. While the New England Indians were not particularly talkative unless they had something to say, they were exceptional mimics. Some could repeat whole sentences back verbatim even though they had no idea what was being said.

In 1615, a French ship ran aground on Cape Cod. In response to what Captain Hunt had done the year before, the Indians there killed almost all the crew and burned their ship. At about that same time, another French ship stopped in Boston Harbor, where Indians killed the entire crew and burned the ship. The Virginia Company blamed the failure of their venture in Maine on the fact that Hunt had ruined relationships with the Indians.

Meanwhile, Squanto was convincing his benefactor in London of the riches to be had in Cape Cod Bay and of his ability to help him tap into them. So, he was allowed to board a ship to Newfoundland. He eventually made his way to Maine and then sailed south in 1619 with a man named Dermer. Dermer described who described the coast as they sailed south:

we passed along the coast where we found some ancient plantations, not long since populous now utterly void; in other places a remnant remains but not free of sickness. Their disease the plague, for we might perceive the sores of some that had escaped, who descried the spots of such as usually die. When we arrived at my savage's native country, all were dead.

They were sailing by what was essentially a cemetery for 200 miles along the coast that stretched 40 miles inland. Where there had been thriving communities shortly before, skeletons were now bleaching in the sun. It must have been a shock for Squanto to find his hometown totally gone, with just scattered skeletons remaining. The pestilence started in 1616 and took three years to burn out.

As people got sick and began to die, those still alive fled, leaving their dead wherever they lay but unknowingly carrying the disease with them to the next settlement. The epidemic killed up to 90 % of those along the coast from Cape Cod to Portland, Maine. Like Plymouth, over 50 more of the first English settlements in New England would arise on the sites of these obliterated Indian communities.

As was typical for that era when there was no understanding of what caused disease, most saw a spiritual aspect to it. As one of the Pilgrims put it, *"The good hand of God favored our beginnings by sweeping away a great multitude of the natives that he might make room for us."* Another Englishman wrote that the epidemic left the land *"without any to disturb or appease our free and peaceable possession thereof, from which we justly conclude that GOD made the way to affect his work."*

Massasoit had seen his immediate domain at Pokanoket shrink from a few thousand to less than a hundred, while his whole Pokanoket people had shrunk from about 20,000 to less than a thousand. However, due to the extremely limited interactions, because of tensions along their western border with the Narragansett, the Narragansett were virtually unaffected by the epidemic. That enabled the Narragansett to begin bullying Massasoit and his people. Squanto took Dermer to visit Massasoit at Pokanoket. Then Squanto and Dermer sailed back to Maine. Squanto then decided he really did still want to be home. So he walked all the way back to Pokanoket alone.

By the time Dermer returned to the area in the summer of 1620 (just months before the Pilgrims arrived), the Pokanoket had developed an *"inveterate malice to the English."* And for good reason. Just that spring, an English ship had sailed into Narragansett Bay (Providence). After its sailors invited a large group of Massasoit's people aboard, they just shot and killed them all. So Dermer would have been killed when he returned had Squanto not intervened for him. Everywhere Dermer went, he came under attack even though Squanto went with him. On Martha's Vineyard, Dermer was attacked and gravely wounded, most of his men were killed, and Squanto was taken prisoner. Dermer died shortly after making his way back to Jamestown. That fall, Squanto was moved from Martha's Vineyard back to Pokanoket. So, when the Mayflower first arrived in November, the Indians initially assumed it was there to avenge the attack on Dermer.

Massasoit had been keeping track of the Pilgrims since they first arrived. That interest increased when they moved into his territory in December and began to settle in. They were different. First of all, they had women and children with them, the first European women and children they had ever seen. And they were constructing buildings. They clearly intended to stay. He had a decision to make. He had sent Samoset because he spoke a little English. He also had Squanto as a prisoner. However, even though Squanto had grown up in Patuxet and spoke excellent English, Massasoit didn't trust him enough to have him make that first contact.

On Samoset's first visit, he stayed the night despite the Pilgrims' polite efforts to dissuade him. On March 22, he returned with four other Indians, including Squanto. Squanto immediately charmed the Pilgrims as he discussed with them, in fluent English, places in England where he had been. He then informed the Pilgrims that Massasoit was coming.

Massasoit appeared on a nearby hilltop surrounded by 60 warriors. He was *"a very lusty man, in his best years, an able body, grave of countenance, and spare of speech."* His face was painted dark red. His whole head glistened with bear grease. He wore a wide necklace of white shells. His warriors were *"all strong, tall men in appearance"* whose faces were also painted; *"some black, some red, some yellow, and some white, some with crosses, and other antic works."* Some had furs draped over their shoulders, while some were naked. All had a bow and a quiver full of arrows. It was an intimidating display. As requested, one of the Pilgrims went with Squanto to greet Massasoit. He went, clad in full armor with a sword at his side, where he presented Massasoit with a pair of knives, copper chains, some alcohol, and a few biscuits *"which were willingly accepted."*

After some discussion, with Squanto translating, the Pilgrim stayed with the Indians as a hostage while Massasoit went with 20 of his men, minus bows, to meet the Pilgrims' governor. In all, they had put together a surprisingly impressive reception for the man they considered the *"Indian King."* There was another exchange of seven hostages before a small procession, complete with a drummer and trumpeter and a few musketeers, ushered the two leaders together, where they kissed each other's hand before sitting on pillows on a green rug. Squanto translated. They worked out an agreement that required that each side do no physical harm to the other side, not steal from the other side, come to each other's defense if others threatened either side and that Massasoit notify other Indian groups of this agreement.

So why did Massasoit agree to this deal that not only let the Pilgrims stay at Plymouth but obligated him to defend them if attacked by other Indians? Just like the Athenians, 2,000 years before, when they let the settlement on Lesbos survive, he did it not out of charity but because he felt it was in the best self-interest of both himself and his people. He needed their support against the Narragansett. And, in the short term, it turned out to be a good deal for him.

Now back where he grew up, Squanto lived with the Pilgrims, helping them plant corn and better understand how to utilize the resources around them. The Mayflower sailed for England on April 5. The Pilgrims had several more successful interactions with Indians that summer, including once where they had to come to Massasoit's defense against his neighbors. It even brought the Pilgrims newfound respect from those neighbors. Their corn did well, while their wheat and peas did not. They celebrated that first fall (their first chance to see a New England fall with all its glorious colors – far more spectacular than any fall in England) with a feast. Massasoit, along with about 100 Indians, came with five freshly killed deer.

There were more than twice as many Indians as Pilgrims at that first Thanksgiving. By then, they no longer viewed these Indians as just a despicable pack of savages, despite their refusal to wear clothes. They now regarded them as *"very trustworthy, quick of apprehension, ripe witted, just."* They were also adjusting to the Indians' appearance. As one Pilgrim put it, the Indians were *"more amiable to behold (though only in Adam's finery) than many a compounded English dandy in the newest fashion."* A few weeks later, a small English ship arrived with 37 more settlers who had heard from the return of the Mayflower that a successful settlement had been established and that there was peace with the Indians.

The flow of English settlers to New England had begun. However, it was another two years before they were really on solid ground, both in their relations with Indians and in their ability to feed themselves.

The next year (1622), along with more settlers, chickens, goats, and pigs arrived from England. However, because their harvest was still quite limited, they continued to suffer crippling food shortages through their third winter. Those first two summers, they had grown crops communally as had been done at Jamestown. Then, in April 1623, the governor decided to assign each household its own plot of ground with the understanding that each one could keep whatever it grew. *"The change in attitude was stunning. Families were now willing to work much harder than they had ever worked before...The Pilgrims had stumbled upon the power of capitalism. The inhabitants never again starved."*

And this change was within a close-knit religious group committed to looking after one another. The Pilgrims were still willing to share their own food with a family in need after the harvest was in, but that was quite different than splitting the harvest of a communal crop. This is an obvious lesson many are still struggling to learn and relearn. Michael Shellenberger, who was a committed socialist, has described his experience in Brazil in the 1990s as follows:

In Brazil, as in Nicaragua, my enthusiasm for socialist cooperatives was often greater than that of the small farmers who were supposed to benefit from them. Most of the small farmers I interviewed wanted to work their own plot of land. They might be great friends with their neighbors, and even be related to them by birth or marriage, but they didn't want to farm with them. They didn't want to be taken advantage of by somebody who didn't work as hard as them, they told me.

Meanwhile, it turned out that Massasoit had good reason not to trust Squanto, who had been plotting to overthrow Massasoit and become Sachem in his place by convincing the Pilgrims that Massasoit was joining forces with the Massachusett to drive the Pilgrims out. He had also apparently told Massasoit and other Indians that the Pilgrims kept the plague in barrels in their storehouse and could bring it out anytime they wanted to kill the Indians. When the plot was uncovered, Massasoit demanded that Squanto be turned over to him for execution. However, the governor of the Pilgrims had become so dependent on Squanto as a translator and confidant that he refused to turn him over. Then, Squanto suddenly fell ill and died. Was he poisoned? So, by the fall of 1622, relations were very tense between Indian groups and with the Pilgrims. The trust of the previous fall had completely evaporated.

Then Massasoit fell deathly ill. Edward Winslow, a prominent Pilgrim who had dealt with Massasoit before, went to Pokanoket to see him. He found Massasoit, who had not eaten for days, expecting to die soon. He was very weak, blind, and had thick white fur all over his tongue (we now know that is a symptom of typhus). Winslow scraped his tongue and fed him chicken broth and some preserves. As he was treating Massasoit, Indians poured in from as much as a hundred miles away to pay their final respects to Massasoit. However, Massasoit made a remarkable recovery over the next two days. He had asked Winslow to treat others in the village who were sick. So, Winslow found himself scraping the tongues of several other Indians. This changed everything. Massasoit said before all the crowd that had gathered:

Now I see the English are my friends and love me. And whilst I live, I will never forget this kindness they have showed me.

This event had a tremendous effect on all the Indian groups and diffused an explosive situation. Plymouth continued to grow. They got cows and horses in the fall of 1623, along with more settlers. However, several of the "others" grew tired of the Puritans' restrictive lifestyle and went back to England or to Jamestown. A few moved in with Indians.

So, in this short summary of history, why have I spent so much space on this story of the Pilgrims at Plymouth? Let me editorialize a bit. The Pilgrims were able to establish Plymouth and survive there for two reasons rolled into one. The epidemic opened a place to settle and, because of the desperate situation that epidemic had placed him in, Massasoit decided to let the Pilgrims stay. Even in his weakened situation, he could have easily driven them out. The Pilgrims had less than twenty able-bodied men. The Indians' arrows had as much killing power, accuracy, and range as the matchlock muskets of that era. And an Indian could fire half a dozen arrows in the time it took to reload a musket. Most of his people and all the neighboring Indian groups would have preferred he push the Pilgrims out. Yet, he made peace with them.

While preparing this review, I have become convinced that, but for Massasoit's decision to let the Pilgrims stay, there would be no USA as we know it. The USA owes its very existence to Massasoit's decision. Over the next few decades, the English poured into New England while Jamestown continued to grow. Other than Maryland's eastern shore, which was opened up for English Catholics in 1634, the English went nowhere else for over 40 years. If Massasoit had decided to attack, any surviving Pilgrims would have retreated to the Mayflower, which was still in the harbor. The Mayflower, with any survivors, would then have limped home with its tail between its, legs, a total loss for the venture's investors. That would have made two failed efforts in New England. The Virginia Company, with Jamestown still sucking up resources along with an 80% death rate, would have been unable to finance any new ventures. It was abolished by the King in 1624. Other English investors would have been hard to find. Spain was already in Florida.

The Dutch, who were already in Albany, established another trading post in Delaware in 1624, "bought" and settled Manhattan Island in 1626, and settled in New Jersey in 1630. Sweden settled in Delaware in 1634. The French were already in Quebec and were fishing along the New England coast. While it is likely that Europeans would still have eventually swept across North America, the entire Atlantic coast would not have been controlled by 13 British colonies able to unite against one mother nation.

There would have been no Declaration of Independence written on July 4, 1776, for us to now celebrate. The United States of America would not exist. Instead, north of the Rio Grande, America would be a patchwork of countries, like South America, but speaking several different European Languages, as we now see in Africa. Thus, the USA owes a huge debt of gratitude to Massasoit. And his people did benefit in the short term.

However, as we shall see, Massasoit's decision ended up being a disaster, not only for the Pokanoket and Indians in general but for his own children and grandchildren.

OTHER ENGLISH COLONIES ON THE ATLANTIC COAST OF NORTH AMERICA – In 1630, a fleet of 17 ships brought about a thousand English men, women, and children, all Puritans, to Boston Harbor, where they established the Massachusetts Colony. It was instantly three times the size of Plymouth Colony. The mouth of the Charles River was a much better harbor. It was well protected, while large ships could pull up close to the shore. It quickly became the center of an expanding New England. New Hampshire Colony was established a year later, with settlements soon extending into what is now Maine. Connecticut Colony was established in 1633 as more Puritans continued to arrive and spread out. Harvard College was also established in 1636, just six years after Boston was colonized. Over the next decade, as King Charles (who became king in 1625) clamped down on religious non-conformists in England, about 21,000 Puritans flooded into New England.

However, King Charles, who believed strongly in the absolute divine right of Kings, generally ignored parliament, which forcefully deposed him in 1645, after a three-year civil war between the armies of King Charles and Parliament. He was beheaded in 1649, after the monarchy had been abolished and the Commonwealth of England established as a republic. Oliver Cromwell, a Puritan, became head of state. With this dramatic political change, Puritan migration to New England abruptly stopped. The English Monarchy was reestablished in 1660, with Charles II as King, following the death of Cromwell.

It turned out that the Puritans were not very tolerant of divergent religious views either. And they enforced conformity. Roger Williams was kicked out of the Massachusetts Colony and established Rhode Island in 1636 as a colony with far fewer religious restrictions.

Thus, all five of the New England colonies began from Puritan stock. Rather than men just seeking adventure and profit, the settlers were families with deep religious convictions that influenced their approach to life in this new land. They believed idleness was the *Devil's workshop* and behaved accordingly. They were always doing. They came from England's better farmlands and were not destitute like the indentured servants going to Jamestown. They also included skilled craftsmen and professionals. However, New England had poor farmland. The area had been scraped down to bedrock during the last ice age, with its soil pushed down to create Long Island, Martha's' Vineyard, and Nantucket. Over the ensuing few thousand years, only thin scrabble soil had developed. Thus, while they were able to feed themselves, there was no cash crop, like tobacco, that would sustain the economy. So, New England's economy became far more diversified. Fishing, timber, livestock (meat), and shipbuilding became important factors. They could build a ship for about half the cost of building one in England. By 1700, New England had 15 shipyards and was producing 40 ships a year. However, it still needed to import iron and most manufactured goods. Although there was little new immigration into New England after 1645, the colonists had many children there. By 1700, the population was 90,000.

Meanwhile, Maryland was established in 1634 as a destination for Catholics who wanted to immigrate to North America. It developed more slowly because King Charles was more tolerant of Catholics than Puritans.

The Dutch colony of New Netherlands primarily stretched along the Hudson River from Manhattan to Albany. However, they also made some ventures around Delaware Bay and up the Delaware River. Their settlement on the west side of Delaware Bay was wiped out by Indians. New Sweden was established on both sides of the Delaware River near Wilmington. However, its total population never exceeded 400. The Dutch took over New Sweden in 1656 without much fight after the Swedes had captured a Dutch fort along the Delaware River the year before. Then, again without much resistance, the English took over all of New Netherlands in 1664 and renamed it *New York.* In that era, "*the Dutch had the most advanced and the most market-oriented economy in Europe.*" They had developed new levels of stock and commodity exchanges, as well as insurance and corporate government, along with a tolerance for religious diversity. *"Both the Dutch capitalist spirit and religious freedom"* that had been firmly planted in New Netherlands were retained as it became New York. The 8,000 Dutch already living there were there to make money, not fuss about religion. And that city they founded on Manhattan Island has retained that character ever since.

Over the next several decades, by various Royal decrees to favored subjects (which sometimes shifted boundaries), the English Crown divided what had been the New Netherlands area, comprising all the settlements between Maryland and New England, into three colonies: New York, New Jersey, and Delaware as new colonists from England continued to arrive.

In 1681, the king granted William Penn, a Quaker, an enormous area west of the Delaware River (now Pennsylvania) in exchange for canceling a large debt the king owed him. Penn had two goals in promoting a colony there: to extend religious freedom and to make money. The soil there was far better than in New England, and the climate was more moderate. Colonists poured in by the thousands, mostly families. Within six years, it had a population of over 6,000. In addition to Quakers, it attracted many Germans and Anglicans. Like New England and New York, it developed its own merchant class and an economy far more diverse than the plantation colonies in the South.

The two Carolina colonies have a separate history. Under the direction of Sir Walter Raleigh, a settlement was established on Roanoke Island in 1587 (20 years before Jamestown). However, due to the Spanish Armada invasion and other complications, it was three years before anyone returned with more supplies to check on it. The colony had simply disappeared. Not much happened for the next 75 years. Both Carolinas were part of the Carolina Land Grant by King Charles II in 1665. However, North Carolina developed almost entirely from colonists moving south from Virginia beginning in the 1660s, first into the Albemarle area and then to the mouth of the Cape Fear River (Wilmington). There was little direct colonization from England. The economy, like Virginia, was dominated by tobacco.

The history of South Carolina begins with English colonists moving into the Caribbean, particularly the Island of Barbados, in 1625. By then, it was largely uninhabited since the Portuguese, through disease and enslavement, had basically eliminated the native population. Many came as indentured servants since they were promised land upon completion of their servitude. By 1650, there were about 12,000 English colonists around the Chesapeake Bay (Jamestown), 23,000 in New England, and 44,000 in the West Indies, primarily Barbados (where thousands of African slaves were also brought in). In sum, substantially more had gone to the West Indies than to North America. Then, in 1665, when England took Jamaica from Spain, English settlers also began to flow there.

By 1670, sugarcane had replaced tobacco and cotton as the primary crop on Barbados. England now had its own supplies of sugar. With that change, there was a major consolidation of plantations occurring on Barbados, with many of the smaller operators being crowded out. So, about 200 of these displaced landowners left Barbados and established a new colony at Charleston in the Carolina land grant. They were already well-versed in plantation operations and slave management. Although the two Carolina colonies had thought of themselves as separate from the beginning, the official split into North and South Carolina occurred with a proclamation by the Crown in 1719. The primary cash crop and chief export of South Carolina's plantations was rice.

So, with Rice in South Carolina and tobacco in North Carolina and Virginia, both cash crops for export well suited to plantation agriculture, all three states developed plantation economies relying on slave labor. They failed to diversify agriculturally and developed little industry.

The thirteenth colony was Georgia. The first colonial effort by Europeans in Georgia was by Spain in 1526, when 300 colonists, along with 100 African slaves, were brought in. However, it was abandoned after just a few months. After decades of competing claims between England and Spain over the Georgia coast, in 1707 the English destroyed the Spanish missions there. Then, around 1715, South Carolina colonists and their Indian allies went to war with the local Indians, who then fled to Spanish Florida, which left the Georgia coast largely depopulated.

By 1730, England's debtor prisons were overflowing. James Oglethorpe, a member of parliament, proposed a colony in Georgia for the "noble poor" that could also be an alternative to prison for delinquent debtors. While it was not established as a penal colony, it was intended to promote the concept of "agrarian equality" for poor immigrants. A colony was established at Savanah in 1733. Slavery was prohibited, while land grants were limited to 50 acres. Those who went there as indentured servants could receive such a grant upon completion of their service. Initially, the primary crop was rice. The King lifted the ban on slavery in 1750. By 1776, black slaves were about a third of the population as it too shifted to a plantation economy.

In sum, migration into the thirteen British colonies that would become the United States has been described as occurring in four waves. One, the Puritans who came to New England from East Anglia seeking religious isolation, primarily between 1620 and 1650. Two, the Cavaliers seeking fortune, along with poor indentured servants, who came to Virginia from southern England in the seventeenth century. Three, the Quakers who came to the Delaware River Valley from England's North Midlands in the decades around 1700, where they mingled with the Dutch and Swedish immigrants already there. Many German immigrants also came into this area in that time period. And four, also in the decades around 1700, immigrants from Scotland (including some who had settled around Ulster, Ireland for a few generations – the Scotch-Irish) and England's northern borderlands, who settled some of the Carolina Piedmont and throughout Appalachia from Pennsylvania to Georgia where they made up a majority of the population in many counties.

These four distinct waves brought vastly different cultures, impacting the colonies' regional development. *"It is not uncommon for a culture to survive longer where it is transplanted and retain characteristics lost in its place of origin."* This cultural impact will be discussed later.

KING PHILLIP'S WAR – This war (which Nathanial Philbrick describes in detail), was between some Indian groups and New England colonists aided by other Indians. It began in June 1675 and lasted 14 months. On a *per capita* basis, it is the bloodiest war in our history. I can say "our" because I had several ancestors living in New England by 1675. I discuss it here for four reasons. First, it demonstrates the dramatic shift in the balance between colonists and Indians that had occurred in just 55 years. Second, it stands as an example of how the decisions of one or two leaders can not only have disastrous consequences for their people but shift history. Third, it stands as a horrific example of the disastrous consequences that can flow from presuming racial identity defines who people are (a critical component in the current debate about racism in the USA). Fourth, it demonstrates that, among the colonists, a unique American culture and identity was already forming just one or two generations removed from their very English progenitors.

On the issue of balance between colonists and Indians, from the moment the Pilgrims settled at Plymouth, the ways of life for both the colonists and the Indians around them began to irreversibly change. Indians grew attached to, and depended on, things only the colonists could provide, particularly metal tools, weapons, and fabric. The colonists had adopted corn as an essential crop and adjusted to living in a foreign wilderness surrounded by Indians. They constantly sought things to export back to England, primarily furs, fish, timber, and grain, to pay their debts and buy supplies. Within a few decades, the fur-bearing animals had been practically wiped out by Indians seeking furs to trade for colonist goods.

By this time, the new flintlock muskets were available. It was a weapon far superior to the old matchlock muskets colonists first brought. However, the conservative colonists tended to stick with their old guns, which the Indians considered no better than their bows and arrows, while the Indians bought as many flintlocks as they could possibly afford. Suddenly, the colonists found they no longer had a technological advantage in weapons, which made them nervous. Still, selling flintlocks and ammunition to the Indians was highly profitable, so they kept selling.

As Spain and Portugal had moved into the Americas, along with African slaves, it was done primarily with young men seeking fortune, resulting in generations of mixed-race children through social intermingling with native populations. However, since Puritans came as families and often settled in areas abandoned by Indians (a smallpox epidemic in 1634 again drastically reduced the local Indian population), there were few mixed-race children resulting from social intermingling between colonists and Indians. Although interactions were frequent, the two groups generally lived quite separately.

The next generation of colonists had lost their Puritan fervor, much to the dismay of their elders. The next generation of Indians had grown up during the boom times of the fur trade with colonists living around them. They viewed English goods as essential. Though the Puritans did not proselytize to Indians with the fervor of Spanish priests, some Indians, particularly around Cape Code and the Islands to the south, had converted to Christianity. They were generally referred to as Praying Indians.

From the beginning, the colonists recorded all land purchases from Indians. Initially, the Indians had no concept of private land ownership. However, after being snookered several times, they began to learn. A couple of sales are instructive. In 1650, Massasoit sold the site of Bridgewater for seven coats, nine hatchets, eight hoes, 29 knives, four moose skins, and 10 ½ yards of cotton. Two years later, he sold the site of Dartmouth for 30 yards of cloth, eight moose skins, 15 axes, 15 hoes, 15 pairs of shoes, one iron pot, and ten shillings' worth of assorted goods.

Let's just say 30 years after arrival, Massasoit was still being taken to the cleaners on land sales. As the fur trade collapsed, a finite and diminishing supply of land was all they had left to bargain with.

In short, by 1675, the growing colonist population no longer felt dependent on Indians for survival. Instead, they coveted the remaining Indian lands. On the other hand, internal Indian rivalries remained as Indians became accustomed to having colonists nearby and being dependent on their goods.

On the second point, this war was the result of two obstinate leaders. Each contributed to the circumstances that led to war. Either could have prevented it. One was Massasoit's son, Phillip, who had become the sachem of Pokanoket. The other was Edward Winslow's son, Josiah Winslow, who had become the governor of Plymouth. It is ironic that, but for their fathers saving each other's lives over 50 years before, neither of these men would have ever been born.

By 1662, Massasoit had been replaced as Sachem by his son Alexander, while Josiah Winslow had become the chief military officer of Plymouth. On two occasions, Alexander had sold land to members of the Rhode Island colony, which Plymouth viewed as a violation of their mutual agreement that supposedly prevented the Pokanokets from selling land to anyone but them. After the second sale, Alexander was ordered to appear in court in Plymouth. When he did not show up, Josiah was sent, with ten armed men, to get him. An enraged Alexander was brought in at gunpoint. After court, Alexander spent the night at Josiah's house, where he got sick. He died a few days later. His younger brother, Phillip, became sachem.

Thousands of Indians gathered to mourn the death of Alexander. While there, they celebrated the rise of Phillip, who was just 24 years old, to sachem. The *"flocking multitudes"* were so uproarious, and carried on so long that the leaders in Plymouth feared Phillip was convening a war council. They issued an order that he be brought into court. In court, he refused to cower before Plymouth magistrates. He made clear that he considered himself on a par with King Charles II, that the leaders in Plymouth were *"but subjects"* of King Charles II and therefore unfit to tell him, a fellow monarch, what to do. Thus, the Plymouth colonists came to mockingly call him "King Phillip," a nickname he never claimed for himself.

For the next decade, Phillip, who hated Josiah and was convinced that he had poisoned his brother, had to sell more and more land to try to maintain his people. However, he drove much harder bargains than his father or brother had done. He actually got reasonably fair prices. Then, in 1673, the governor of Plymouth died, and Josiah became governor. That meant Josiah and Phillip, who detested each other, now had to deal directly with each other. After Josiah ordered a confiscation of Phillip's guns, Phillip began to quietly prepare for war by accumulating weapons and ammunition while reaching out to other Indian groups for support.

Things came to a head before Phillip was ready when, in early 1675, a Harvard-educated Indian, Sassamon, who knew English very well and who had cheated Phillip in the past while acting as his interpreter, told Josiah Winslow that Phillip was preparing for war. Soon after, Sassamon turned up dead in suspicious circumstances. Another Indian of dubious loyalties came forward to say he had seen three of Phillip's close associates commit the murder. Although English law at that time required two witnesses to convict someone of murder, the Plymouth court, with Josiah presiding, convicted the three Indians on the dubious testimony of one Indian and promptly hung them. For a colonist court to convict and execute three Pokanoket Indians for allegedly killing another Pokanoket Indian, based solely on the testimony of a disaffected Pokanoket Indian, was so far beyond what the Pokanokets saw as Plymouth's jurisdiction that it put all of Phillip's people in an uproar. They were all ready for war.

After three weeks of war dances, on a Sunday in June 1675, Pokanoket Indians raided a few outlying colonists, killing cattle and burning a few houses. But they were careful to kill no settlers. Colonists responded by killing a few Indian raiders. So, Indians killed those colonists. And the war was on. Within days, the Massachusetts and the Rhode Island colonies sent forces to assist Plymouth. This force drove the Pokanokets, including women and children, from their home territory and into the areas of two female Sachems to the southeast, who then found themselves reluctantly having to back Phillip even though they had tried to stay out of the fight. Then, at the end of July, with his fighting force whittled down from 250 to about 40 warriors accompanied by about a hundred hungry women and children, Phillip managed to sneak them all past the colonist forces and lead them into the area of the Nipmuck, who had built close ties with Massasoit, in central Massachusetts. The fight between Phillip and Josiah had quickly gotten out of hand and suddenly was well beyond Pokanoket vs Plymouth.

My third point is that the real tragedy was that the New England colonists, who were all English Puritans, immediately assumed this was a war between the English and all Indians rather than a localized political dispute between Plymouth and the Pokanoket. Therefore, even though those in the Massachusetts and Rhode Island colonies generally felt that Josiah had been unduly severe in his treatment of the Pokanoket, they immediately came to Plymouth's aid when fighting broke out. They made the same mistake the Indians of Cape Cod and around Boston Harbor had made in 1615 when they burned French ships and killed the crews in response to what an English ship had done the year before. Both groups of Indians had assumed that because the crews of both ships looked the same (they were all European), burning these ships and killing the French crews somehow hurt the English. Instead, it helped the English by keeping the French out of the area until Plymouth was established. The Indians simply did not understand the level of animosity between various European nations, who were all white.

If the New England colonists had included separate Irish, Celts, Welch, Scotts, and English (or even French and Dutch), who had been fighting each other for centuries, they might not have been so quick to come to each other's aid or to assume that all the various Indian groups around them would quickly support one another. But they were all a very homogenous group of English Puritans sharing every ethnic trait, and some simply hated all Indians. So, to them, it was a clash of civilizations, while to the surrounding Indians, it was a local fight between the Pokanoket and Plymouth. And many of them weren't that fond of the Pokanoket, so they did their best to stay neutral until attacked by colonists. In fact, if the Indians had actually all banded together in this war, as the colonists thought they would, they could have easily wiped New England clean of colonists. But they had become too fond of English goods for that to be their objective. Many saw no reason to support their traditional enemies against their new English friends. The Mohegan even quickly joined colonists in fighting the Pokanoket. However, as the colonists ramped up the fight, Indians across New England discovered that, rather than thinking of them as valued allies, the colonists had suddenly begun to regard them all as potential foes.

The English colonists were also upset that the Indians refused to fight a proper war (different rules of engagement). They refused to line up their forces in a straight line in an open field so the competing forces could march forward and mow each other down. Instead, Indian warriors set up ambushes where, hidden behind rocks and trees, they fired from unseen positions. Then, when chased by colonist forces, the Indians retreated into swamps where the colonists couldn't find them. How unfair!

Through the rest of summer and fall, while things were now quiet around Plymouth, Indians raided many outlying communities across Massachusetts on into the Connecticut River Valley and north along the coast. Battles raged. After one battle, 64 Englishmen were buried in a single grave. Over generations of fighting one another, these Indian groups had never let their battles get so out of hand as to have casualties of that magnitude. As towns were sacked and burned, surviving refugees flocked to Boston, which was soon so overrun that it banned any more seeking refuge there. After Springfield was sacked in October, all Indians were suspect. The Praying Indians around Boston were rounded up, despite their protests of loyalty to the colonists, and placed on an Island as an internment camp, much like the Japanese were rounded up during World War II. Hundreds died there of starvation and exposure.

The Narragansett, the most powerful Indian group in New England and a longstanding adversary of the Pokanoket, had stayed out of the fight. However, by December, the paranoid colonists decided to take the fight to them. Many had bought into the view personified by Captain Samuel Mosely: *"The only good Indian is a dead Indian."* An army of 1,000 colonists, headed by Josiah Winslow, marched into Narragansett territory. Directed by a captured Indian, they finally found a large group deep in a swamp far from any colonist settlements. About 3,000 men, women, children, and elderly were holed up there, with extensive provisions, in an ingenious fort of mixed Indian and English design on an island in the swamp. *"Instead of joining the Pokanokets and Nipmucks, the Narragansets had spent the fall and winter doing everything in their power to defend themselves against an unprovoked attack. If ever there was a defensive structure, it was this fort."*

Because the weather was unusually cold, the frozen ground enabled the colonist army to march through the swamp to the fort and attack. It was a bloody standoff (the colonists lost over 200 fighters) until the Indians ran out of ammunition. Then, the colonists were able to take the fort and burn it to the ground. While many Indians were able to escape, some 350 to 600 men, women, children, and elderly were killed in the fight or incinerated in the fire. While the colonists hailed this as a great victory, in truth, it drove the thousands of remaining Narragansets into the arms of their enemy, more than doubling the size of its forces.

My fourth point is that a new American character was emerging among the colonists. Phillip and his little band of survivors were fast becoming irrelevant to the war he had started. He was off in the Hudson River Valley that winter trying to recruit both the French, along with their Indian allies to the north, as well as the powerful Mohawks (the easternmost tribe of the Haudenosaunee alliance of Iroquois tribes) around Albany, to his cause. The French agreed, with the understanding that they would then come in and occupy all the English settlements in New England when the war was concluded. Phillip's plan to recruit the Mohawks, who hated the French and their Indian allies, was to kill a few Mohawks and blame it on the English. Unfortunately for him, one Mohawk got away and pointed the finger at Phillip. The Governor of New York, stationed at Albany, where most of the colonists were Dutch, did not see this war in racial terms. He had carefully cultivated a close relationship with the Mohawk for years and was not about to see that wrecked by this war. With the exposure of Phillip's treachery, he got the Mohawk to confront the several hundred Indian allies of the French who had come down and joined Phillip. The Mohawks won in a rout, so Phillip had to go back to Massachusetts without any additional support. Only New England colonists viewed this as a racial war.

Over the remainder of that winter and into spring, the colonists suffered terrible losses, including some close to Plymouth, with no real victories. Prior to the war, a young carpenter from Plymouth named Benjamin Church had settled with his young family at what is now the southeastern tip of Rhode Island, where he was surrounded by Indians and isolated from other colonists. There, he had cultivated close ties with his Indian neighbors and their leaders. Then, when war came, he joined the fight. However, he was in constant conflict with colonist leaders over their treatment of friendly Indians and those leaders' unwillingness to use or rely on them. In February, he was offered command of a militia to be sent to outlying towns in the Plymouth colony to defend against Indian attacks. He refused. He felt it was a waste of time and men stationing militias in town garrisons. While they could protect the town, they did nothing to limit Indians' activities. He said the only way to conduct this war was to

lie in the woods as the enemy did. If they intended to make an end of the war by subduing the enemy, they must make the business of war as the enemy did.

He asked for an army of 300 men with at least a third being friendly Indians. He was turned down, so he went home and took his family to an Island inhabited by friendly Indians.

In February, the colonist leaders reluctantly agreed to let two Praying Indians serve as spies. Then, one settlement was destroyed because they failed to believe the intelligence those spies brought back. By April, attitudes towards Indians who had been friendly began to shift. They began to use Praying Indians as scouts and to handle negotiations on prisoner exchanges with the Nipmucks, who, despite their overwhelming victories, were running desperately short of food and supplies because they had to stay on the move with their women, children, and prisoners. In May, the tide of war began to shift in the colonist's favor with a successful attack on an Indian camp that killed hundreds. The Boston colonists let all the Praying Indians leave the internment camp and return home. Throughout the first year of the war, Cape Cod and the Islands to the south remained free of violence. *"Instead of treating their large Praying Indian population with cruelty and distrust, the English inhabitants there had relied on them for protection. As a result, the Cape had become the colony's one oasis of safety."*

In June, the Nipmucks, out of food and ammunition, sued for peace. Phillip, who refused to go along, went back to his home territory with about a thousand Indians from various groups unwilling to give up the fight. There, they sacked a couple of settlements. The war was now back where it had started. Also, Benjamin Church found that the Sakonnet, from around his home and who had been driven out with Phillip, had snuck back home. Church convinced them to now go to war with him against Phillip. With his band of Sakonnets and a handful of colonist volunteers, he went where no colonist fighters had gone before. He learned from the Sakonnet *"how they got such advantage of the English in their marches through the woods."* They kept their forces *"thin and scattered"* while the English *"always kept in a heap together,"* so it was as *"easy to hit them as to hit a house."* The Sakonnet insisted on absolute silence. They even had to abandon their squeaky English boots for moccasins. They used an ever-changing vocabulary of wildlife sounds to communicate while learning how to track the enemy. They also learned that to avoid ambush, they must never leave a swamp the same way they had entered it. On their first outing, they captured several Indians. One, named Jeffrey, told Church of a nearby camp of fighters. Church told Jeffrey that if he joined him in the fight, he would not be turned over with the rest of the captives to be sold as a slave (the colonists sold over a thousand captured Indians as slaves, who were then sent to the Caribbean – it helped pay for the war). Jeffrey ended up being a part of the Church household for the rest of his life. Church then got permission to offer this same deal to other captured Indian fighters. Over the next two months, Church and his band captured 700 Indian fighters. Then, on August 12, 1676, they finally caught and killed Phillip. With his head on a spike outside Plymouth, the war was over.

So why did the colonists win? As described by Nathanial Philbrick:

In the end, the winner of the conflict was determined not by military prowess but by one side's ability to outlast the other. The colonies had suffered terrible defeats, but they had England to provide them with food, muskets, and ammunition. The Indians had only themselves, and by summer they were without the stores of food and gunpowder required to conduct a war. If Phillip had managed to secure the support of the French, it might have turned out differently. But the sachem's dream of a French-Pokanoket alliance was destroyed when, at New York governor Andros's urging, the Mohawks attacked him in late February. The Puritans never admitted it, but it had been Andros and the Mohawks who had determined the ultimate outcome of King Phillip's War.

While we can now see that the ultimate outcome was established by the Mohawk's victory months before, the war was finally brought to closure because some colonists were willing to abandon their English ways and learn from their Indian neighbors, whom many regarded as savages. Benjamin Church became a legend and the prototype for the uniquely American hero. Again, as expressed by Philbrick at the end of his description of this war:

There are two possible responses to a world suddenly gripped by terror and contention. There is the Mosely way: get mad and get even. But as the course of King Phillip's War proved, unbridled arrogance and fear only feed the flames of violence. Then there is the Church way. Instead of loathing the enemy, try to learn as much as possible from him instead of trying to kill him, trying to bring him around to your way of thinking. First and foremost, treat him like a human being. For Church, success in war was about coercion rather than slaughter, and in this he anticipated the welcoming transformative beast that eventually became – the United States.

So, what were the impacts of this war? The Plymouth colony lost eight percent of its men. Across New England, hundreds more died, and thousands lost their homes and became refugees. It took another hundred years before the average per capita income in New England returned to where it had been before the war. The Crown appointed a royal governor to preside over New England (they lost self-rule), and in 1692, Plymouth colony was absorbed into Massachusetts colony. More small wars with Indians followed. Those in outlying communities lost their sense of safety. But the war was far more catastrophic for the Indians. Through death in battle, sickness, and starvation, along with those shipped out as slaves and those who fled the area, Southern New England lost over half of its Indian population in just 14 months. The Pokanoket, who 55 years before greeted the Pilgrims with *"Welcome Englishmen,"* were obliterated. Phillip's wife and nine-year-old son, Massasoit's grandson, were shipped to the Caribbean as slaves, a sad legacy for the man responsible for allowing English settlements in New England.

So, were these Puritan colonists ethnocentric (which includes bigotry based on race)? Of course they were! Ethnicity is based on race, religion, language, culture, nationality, or tribe. The Puritans not only believed God was on their side and had cleared the way for them through plagues so they could establish their initial settlements, but they were also a uniquely homogenous group sharing all of six ethnic characteristics when compared to the Indians around them. In addition, they had a written language, ships, metal tools and weapons, gunpowder, glass, fabrics, and domestic animals, while the Indians had none of these. They felt their culture was vastly superior. In 1675, when being ethnocentric was as widespread and socially acceptable around the world as family loyalty, they were living in a foreign land surrounded by vastly different people. How could they not be ethnocentric (based on far more than just race)? But what is the point of judging or condemning these people, who have now been dead for over 300 years? Nor am I trying to excuse them. Instead, we need to understand and learn from the terrible cost of their being so ethnocentric. From their failing to understand that their common humanity, and the uniqueness of each individual, trumps ethnicity. We also need to recognize that, to varying degrees, some were coming to that understanding, while for many others, their bigoted feelings were only hardened by the war. But war usually does that.

INDIANS OF NORTH AMERICA – There are a few more points about Indians, as described by Mann, particularly those in what is now the northeast of the U.S., that need to be elaborated on further because they relate to the founding of the USA and our current controversies.

So, what was life like for the Indians that the pilgrims encountered? Colonists were very curious about their new neighbors and their *"wholly novel ways of being human."* They tried to understand, as a sociologist-historian in Quebec has put it "the *very existence of these relatively egalitarian societies, so different in their structure and social relationships than those of Europe."*

From records left by the pilgrims, we know that they lived in dome-shaped houses, wigwams, that were *"warmer than our English houses"* because they were covered with multiple layers of mats that *"deny entrance to any drop of rain, though it come both fierce and long."* Pilgrim families, who expected children to be hard at work all day every day, thought Indian families were way too lax since they let children spend much of their time playing until they reached puberty. The goal of Indian education was to build character, to create adults who were brave, hearty, honest, uncomplaining, and avoided gossip. *"He that speaks seldom and opportunely, being as good as his word, is the only man they love."* Children were taught to endure hardship. Family games included tossing naked children into snowbanks. When boys came of age, they would spend an entire winter alone in the forest, equipped only with a bow, a hatchet, and a knife. Apparently, it all worked. *"Beat them, whip them, pinch them, punch them, if they resolve not to flinch for it, they will not."*

Many Europeans noted that, throughout the Northeast, Indians enjoyed a level of personal freedom unknown in Europe. There were no slaves nor even a class structure among them. A Dutchman living among the Mohawks (part of the Haudenosaunee alliance) around Albany in the 1640s was fascinated by their dedication to personal liberty. They are *"all free by nature, and will not bear any domineering or lording over them."* A frontiersman explained the Indian view to an aghast British audience: *"Every man is free. No one has any right to deprive another person of his freedom."* In describing the Haudenosaunee, one administrator declared they had *"such absolute Notions of Liberty, that they allow no Kind of Superiority of one over another, and banish all Servitude from their Territories."*

Some saw all this Indian love of freedom in a negative light. One Frenchman complained in 1670 "*The Savage does not know what it is to obey. They think everyone ought to be left to his own Opinion.*" One priest complained that Indians "*believe what they please and no more.*" Another priest complained "*All these barbarians have the law of wild asses – they are born, live, and die in a liberty without restraint; they do not know what is meant by bridle and bit.*"

These northeast Indians, on the other hand, were appalled by European class structure. One Frenchman wrote of the experience of some Indians who visited France. They complained that "*among us some men gorged to the full with things of every sort while their other halves were beggars at their doors, emaciated with hunger and poverty. They found it strange that these poverty-stricken halves should suffer such injustice, and that they did not take the others by the throat or set fire to their houses.*"

One French Baron, who spent a decade interacting with the Huron around 1690, tried to explain the superior government structures of Europe to them. He later reported that the Indians could not understand why "*one man should have more than another, and that the Rich should have more Respect than the Poor...They brand us for Slaves, and call us miserable Souls, whose Life is not worth having, alleging That we degrade ourselves in subjecting our selves to one Man (a king) who possesses the whole Power, and is bound by no Law but his own Will...Individual Indians value themselves above anything that you can imagine, and this is the reason they always give for 't,* **That one's as much Master as another, and since Men are all made of the same Clay there should be no Distinction or Superiority among them.** (Emphasis in the original).

Although Benjamin Franklin referred to Indians as "Savages" and initially held them in low regard, he did write the following in 1753:

When an Indian Child has been brought up among us, taught our language and habituated to our Customs, yet if he goes to see his relations and makes one Indian Ramble with them, there is no perswading him ever to return. When white persons of either sex have been taken prisoners young by the Indians, and lived a while among them, tho' ransomed by their Friends, and treated with all imaginable tenderness to prevail them to stay with the English, yet in a Short time they become disgusted with our manner of life... and take the first good Opportunity of escaping again into the Woods, when there is no reclaiming them.

It should be noted that most of these northeast Indian groups were ruled by one person, the sachem, who ruled with the consent of the governed. In short, they were governed by consensus, not majority rule, as in a democracy. In many cases, beginning as early as 1622, when colonists found living under Puritan restrictions too much to bear, they simply voted with their feet by leaving their settlements and moving in with nearby Indians. Colonists in the northern colonies, whether they admitted it or not, really learned about equality and individual freedom from their Indian neighbors. How else can one explain how those stuffy structured Puritans invented the *"raucous, ultra-democratic New England town meeting"* as a system of governance that an Ivy League historian characterized as displaying *"more attributes of Algonkian government by consensus than a Puritan government by the divinely ordained."*

Battles between Indian groups were frequent minor skirmishes that colonists recognized were *"farre less bloudy and devouring than the cruell Warres of Europe."* Captured women and children were rarely killed. Usually, they were required to join the winning group. Captured men were often tortured, then adopted or killed, depending on whether they bore the torture well.

On the other hand, Indians in the Southeast, who descended from Mississippian societies, were far more hierarchical and autocratically ruled than those of the Northeast. They had also been practicing slavery for generations. They happily captured other Indians and traded them as slaves to the colonists for hatchets, pots, guns, ammunition, and horses. They were also happy to catch and return runaway African slaves for a price. In short, colonists in the Carolinas (many of whom had been slave owners in Barbados before going there) and Georgia found full support and cooperation for slavery among their Indian neighbors. Some southern Indians acquired black African slaves. Later, in the 1830s (as a result of President Andrew Jackson's defiance of the Supreme Court), when the

Cherokee were driven west out of northern Georgia to Oklahoma, along what would become known as *The Trial of Tears* because of the death and suffering they endured, slave-owning Indians took their black slaves with them to Oklahoma.

As previously noted, along the Atlantic coast from Jamestown to New England, trees were cleared from large areas along the coasts and riverbanks for farming. The understory in wooded areas was also burned annually, so the forest was open and park-like, with large trees and a high canopy. However, as Indian populations were decimated by disease and displacement, there were no longer enough left to continue the annual burning of most forests and fields. Thus, by 1800, there was far more "wilderness" in what is now the eastern USA than there had been in 1600. The dark, dense woods around Walden Pond, loved by Thoreau, did not come into existence until after the Pilgrims arrived and the Indian population had been dramatically thinned out. Further, the deer, wild turkey, and passenger pigeon populations exploded (along with other game species) as Indian populations declined. Indians had aggressively hunted these, not only for food but to keep them out of their crop fields. While they valued them for food, they had intentionally kept the populations limited and away from their crops. While the Frenchmen who came up the Mississippi River in 1682 did not see any Indians where Desoto had found Indians everywhere in 1540, they frequently saw herds of buffalo, which Desoto never mentioned. Buffalo are so distinctive that if Desoto had seen them, he would have mentioned them. In short, the "wilderness" encountered by white pioneers as they moved inland toward and into the Appalachian Mountains after 1700 was not an ecologically balanced natural world as we have been taught. It was a natural world in transition after having the Indians' finger largely lifted off the scales, and that had not yet found a new equilibrium.

SLAVERY IN THE THIRTEEN COLONIES – In August 1619, about 20 black Africans (one source says 20 men and three women), taken from a raided Portuguese slave ship bound for Mexico, were sold at Jamestown. Thus, the title of the New York Times *1619 Project,* which was published in August 2019 to commemorate the 400th anniversary of this event. What the *1619 Project* fails to do is provide any context for that event, as if, somehow, these were the first slaves in the world. So, some context. First, those first Africans were not sold as slaves, but as indentured servants obligated to serve for a specific time, probably seven years. Initially, most, if not all, buyers honored their contract to release those black servants at the end of their term of service (they would have been lifelong slaves in Mexico). So, there were soon some free blacks at Jamestown. However, that had shifted by 1650 as many settlers stopped allowing the Africans they bought as indentured servants to go free at the end of their service and began keeping them as permanent slaves. However, Virginia would not have any laws expressly authorizing or governing the ownership and sale of slaves until 1655. Massachusetts, in 1641, was the first colony to explicitly legalize slavery. Some of those Africans who were freed at the end of their service obligation went on to own land and slaves themselves.

Second, in 1619, slavery was a socially acceptable and common practice around the world in most nations and among most groups. There had already been over half a million black Africans shipped to other parts of the Americas, mostly by Portugal. In fact, of all the black Africans shipped to the Americas during the 350 years of the transatlantic slave trade, only about 5% of them came into the area that would become the USA. Initially, there weren't that many Africans brought in. By 1650, after 31 years, there were only about 300 Africans in Virginia, while the much smaller Dutch colony of New Netherlands (now New York) had about 500 African slaves.

In 1660, a young woman in Virginia won her freedom in court since she was the daughter of an African slave mother and an English father. Under English law at the time, children's rights came through their fathers. Since her father acknowledged paternity, that made her English, so she could not be enslaved in an English colony. In response, Virginia law was changed two years later so that all children born to slave mothers, regardless of paternity, were slaves at birth. The number of African slaves in the colonies remained relatively low until at least 1680. While there was a need for laborers, that need was largely met by indentured servants from England and enslaved Indians.

As previously mentioned, Plymouth Colony sold over a thousand Indians into slavery during King Phillip's War. Most went to the Caribbean. The initial settlers of South Carolina, who were experienced slavers from Barbados, soon began buying slaves from local Indians, who captured them from other tribes, starting up a vigorous slave market there. Over the first 40 years of the colony, South Carolina exported at least ten times more Indian slaves (over 30,000) than the African slaves it imported. By 1700, slaves were common throughout all the colonies. However, Indian slaves were falling out of favor. The four New England colonies, along with Pennsylvania, banned the importation of Indian slaves. In doing so, Rhode Island complained about the *"conspiracies, insurrections, rapes, thefts and other execrable crimes"* committed by Indian slaves, while the Massachusetts law said Indian slaves were *"malicious, surly, and revengeful."* Indian slaves, particularly in the South, also died at an increasingly alarming rate, as did indentured servants. It turned out that, with those Africans that were being brought in, malaria came along for the ride. The impact of malaria on the transatlantic slave trade will be discussed later as that trade increased in volume over the next century.

While slavery was common throughout all the colonies in the seventeenth century, the nature of farming in Virginia and the Carolinas contributed significantly to its greater importance there. Rice, which is well suited to plantation farming, quickly became the primary cash crop in South Carolina. Further, many slaves coming from West Africa were already experienced rice farmers. In Virginia and North Carolina, the only cash crop from the beginning was tobacco, another plantation crop. Tobacco wore out the land so fast there could never be enough. So, plantations there were huge, usually starting as large land grants from the Crown. After cutting down the trees, tobacco was planted without removing the stumps. After three years of tobacco, they would move on to clearing new forested land for tobacco while growing wheat or corn to feed the slaves for a year or two on the old field before letting it go back to forest. Thus, they burned through vast amounts of land and slaves. George Washington owned over 20,000 acres. Thomas Jefferson owned about 16,000 acres. And those were typical for plantations of the era. Slavery was an integral part of these destructive farming practices.

But it didn't have to be that way. Like farmers in the northern colonies, German immigrants in the Shenandoah Valley in the eighteenth century had a much different relationship with the land than did the English plantation owners to the east. They had not received large land grants. They had to buy their farms, so they were relatively small. Plus, they came from a tradition where a family would keep the farm for generations, if not centuries. They cleared the stumps, plowed deep to minimize erosion, housed their livestock in barns, used manure on their fields, and practiced a precise scheme of crop rotation. Because they were subsistence farmers, eating what they grew and only selling surplus, they produced a far greater variety of crops and livestock than was done on the large tobacco plantations of English immigrants. They and their children worked with their own hands on their own land without slaves. By the time of the Civil War, a century later, the Shenandoah Valley was the breadbasket of Virginia and crucial to feeding the Confederate army.

Racism did not cause slavery. Slavery had existed for thousands of years around the world, with slaves and masters all being of the same race. However, when slaves are all from one race and masters from another, virulent racism is inevitable, particularly in a chattel slave system where slaves are bought and sold like cattle at public slave markets. Coming to believe the other race is inferior is inevitable to justify what has been, and is being, done to them. This was becoming evident in Virginia by 1670, as free blacks found themselves beginning to face restrictions they had not seen before. Racial bigotry is fostered by race separate chattel slavery, as was first developed with sugar plantations on islands off the African coast in the fifteenth century and then transplanted across the Atlantic to the Americas. Slavery, and the bigotry it fosters, were in full bloom across this new Nation at its founding in 1776. While that slavery was not unique, and was only a small part of such chattel slavery in the Americas and the world, the racial line between slave and master was as sharp, if not sharper, in the USA than in the rest of the Americas, which eventually made racial bigotry particularly intense here. While, by the end of the nineteenth century, legal slavery had ended throughout the Americas, Europe, and most of the world, the racism and bigotry that was magnified by that slavery did not end with it.

THE FRENCH AND INDIAN WAR – The Appalachian Mountains, which stretch from northern Georgia into central New York, constituted a significant barrier to the westward movement of British colonists. By 1750, there were close to two million British colonists spread out in Britain's thirteen colonies along the Atlantic coast east of the Appalachians. Yet, there were less than a hundred thousand French colonists in New France to the north. Because the fur trade with Indians dominated the New France economy, they created a much lighter footprint as they spread west and were beginning to expand into the area between the Ohio River and the Great Lakes by 1750: an area also claimed by Britain and its colonies. While both the French and British had cultivated alliances with various Indian tribes, the Indians were critical to the success of the French fur trading, while the British cultivated such relationships as a means to avoid war and as a buffer against the French. After almost a decade of increasing conflict and disputes, in 1754, armed military forces engaged in open battle near where the French were in the process of building Fort Duquesne, at the point where the Monongahela and Allegheny Rivers joined to form the Ohio River. Over the next six years, with a young George Washington gaining his first military experience, battles were fought from Fort Duquesne to Lake Champlain to Quebec.

Meanwhile, in 1756, Britain declared war on France, which took the war directly to Europe and many European colonies around the world in what became known as the *Seven Year War.* Spain aligned with France and Prussia with Britain. It was the world's first global war, ending with a 1763 treaty between France, Britain, and Spain that was a concession to Britain.

France gave up all its claims in the North American continent, with New France (now Canada) going to Britain and Louisiana to Spain. Fort Duquesne was then renamed Pittsburgh. Britain had conquered Cuba and Manila from Spain during the war but gave them back in exchange for Florida (which had less than a thousand Spanish colonists at Fort Augustine, who then moved to Cuba). Both Britain and Spain would have open access to the Mississippi River. Beginning in 1755, Britain started expelling French colonists from Acadia (New Brunswick and Nova Scotia) by the thousands. While they were sent to several different places, many ended up in Louisiana, around New Orleans, where they were initially referred to as Acadians. That soon became *Cajuns*.

While Britain was largely victorious, the war had been costly. Britain had financed the war by borrowing money, leaving it deeply in debt. In response, Britain began to raise taxes, not only in Britain but throughout its colonial empire, including the thirteen colonies in North America, to address that debt. The colonists' taxes were only a small fraction of what citizens living in England were paying. Still, these colonial taxes were a significant contributor to the Revolutionary War.

CHIEF PONTIAC'S WAR – Following the French and Indian War, the Indian tribes who had aligned with the French lost their ally as the British military and colonists moved west. Further, the tribes, like the Iroquois alliance that had aligned with the British, found the British no longer needed them as a buffer against the French and their Indian allies. They were now just in the way of British colonists moving further west. In 1763, the Ottawa, led by Chief Pontiac, pulled together a coalition of tribes to expel the British military and settlers from the area drained by the Ohio River. Because their goal was to terrify colonists as well as to defeat the military, they employed gruesome practices, including scalping, torture, mutilation, and drinking of blood. They quickly gained control of all the area west of Pittsburgh while killing about 2,000 settlers and 400 soldiers in the process. Thousands of other terrified settlers fled east, many over the mountains. This campaign strongly reinforced colonists' view of Indians as *"merciless savages"*, as expressed in the Declaration of Independence a decade later.

The British response was twofold. First, they banned settlements west of the mountains. Second, they initiated what we would now consider biological warfare. There had been a recent outbreak of smallpox in Pennsylvania. British military leaders took blankets that had been used by smallpox patients and distributed them in Indian villages. Smallpox soon decimated Indian communities throughout the region. And peace was restored. However, distrust on both sides was heightened.

6: EUROPE COLONIZES THE WORLD

A thorough discussion of Europe's worldwide colonial empires built after 1492 could fill volumes. Here, I will just emphasize a few points, including some that are often not addressed, again with the intent to neither excuse nor condemn, but to understand.

Colonialism is as old as mankind. People have been pushing other people around for thousands of years. The *Right of Conquest* principle was simply the way of the world with ethnocentrism at the heart of all colonial efforts into already inhabited lands. Those coming in believe they are superior and, having the might, have the right to impose their will. Groups large and small have been conquering and colonizing for various reasons: to extract wealth to send back home, to obtain things they don't have back home, for better lands than they currently have, the group is outgrowing its home territory and needs new lands to spread into, to expand empires, or to spread religious convictions (Islam, Christianity, etc.). Occasionally, a small group (like the pilgrims) just wants to separate themselves from their home group. Sometimes it has occurred for several of these reasons combined. When colonists have a conviction that they are spreading the true word of God, it helps them justify such intrusions. However, even then, the invading groups have been centered on their own interests with limited concern for those already there.

Colonial efforts have taken several forms: move in and exterminate those already there, move in and enslave those already there, move in just enough to take control and then extract wealth to send back home, or just crowd into open spaces in the neighborhood as was done at Jamestown and Plymouth. The responses of the natives already there have also varied widely. When the newcomers brought new unheard-of technologies and goods like fabric, domestic animals, or metal weapons, tools, and containers, they have often been cautiously welcomed – and their culture immediately begins to change with these new technologies and goods. The Athenians colonized Sicily. The Romans invaded other lands on a massive scale, then usually left enough behind to collect tribute. However, they also extensively colonized a few areas, such as along the east side of the

Adriatic Sea and the west side of the Black Sea, where they left populations with Latin-based languages behind (Albania and Romania) when the empire collapsed. John Steele Gordon summarized colonialism this way:

Rome conquered the known world by force of arms. Its power arose from its military machine, epitomized by its legions. And every Great Power since has exercised formal political hegemony over alien peoples to advance its own interests.

Islam spread primarily through military conquest, but they also colonized some areas, such as Spain, and extended the Ottoman Empire into Europe. The Vikings, Germans, and French colonized the British Isles. The Comanche, after becoming the best horsemen on the Great Plains, terrorized and pushed aside the Apache. The Apache and Navajo moved into what is now New Mexico, compressing the Indian pueblos already there (and selling captured local Indians to the Spanish as slaves). After adopting a horse culture, the Lakota Sioux moved west onto the Great Plains, across the Missouri River, and then on into the Black Hills, much to the chagrin of the tribes (recently decimated by disease) that were already there. The Inca and Aztec empires were also colonial in nature. The Japanese conquered Korea. China built the Great Wall to keep out invaders. And the list goes on and on over the centuries, including in Africa.

However, the scale and reach of human colonization into the rest of the world accomplished by Europeans in the first four centuries after Columbus is levels of magnitude beyond anything ever known before. And, by the millions, they took Africans with them into much of the Americas. The slave trade was a major part of the black African economy for centuries. The transatlantic slave trade ended in 1853, not because black leaders in Africa quit selling but because European colonists in America quit buying. Sometimes, colonization was done as a national effort (Spain and Portugal), and sometimes it was authorized private ventures. The British East India Company ruled much of India for over two centuries before the British government took direct control.

By 1900, Europeans (whites) were scattered all over the world, and a few European countries were in charge across these colonial empires. While those national empires have now essentially disintegrated, the descendants of those white colonists are still in charge in some places. The entire Americas exemplifies this (though in parts of the Caribbean, it is the descendants of African slaves involuntarily brought there who are now the ruling population). Even where Europeans are no longer in charge, changes that came with that colonial past are still evident. Some of those residual effects are positive, like technology. Others, not so much.

INITIAL COLONIAL EFFORTS BY EUROPE – Europe's first step in colonialism that shaped today's world was Portugal's move to uninhabited Madeira in 1450. Then, with Columbus' voyages to the Americas, the race for European countries to lay claim to its riches and lands was on. However, much of Europe was not involved. European Colonialism was initially limited to two countries: Portugal and Spain. Why them? Because they were the two countries with the greatest (and growing) resources and expertise in shipbuilding and navigation. Why did they do it? For wealth, power, adventure, and because they could. It took a lot of hubris for Spain and Portugal, in 1494, to divide up ownership of the Americas (which they knew practically nothing about) between them with absolutely no consideration of the people who already lived there or the interests of any other country. But they did it. Then, in 1524, they tried to do the same with the rest of the world, including Asia and Africa.

Spain went west across the Pacific, and Portugal went east around the horn of Africa into India and Indonesia. Spain began shipping silver across the Pacific to the Philippines around 1565 and established Manila in 1571. Portugal established settlements and sugar plantations in Brazil, dominating the transatlantic slave trade for a century. Portugal also went around the southern tip of Africa (establishing an outpost in South Africa in 1500) and into the Persian Gulf, India, Malaysia, and even Japan. It was a far-flung empire for a tiny nation of two million people along the western edge of the Iberian Peninsula. However, due to a lack of successors with a claim to the throne, Portugal was then ruled by Spanish kings for 60 years, beginning in 1580, before again gaining full independence. Meanwhile, much of its worldwide influence was lost.

Around 1600, the Dutch, French, and English began to get involved in colonization as Portugal's influence outside Brazil began to wane. Since each wanted its own supply of sugar, they all went to the Caribbean. A few other countries also established settlements but with marginal success. These European countries sometimes fought with each other, even on foreign soil, over their colonial claims.

In addition to their colonization around the Hudson River and the Caribbean, Dutch efforts included Australia in 1606, Malaysia in 1641, and South Africa in 1650. The Dutch East India Company, formed in 1602, was the world's first formal public company and was a significant player in worldwide trade for two centuries. One notable long-term impact of Dutch colonialism is the Afrikaner population in South Africa.

The French, in addition to the Caribbean, went into Acadia, Quebec, and on down the St. Laurance River, beginning after 1600. They focused on the fur trade by establishing close ties with Indians throughout the area. Therefore, the total number of French colonists in Canada was limited. A century later, the French began pushing up the Mississippi River to establish their own source of tobacco. They were concerned about all the money their citizens spent on English tobacco. They founded New Orleans in 1719. However, the lower Mississippi turned out to be poor land for tobacco, so they switched to sugar. French missionaries had begun moving into southeast Asia by the mid-1700s. Then, following the murder of two missionaries, France took control of Vietnam in 1858.

English efforts beyond Europe began with the formation of the East India Company, chartered by Queen Elizabeth in 1600, to get England involved in Asian trade. It moved into India in 1608 and, over the next century, established the cities of Madras, Bombay, and Calcutta (all renamed in 1995 with Indian names) to handle that trade. The East India Company basically ruled an ever-expanding portion of India for the next 250 years until the British Crown took direct control of India (in 1858). From 1750 to 1830, the East India Company handled a full 50% of the World's trade in sugar, silk, tea, spices, cotton, indigo dye, salt, and opium. They managed to get China addicted to opium and then supplied that huge market. As previously discussed, in 1606, King Charles chartered the Virginia Company (named after Elizabeth, the Virgin Queen) for colonial ventures into North America. However, the British colonies in North America that became the USA were never as economically important to Great Britain as either the East India Company or its colonial holdings in the Caribbean, led by Barbados and Jamaica.

England made two changes in its financial structure that dramatically improved its financial position at home and in relation to other European nations in the latter part of the seventeenth century. First, it changed its tax collection structure from one in which it granted the right to collect taxes in exchange for a commitment to deliver a certain amount to the treasury, with the collectors keeping the surplus for themselves (the historical pattern across Europe) to one where the tax collectors were bureaucrats who were judged on how much they turned into the treasury. Tax collections soared. Second, it left behind the system where government debts were personal debts of the sovereign and shifted such debt to the nation. In 1694, England gave the Bank of England a corporate charter, which evolved into the Nation's central bank. This essentially liquified wealth across England and made borrowing money much easier for the government. It enabled England to finance its endless wars with France by increasing national debt. And money is at the heart of being able to fight and win a war. *"Because of its national debt, Britain became the linchpin of European power politics."* Thus, the British Empire was able to expand for over two more centuries. John Steele Gordon on the British Empire:

A century ago, the British Empire covered a quarter of the globe's land area, while a third of the world's people were subjects of King Edward VII. But only a small minority of those people spoke English or regarded themselves as British.

It is noteworthy that in the first two centuries of colonization (until 1700), except for the Atlantic coast of North America, about ninety percent of those who crossed the Atlantic to live in the Americas were African slaves. In many areas, only enough Europeans came to manage the slaves on the plantations, ports, etc., established to extract wealth from these new lands, convert the natives, or explore for riches and a passage to the Pacific Ocean. With all this, by 1650, Mexico City was by far the most cosmopolitan city in the world, with a broad mix of native peoples, Europeans, Africans, and Asians (primarily Chinese) across all classes and castes. And that included many of mixed race of all possible combinations.

AFRICAN SLAVERY AND THE TRANSATLANTIC SLAVE TRADE – As in the rest of the world, slavery had been endemic within Africa throughout recorded history. Quoting Thomas Sowell:

It was not because people thought slavery was right that it persisted for thousands of years. It persisted largely because people did not think about the rightness or wrongness of it at all. In very hierarchical societies, where most people were born into their predetermined niches in the social complex, slaves were simply at the bottom of the long continuum of varying levels of subordination based on birth.

In Africa, unlike Europe where private ownership of land was the accepted norm, the societies of Central Africa had no concept of private land ownership. Therefore, wealth among the upper classes and elites was measured by the number of slaves owned. In some kingdoms, as much as a third of the population were slaves. Europe and Africa operated with two very different economic systems. While Europeans primarily measured wealth in terms of land owned, which they bought and sold, Africans measured wealth in the number of laborers owned and thus bought and sold labor. In discussing the inception of the transatlantic slave trade, Charles C. Mann notes:

Few Europeans or Africans at this time viewed slavery as an institution that needed to be explained, still less as an evil that needed to be decried. Slavery was part of the furniture of everyday life; in both Europe and Africa. Depriving others of their liberty wasn't' morally problematic, though it was bad to enslave the wrong person. Christians, for example, were generally not supposed to enslave fellow Christians.

And virtually all Europeans were Christian. While slaves were an integral part of everyday life in Africa, they were also exported in all directions in astounding numbers. Detailed estimates, with some variations, have been made to try to document how many slaves were taken from Africa. As African journalist Elikia M'bokolo wrote in *Le Monde diplomatique*:

> *The African continent was bled of its human resources via all possible routes. Across the Sahara, through the Red Sea, from the Indian Ocean ports and across the Atlantic. At least ten centuries of slavery for the benefit of Muslim countries (from the ninth to the nineteenth)... Four million enslaved people exported via the Red Sea, another four million through the Swahili ports of the Indian Ocean, perhaps as many as nine million along the trans-Saharan caravan route, and eleven to twenty million (depending on the author) across the Atlantic Ocean.*

Thus, only about half, maybe less, of the slaves exported from Africa during that thousand-year period crossed the Atlantic. However, most of the shipments across the Atlantic occurred in the last 300 years of that period. *"The European demand for slaves provided a large new market for an already existing Trade."* While the export of slaves from Africa in any direction was drawing to an end by 1900, there were still two million slaves in the Caliphate covering what is now Cameroon and Nigeria. Legal slavery continued in Africa well into the twentieth century. As late as the 1930s, ten to twenty percent of the population of Ethiopia were slaves.

Contrary to the portrayal in Alex Haley's 1976 bestseller *Roots,* virtually none of the slaves crossing the Atlantic were captured by Europeans. Although Portugal initially made a few attempts, such efforts were met with strong resistance from local African leaders who wanted control of any slave exports. So, Portugal began to buy slaves from those local black leaders who would capture, transport, and hold slaves at ports along the western coast of Africa for sale to slave traders for transport across the Atlantic. Other European nations followed that pattern. Thus, the source of slaves was largely met by preexisting tribal conflicts within

African society. However, some conflicts were started for the express purpose of capturing slaves. *"African merchants bought slaves from African armies, raiders, and pirates and paid Africans to convey them to African-run holding tanks. Once a contract was arranged, Africans loaded the slaves aboard the ships, which often had crews with significant numbers of Africans. Other Africans supplied the slave ships with food, rope, water, and timber for the voyage out. Europeans naturally played a role: they were the customers."* As one African king said in the 1840s: *"The slave trade is the ruling principle of my people. It is the source and glory of their wealth...The mother lulls the child to sleep with notes of triumph over the enemy reduced to slavery."*

It should be noted that African elites and Europeans with plantations in the Americas viewed slaves quite differently without either understanding the other's point of view. African elites saw intrinsic value in their slaves beyond their ability to work: they were part of their wealth and influence. In the colonies slaves were viewed quite differently, as explained by Charles C. Mann:

Chattel slavery on colonial plantations, by contrast, made slaves anonymous – they were, so to speak, something bought in a store, selected purely on physical characteristics, like so many cans of soup...European slaveholders usually didn't even see their human property; they were thousands of miles away, safe from disease in London, Paris, and Lisbon. When they wanted to expand production of sugar or tobacco, they borrowed money from equally distant financiers and dispatched written instructions to acquire so many pieces at such-and-such price. This transformation was not understood as it occurred. But it removed a bond, however tenuous, between slave and owner. No longer were captives an owner's relatives or vanquished enemies. Instead, they were anonymous units of labor, production inputs on a balance sheet, to be disposed of purely according to an estimate of their future economic value.

The attrition rates in the Transatlantic slave trade, between initial capture by other Africans in Africa and arriving at a plantation in the

Americas, were horrendous. At least 10% died in the process of capture and transport to the slave ports. Another 5% died in the port stockades while awaiting sale to a slave trader. About 15% died at sea during transport. Over 10% died in the slave market process between leaving the ship and finally arriving at a plantation where they began work. Thus, less than two-thirds survived the whole process from capture to beginning work as a slave. However, that was still far better than the Arab slave caravans taking millions of black Africans north across the Sahara, which had attrition rates of 70% to 90%.

While there are published claims ranging from six million to twenty million African slaves being sent to the Americas, the most detailed reconstruction of transatlantic slave trade records I found online shows 12,356,910 being shipped from Africa to the Americas, but only 10,538,224 arriving (a loss of 15%). According to this record, 47% of slaves shipped were aboard Portuguese ships, 26% aboard British ships (although Britain was the largest shipper for a century – from the late 1600s to the late 1700s), 11% aboard French ships, and 8% aboard Spanish ships. The other 8% were split among Dutch, Danish, and American ships. Of those slaves who arrived in the Americas, 46% went to Brazil, while 22% went to the British Caribbean. Only 4% came to North America. The other 28% went to the French Caribbean or the Spanish or Dutch Americas. In addition, 9,000 were shipped to Europe and 155,000 to other parts of Africa.

While shipping slaves across the Atlantic to the Americas apparently began in 1502, the slave trade had become part of a shipping triangle by the late 1500s that then lasted for almost three centuries. Each leg of the trip was highly profitable. The triangle began with ships leaving their home ports in Europe loaded with manufactured goods: weapons, ammunition, other metal goods, dyed fabric (mostly cotton), and rum. In African ports, they would trade these goods for slaves and sail for the Americas (the leg of the journey often referred to as the *middle passage*). In the Americas, they would sell their slaves and then load up with sugar, rum, molasses, timber, or raw cotton for the return trip to Europe.

African slaves in the Americas escaped from their plantation overseers in huge numbers. And these escaping slaves often encountered Indians.

Several different names have been applied to communities of escaped slaves. In English, they are usually called Maroons. Again, in the words of Charles C. Mann:

American history is often described in terms of Europeans entering a nearly empty wilderness. For centuries, though, most of the newcomers were African and the land was not empty, but filled with millions of indigenous people. Much of the great encounter between the two separate halves of the world was less a meeting of Europe and America than a meeting of Africans and Indians – a relationship forged both in the cage of slavery and the uprisings against it. Largely conducted out of sight of the Europeans... Africans and Indians fought with each other, claimed to be each other, and allied together for common goals, sometimes all at the same time. Whatever the tactics, the goal was constant: freedom... Slaves vanished from the ken of their masters by the tens or even hundreds of thousands in Brazil, Peru, and the Caribbean. Spain recognized autonomous maroon communities in Ecuador, Colombia, Panama, and Mexico.

Numerous communities of escaped slaves developed in the jungles of Brazil where it was relatively easy to avoid capture. This, along with a much higher death rate among slaves there (over a third of slaves sent to Brazil died within the first five years), was a significant factor in why Portugal shipped so many more slaves than any other country and why it continued to do so after other countries had stopped. Many escapees in Brazil mixed with native Indian jungle communities. As late as the 1970s, much of the Amazon jungle was just a blank on Brazilian maps, with practically nothing known about the areas. As part of efforts to promote economic development (timber and grazing), the government began to sell off large sections. However, when the new owners went in, they found many areas already full of people (African or mixed race) who had been living there for centuries and had often divided the land into individual plots. Brazil is still wrestling with the fallout from this.

Escapees on Caribbean islands or in North America met with less success (Haiti was an exception). However, some communities of escaped slaves did develop in remote areas. In North America, escapees also went south to Florida, where they were often able to mix with Indian communities there that were under the protection of Spain.

Great Britain banned participation in the transatlantic slave trade in 1807. It then began active efforts to disrupt the transatlantic slave trade by other nations. Over the next several decades, it seized over 1,500 slave ships and freed about 150,000 Africans that were on board.

In 1806, the USA, with strong support from President Jefferson, banned participation in the international slave trade, effective in 1808. As described by historian H. W. Brands:

During the early nineteenth century, American practices and attitudes involving slavery continued to change. Additional northern states mandated an end to the institution, although most allowed owners to keep current slaves for years or decades. Congress outlawed the importation of slaves in 1808, a move that assuaged American consciences but posed little hardship to slaveholders, as American slaves reproduced fast enough to meet the needs of the domestic market. (In the West Indies and Brazil, by contrast, the far higher death rate necessitated regular replenishment of slave ranks to sustain the institution.)

African slaves in the USA, like European immigrants, were taller on average and had higher birth rates than their Old-World counterparts. Also, unlike African slaves sent to the rest of the Americas, the slave population in the USA expanded independent of new imports because of the high birthrate and higher survival rates of slaves and their children. The only exceptions to this were the rice and sugar plantations in South Carolina and Louisiana, where the severe working conditions (and thus the death rates) resembled the West Indies.

After Britain abolished slavery throughout the British Empire in 1833 (except in India, where slavery was not banned until 1843), freed slaves often declined employment in the cane fields. This led to the importing of indentured labor, mainly from India and China. The transatlantic slave trade came to an end around 1853 when Brazil banned the importation of slaves from Africa, the last country in the Americas to do so.

But why had the British ever embraced the transatlantic slave trade so completely? Slavery within the British Isles was being eliminated by the time of the Crusades while they deeply resented the thousands of British citizens being enslaved by Islam for several more centuries. Yet, for a century (from about 1680 to 1780) the British dominated the transatlantic slave trade, with only 10% of the slaves it shipped coming to its colonies in North America. Why? For the same reason, so many African slaves were imported to South and Central America, Mexico, and the Caribbean by other European countries. The one dominant factor that overrides all others in answering that question is – malaria (helped by yellow fever).

MALARIA – While malaria did not cause African slavery in the Americas, it was a huge factor in the magnitude of that slavery. It is now apparent that malaria was why Africans and Europeans ended up in the numbers they did in the places they did within the Americas during the three and a half centuries of the transatlantic slave trade. It also affected who won and who lost various wars and/or in the magnitude of those wars. Whoever you are and wherever you live in the Americas, malaria has played a role in shaping the circumstances of your life.

Adam Smith, in 1776, made a strong economic argument against slavery. He argued that the cost of purchasing slaves, combined with the cost of providing year-round room and board for them when the need for labor was seasonal in an agrarian society, did not make economic sense. And, but for malaria, his argument was largely proved to be true in both North and South America. While slavery was a small factor in Canada, slavery was quite extensive in all the British colonies along the Atlantic coast by 1700. However, slavery phased out in those states north of the Mason-Dixon line in the first few decades after the Revolutionary War. That line also largely corresponds to the northern reach of malaria. From all along the Chesapeake Bay and extending south, where malaria flourished, slavery also flourished and was seen as essential to the economy. The same was true in South America, where Argentina, which is beyond the reach of malaria, initially had African slaves brought in.

However, they were never an essential part of the economy and, over time, were phased out. In contrast, the economy in Brazil, where malaria became endemic, was heavily dependent on slavery. It was the same for the Caribbean and those areas of Mexico, Central America, and Spanish South America, where malaria became endemic. Africans survived malaria at a much higher rate than Europeans or Indians.

Malaria is a rather unique disease. Its primary symptom is recurring chills and fever, which come in waves at 18 to 24-hour intervals. These waves will continue until recovery or death, but prolonged cases can cause damage to other organs or the brain. The body's immune system is weakened battling the disease so that those infected are quite susceptible to other infections, which may be the actual cause of death. One type of malaria (vivax) can become dormant in the liver and resurface again weeks, months, or even years after the initial infection. Malaria is particularly deadly for children under five years old. Because many diseases cause fevers, it was misunderstood and poorly understood for centuries, and was known be a variety of names. It didn't even get its current name until 1929. Much of what we now know of the history of malaria has been put together by medical historians now that we understand its cause, symptoms, and transmission.

It is never transmitted through the air or by contaminated food or water, or even by direct contact with someone who has it. You simply cannot get malaria from being around someone who is sick with it. The only way to catch malaria is to be bitten by a malaria-infected *Anopheles* mosquito (or through a blood transfusion), something that wasn't understood until the 1890s. Thus, unlike smallpox or many other diseases, malaria does not come in epidemic waves and then disappear. Instead, it becomes endemic and seasonal wherever there are *Anopheles* mosquitos that have become infected.

There is no vaccine, though efforts to develop one continue. Nor is there a cure beyond each human body's ability, or not, to fight off the infection. There are only antimalarial drugs (quinine being the first with large-scale use beginning after 1850) that can significantly limit its severity and greatly increase the potential for the body to overcome the infection. Overcoming a malaria infection provides immunity for that particular strain. *"In malaria zones, the primary victims are children. Adults, as a rule, have already contracted the disease and become immune upon survival."* So, most surviving adults living in areas where malaria is endemic function quite normally. However, there are many different strains, so subsequent infections are possible. Other than drugs, mosquito eradication and nets are the only means of controlling malaria.

Single-celled organisms of the genus *Plasmodium* cause malaria. These organisms have a very complicated life cycle, which involves several different forms of the organism. Part of the life cycle can only be completed inside the body of a mosquito, while other parts of the life cycle can only be completed inside the human body, which is why malaria can only be contracted through a mosquito bite (and a mosquito can only become infected by biting someone with malaria). The organism cannot survive outside a human or mosquito body. Since a mosquito's body is the same temperature as the air and the *Plasmodium* lifecycle slows dramatically at cooler temperatures, it cannot complete its life cycle inside the mosquito in cool air before the mosquito dies of old age (about two weeks). Thus, malaria is limited to warmer climates.

There are two primary types of Malaria, one caused by *Plasmodium vivax* and the other by *P. falciparum*. Vivax malaria can survive in more temperate climates, while falciparum malaria is more deadly. About 95% of black Africans are immune to vivax malaria. However, the extent of that immunity and its mechanism were not understood until the 1970s. Sickle cell anemia is a genetic disorder that, in its light form, provides immunity to falciparum malaria because an infected red blood cell immediately dies before *P. falciparum* can reproduce itself by the thousands as it would inside a normal infected red blood cell before it ruptures releasing all those new parasites into the bloodstream to cause chills and fever. Thus, through generations of exposure to falciparum malaria in Africa, sickle cell anemia is much more prevalent among black Africans and their descendants in the Americas than other populations.

It is now believed that vivax malaria reached coastal lowlands in southern England in the 1500s. Maps have even been developed showing areas in southern England where vivax malaria was probably endemic by 1600. About a third of the first two waves of Jamestown settlers came from these areas. Because of the symptoms described in contemporary records of the deadly illness that swept through Jamestown settlements during its first 15 years, it now is believed to have been malaria that, unknown to the first settlers, had come with one or more of them and then found the right mosquitoes living in ideal conditions in the tidewaters and swamps of the area. Those early reports repeatedly talked about how new arrivals had to be "seasoned" and the survivors would be okay. Falciparum malaria came later with slaves from Africa. With both types, malaria had become endemic along the coastal plain in Virginia and the Carolinas by 1700.

There was always a labor shortage in the colonies, which was particularly acute in Virginia and the Carolinas since growing rice and tobacco was labor intensive. Also, tobacco soon exhausted the soil, so new land constantly needed to be prepared for tobacco. Since African slaves had much higher survival rates for malaria than English indentured servants or native Indians, they became the labor force of choice. Just as with the Sugar plantations in the Caribbean and Brazil, malaria was a major factor in why so many Africans ended up being shipped to these southern colonies, even though the initial purchase price of an African slave was higher than that of an Indian.

Malaria even played a significant role in the merger of Scotland and England to form Great Britain in 1707. By the late 1600s, Scotland was a very poor country compared to England, which was constantly pushing for a merger. However, patriotic Scots resisted. Then the idea was pushed for Scotland to get in on the international trade of Asian goods and American silver by establishing a Scottish colony in Panama that could control a significant amount of the trade going back and forth between the Pacific and Atlantic oceans. After rounding up investments of as much as a third of the capital of the nation, in 1698, a colonial effort was launched that included two waves totaling 2,500 Scottish settlers with a year's supply of food and extensive provisions for trade to get them established. Unfortunately, the bulk of their trade goods were 25,000 pairs of leather shoes, the finest woolen socks, and woolen blankets. There was not much demand for any of those in tropical Panama. But the real culprit was a disease, primarily malaria. Settlement efforts were abandoned after less than a year, with less than 20% of the colonists surviving to make it home.

The effort resulted in a total financial loss, which set off riots in Scotland. Then England promised to reimburse the venture's investors as part of a merger, which overcame the resistance of Scottish leaders. As one historian wrote: *"Thus Great Britain was born, with assistance from the fevers of Panama."*

Malaria played a significant role in the Revolutionary War. In 1778, Henry Clinton was put in charge of the British forces. After deciding on a southern strategy, he moved much of his army south and took Charleston in 1780. He then left the area and put Cornwallis in charge with instructions to move inland and take control of the Carolinas. Cornwallis moved in June, the height of mosquito season. By August, he complained that disease had *"nearly ruined"* his army. The only ones capable of fighting were the local loyalists who had hooked up with his army (and were already malaria survivors), including Tarleton's green-coated dragoons. But they were not enough to win the war. As one historian put it: *"There was a big imbalance. Cornwallis's army simply melted away."* So, Cornwallis abandoned the Carolinas and, under orders from Clinton, took his army to Chesapeake Bay in June 1781. At Yorktown, which was described as *"some acres of unhealthy swamp,"* he set up camp while Washington marched south from New York with the continental forces, and a French fleet arrived off Chesapeake Bay. By the time of the battle, which began in late September, less than half of Cornwallis's 7,700 troops were fit to fight, thanks to raging fevers in the rest. As one historian put it, along with the bravery and skill of the continental forces, *"revolutionary mosquitoes stand tall among the Founding Fathers"* because of their role in the Revolutionary War.

Malaria played a huge role in Haiti gaining its independence and in the USA being able to make the Louisiana Purchase. As the French Revolution got in full swing in 1791, French Colonial Haiti (then called St. Domingue) was a classic extractive endeavor with forty thousand rich Europeans overseeing half a million African slaves working the sugar plantations there. As the monarchy fell in Paris, those rich colonists decided to declare their independence from France, while their slaves undertook a revolt of their own. Britain and France were soon at war, so Britain cut off France's Caribbean sugar revenue and took control of

Haiti's major cities. However, its armies there were continually decimated by malaria and yellow fever as fast as they could send reinforcements. *"The newly arrived died with astonishing quickness, seemingly disembarking from ships straight to their graves."* Thousands died. Britain abandoned Haiti in 1798 as the slave revolt continued. After taking control in Paris, Napoleon wanted to retain Haiti as a French colony because of the highly profitable sugar business there, so he sent 65,000 troops there in early 1802. By then, the fight was with the slave revolt. However, his army met the same fate the British had. After 18 months, with 50,000 dead from disease, his 15,000 remaining feverish troops limped home while, with his dreams of an American empire in ruins, he sold all France's interests in North America to the USA: the Louisiana Purchase. Malaria and yellow fever, which had been the cause of so many Africans being enslaved, ended up being the primary means of their deliverance from slavery in Haiti.

The Civil War was fought almost entirely in the South, while the Union army came largely from portions of the USA that were malaria-free. In the four years of the Civil War, for every Union army combat death, two soldiers died of disease, while the Confederate army was made up of malaria survivors. Thus, they had far fewer deaths from the disease.

QUININE AND COLONIALISM IN AFRICA – As Europeans spread their colonial empires around the world, colonial efforts in Africa came rather late. While there had been various ventures into Africa by a few Europeans over the centuries, as late as 1870, only ten percent of Africa (and none of central Africa) was under colonial rule by European nations. In fact, Africa was sometimes referred to, with good cause, as *"white man's grave."* Then, just 30 years later, by 1900, ninety percent of Africa was under colonial rule by Europe. Why the sudden change? And the answer is – quinine!

Within a few decades of the fall of the Inca Empire, Spanish priests became aware that the natives there used the bark of the cinchona tree, a tree native to Peru, to treat shivers. They tried it to treat fever and chills (malaria) and discovered it helped dramatically. We now know it blocks *P. falciparum's* ability to attack hemoglobin. However, it also works well against fevers from some other diseases. By the early 1600s, malaria had become endemic in the swamps around Rome and had killed high church officials, including popes. A priest in Peru sent some cinchona bark to Rome as a possible treatment. It worked very well and became known as *Peruvian bark.* It was used in London in 1690 to save King Charles II, who was suffering from malaria. This increased its popularity, but its availability was still limited. The very bitter bark was often pulverized and mixed with wine to get it down. In 1803, it was the primary fever medicine taken along on the Lewis and Clark expedition.

The active ingredient in the bark that helped control fevers was first isolated by chemists in 1820, who named it *quinine*. By then, Peru and surrounding countries had outlawed the export of cinchona seeds to try to control production. Quinine did not come into general use as a widely available treatment for malaria until after 1850. With quinine in hand, European nations began to move into West and Central Africa in a serious way. Quinine was also essential to the construction of the Panama Canal. It simply would not have been built without it.

The Dutch government succeeded in smuggling cinchona seeds out of Peru and, by the late 1800s, had established plantations in Indonesia. By the 1930s, thanks to those plantations, the Dutch controlled 97% of the world's quinine production. There were also some plantations is the Philippines. During World War II, with Germany conquering Holland and the Japanese taking the Philippines and Indonesia, the Allies were cut off from quinine supplies. Tens of thousands of U.S. troops died from malaria in North Africa and the South Pacific due to a lack of quinine. Efforts to develop new plantations in Costa Rica were too late. After the war, synthetics like hydroxychloroquine were developed. They have now largely replaced quinine to treat malaria.

7: THE FOUNDING OF THE UNITED STATES OF AMERICA

David McCullough described the founding fathers this way:

None of them had any prior experience in either revolutions or nation-making. They were, as we say, winging it. And they were idealistic, and they were young. George Washington, when he took command of the Continental Army at Cambridge in 1775, was 43 years old, and he was the oldest of them. Jefferson was 33 when he wrote the Declaration of Independence. John Adams was 40, Benjamin Rush, one of the most interesting of them all and one of the founders of the antislavery movement in Philadelphia, was 30 years old when he signed the declaration. They were young people. They were feeling their way, improvising, trying to do what would work. They had no money, no navy, no real army. There wasn't a bank in the entire country. There wasn't but one bridge between New York and Boston. It was a little country of 2,500,000 people, 500,00 of whom were held in slavery, a little fringe of settlement along the East Coast. What a story. What a noble beginning. And think of this: Almost no nations in the world know when they were born. We know exactly when we began and why we began and who did it.

Yet, I will begin this discussion of the creation of the USA with Benjamin Franklin, the old man of the group (age 70 in 1776), for four reasons. First, he is the only one of our founding fathers to have signed (and played a significant role in developing) all three documents creating this nation: 1) the Declaration of Independence in 1776, 2) the 1783 Paris treaty with Great Britain that ended the Revolutionary War and acknowledged to the world that these 13 united colonies were now an independent nation, and 3) the Constitution in 1787 (there were only five others who signed both the Declaration of Independence and the Constitution, none of them well known). Franklin was simply indispensable to the founding of the USA. Second, his pioneering work with electricity vastly expanded human understanding of this energy source so essential to our modern world. Third, his personal story personifies the *rags to riches* American dream as he rose from humble origins to become not only wealthy but the most famous American throughout the world by the time of the revolution. And finally, he was just an incredibly interesting character. At age 17, he was a fugitive from justice. He owned slaves. As a young man, he fathered two illegitimate children with two different women. Later, he only had a common-law marriage with another woman (they never officially married; they just moved in together) that he lived with for decades because she already had a husband who had disappeared in the Caribbean. Yet, he was continually committed to self-improvement. In that, he foreshadowed the improvements the USA would need to undertake, particularly as they related to race and slavery.

BENJAMAN FRANKLIN – Franklin was born in Boston on January 17, 1706; he was his father's 15th and last child and the eighth child of his mother, his father's second wife. This large Puritan family lived in a four-room house. He was reading the bible by the time he was five. Because he was so bright, his father sent him to school at age eight in hopes that he would enter the ministry. However, after just two years, due to a lack of funds, he left school to work full-time in his father's candle shop. At age twelve, he signed an apprentice agreement to work in his older brother's printshop for nine years as an indentured servant. There, he learned all aspects of the printing business. He spent all the money he earned on books and read incessantly, often borrowing books as well.

When Ben was 15, his brother started his own weekly newspaper, the first independent newspaper in Boston. A year later, Ben began secretly writing letters under the pseudonym *Silence Dogood,* supposedly a middle-aged widow, that were published in the paper. They quickly became very popular. In one, he criticized Harvard and its students:

Most of them consulted their own purses instead of their children's capacities. At Harvard they learn little more than how to carry themselves handsomely and enter a room genteelly. And from whence they return after an abundance of trouble and charge, as great blockheads as ever, only more proud and self-conceited.

That is rather cheeky for a 16-year-old indentured servant with only two years of schooling. Later, when his brother was arrested and spent three weeks in jail for criticizing prominent leaders in Boston, young Ben, as Mrs. Dogood, wrote a stirring defense of freedom of the press. However, his brother was furious when he learned that Ben was Mrs. Dogood. He became tyrannical, even physical sometimes. So, young Ben ran away, breaking his indentured service contract, and caught a ship to Philadelphia.

In 1723, Philadelphia, with 6,000 residents, was totally different from stuffy Boston. It included Indians, Quakers, Anglicans, Germans, slaves, and free blacks. There, at age 17, totally alone, homeless, and a fugitive from justice, Franklin found a print shop to work in, a room to rent, and began courting his landlord's 15-year-old daughter. He loved being on his own in Philadelphia.

After a year, Franklin had managed to catch the eye of Pennsylvania's governor, who sent him to London to buy supplies to set up a new printshop. However, after arriving in London at age 18, he discovered that his benefactor had no credit there and a poor reputation. So, he was again on his own, this time in a city of 600,000 that was the bustling hub of a global empire and home to many enlightened philosophers. He again found work in a print shop. And read and explored the city. After 18 months, he bought a passage home. During the twelve-week voyage, he wrote out the four principles that he intended to live by as a guide to a proper life. In short, they were frugality, commitment to the truth, being industrious, and speaking no ill of anyone.

Franklin, now age 20, found work in a printshop again. While Franklin was strongly committed to self-reliance, he was very sociable and believed in the value of community – of people working together for the common good. At age 21, he led the founding of the *Leather Apron Club,* a group of shopworkers who met every Friday evening to discuss whatever. At Franklin's urging, they pooled their books for sharing, which soon evolved into America's first public subscription library. They led the founding of a volunteer fire brigade and other public services, including a hospital. Later, Franklin took the lead in establishing a college that would become the University of Pennsylvania. He was president of its first board of governors.

At age 22, with a financial backer that he was soon able to buy out, Franklin opened his own printshop. The next year, he started his own newspaper, the Philadelphia Gazette. It was an immediate success, including not only local news, but stories from Britain and other colonies, along with witty letters (many of which he wrote himself under such names as *Anthony Afterwit* and *Alice Addertongue*). The paper also included commercial and private advertisements, including ads to buy and sell slaves. In 1728, slaves were just part of life. He would later own a few, using them in his printshop and his household. He began publishing *Poor Richard's Almanac* annually in 1733, which gave him another outlet for his wit and ideas on a wide range of topics while spreading his name throughout the colonies. He was made Philadelphia's postmaster in 1737. He developed links to print shops in other cities throughout the colonies. Then, having become a wealthy man, in 1748, at the age of 42, he retired from managing the printshop to pursue new interests.

Though his interests and inventions varied, his explorations of electricity would earn him worldwide fame. He was the first to identify that electricity had a positive and a negative charge and that it flowed from one to the other. He coined the term *battery* for a series of glass jars in which he tried to capture electricity. His kite experiment demonstrated that lightning is indeed electricity. He then invented the lightning rod, which was soon saving lives and church steeples (and other tall buildings) throughout the colonies, Britain, and Europe. He vastly expanded human understanding of electricity, which brought him world renown. Some in Europe even labeled him the modern *Prometheus*. Oxford University granted him an honorary doctorate, after which he was generally referred to as Dr. Franklin. He refused to patent any of his many inventions because he felt they should be free to benefit all mankind.

In 1752, he was appointed postmaster for the colonies. At the time, to get a letter from Boston or New York to Charleston, it would probably go through London. There was little interaction or traffic between colonies. He took months long trips going both north and south to establish a postal network. Far more than any other American, he came to understand the diversity and reach of the thirteen colonies. A colonial postal system began to work.

When the French and Indian War broke out in 1754, Franklin played a key role in defending eastern Pennsylvania, which only added to his popularity. He was also part of a small group that reached out to several Indian tribes, including the Haudenosaunee alliance, to try to win their support for the British in the war. He was very impressed by this alliance of Iroquois tribes and their joint commitment to their freedom. He then led an effort to create an alliance between the colonies. In the process, he created a flag with the image of a snake on it cut into pieces with the name of each colony on a snake segment and the words "*Join or Die.*" However, his efforts to unite the colonies in any kind of structured way failed. He lamented:

It would be a very strange thing if six nations of ignorant savages should be capable of forming a scheme for such a union and be able to execute it in such a manner as that it has subsisted for ages and appears indissoluble, and that a like union should be impracticable for ten or a dozen English colonies to whom it is more necessary and must be more advantageous.

In 1757, the middle of the war, he returned to London to represent Pennsylvania's interests there. He took two slaves with him on this trip to London. However, to his great frustration, one ran away. He again found that he loved London society. And stayed five years and wrote:

Why should this island, which compared to America, is but like a stepping stone in a brook, enjoy in almost every neighborhood more sensible, virtuous, and elegant minds that we can collect in ranging 100 leagues of our vast forests?

Franklin returned to Philadelphia, now a city of 20,000 and the largest city in the colonies, in 1762. He only stayed two years before going back to London. Before he left, his wife had enrolled a child of one of their slaves in a new school for black children. At her urging, Franklin visited the school. And then wrote the following:

I was on the whole much pleased and from what I then saw I have conceived a higher opinion of the natural capacities of the black race than I had ever before entertained. Their apprehension seems as quick, their memory as strong, and their facility in every respect equal to that of white children. You will wonder perhaps that I should ever doubt it, and I will not undertake to justify all my prejudices nor to account for them.

Franklin was an intensely curious man of science who was always looking for new truths. And here he was confronted by a nearby truth that had never even crossed his mind before. He also came to recognize the plight that the colonies had placed on Indian tribes.

If an Indian injures me, does it follow that I may revenge that injury on all Indians? These poor people have been always our friends, their fathers received ours when strangers here with kindness and hospitality. Behold the return we have made them.

Back in London, he represented the interests of four colonies before Parliament and the Crown. He loved being British but was deeply concerned that his fellow Americans were not being accorded their full rights as British citizens.

Being born and bred in one of the countries and having lived long in the other, I wish all prosperity to both. But I do not find that I have gained any point in either country except that of rendering myself suspected by my impartiality, in England of being too much of an American, and in America of being too much of an Englishman.

This time, he stayed in London for ten years. He did his best to avert armed conflict and represent the colonies' interests as tensions rose. Then, in late 1774, he was publicly ridiculed for all the perceived belligerence of the colonies. He finally returned home in early 1775, convinced that reconciliation with Britain was not possible. He was now a fully committed patriot and represented Pennsylvania in the second Continental Congress held in Philadelphia later that year.

In late 1776, just a few months after signing the Declaration of Independence, he was sent to Paris to try to win France's support. The French loved him. He was in constant social demand everywhere. He understood his role, loved it, and played it perfectly. France sent arms, supplies, and money long before they finally provided the military support crucial to victory at Yorktown. Franklin was there until 1785, and then he finally returned home, where he participated in the Constitutional Convention two years later.

The colony's first abolitionist society was formed in Philadelphia in 1775. In 1787, Benjamin Franklin became its president and, at the end of his life, was working to abolish slavery. He died in 1790 at the age of 84. Near the end of his life, he wrote the following:

I begin to be almost sorry I was born so soon since I cannot have the happiness of knowing what will be known 100 years hence, but it is the will of God and Nature that these mortal bodies be laid aside. Whether I have been doing good or mischief is for time to discover. I only know that I intended well and hope all will end well.

WHAT LED TO THE DECLARATION OF INDEPENDENCE BEING WRITTEN? – A basic question about the American Revolution is: what did the colonists really want? Primarily, they wanted their *rights as Englishmen!* They were upset about taxes that had been levied on them to pay off British debt for the global Seven-Year War (which included the French and Indian War) two decades before, as well as the heavy-handed British overlords and governors imposed upon them by the King. That was particularly true in New England. When tons of tea were thrown off a British merchant ship into Boston harbor in 1773, they were complaining about taxes. *Taxation without representation!* In Virginia and North Carolina, where growing tobacco soon wore out the soil, settlers had a continuing interest in moving west. They were beginning to pour over the Appalachian Mountains into what is now Kentucky and Tennessee.

When the first Continental Congress finally met in 1774 in Philadelphia, it was to develop a united front for the 13 colonies in presenting their grievances to Britain. And each colony had sent its best and brightest as delegates. After a month of discussions, John Adams, a prominent attorney who led the Massachusetts delegation, wrote to his wife, Abigail:

This assembly is like no other that ever existed. Every man in it is a great man – an orator, a critic, a statesman, and therefore every man upon every question must show his oratory, his criticism, and his political abilities.

The consequence of this is that business is drawn and spun out to immeasurable length. I believe that if it was moved and seconded that we should come to a resolution that three and two make five, we should be entertained with logic and rhetoric, law, history, politics, and mathematics, concerning the subject for two whole days, and then we should pass the resolution unanimously in the affirmative.

While the Congress succeeded somewhat in getting the colonies to work together, it had little impact on British policies toward the colonies. That year, Britain passed the Quebec Act *"to stem the flow of Virginians across the mountains, by extending the boundary of Canada south to the Ohio River."* By the time the Continental Congress met the next year, blood had already been spilled at the battles at Lexington and Concord. Bunker Hill soon followed. So, in 1775, Congress was kept busy raising an army and putting George Washington in charge. However, independence was not yet the goal. In fact, support for the idea was still quite limited.

However, by the time Congress met again in February 1776, things had begun to change. And a leading cause of that change was a 47-page pamphlet titled *Common Sense* by Thomas Paine, an immigrant from

Britain who had met Ben Franklin in London in 1774, and then came to America with Franklin's help. It first appeared on January 9, 1776. By the time Congress met again a month later, over 100,000 copies were circulating throughout the colonies. It attacked the very idea of hereditary monarchy as absurd and evil while boldly calling for independence in a way that had never been seen before in print. In a letter to Abigail, John Adams described it as:

A ray of revelation that has arrived to clear our doubts and fix our choice.

Yet, there was still considerable resistance. As the delegates arrived that February, those from New York, New Jersey, Pennsylvania, Delaware, Maryland, and South Carolina were under specific instructions not to vote for independence. But the issue was now openly being debated. On March 4, Congress voted to disarm all Tories. On March 23, they voted to outfit armed vessels to prey on *"the enemies of the United Colonies."* On April 6, Congress opened all the colonies' ports to trade with all nations but Britain. That month, the delegates from South Carolina, North Carolina, and Georgia received clearance to vote for independence. The Congress also learned that Britain had contracted to bring 17,000 Hessian mercenaries to help subdue the rebellious colonies. On May 8, they could hear the thunder of cannons from 30 miles away where two British warships were trying to break through the blockade on the Delaware River. Had they succeeded, it would have enabled them to reach Philadelphia. By then, the British had evacuated Boston, and most had gone to Halifax to re-arm for an attack on New York.

So, On May 10, Adams, who had become the principal advocate for independence and a powerful voice in the Congress, began to formally move the Congress toward independence with a resolution recommending that the individual colonies assume all powers of government to secure *"the happiness and safety of their constituents in particular, and America in general."* It passed unanimously. Then, on May 15, a more detailed preamble expanding that resolution was approved. However, it still made no mention of severing ties to Britain. On May 24, General Washington arrived to discuss with Congress his grave concerns about being able to defend New York, where they were expecting a British attack in the near future. On May 27, the Virginia delegation said they were now to support independence.

On June 7, 1776, a resolution was introduced before the Congress that would resolve:

That these United Colonies are, and of a right ought to be, free and independent states, that they are absolved from all allegiance to the British Crown, and that all political connection between them and the state of Great Britain is, and ought to be, totally dissolved.

With independence now squarely on the table, the heated debate began. However, there was some strong opposition from Pennsylvania and New York. On June 10, three things were agreed to: 1) a final vote would be delayed until July 1 in order to give delegates time to seek further instructions from their respective colonies, 2) work should begin on drafting a formal Declaration of Independence, and 3) a committee of five, that included Thomas Jefferson, Benjamin Franklin, and John Adams, was appointed to prepare that draft formal declaration. That committee then agreed that Jefferson should write a draft for the committee to work on.

We should note here that Jefferson did not have to start completely from scratch. He would have been familiar with the writings of John Locke (once described by George Washington as *"the greatest man who ever lived"*), who had used the phrase *"life, liberty, and the pursuit of property,"* and Locke's ideas on the *social contract* in which the sovereign serves the people instead of the people serving the sovereign. He would have also been aware of the 1689 English *Bill of Rights,* influenced by Locke, and agreed to by William and Mary as the new sovereigns as they replaced James II, who was deposed. That bill included a long list of charges against King James II and clarified the relationship of the sovereign to Parliament. It also included several rights now contained in the Constitution's Bill of Rights as laid out in its first ten amendments.

The debate over independence resumed on July 1. After a long day of arguments, a preliminary vote showed that only nine states supported independence, and three opposed it, with New York abstaining. The proponents wanted more unanimity and quickly agreed to delay the final vote to the next day. Word came that night that 100 British warships were coming into New York harbor. The next morning, July 2, two opposing delegates from Pennsylvania did not attend, one new delegate from Delaware supporting independence arrived (he rode all night to get there), and South Carolina shifted its position. So, the final vote had twelve states supporting independence and New York abstaining. There is no record of whatever backroom deals were made the previous night to enable to enable a vote for independence, with no states voting no. The Congress had finally voted for independence to separate themselves from Britain. In fact, John Adams wrote to his wife that night:

The second day of July 1776 will be the most memorable epocha in the history of America. I am apt to believe that it will be celebrated by succeeding generations as the great anniversary festival.

Now that they had finally agreed on independence, the next day, July 3, was spent with the whole Congress marking up the draft Declaration since they were all now committed to signing the final version. As the day wore on, about a fourth of Jefferson's latest draft was cut entirely. Jefferson sat quietly alone as the Congress marked up his work. In all, about 80 changes were made from Jefferson's first draft in June. Then, on July 4, after a little more debate, Congress voted to approve the Declaration of Independence as modified. After the vote, only John Hancock, as President of the Congress, and Charles Thomas, as Secretary, signed the Declaration that day to authenticate it for printing.

It was printed that night, and copies began to be distributed the next day. The entire Declaration was printed as the front-page story of a Philadelphia newspaper on July 6. George Washington read it to his troops in the Continental Army in New York City as they were preparing to defend it against British forces that had begun to arrive in New York Harbor. The approved Declaration was later handwritten (with slight punctuation differences) by someone with elegant penmanship on a large piece of parchment. Most of the delegates then signed that parchment document on August 2, though a few signed later. That is the document in the National Archives.

THE DECLARATION OF INDEPENDENCE – So, on July 4, 1776, the Continental Congress voted to approve the final version of the Declaration of Independence. The 56 delegates who later signed that Declaration represented 13 separate British colonies scattered along the Atlantic coast of North America, from Georgia to New Hampshire. They were all British citizens – subjects of their British king, so they were all white men. They were also quite young, with more under 40 than over 50. The youngest was 26. They were there representing about two and a half million British colonists scattered across those 13 colonies. Those colonies also contained over half a million black African slaves and about 50,000 free blacks. While slaves were primarily in the southern colonies, there was legal slavery in each of the 13 colonies. There was also an untold number of Indians along the frontiers of the colonists.

The Declaration is just what the title says: a united declaration that these 13 British colonies are now independent of their British King. Before launching into a long list of grievances against their king, the Declaration contains the following remarkable sentence that is still reverberating around the world:

We hold these Truths to be self-evident, that all Men are created equal, that they are endowed by their Creator with certain unalienable Rights, that among these are Life, Liberty, and the Pursuit of Happiness – That to secure these rights, Governments are instituted among Men, deriving their just power from the Consent of the Governed, that whenever any Form of Government becomes destructive of these Ends, it is the Right of the People to alter or abolish it, and to institute new Government, laying its Foundation on such Principles, and organizing its Powers in such Form, as to them shall seem most likely to effect their Safety and Happiness.

That sentence is even more profound than it is long (this is all one sentence as shown above in the Declaration as printed that first evening and widely distributed on July 5. The handwritten parchment document prepared later and signed by all delegates has this as two sentences with a period instead of a dash). There may well have never been another sentence that said so much and had such an impact. When these radical and earth-shattering ideals were laid out in 1776, virtually every nation in the world had autocratic rule by a monarch, emperor, or dictator. There had been no democracies for two thousand years. The divine right of kings had rarely been questioned. These remarkable new ideals have been tumultuously reverberating around the world ever since. As noted by Charles C. Mann:

So accepted now around the world is the idea of the implicit equality and liberty of all people that it is hard to grasp what a profound change in human society it represented.

Not only does this sentence lay out the ideals of equality and liberty for all, but it also states that governments are instituted to secure these rights, and that Governments derive their power from the consent of the governed. People have the right to change or replace their government when it is destructive of those rights. And that these are all self-evident truths! (The term *self-evident* was Franklin's edit of a much longer explanation in Jefferson's original draft.) Thus, it expressly and clearly states our democracy's founding ideals. It is the sentence that has changed the World. The last sentence of the Declaration states:

And for the support of this Declaration, with a firm Reliance on the Protection of divine Providence, we mutually pledge to each other our Lives, our Fortunes, and our sacred Honor.

The 56 men who signed that Declaration knew full well that their signature meant they would be hung if captured by the mighty British army currently moving into New York Harbor. The ideals in that first sentence and the scope of the commitment in that last sentence, along with all that followed, are why we have celebrated the fourth of July ever since. It was clearly a declaration of, by, and for British colonists against their

British king, and it included a long list of grievances against him, along with soaring rhetoric about the inalienable rights of mankind. And the Nation was born.

So, it was a big deal when, in 2019, the New York Times, the most prominent newspaper in the USA, published the *1619 Project* with its banner headline stating the Nation's *"founding ideals were false when written";* when, in 2020, that paper received a Pulitzer Prize for that publication; and then, in 2021, the federal government itself began to promote teaching the *1619 Project* in the Nation's schools.

Although the *1619 Project* claims that the primary reason for the Revolutionary War was to preserve slavery against British plans to abolish the practice, that claim is patently false (the Times has since softened the online language of that claim without acknowledging any change). The evidence cited for this claim is that Britain had offered freedom to slaves who would revolt against their masters and help Britain quash the colonists' rebellion. However, that offer was just looking for an edge in the fight. The list of issues that led to the battles the previous year between the colonists and their British rulers at Lexington, Concord, and Bunker Hill, or their successful expulsion of British troops from Boston earlier that spring, did not include slavery at all. In fact, Great Britain was not only deeply involved in the transatlantic slave trade but had been the trade's largest player for a century, with most of those slaves being shipped to the Caribbean. When King George announced to Parliament in October 1775 (and Parliament, after a raucous debate, approved by a margin of more than two to one) that the rebellious colonies must, and would, be brought into submission, slavery was not even mentioned as a factor in the conflict. In short, slavery, a common and socially acceptable practice around the world in 1776, was simply not a factor in why the colonies were rebelling against Great Britain.

While that first *1619 Project* banner headline is quite sweeping by stating our founding ideals were false when written, the first sentence of the essay narrows that charge of being false when written to the ideals of liberty and equality. It is certainly true that the Declaration says nothing about slaves or slavery and that the founders only applied those ideals of liberty and equality to themselves (British colonists rebelling against their

British king), and not their black slaves nor their Indian neighbors they were pushing aside. But that does not negate the validity of the ideals. It only shows that the colonists were so ethnocentric that the irony of truly believing in those ideals without extending those ideals to their African slaves or the *"merciless Indian Savages"* (the phrase used in the Declaration) around them was beyond their current concerns. But the fact that they were so ethnocentric is not surprising or even news since they were living in a very ethnocentric world where they were colonists pushing aside the original inhabitants. These were still world-shattering ideals even though they only applied them to themselves.

The ideals expressed in that sentence are what have enabled the transformation from those 13 British colonies into what the USA was to become over the next 200+ years. These ideals encouraged initiative, innovation, and entrepreneurial activity like never before. The promotion of those ideals among a very imperfect population enabled those people to try harder and reach further than they otherwise would have. Those ideals also encouraged others from around the world to take the initiative to chase their dreams and come here to do it. *"Those with get up and go, got up and came."* Martin Luther King understood that. Frederick Douglas understood that, as evidenced by his July 1852 Independence Day speech. His whole speech was praising the USA's revolutionary ideals while chastising the nation for not applying them to their human slaves (this eloquent speech should be required reading in our high schools and colleges). The truth of these ideals is also shown in how much they have altered the entire world since then to the benefit of all mankind. These ideals have been the starting point for many democracies that have risen since then. They also helped abolish slavery in the world.

English (or British) society, in the seventeenth and eighteenth centuries (in 1707, England and Scotland joined to form Great Britain), like all European societies, was divided by class, with a few extraordinarily rich and titled, lots very poor, and a range of layers in between. The lower classes served those above them. This was simply the accepted way. To the deeply religious Puritans, while God loved everyone, all were not to play equal roles in society. As expressed by John Winthrop, the founder of Boston, who had deeply held religious principles:

GOD ALMIGHTY in his most holy and wise providence, hath so disposed of the condition of mankind, as in all times some must be rich, some poore, some high and eminent in power and dignitie; others mean and in submission.

The social ideal was responsible adherence to religiously inspired authority within a class-structured society, not classless democratic self-rule. The Pilgrims on the Mayflower, just like the settlers at Boston, included families and the servants of families. Yet, by 1776, colonist society, at least in the north, was quite different with far less class structure. So, where did the founders get those ideals in the Declaration about government, equality, and man's inalienable rights of life, liberty, and the pursuit of happiness? They did not bring those ideals (of a classless society governing itself with equal opportunity for all) with them from the British Isles.

Some have suggested that those ideals came from, or were at least influenced by, the frequent and almost constant interactions of colonists with Indians living around and among them, particularly along the porous and ill-defined frontiers in the northern colonies throughout the 150+ years leading up to the Declaration of Independence.

What role, if any, Indian values of freedom and equality, particularly the Haudenosaunee, had on the ideals expressed in The Declaration of Independence can only be guessed at (and I am not the first to guess). I find it easy to believe Indians had some influence. Boston colonists dressed as Mohawk Indians (part of the Haudenosaunee coalition) when they threw that British tea into Boston harbor. New England led the colonies' conflicts with their mother country from the beginning. John Adams was the principal protagonist of independence. I expect the committee assigned to draft the Declaration met to discuss what it should say before Jefferson went off to write the first draft. In any case, these founding ideals were a dramatic departure from the British title and class structure that was still evident well into the twentieth century, as exemplified by the hit TV show *Downton Abby*. Protesters seeking freedom around the world, even in China, over the last few decades have often dressed as Native Americans. It is true that the idea of citizens having some role in their government, at least for the upper classes, was expressed in the *Magna Carte,* and in the *Mayflower Compact.* There was also Parliament's revolt against King Charles over a century before, but England soon reinstated the monarchy. In any case, the ideals of equality and liberty for all, embodied in Fourth of July celebrations ever since 1776, were world-changing concepts that, other than the Athenians 2,000 years before, had no roots anywhere in Europe, Asia, Africa, the Inca, or the Aztecs. Instead, they sprang from British colonists living for over a century among Indians who abhorred class and valued individual freedom above all else for generations.

JOHN ADAMS AND THOMAS JEFFERSON – These two men were far more responsible for the Declaration of Independence than any others. Adams was the primary force that led to it being written and approved, and Jefferson was its principal author. It seems providentially fitting then that these two men died on the same day, July 4, 1826, exactly 50 years after that Declaration was approved – the 50th birthday of the USA. While they had a few things in common, they came from very different backgrounds and viewed life quite differently. Life in eastern Massachusetts was unimaginably different from the tobacco plantation life of Virginia.

In July 1776, John Adams was 40 years old, 5' 7", nearly bald, and somewhat portly. He loved books, would always have some with him, and read the classics in the original Greek and Latin. He considered Greek the greatest of languages. He was always thinking and would fill his diaries and letters to his wife, Abigail, with his innermost thoughts and feelings. He loved to talk and the back-and-forth exchange of ideas and arguments. His ancestry dates back to the early days of Puritans, who came to Boston in 1638. He was the son of a farmer of modest means. He had learned to work with his own hands as a child and detested the institution of slavery. Frugality, independence, honesty, chastity, and hard work were cherished virtues. He was bright and loved books so that, through the application of those virtues, he went to Harvard on scholarship, managed to become a licensed attorney, and established an excellent reputation. The Adams lived in a modest home. Although he had never been outside of New England before and knew little about other colonies, he quickly became a force in the Continental Congress from its inception. He had strong reservations about human nature and *"was not inclined to believe mankind improvable."* He believed that the best form of government would be one that would provide the most people the best chance for happiness, and that would be a republic governed by the *Rule of Law*. He felt a simple majority-rule democracy like Athens would be too fickle.

In July 1776, Thomas Jefferson was 33 years old, almost 6'3", lean and long-limbed with a full head of thick coppery hair. An aristocrat, he was raised as a perfect landed gentleman of Virginia. He was always gracious and abhorred personal confrontation. He was never blunt or assertive, as Adams could be. He was born into wealth and married into more wealth. He had never done any manual labor. He was an excellent horseman. He sang. He played the violin. He was also an attorney and read the classics in the original Greek and Latin. In addition to English, he spoke French, Italian, and Spanish. He was working on German. He kept detailed records and ledgers but rarely wrote about his thoughts or feelings as Adams constantly did. He was building a colossal mansion he called Monticello. He owned about 16,000 acres and 200 slaves. Slaves not only worked his fields but also *"cut his firewood, cooked and served his meals, washed and ironed his linen, brushed his suits, nursed his children, cleaned, scrubbed, polished, opened and closed doors for him, saddled his horse, turned down his bed, and waited on him hand and foot from dawn to dusk."* He arrived at the Congress on May 14, 1776, with a 14-year-old slave as his personal servant. Jefferson was intensely curious about natural science, exploration, history, and philosophy. He was an inventor, always tinkering with new things. He admired Benjamin Franklin above all men. Jefferson was: *"devoted to the ideal of improving mankind but had comparatively little interest in people in particular."* Yet, Jefferson had severe reservations about slavery's impact on both master and slave:

The whole commerce between master and slave is a perpetual exercise of the most boisterous passions, the most unremitting despotism on the one part, and degrading submissions of the other. Our children see this, and learn to imitate it...If a parent could find no motive either in his philanthropy or his self-love, for restraining the intemperance of passion towards his slave, it should always be a sufficient one that his children is present. But generally it is not sufficient. The parent storms, the child looks on, catches the lineaments of wrath, puts on the same airs in the circle of smaller slaves, gives a loose to his worst of passions, and thus nursed, educated, and daily exercised in tyranny, cannot but be stamped by it with odious peculiarities. The man must be a prodigy who can retain his manners and morals undepraved by such circumstances.

So, maybe it is unsurprising that Jefferson attempted to address slavery in the Declaration of Independence. His initial draft of the Declaration of Independence contained a longer list of grievances against the King that included the following passage:

*He has waged cruel war against human nature itself, violating its most sacred rights of life and liberty in the persons of a distant people who never offended him, captivating and carrying them into slavery in another hemisphere, or to incur miserable death in their transportation hither, this piratical warfare, the opprobrium of **infidel** powers, is the warfare of the **Christian** king of Great Britain. Determined to keep open a market where MEN should be bought and sold, he has prostituted his negative for suppressing every legislative attempt to prohibit or to restrain this execrable commerce: and that this assemblage of horrors might want no fact of distinguished die, he is now exciting those very people to rise in arms among us, and to purchase that liberty of which **he** had deprived them, by murdering the people upon whom **he** also obtruded them: thus paying off former crimes committed against the **liberties** of one people, with crimes which he urges them to commit against the **lives** of another.* (emphasis in original)

It was a remarkable statement for a man whose entire life was built around slaves. Although the rest of the committee made numerous edits to the first draft, that charge about slavery was retained in the draft the committee submitted to the full Congress. However, deleting this charge against the King regarding slavery (led by South Carolina and Georgia) was among the long list of changes made by Congress on July 3. While John Adams, the primary mover behind getting Congress to agree to declare independence, opposed slavery and supported including the slavery charge in the Declaration, he was not about to lose it all over a fight to keep that language in. John Adams and Thomas Jefferson had achieved something quite remarkable that is still reverberating throughout the world.

THE REVOLUTIONARY WAR – Just a few comments about the Revolutionary War that aren't often noted or that warrant a highlight. Going into the war, Independence from Britain wasn't all that popular with the general public. As estimated by John Adams, a third supported independence, a third were Tories opposed to independence (some of my New England ancestors moved to Canada shortly after the war ended), and a third were ambivalent or timid.

The outcome of the Revolutionary War was far from certain. By late 1776, things were looking incredibly bleak. After barely escaping from New York City, Washington's army had been on the run for months to avoid being crushed. Then Thomas Paine wrote the following:

THESE are the times that try men's souls. The summer soldier and the sunshine patriot will, in this crisis, shrink from the service of their country; but he that stands by it now, deserves the love and thanks of man and woman. Tyranny, like hell, is not easily conquered; yet we have this consolation with us, that the harder the conflict, the more glorious the triumph. What we obtain too cheap, we esteem too lightly: it is dearness only that gives everything its value. Heaven knows how to put a proper price upon its goods; and it would be strange indeed if so celestial an article as FREEDOM should not be highly rated.

These words came to embody the spirit of the Revolution (and show what has been lost to much of our current generation in 2024). Soon after these words were widely published, Washington snuck his army across the Delaware River in the middle of the night and won a surprise Christmas attack that provided a little hope. But things were still bleak. In the spring of 1777, Abigail Adams wrote the following to her husband, John Adams, concerning the war:

I want a bird of passage. Posterity who are to reap the blessings will scarcely be able to conceive the hardships and sufferings of their ancestors.

And that has certainly proved to be true. Then, in November 1779, John Adams was sent back to France again to support Franklin's efforts to gain support from France. He again took their eldest son, John Quincy Adams, now 12, along with their next son, who was nine. John Quincy had gone with his father the year before when they were nearly lost at sea during a storm, so he did not want to go. Crossing the Atlantic late in the year was always dangerous, especially so now that the British were attacking any colonial ship they saw. Yet, his parents insisted. Abigail, one of my favorite people from that period, felt strongly that the experience would be good for him. She wrote the following in a letter to young John Quincy as they departed:

It will be expected of you, my son, that as you are favored with superior advantages under the instructive eye of a tender parent, that your improvements should bear some proportion to your advantages.
These are the times in which genius would wish to live. It is not in the still calm of life, or the repose of a pacific station, that great characters are formed. The habits of a vigorous mind are formed in contending with difficulties. Great necessities call out great virtues. When a mind is raised, and animated by the scenes that engage the heart, then those qualities which would otherwise lay dormant, wake into life and form the character of the hero and the statesman.

Those are remarkable words for a loving mother to write to a twelve-year-old boy as she sends him away on a very dangerous ocean crossing.

First, it is not written in simple words and sentences, which most of us might use with a twelve-year-old. The fact that she expected a boy that age to even understand what she was saying speaks volumes about her confidence in him. Now, we seem to try to provide excitement without any risks for our children. She understood the value of risk and challenges in making her son into the kind of man she hoped he would become. She saw opportunity in these challenges and wanted him to make the most of them. And he did.

The colonists won the Revolutionary War because Washington and his armies quickly learned the lessons the Indians in King Phillip's War already knew. They could not beat the British, the most powerful army on earth at that time, by facing them head-on. Instead, they learned to run, hide, and strike, then run, hide, and strike again. And again. Until they outlasted the British. Also, As the Athenians learned over two thousand years before when they invaded Sicily, and as the USA should have learned in Vietnam and Afghanistan (and as President Roosevelt feared during World War II), wherever popular support is critical to a government, know that the population back home will grow tired of an endless war far from home. The British got tired of this war far from home. They were far less invested in it than the people who lived here. John Steele Gordon described it this way:

The United States only had to avoid losing the war until the British government and people tired sufficiently of the struggle and its mounting costs. Britain had to defeat and pacify a vast country awash in rebellion.
The United States had won by not losing.

The colonists won the war because, unlike the Indians in King Phillip's War, who were destitute after a few months of victories, the colonists, thanks to France, had the reserves, food, shelter, and weapons, though sometimes scarce, that enabled them to grit it out with steely resolve and survive until they could win a significant battle that sucked the will out of the British.

The colonists won because of Washington's strong discipline, unyielding character, and steadfast resolve. And his demand for discipline in his troops. When, after years of bad food, limited supplies, and hardly any pay (Congress had a hard time raising money to pay for the war), some of his troops were on the verge of revolt. He forcefully restored discipline.

The colonists won because Washington finally realized that, as much as he wanted to, he did not need to retake New York City to win the war. He only needed to force the British army into surrender in a significant battle, wherever that happened to be.

The colonists won the war because France finally provided military assistance, in addition to the arms and supplies they had provided for years, in that significant battle at Yorktown. And because patriotic mosquitoes had decimated Cornwallis' army in time for that battle.

Paper also played a critical role. It has not only been essential to growth and dissemination of accumulated knowledge but also in the spread of ideas. Newspapers were used to spread the Declaration of Independence and Thomas Paine's words to the public to inform and inspire them. And on and on. The nation and the world we live in could not have come to be without that Chinese invention: paper.

While the fight had gone out with the British, the British army continued to occupy New York City for another two years while a treaty conceding victory was worked out in London and Paris. That meant Washington had to maintain his army not far away that whole time, even though there was limited fighting. And they still weren't getting paid. After 18 months, Washington had to stare down his officers to keep them from marching on Congress in a military coup. His resolve and character maintained civilian control of the nation. By the time the British army finally left New York City in November 1783, after over seven years of occupation, the city was only half the size it had been when they arrived. Many of the city's merchants and elites left with them.

The 13 former British colonies were now 13 free and independent states loosely linked together by the Articles of Confederation they had each agreed to during the war. Each state retained its *"sovereignty, freedom, and independence, and every power, jurisdiction, and right not expressly delegated to the United States, in Congress assembled."* Among the powers expressly not delegated were taxing, raising troops, or regulating commerce. As previously noted, the ability to create and control money is key to the success of any nation. The new United States not only lacked the authority to tax, it also could not mint, print, or borrow money or regulate the supply of money. In short, the national Congress, which was the only body of national government, was left to beg states for money and had no power to enforce anything.

It soon became apparent that something more was needed if they were to survive, individually as states and collectively as one nation. On the issue of slavery, as one historian has phrased it: *"While there were some people who spoke against slavery before the Revolutionary War, it was never a major public issue. After the Revolution, there was never a time when it wasn't a major public issue."*

That was the impact of the Declaration of Independence.

THE UNITED STATES CONSTITUTION – Eleven years after the Declaration of Independence, another convention was held in the same place with representatives of those newly independent states that had now achieved their freedom from Britain. The goal this time was to establish a constitution that would bind these states together into one nation. The host for the convention was Benjamin Franklin, now 81 years old and the President of Pennsylvania. George Washington was elected President of the convention on its first day, May 25, 1787. The convention began with three main rules in place: 1) a quorum would consist of seven or more states, and any question would be decided by a majority of the quorum present, 2) each state would have only one vote; and 3) the proceedings were to be kept secret. Secrecy was essential so that delegates could argue, debate, and compromise without locking themselves into public positions that it would be very difficult to backtrack from. Washington took stern actions to enforce secrecy and the protection of written notes. Throughout the convention, various committees were formed on issues that would then report back to the entire convention.

All three rules proved critical to the convention's success. The convention began with only seven states being present on that first day. While 55 delegates attended sometime during the convention, at any given time, only about half that number were present. No more than 11 states ever voted on any issue. Rhode Island never sent any delegates. By the time delegates from New Hampshire finally arrived in late July, the New York delegation had already left the convention and did not return. On the convention's last day, September 17, 1787, 38 delegates signed the constitution that had been agreed to two days before and then written out on parchment in its final form the day before. However, three delegates opposed the final version and would not sign. This dissent was glossed over in the public release, which stated that the constitution was adopted *"by the unanimous consent of the States present"* so that there was no mention of absent states or dissenting individuals.

The convention had lasted almost four months. On May 29, Virginia (James Madison) presented its draft plan, which became the working model. It provided for a national legislature with two branches, the first elected by the people and the second elected by the first. On May 30, the convention overwhelmingly agreed to the proposition that "*a national government ought to be established consisting of a supreme legislative, executive, and judiciary.*"

Then came the hard work. On June 19, by a 7 to 3 vote, the convention agreed to abandon the initial plan of modifying the existing Articles of Confederation and, instead, develop a completely new Constitution. However, the small states still wanted equal representation in the legislature, while the large states wanted representation based on population. On June 29, by a 6 to 4 vote, they agreed to have the first branch of the legislature based on "*some equitable ratio*" of the population. Then came the Great Compromise. On July 16, after a few weeks of heated debate, on a 5 to 4 vote, with the Massachusetts delegation split, the convention agreed to equal representation for each state in the second branch of the legislature whose members would be chosen, not by the people, but by the state legislatures. Members would serve six years.

At the end of July, the Committee on Detail came back with the names, *Congress, House of Representatives, Senate, Supreme Court,* and *President of the United States of America.* Debates followed on a range of issues, slavery, taxing authority, imports and exports, nobility, etc. They finally agreed that Congress would be forbidden from prohibiting the importation of slaves for 20 years, that a census would be taken every ten years for the purpose of apportioning seats in the House of Representatives, and that three-fifths of the number of slaves would be included in apportioning those seats. The nation's granting of titles of nobility, which was common throughout Europe, was prohibited. A big concern was how to select the president. They settled on election by the states, with each state getting as many votes as it had members in Congress, rather than directly by the people. Finally, through compromise (Franklin's key role), the Constitution was finished, approved, and signed.

Between October 27, 1787, and May 28, 1788, 85 separate *Federalist Papers* were printed and widely distributed, laying out the case for ratifying the Constitution. Most were written by Alexander Hamilton.

The debate over ratification was heated and important. Delaware became the first state to ratify the Constitution on December 7, 1787 (by a vote of 30 to 0). On June 29, 1788, New Hampshire became the ninth state to ratify (vote of 57 to 47) the new Constitution, making it binding on the states that had ratified it so that this new framework of federal government under the constitution went into effect. Thus, this new constitutional democracy with nine states was born that day. Five days later Virginia (vote of 89 to 79) and New York (30 to 27) ratified the Constitution. On April 6, 1789, quorums of both houses of the new Congress met for the first time. On April 30, George Washington was inaugurated as the Nation's first President. On September 25, Congress sent twelve proposed amendments to the Constitution to the states for ratification. On May 29, 1790, Rhode Island became the last state to ratify the Constitution (vote of 34 to 32). So, George Washington had already been President for over a year before Rhode Island narrowly decided to join the Nation (North Carolina had finally ratified and joined the nation six months earlier). On December 15, 1791, ten of the twelve proposed constitutional amendments, the Bill of Rights, were ratified. These ten amendments were all in response to concerns that the new Constitution fell far short of adequately protecting individual and minority rights against the tyranny of the majority or states' rights against overreach by the newly established federal government.

It is noteworthy that, over 230 years later, the Oath of Office for any appointed or elected position in the Federal Government still includes the phrase *"I will support and defend **the Constitution of** the United States against all enemies, foreign and domestic;"* rather than just defending and supporting the country. Having taken that oath, it makes me uncomfortable when I hear others who have also taken that oath refer to the Constitution as *fluid* or *evolving*. There is a mechanism to amend it, but it is not easy. Over 10,000 amendments have been introduced in Congress, only 33 of those have been adopted by Congress, and just 26 have been ratified by three-fourths of the states and become part of the Constitution. The last, lowering the voting age to 18, was ratified on July 1, 1971, over 50 years ago.

So, what has been the effect of the U.S. Constitution developed in Philadelphia in 1787 on this country and the World? A 2022 paper on the Constitution by law professor Justin Collings included the following two statements:

The very idea of a written constitution – a fundamental law, enforced by an independent judiciary, that both creates and limits government power – is an American original.

The U.S. Constitution is to modern governance what Homer is to Western literature: the influence that influenced all other influences...Not the least miraculous product of the "miracle of Philadelphia" has been the U.S. Constitution's role in spreading constitutional principles around the world. That too remains a work in progress...Since 1945, constitutionalism has swept the planet. Virtually every sovereign state on earth now has a written constitution.

The Constitution preamble begins with the phrase *"**We the People of the United States"*** and goes on to list its purposes, including *"secure the Blessings of Liberty to ourselves and our Posterity."* So, who was included in *"We the People of the United States"* when it was being written? The Constitution expressly identifies three categories of people: 1) *"Free Persons, including those bound to Service for a Term of Years, excluding Indians not taxed"*, 2), *"all other Persons"* (slaves), and 3) those *"Indians* *not taxed"* excluded from the first category. Thus, the Constitution does not distinguish between black and white but between free people (including free blacks) and slaves (without using the word slaves). For Indians, it distinguishes those living in separate Indian societies, and thus not taxed, from any free Indians who might be living among the communities of the USA and thus subject to taxes. The Constitution also mandates that a census be taken every ten years for the purpose of apportioning seats in the House of Representatives within Congress. Since *Indians not taxed* were not to be counted in the census, they were not to be considered in apportioning seats in the House of Representatives. It is apparent they were not considered part of *We the people of the United States* even though they were the original inhabitants and still lived here. Instead, Congress was given the authority to regulate commerce with *"Indian tribes."* Only three-fifths of the number of slaves were to be included in the apportioning of House seats. Thus, slaves were not part of *We the people of the United States*. But free blacks were. The Constitution barred Congress from prohibiting any state's participation in the international slave trade for the first 20 years after ratification. In 1806, Congress did pass a law banning such trade, effective in 1808, the first year such a prohibition could take effect under the Constitution.

The 1790 census, taken just two years after the Constitution was ratified and the year after George Washington became its first President, was the first count of the population of this brand-new nation. It counted 3,140,207 *"white persons"* (51% male and 49% female), 59,150 *"other free persons"* (free blacks), and 694,280 *"slaves."* Although they were not yet states, Kentucky, Maine, and Vermont were each included separately in the count. The five largest cities were New York City (with 31,131 people), Philadelphia, Boston, Charleston, and then Baltimore (with only 13,503 people). If any Indians were counted, it was only those few living within white settlements and therefore included either in *"white persons"* or *"other free persons"* as listed in the census tables. Massachusetts was the only state without any slaves (it had fully abolished slavery in 1783). It had 5,463 free blacks (Maine, which was not yet a state, also had no slaves and 538 free blacks). Connecticut was the only New England state with more slaves than free blacks: 2,764 to 2,508. Pennsylvania was the only state outside New England with more free blacks than slaves: 6,573 to 3,737. New York had 21,324 slaves (about 7% of the state's population). Thus, while over 90% were in the South, slaves were scattered across much of this new nation.

LIFE IN THE NEW UNITED STATES OF AMERICA – By the time of the second census, in 1800, there were 4,308,081 whites, an increase of 37% in just ten years, while the number of slaves had increased by 29 % and the number of free blacks had increased by 77%. The number of people in those five largest cities had increased by 57%. New states, Vermont, Kentucky, and Tennessee, had been added. The new USA was growing.

White people thought of themselves as equals and considered themselves *citizens* rather than subjects. Shaking hands replaced bowing. But daily life was still tough and had changed little. Daniel Walker Howe described life in the early years of nineteenth-century America this way:

Life in America in 1815 was dirty, smelly, laborious, and uncomfortable. People spent most of their waking hours working, with scant opportunity for the development of individual talents and interests unrelated to farming. Country people of ordinary means went barefoot most of the time. White people of both sexes wore heavy fabrics covering their bodies, even in the humid heat of summer, for they believed sunshine bad for their skin. People usually owned few changes of clothes and stank of sweat. Only the most fastidious bathed as often as once a week. Since water had to be carried from a spring or well and heated in a kettle, people gave themselves sponge baths, using a washtub. Some bathed once a year, in the spring, but as late as 1832, a New England country doctor complained that four out of five of his patients did not bathe from one year to the next. When washing themselves, people usually only rinsed off, saving their harsh homemade soap for cleaning clothes. Having an outdoor privy signified a level of decency above those who simply relieved themselves in the woods or fields. Indoor light was scarce and precious; families made their own candles, smelly and smokey, from animal tallow. A single fireplace provided all the cooking and heating for the common household. During the winter, everybody slept in the room with the fire, several in each bed. Privacy for a married couple was a luxury.

Whether producing for a market or their own consumption, their way of life depended on the practice of thrift. When a husband hammered together a stool and his wife made the children's clothes, they were not being "thrifty" in the same way someone shopping for groceries today is thrifty by remembering to use a coupon. They were performing their occupations, earning a living, just as much as when the man plowed a field or the woman churned butter to sell in the village. Their thrift was a necessity, not an option. Thrift demanded the family set aside enough corn or wheat to be able to seed next year's crop, feed the animals, and go on farming. Two thirds of all clothing and linens were produced in households.

This was not a relaxed, hedonistic, refined, or indulgent society. Formal education and family connections counted for comparatively little. The man who got ahead in often primitive conditions did so by means of innate ability, hard work, luck, and sheer will power. An important component of his drive to succeed was a willingness – surprising in an agrarian people – to innovate and take risks, to try new methods and locations. For most white men, this proud, willful independence derived from having one's own land.

The prevailing versions of Protestantism preached a stern morality and self-control. Such austere religion did not foster the traditional high arts of music, painting, and sculpture. It did foster literacy for Bible-reading, broad participation in decision-making and a sense of equality among the lay members.

Most farms of the era, particularly in the North, were individualistic, operated by a nuclear family rather than extended family groups or communities. Running a farm required both a man and a woman. And it was prudent to have lots of children to help run the farm. The birth rate for white women in 1810 was seven per woman. And each birth was a walk through the valley of the shadow of death. Death during childbirth led to life expectancy being (unlike today) shorter for women than men. Children were born at home, hopefully with the help of a midwife. Over a third of white children died before reaching adulthood. It was a young society. The median age was only 16. Only 12% were over 43. Single adults, both men and women, found themselves needing to hire out to others where they performed labor typical for their gender. Remaining single was avoided if at all possible. In most village stores, accounts were still kept in shillings and pence while a wide variety of currencies were in circulation.

The single largest economic problem for this new nation, stretching from New Hampshire to Georgia and westward across the Appalachians, was transportation. *"Transportation is what economists call a 'transaction cost,' one that adds to the cost of an item without adding to its intrinsic value. Advertising, sales, and packaging are all examples of transaction costs. The lower these transaction costs, obviously the lower the final price, and thus the higher the demand."* Overland roads in this new country *"were rutted and dusty in the summer and often a morass of mud in the spring and fall. Wagons and stagecoaches, when they were able to negotiate the roads at all, could take hours just to go a few miles. Travel was often easiest in the winter, when the ground was frozen hard."*

Which is why farmers in western Pennsylvania would distill their grain crops into whiskey before trying to ship it east over the mountains to urban markets there. The value per pound was vastly increased so that they could afford the transportation costs and still compete in those markets. When the new federal government imposed a tax on distilled spirits, these farmers went to war against tax collectors in what became known as the *Whiskey Rebellion.* In 1794, President Washington, as Commander in Chief, led the army into western Pennsylvania to quickly put down these rebellious farmers.

While the building of toll roads in the early 1800s, followed by canals, helped the transportation problem considerably, dramatic improvements in transportation that would drastically reduce its costs with corresponding reductions in the ultimate sale price and availability of products to the consumer were yet to come with the First Industrial Revolution.

People in the North ate wheat, beef, and potatoes. Those in the South ate corn, pork, and sweet potatoes. Other than some preserves, most fruits were eaten only in season, as were green vegetables. Families, particularly in the North, might have a *root cellar* for storing cabbages, root vegetables, and apples. Their diet was monotonous and constipating, too high in fat and salt. Still, it was more plentiful and nutritious, with more protein, than found in most of the world. At 5'8", the average American man was four inches taller than his English counterpart.

Then there was the world of the southern plantation owners. They owned lots of land and slaves, focused on one commercial crop, lived a privileged life, and borrowed extensively against next year's crop. They were always deep in debt. Again, in the words of Daniel Walker Howe:

The plantation owners were the great consumers of the American economy, with their big houses, their lavish hospitality, their horse races, and hordes of domestic servants. In a nation of austerity and thrift, they opted for extravagance and elegance, honor, and refinement. Like their exemplar Thomas Jefferson, many American plantation owners lived well and died broke. Americans of the 21st century may look back upon them as our precursors in some ways, for like them we too spend even more than our relatively high average incomes and slide more and more in debt to outside creditors.

Only a third of white families in the South owned at least one slave. Most of the rest aspired to own slaves. About one in eight white families owned 20 or more slaves, while about half of all slaves lived on plantations with at least 30 other slaves. About half of slave children died before becoming adults. Still, the high birth rate among American slaves produced a natural population increase of two percent per year, which was almost the same as the white population. And most were relatively well fed and thus *"were taller on average than their Old World counterparts."* With the 1808 ban on the importation of slaves, *"Alone among New World slave societies, the enslaved population of the United States grew independent of importations from overseas."*

There were also other sharp cultural differences affecting daily life between whites living in the South and Appalachia compared to those living in the North, particularly New England. These will be discussed in more detail later.

As moral opposition to slavery increased in the North, a new pernicious rationale for slavery developed in the South beyond just profit. Paternalism. Again, in the words of Howe:

Slaveowners, in response to moral criticism, sought to explain their relationship to "their people" as one of caring for those who could not look after themselves. Negroes as a race, they insisted, were childlike.

They were seen as inferior beings that needed to be taken care of because they couldn't make it on their own. It doesn't get more racist than that. But we increasingly see some of that attitude today in different ways. As the years went by, the number of free blacks increased in cities. By 1830, 80% of Baltimore's black population were legally free, as were 40% of those in New Orleans. Slavery was an agrarian institution that increasingly made little economic sense in cities where maintaining control of slaves was more difficult.

The First Amendment to the Constitution includes the phrase *"The right of the people peaceably to assemble."* This amendment prohibits Congress from passing any law impacting that right. Today, this is generally viewed as the right to protest. However, it is much broader than that. Historically, it has been viewed as the right to get together with whomever we want for whatever reason we want. The right of *association*. When Alexis de Tocqueville visited America in the 1830s, he was amazed at how much Americans associated with each other. He wrote:

of all countries in the world, America has taken greatest advantage of association and has applied this powerful means of action to the greatest variety of objectives.

Wherever, at the head of a new undertaking, you see in France the government, and in England, a great lord, count on seeing in the United States, an association.

Americans of all ages, of all conditions, of all minds, constantly unite. Not only do they have commercial and industrial associations in which they all take part, but also they have a thousand other kinds: religious, moral, intellectual, serious ones, useless ones, very general and very particular ones, immense and very small ones; Americans associate to celebrate holidays, establish seminaries, build inns, erect churches, distribute books, send missionaries to the Antipodes; in this way they create hospitals, prisons, schools. If, finally, it is a matter of bringing a truth to light or of developing a sentiment with the support of good example, they associate.

This inclination to formally associate was uniquely American. By 1791, when the First Amendment was ratified, Americans had been practicing self-government for over 150 years, beginning with the Mayflower Compact. They had no aristocrats, nor did they want them or need them. Nor did they want the colonial governors appointed by the Crown in charge of everything. By getting together in associations, they could manage their affairs without government help or interference; thank you very much! This right to associate in order to address and solve community problems in a nation that was constantly expanding west beyond the reach of governments was critical to that successful expansion. This freedom to associate to solve community problems also promoted innovation and change. And the new USA, made of immigrants who came here because they were willing to change, quickly developed the most mobile, innovative, and inventive culture the world has ever known.

Further, the right to assemble is a protection against tyranny. Tocqueville noted that a great danger in democracies was that, with majority rule, the majority would oppress minorities. One of the great securities against this danger is the freedom of association and assembly. It has played a critical role in social movements for over two centuries. Tocqueville also wrote:

America is not great because it is more enlightened than any other nation, but rather because it has always been able to repair its faults.

8: THE FIRST INDUSTRIAL REVOLUTION

Thanks to the Industrial Revolution, our complex modern world came about and continues to innovate. But what was it, or is it? How did it happen? So what? All that differentiates how we live now (2024) from how those colonists lived who declared their independence in 1776, as outlined in the first two pages of this paper, is a result of the Industrial Revolution. Before that revolution, *"A newborn child entered a world that was almost medieval: a dim world lit by candlelight, in which folk remedies treated health problems and in which travel was no faster than possible by hoof or sail."* The Industrial Revolution's impact on humankind has been compared to the discovery of fire, the invention of farming, the domestication of animals, and the invention of the wheel. It wasn't always pretty, but it was amazingly transformative of human societies. *"Something transformative took hold in Britain between about 1780 and 1830. From this point on, means of production would grow larger and more mechanized as factories replaced handicraft industries. People would move to the cities in droves and into ever larger workforces. Markets would become increasingly global, and for many, material wealth would reach undreamed of heights."* Some consider it the most important event in human history.

Let's start with a simple yet profound monument to the first 150 years of the Industrial Revolution and the free-market capitalism that enabled and financed that revolution. That monument is the Pencil. No one can make a pencil. It would take days to get it done if they could, making it very expensive. No one person even knows how to make a pencil. Yet, pencils are made by the billions while thousands upon thousands of people are involved in, and are getting paid for, some small part of pencil making. Pencils are sold everywhere, which means they must be shipped everywhere from where they are made. Yet, pencils cost practically nothing. Pencils are an integral part of daily life for millions of people, particularly school children (though not as important now as they were in the twentieth century). The wood, lead, erasure, glue, paint, lettering, and metal band that crimps the erasure to the wood all have complex trails involving various machines and skills that led to the creation of each from a variety of basic materials available within our human environment into being part of a pencil through the application of energy, machines, and diverse skills (accumulated knowledge). That is the magic of the Industrial Revolution. (See Leonard Read's 1958 essay "*I, Pencil*")

The Industrial Revolution is generally thought of as occurring in three phases, generally referred to as three revolutions, with each building on what came before. Each spurred enormous leaps in economic growth, particularly the second one. And the revolution continues. Many feel that the Fourth Industrial Revolution is just getting underway in the twenty-first century.

Early in this paper, I noted that a society could only become more complex by increasing productivity – and that productivity depended on materials, energy, and accumulated knowledge. Thus, the Industrial Revolution and our modern way of life were developed and are sustained by ever-expanding know-how (accumulated knowledge) in using energy and materials to maintain and increase productivity – fewer people needing less time to make and/or move more stuff and/or get more done. Complex societies, specialization, and urbanization require much greater productivity than hunter/gatherer or agrarian societies. Over millennia, various peoples developed tools and machines to magnify the efficiency of the energy they expended using muscle power (human and animal) so that they could increase productivity. Many cultures also developed sails to power their boats and ships. Waterwheels and windmills were developed in a few societies to power some machines. A few have also developed ingenious ways to use gravity to power specialized machines such as weighted clocks and trebuchets. But, along with fire, that was it! A few societies had black powder, which would burn suddenly with explosive force, and developed cannons and muskets to utilize that explosion. However, until the eighteenth century, fire, muscle power (humans and domestic animals), wind, water, and gravity were the only sources of energy known throughout mankind. And no one had figured out how to use fire to power a machine – to turn heat into motion and turn a wheel. Machines were the key to further increases in productivity, but the size, location, and variety of machines were limited by the fact that they could only be dependably driven by muscle power or water wheels. That was the situation around the world in 1776 (with one recent exception, as explained below).

It has been said that *"necessity is the mother of invention."* While that is often true, opportunity, culture, and just one person's imagination and ingenuity are also major factors. Is a culture open to change? For all the intellectual and philosophical advances within the Aztec empire, apparently, no one had thought to make a cart with wheels to carry things even though they made children's toys with wheels on them. How could that be!? Quite possibly because they had no domesticated animals to pull such carts. Since wheels and axels are essential to almost all machines (at least until our digital age), they, therefore, had no machines. How could the Inca and the Aztec have accumulated considerable expertise in metallurgy for ornamental purposes, yet not thought to develop metal weapons, tools, or containers? Someone, sometime, must come up with a new idea and have the resources to implement it. Culture can also kill or severely restrict the adoption of great new ideas. In the 1980s, I took three trips to India, which has rich cultural and intellectual traditions going back over a thousand of years. I was in several large cities across northern India and spent hours on the road through a wide range of settings. I saw numerous construction projects, ranging from large multistory buildings to road paving. At ALL of them, construction materials were moved by women carrying stuff on their heads. I never saw a wheelbarrow or any kind of handcart. Huh? The Inquisition's punishment of Galileo for his claim that the earth revolved around the sun ended scientific and technical development in Italy and much of the Catholic world for centuries. So, how did the Industrial Revolution happen?

Although the Industrial Revolution began in Great Britain in the late 1700s, its seeds were planted there six centuries before, with what would ultimately lead to developing a completely new source of energy that would lead to a complete transformation in how people lived. Without that new energy source, there would have been no industrial revolution as we know it for the same reason there were no wheels, machines, or metal weapons or tools in the Americas before 1492. Nobody would have thought of it. This is a story largely pulled together by Barbara Freese.

HOW THE STEAM ENGINE CAME TO BE – Coal, a dirty black rock that burns, is found in many places throughout the world. Yet, no one anywhere understood why it burns (and would not until the late 1800s when scientists in the new field of geology first began to realize that coal was dead plant material that had been buried for millions of years). Because it comes out of the earth and burns with an acrid smell, it was sometimes given a spiritual aspect associated with the dark forces of the underworld. A few societies used it a little, but none had used it enough for it to be a significant factor in their civilization. It was largely ignored, if not outright avoided.

That began to change in Newcastle, England, a city located at the navigable tidewaters of the Tyne River along the northeast coast that had coal everywhere, including thick seams outcropping just above the waterline of the river. Almost a thousand years ago, the locals began to burn it for fuel rather than wood. Then, sometime in the twelfth century, someone got the idea of loading a ship with coal and sailing to London to sell it. Moving coal by ship 300 miles to London cost about the same as hauling wood three or four miles overland from the surrounding forest, making coal from ships competitive there. It sold. So, more was shipped. It was called *sea coal* to distinguish it from charcoal made from wood, which they called *coal*. It was not popular with homeowners because of its acrid smoke. English homes at that time had no chimneys. They just had a fire in the middle of the room, and smoke seeped out through the cracks. However, coal quickly became popular with breweries and blacksmiths since they consumed a lot of fuel, and wood was getting more expensive and harder to come by as the growing population of London was depleting the surrounding forests. A modest market for coal became established in London and other English port cities that would fluctuate as opposition to burning coal would rise and fall as the local forests were depleted. *"Coal sellers, watching cities expand and forests shrink, may well have assumed that their industry was in for a long period of growth."*

Then the plague arrived around 1350. Three waves of the plague, along with other diseases, had cut the population of England in half by 1500. Forests had expanded again while coal sales slumped. Further, after over 300 years of mining, much of the easily accessible coal near the surface had been mined. Almost all the coal was owned, and the mines controlled, by the Catholic Church, a very conservative organization that had little interest in making the investments necessary to dig deeper for coal or in developing and funding ways necessary to deal with the groundwater that would inevitably seep into deeper mines, flooding them.

Then, in the new century that began in 1500, with Portugal and Spain moving into the Americas, three things happened in England that would also significantly alter the course of world history: 1) the English population started to grow again, renewing pressure on England's forests, 2) the common people were adding chimneys to their houses, and 3) in 1527, King Henry VIII decided he wanted an annulment because his wife could not produce an heir.

The Pope refused his request. Over the next few years, the King broke from the Catholic Church and took England with him. At the time, the Church owned about 20% of England's land and wealth. It had an income about three times that of the cash-strapped Crown. So, the King confiscated the Church's property. The Crown then owned the best coal mines in England. He soon sold them to merchants keen to invest and develop them for long-term production at a time when coal demand increased as London grew faster than the general population.

By the time Elizabeth assumed the throne in 1558, England's forests were again under heavy pressure. England's growing iron industry consumed massive amounts of fuel. There was enormous demand for wood as a building material as London doubled in size between 1550 and 1600 (to 200,000 people). The cold winters of the *Little Ice Age* substantially increased the need for fuel. Further, *"even in modest English homes, chimneys had become common by the mid-1500s."* In short, coal sales boomed. By 1600, coal had become the main source of fuel for London. There were not enough forests in all of England to provide the wood fuel necessary to enable London's growth. The large number of ships built and the increased shipping expertise that resulted from all this coal transport contributed to England's ability to defeat the Spanish Armada in 1588. That increased shipping capacity and expertise, along with the dramatic growth of London, also positioned England, with the launch of the East India Company chartered by Queen Elizabeth in 1600, to become a significant player in international trade for centuries. *"The coal trade may be regarded, in short, as the magnet which helped draw Englishmen to seek their profits and their livelihood in ocean commerce."*

Over the next centuries, both England and London continued to grow as the use of coal accelerated, and London became a world center for intellectual pursuits and financial activity. *"By the mid-1600s, Londoners did not merely welcome coal into their homes, they were desperate to have it"* because it was so much cheaper than wood from the depleted forests. However, all this use of coal came with two terrible consequences. First, for centuries, London had the worst air quality on the planet as England was burning five times more coal than all the rest of the world combined. It not only smelled awful but was devastating people's health. Even gardens were seriously blighted. The whole field of statistics first came into being as a few began to analyze London's death and illness records in the 1600s. Volumes have been written on the disastrous effects of London's air quality and infamous *fogs*.

The second terrible consequence was creating a new class of blighted people: *coal miners*. However, unlike the silver mines of Potosi or the mercury mines of Huancavelica, where foreign Spaniards made slaves of the locals and brought in slaves from Africa, this degraded subclass were English citizens segregated into ramshackle housing as rural peasants came looking for consistent work. They even came to be seen as a separate race and were ostracized by the rest of society. *"Coal created a new gulf between classes. The medieval peasants and artisans, whatever their disabilities and trials may have been, were not segregated from their neighbors to anything like the same extent as were coal miners of the seventeenth century."* They were so segregated that they developed different habits and speech styles. As social outcasts, they also developed a fierce sense of solidarity, which led to the beginning of labor movements around the world. *"It is hard to imagine a workplace more dismal and dangerous than a seventeenth century coal mine. Dark, damp, cramped, and chilly, the mines had ceilings that could collapse on your head, air that could smother you, poison you, or explode in your face, and water that could rush in and drown you or trap you forever."* Deadly mine explosions became so common that, in 1767, the Newcastle *Journal* even announced that *"as we have been requested to take no particular notice of these things, which, in fact, could have very little good tendency, we drop the further mentioning of it.* After all, it was just coal miners who were dying in these mine explosions, so why should they be mentioned in the news?

Coal mining was a family affair, with children starting in the mines as young as five or six. Children could work coal seams too narrow for adults. One contemporary report described children in the mines as *"chained, belted, harnessed like dogs in a go-cart, black, saturated with sweat, and more than half naked – crawling upon their hands and feet, and dragging their heavy loads behind them – they present an appearance indescribably disgusting and unnatural."* In Scotland, until 1799, coal miners were essentially slaves that were legally owned by the mine once they entered a mine to work as a child. If a mine was sold, they were sold with it. Runaways were legal fugitives who, upon capture, were subject to *"torture in the irons provided only for coal miners, witches, and notorious malefactors."* Bigotry and man's inhumanity to man are not limited to race, religion, or other ethnic distinctions. Bigotry based on caste or class within an ethnic group also has a long and painful history in many societies around the world.

But enough on that. The coal mine issue that led to a new source of energy that would power the Industrial Revolution was water. Any coal mine that slopes down is going to fill with water. By 1600, that was pretty much any coal mine in England. By the seventeenth century, every known technique for getting water out of mines had been tried, from carrying out in buckets to digging drainage tunnels up to five miles long. Various designs of water pumps had been around for thousands of years. By 1600, most large mines were using hundreds of horses to power their pumps. Mine operators were constantly looking for new ways to remove water. It was such a serious problem that it was threatening the nation's coal supply. A new solution was desperately needed. By then, *"England had become a good place to be a scientist or an inventor"* with the creation, in 1660, of the Royal Society to promote the theory and application of science. By 1700, British scientists had discovered that air has weight and were beginning to experiment with the force created by a vacuum. However, no one had yet thought of a practical application.

Instead, it was an obscure small-town ironmonger, Thomas Newcomen, unknown to the scientists of his day, who designed and built the first operating steam engine while working for coal operators. For the first time in human history, man had converted the energy released by fire into motion energy to power a machine. And he built it for one purpose – to pump water from coal mines. But for that problem, it would not have been invented. The first one was installed at a coal mine in 1712. It immediately enabled mine operators to pump water from much greater depths, vastly expanding available coal reserves while replacing as many as 50 horses per pump. Within 60 years, hundreds of these engines were operating at coal mines throughout Britain. However, they were ravenous beasts consuming mountains of coal as fuel because the vacuum cylinder had to be cooled each time to condense the steam and create a vacuum before reheating for the next stroke. Therefore, they were only used in coal mines because there was plenty of readily available fuel right there.

James Watt, a young engineer working on a Newcomen steam engine, came up with a concept for a new kind of steam engine that would be able to stay hot while providing a steady stream of power by using steam pressure to drive the engine rather than to create a vacuum, thus dramatically reducing fuel consumption. However, he lacked the resources and skills to fabricate it. After 10 years and several failed attempts, he finally found a financial backer along with someone with the skills to fabricate his design. His first steam engine went into operation in 1776 and used only a fourth of the fuel needed by a Newcomen engine for the same amount of power generated. With that dramatic increase in fuel efficiency, Watt steam engines could be moved away from coal mines and be used to power other machines anywhere. In 1781, Watt patented the first *rotative steam engine* designed to power a wheel like those used in mills. Steam was the new energy source to power the first industrial revolution.

Let's pause here to consider cause and effect: a *but for* review. In the introduction of this paper, I noted that, in 1500, England was a backward nation far behind its European neighbors in science and technology. I then raised the question: so, how was the British Empire built over the next four centuries until it circled the globe? The answer is simple. Coal. But for England's development of coal as its primary source of fuel, instead of continuing to rely on wood, there would have never been a British Empire circling the world. Nor would there have been an Industrial Revolution. Nor would English have become the dominant language around the world. Entering the seventeenth century, thanks to the shift to coal as its primary fuel source, London was a rapidly growing dynamic city where, despite its terrible air quality, Shakespeare and Isaac Newton were able to thrive, along with a host of others, as London's influence spread around the world through England utilizing its expanding capacity and expertise in shipping to launch a global empire. Further, the steam engine would not have been invented but for the critical problem of water in coal mines, with plenty of coal right there to burn. In short, the British Empire, which reached its peak early in the twentieth century, and the Industrial Revolution, which built our modern world, would not have happened but for London beginning to burn coal in the twelfth century and then, in the sixteenth century, thanks to Henry VIII breaking with the Catholic Church and confiscating its property, moving on to make coal its main source of fuel.

HOW THE INDUSTRIAL REVOLUTION WAS PAID FOR – Paying for a revolution, whether it is a war, or industrial change, costs money. Since at least Roman times, the preferred type of money had been in the form of coinage. And the minting of coins was largely a closely guarded government monopoly across much of the world. It was a defining characteristic, and source of prestige, for political power. China had even used paper money, but then dropped it and went for South American silver that it could turn into coins. However, all the gold and silver that poured into Europe in the sixteenth century from the Americas brought about a new form of money.

Keeping a lot of gold around the house could be risky business. People began to leave their gold with goldsmiths for safekeeping in exchange for paper receipts. Then they found that exchanging these receipts for purchases and sales was easier than going back and taking out the gold. It meant that neither the buyer nor seller needed to actually handle the heavy gold or worry about securing it; they could just deal with paper receipts. Receipts from a trusted goldsmith were *as good as gold* and a whole lot easier to carry around or keep secure. Goldsmiths, who had long been lending out gold to be paid back with interest, began loaning paper receipts instead of gold to those who came to borrow gold with interest owed. In 1704, Britain made such receipts legal tender for sales and purchases. These paper receipts were now *money*. Soon, goldsmiths realized that they could issue more receipts than they had gold in their vaults to cover. As long as all their depositors did not come in at the same time demanding their gold, the smith with a good reputation could lend out receipts on promissory notes far in excess of the amount of gold in his vaults and even pay a little interest to those who deposited gold in his vaults, thus encouraging more deposits. Thus, Banks were born! And these receipts became known as banknotes. They were creating money out of thin air!

Because of that, many people hated banks, including John Adams, who wrote that:

Every dollar of a bank bill that is issued beyond the quantity of gold and silver in the vaults represents nothing and therefore is a cheat upon somebody.

But he was wrong. Banks required collateral that could be taken upon default. So, banks were, instead, converting fixed capital in land and buildings, etc., into liquid capital that could fuel economic activity that could be invested in new assets. But it is all hinged on people not deciding to redeem their deposits all at once: to make a run on the bank. Thus, a bank was only as good as its reputation. It was dependent on the trust of its depositors. Banks, which were first government-chartered in Britain, would provide the capital needed for the Industrial Revolution.

THE REVOLUTION BEGINS – The first industrial revolution began with the invention of larger machines that could manufacture things that individual artisans had previously made in a cottage industry: the creation of the *factory* and the factory system. The world's first factory machines were developed in Great Britain to make textiles.

The first weaving machines to make fabric without directly involving human hands were developed around 1740. The first waterwheel and mule-powered spinning machines to make thread and yarn were developed in the late 1760s. However, as late as 1774, just in Manchester, there were still 30,000 people employed in the individual artisan cottage industry making cotton cloth. Mule powered machines could never be very large while water wheels *"could only be built where the flow was strong, the grade was steep, and where there were no barriers, like other waterwheels. Even in a nation as water rich as Britain, good sites became hard to find. As a result, water-powered mills were dispersed throughout the countryside, often in fairly inaccessible hills, and they were relatively small, causing problems of labour supply, transportation of materials and access to urban merchants."* Then, after 1780, everything changed. Watt steam engines *"enabled mills to be built in urban contexts and transformed the economy of Manchester, whose importance had previously been as a centre of pre-industrial spinning and weaving based on the domestic system. Manchester had no cotton mills until 1783. By 1800 Manchester had 42 mills, having eclipsed all rival textile centres to become the heart of the cotton manufacturing trade."* To place the magnitude of this change in British textile manufacture in context, in 1750, Britain was importing 2.5 million pounds per year of raw cotton for its textile industry. By 1800, that had risen to 52 million pounds per year, a 19-fold increase. By 1850, 588 million pounds were imported. And Britain dominated the world's cotton textile industry. The world had never seen so much fabric of such high quality at such affordable prices before, and it had an insatiable appetite for it. People everywhere could not get enough cotton fabric.

While mills were built in other cities, Manchester was certainly the hub of the new cotton mill industry and became the world's first truly industrial city. And it was a mess. By 1830, the city had seven cotton mills with over 1,000 employees each and another 76 mills with hundreds of employees each. Workers at these mills included displaced artisans and rural peasants flocking into the city seeking regular work. Many children were employed in the mills because they were cheaper and more compliant. The streets were awash in sewage while, thanks to all the steam engine powered mills belching coal smoke, the air quality in Manchester was even worse than

London. *"And the mills were weaving a new social fabric, too, by creating a larger middle class, a richer industrial elite, and an increasingly isolated class of wage-laborers and slum-dwellers."* It is impossible to overstate this colossal revolution, both in productivity per worker hour and in how people worked and lived.

Productivity exploded by orders of magnitude. Suddenly, high-quality cloth was being made at a fraction of previous costs. People in Britain and worldwide could not get enough of this cheap, high-quality fabric. Even common people could afford it, which made them richer.

In short, the factory sweatshop was invented in Manchester (though coal mine sweatshops had been around in Britain for centuries). And just as today in Third World countries, young peasants flocked to the cotton mills for work, grateful for the opportunity to trade the drudgery of their simple lives for the excitement of the city while more than doubling their income. By 1800, William Murdock had discovered that, when heated, coal would give off a gas that would emit a bright flame. This *coal-gas,* distilled from coal, began to be used for streetlights, but also enabled factories to be kept *"as bright as palaces"* with coal-gas lamps throughout the night so that factories could run round the clock. Thus, most operated on two twelve-hour shifts each day. One observer wrote in 1834, *"Whilst the engine runs the people must work – men, women, and children are yoked together with iron and steam. The animal machine – breakable in the best case, subject to a thousand sources of suffering – is chained fast to the iron machine, which knows no suffering and no weariness."* As Barbara Freese described it:

Each production task was broken into its most basic units, achieving much greater efficiencies but limiting many workers' jobs to the most simple, repetitive, machine-like movements all synchronized to the rhythm of the steam engine at the factory's heart. For the first generation of factory workers, the shock of being so thoroughly controlled must have been profound. For many farm workers and cottage craftspeople – people who had worked in relative independence and most of whom had never even owned a clock – were subject to perhaps the tightest daily constraints on personal movement and time that had ever been imposed on an entire class of people.

Alexis de Tocqueville visited Manchester in 1835, shortly after publishing his analysis of American society. He had this to say about Manchester:

From this foul drain the greatest stream of human industry flows out to fertilize the whole world. From this filthy sewer pure gold flows. Here humanity attains its most complete development and its most brutish; here civilization works its miracles, and civilized man is turned back almost into a savage.

Manchester was also a very unhealthy place. By the 1840s, over half of working-class children there died before turning five, while life expectancy for the working class was only 17 years. Rickets, a bone-deforming disease caused by vitamin D deficiency, was rampant among Manchester children because they never saw the sun. With this revolution in how people worked and lived, Manchester went from a small city of artisans to a teeming slum of over 100,000 people long before it finally formed a local government in 1853, to try to manage some of that chaos. For us today, it is impossible to grasp the challenge of living in a chaotic city that is large with no public services or government structure to address public concerns. Since there had never before been such a city in human history, and no one had planned for it, figuring out how to manage such unplanned chaos was trial and error as various crises arose.

At the age of 22, Friedrich Engels came from Germany to Manchester in 1842 to help run a cotton mill partially owned by his family. However, he was already secretly a socialist. In 1844, he published *The Condition of the Working Class in England* based on what he observed in Manchester. Later that year he met Karl Marx, a fellow German who was two years older than Engels and an active socialist. Both Marx and Engels moved to Brussels early the next year where they became close friends. Later that year, Engels took Marx to London and then Manchester to study working conditions there. From that point on, Engels, with resources from his family's mill in Manchester, supported Marx financially for the rest of Marx' life. In 1847, they were both leaders in the founding of the *Communist League* based in London. In 1848, Marx (30) and Engels (28), published their world-changing *The Communist Manifesto,* which they co-wrote. I have found nothing indicating either of them ever labored with their own hands for support. Instead, they were dependent on profits from a cotton mill sweatshop.

Along with coal and cotton, iron was the other material that defined the first industrial revolution. In addition to the growing need for iron in a variety of other uses, building all these cotton mills dramatically increased the demand for iron since it was needed to build both steam engines and mill machines. By 1800, British ironworks had figured out how to make *coke* from coal so that they no longer needed to use charcoal from wood to produce iron. By 1830, while Britain was producing most of the world's cotton cloth, it was also producing 80% of the world's coal and over 50% of the world's iron. Other European nations also began to industrialize, but Great Britain had a good 50-year head start and would maintain its lead for the rest of the century. *"By the time London held the first World's Fair in 1851, Britain was hailed as the workshop of the world, and its markets and its empire reached global scale."* Then, in 1855, British inventor Henry Bessemer developed a new process for mass-producing steel from Iron. With that, steel (mostly an iron-carbon alloy) replaced iron for many uses. However, since steel is made from iron, the demand for iron continued to increase dramatically.

THE COMING OF THE RAILROAD – All of these factories and related activities increased the demand for coal. Between 1700 and 1830, British coal production increased tenfold. It doubled again in just the next 25 years. That was a lot of bulky coal to move around. And it was needed in many places besides port cities. Roads in rainy England in that era were a disaster. They were often so rutted and deep that even the top of a wagonload of hay could not be seen from the side. Again, as with the invention of the steam engine, *"coal created a problem, then helped power a solution, and that solution would have revolutionary consequences far beyond the coal industry."* Beginning with a canal finished in 1765 from coal mines to Manchester, several canals were built around Britain so that horses walking on the banks could pull barges loaded with goods, primarily coal. Wooden rails had been used for hundreds of years in British coal mines and were used extensively above ground around New Castle. After 1800, iron rails began to be used for horse-drawn railways.

Then, a brilliant young man, George Stephenson, from the coal miner slums near New Castle, came along. He had unique mechanical skills. By the time he was 17, he was overseeing a steam engine at a nearby mine even though he had never been to school nor learned to read. So, he went to night school. By the time he was 31, in 1812, thanks to his inventiveness and skill with steam engines, he was put in charge of all machines used by a large coal company. His greatest contribution was the idea of setting a steam engine on a railcar to pull the train rather than using horses. The cars would be able to carry the coal needed to fuel the engine as it moved. In 1814, he invented his first steam locomotive for hauling coal from the mine to nearby docks. It was the first railway with flanged wheels (to keep the cars on the evenly spaced narrow iron rails) that would set the pattern for all future railways. It could haul 30 tons of coal at four miles an hour. However, steam engines were extremely heavy and would sometimes break the iron tracks because of their weight. Stephenson solved the problem of heavy steam engines destroying the iron tracks by 1) using multiple wheels on the engine car to spread out all that weight and 2) replacing brittle cast iron with the more expensive wrought iron (made by repeatedly folding hot molten iron over and over – kind of like kneading bread dough – until many of the impurities are worked out), which is much more flexible so that it would bend rather than break. He also recognized and promoted the need for a standard width or *gauge* for tracks so that engines and rail cars could move from one rail line to another rather than having to unload and reload where different railways met. Although he had built a couple of earlier railways with steam engines, in 1825, he made history with the opening of a 26-mile railway before thousands of people, with a procession of 34 train cars. The top speed was about five miles per hour. On steep sections, the train had to be pulled uphill with attached cables pulled by stationary steam engines.

However, in 1830, the railroad era really got underway with the opening of the Liverpool to Manchester railway. It was built by Stephenson using a steam locomotive of his own design. On its test run, a famous British stage actress, Fanny Kemble, was invited along. The train reached a top speed of 35 miles per hour, a speed totally beyond any previous human experience.

I stood up, and with my bonnet off, drank the air before me. The wind, which was strong, or perhaps the force of our own thrusting against it, absolutely weighed my eyelids down. When I closed my eyes this sensation was quite delightful, and strange beyond description, yet strange as it was, I had a perfect sense of security and not the slightest fear.

Later, a clergyman took his clerk to watch a train pass by for the first time. He wrote that as the train passed by *"spewing dense columns of sulphureous smoke,"* his clerk:

Fell prostate on the bank-side as if he had been smitten by a thunderbolt! When he had recovered his feet, his brain still reeled, his tongue clove to the roof of his mouth, and he stood aghast, unutterable amazement stamped upon his face. After five minutes when he was able to speak, he asked, "how much longer shall knowledge be allowed to go on increasing?"

By 1845, Britain had laid down 2,200 miles of train track. That number would triple to 6,600 miles by 1860. Rail had quickly become the primary means of transporting people and stuff around Britain. And that all required lots of coal and iron. By 1850, London was the world's largest city, with three million people, while Britain had become the first country in world history to have more than half of its population living in urban areas. This was a colossal change, not just for Britain but for all mankind. For the first time in human history, people and things (raw materials and finished goods) could be moved around on land almost as efficiently as they could be moved on water. Transportation on land was forever changed. It was a one-time transformative event for how human societies could organize in the future.

It is noteworthy that these initial events in the Industrial Revolution that would transform human society were developed by working-class people, Thomas Newcomen, James Watt, and George Stephenson, not the intellectual elites in London. In fact, because Stephenson talked like a coal miner, he was still largely ostracized by the upper crust even though he had transformed British society. Other transformative minds from the working class would follow. The Industrial Revolution provided opportunities for bright minds from all classes like never before. As one historian put it: *"Like its American counterpart, the British industrial revolution was to a large extent the creation of the working class."*

THE NEW UNITED STATES JOIN THE INDUSTRIAL REVOLUTION – Britain was intent on keeping its monopoly on mechanized textile manufacturing. Even before the Revolutionary War, Britain had banned the export to America of any tools that might be used in making any kind of fabric. After the war, in addition to banning the export of machinery or even blueprints of machinery, *"Skilled mechanics who worked in textile factories were forbidden to emigrate upon pain of fine and imprisonment."*

In 1790, 95% of the USA's population were farmers. That was fine with Thomas Jefferson, the first Secretary of State, who was intent on maintaining this new country as an *agrarian utopia.* He even went so far as to say it was:

impossible that America should become a manufacturing country during the time of any man now living.

However, President Washington, fully aware of how debilitating supply shortages had been during the War, admonished the first Congress on the need to promote manufacturing enough to make the nation independent, particularly for military supplies. The interests of Alexander Hamilton, the first Secretary of the Treasury, went way beyond that. He felt manufacturing should play a major role in the growth and development of the new nation. *"Certainly no other man in America saw so clearly the significance of the change that was taking place in English Industrialism."* He led the establishment of the *New York Manufacturing Society* in early 1789, and the *Society for Establishing Useful Manufacturers* in April 1791. He envisioned America as a diversified marketplace making all kinds of things that, in his words, would provide:

> additional employment to classes of the community not ordinarily engaged in the business. The promoting of emigration from foreign countries.

Against consistent opposition from Adams, Thomas Jefferson, and Aaron Burr, Hamilton established the framework of government and financial institutions, including the *Bank of the United States* (chartered in 1791 for 20 years), that would enable capital to flow around in the nation while promoting industrialization. This new bank enabled the government to regulate the size of the Nation's money supply while providing a vehicle for government borrowing and managing the national debt. During Washington's administration, about 90% of the Federal workforce was under Hamilton in the Treasury Department as he laid a solid financial foundation for this new nation. It was the primary role of the new federal government.

Hamilton understood banks would be essential to financing industrial development and manufacturing. Britain had not allowed the establishment of any banks in its 13 American colonies. Now that they had won independence, state legislatures were chartering banks. Adam Smith had estimated that a bank could safely issue banknotes equal to five times its capital. Some states limited banks to three times capital. However, some did not. One Rhode Island bank issued $800,000 in banknotes on $45 capital. It, of course, failed. Situations like this are why Hamilton thought the country needed a central bank: to discipline state banks and prevent excess money creation. On the other hand, it is why many bankers opposed Hamilton's federal economic controls, which constrained their financial adventures.

Hamilton also appeared to promote child labor, as was occurring in British mills where over half the workforce were women and children.

It is worthy of particular remark that, in general, women and children are rendered more useful, and the latter more early useful, by manufacturing establishments than would otherwise be, and many of them of a very tender age.

We look at that in 2024 and think, How Awful! Sweatshops using children! However, the idea that this was exploitation of children would have never crossed his mind since children on farms and the children of artisans or other working-class people had always worked from a young age. Instead, he saw it as providing an opportunity to earn a wage for kids who were already expected to work. Viewing child labor as an evil is quite recent (1930s). My own father's first paid job, at age 14, was working ten hours a day, six days a week, in a woolen mill for a dollar a day in 1912.

Despite Britain's best efforts to prevent it, in 1790 (well before the Industrial Revolution got rolling on the European continent), in what might be considered an early international theft of intellectual property rights, Moses Brown (a wealthy resident of Providence, Rhode Island who had built a fortune in the transatlantic slave trade and established Brown University) managed to hire Samuel Slater, an experienced mill operator in Britain. Slater had managed to memorize key aspects of a cotton mill design and then escape from Britain on a ship to America. Brown brought Slater to Providence, where they built a waterwheel-powered mill based on the one where he had worked in Britain. More followed, including many in Massachusetts. Some operators only hired mill girls there because they were cheaper than men. Some were as young as ten. They were required to live in company quarters and work twelve-hour shifts six days a week. Since there was no coal in the area, almost all mills were powered by waterwheels, which limited location and size.

Most efforts to put steam engines on ships were occurring in Europe, with little success. The big problem was figuring out how to get a machine to push a boat through water. Among the many ideas tried were paddle wheels, with little success. Robert Fulton had been in Europe for over a decade working on this problem. Then he heard of the idea of pulling the paddle wheel axle up out of the water so that no more than a third of the wheel was in the water. He then came to America and found financial backing to build a steam-powered boat with such a paddle wheel. In August 1807, Robert Fulton launched the world's first successful steamboat (burning wood), which went from New York City to Albany, attaining a speed of five miles an hour. The 1811 edition of *The Navigator,* an Ohio River guidebook published in Pittsburgh, contained the following paragraph:

There is now a foot a new mode of navigating our western waters, particularly the Ohio and Mississippi rivers. This is with boats propelled by steam. This plan has been carried into successful operation on the Hudson River at New York, and on the Delaware Between New Castle and Burlington. It has been stated the one on the Hudson goes at a rate of four miles an hour against wind and tide on her route between New York and Albany, and frequently with 500 passengers on board. From these successful experiments there can be but little doubt of the plan succeeding on our western waters, and proving an immense advantage to the commerce of our country. . . It will be a novel sight, and as pleasing as novel to see a huge boat working her way up the windings of the Ohio, without the appearance of sail, oar, pole or any manual labor about her – moving within the secrets of her own wonderful mechanism, and propelled by power undiscoverable! This plan if it succeeds, must open to view flattering prospects to an immense country, an interior of not less than two thousand miles of as fine a soil and climate, as the world can produce, and to a people worthy of all the advantages that nature and art can give them.

Then, that October, the first steamboat on the Ohio River departed from Pittsburgh and traveled 2,000 miles down the Ohio and Mississippi all the way to New Orleans in just 14 days, achieving speeds of 12 miles an hour along the way. In contrast, Lewis and Clark, who had returned to St. Louis just five years earlier from their expedition to the Pacific Ocean, spent 20 months of their over three-year expedition traveling aboard boats and canoes on navigable rivers. For a steamboat, just five years later, to go from Pittsburgh to New Orleans in just 14 days demonstrates how quickly steam provided an unimaginable transformation of river travel.

Over the next 40 years, steam and iron would also transform ocean travel, with Great Britain leading the way. For ocean-going ships, underwater propellers began to replace paddlewheels, while iron replaced wood for constructing ship hulls. In 1845, the revolutionary *SS Great Britain* became the first iron-hulled propellor-driven steamship to cross the Atlantic.

Thanks to steam, mankind could suddenly easily move people and all kinds of materials and finished products needed for expanding societies up and down rivers, across oceans, and over land with far greater speed and less cost than had ever been previously imagined. This dramatic rise in transportation productivity improved the standard of living for millions as it spread to other countries. It was also critical to the further development of the Industrial Revolution.

Eli Whitney, a New Englander and son of a farmer/inventor, was a key player in the industrialization of the USA in two ways. First, after graduating from Yale in 1792, he went to Georgia to stay with acquaintances there. That fall, after seeing the challenge of separating cotton fibers from the seeds by hand, he said he was inspired by watching a cat try to pull a chicken through a wire fence and only get a few feathers. In a few weeks, he had fabricated his initial cotton gin, which was small and hand-cranked. Yet, it proved to be 50 times as efficient at separating cotton from its seeds as doing it by hand. He patented his new machine in 1793. At that time, tobacco, rice, and indigo production exceeded cotton as the primary commercial crops in the southern states. The USA was then exporting less than half a million pounds of raw cotton per year while that first cotton mill in New England was just getting underway. By 1810, even though there were now many more cotton mills in New England, the USA exported 93 million pounds of raw cotton. In fact, cotton accounted for over half of the value of all exports from the USA from 1820 until 1860. Most of that raw cotton went to British textile mills like those in Manchester. Since Eli Whitney did not support slavery, it is ironic that thanks to his cotton gin, invented to ease manual labor, King Cotton became the face of, and primary force behind, American slavery until the Civil War as the USA and Britain were clothing themselves and much of the world in inexpensive, high-quality cotton fabric.

Whitney's second contribution to the Industrial Revolution in the USA was promoting the idea of interchangeable parts and the development of milling machines that could produce duplicate metal parts that could be used in both the manufacture and the repair of small arms and artillery. This new method of manufacturing all types of machines was pioneered in the USA and was characterized by the standardization of manufactured goods whose parts were interchangeable and easily replaced when repairs were needed, rather than each machine being the unique creation of an artisan builder and, thus, difficult and expensive to repair. This trend toward standardized interchangeable parts made in large factories would continue throughout the first Industrial Revolution until it dominated manufacturing in the USA by the latter half of the nineteenth century as many new machines were invented for agriculture, home use, and industry.

Like millions of others, a Vermont blacksmith named John Deere moved west and settled in Illinois. While fixing broken plows for farmers trying to plow up the tall grass prairie sod, he experimented with plow designs and came up with one that cut cleanly without scouring. It worked so well that he immediately set up a factory in Moline. His company's motto: "*He gave the world the steel plow*" would be retained for a century.

But the man who did the most to transform American agriculture was Cyrus McCormick. He broke the process for harvesting wheat down into its various components and devised a machine that would do them all. Farmers were skeptical. He didn't sell a machine for ten years. He finally sold seven in 1842. Then, when the international wheat market opened in 1845, he moved to Chicago and opened a factory there. Over the next five years, he sold 5,000 machines and became a very rich man. In 1839, only 80 bushels of wheat were shipped out of Chicago. Ten years later, two million bushels were shipped. Per John Steele Gordon:

With McCormick's reaper, one man could harvest eight acres a day, and the American Middle West would become the breadbasket of the world... The McCormick reaper not only greatly enlarged the potential size of American grain crops, it changed how Americans have earned their livelihoods. With the introduction of the reaper and the endless parade of mechanical Agricultural equipment that followed, the percentage of American workers engaged in agriculture has steadily declined, even while agricultural output has continued to grow. The McCormick reaper thus helped crucially to supply the labor needed in the great expansion of American industry that followed the Civil War.

Europe's view of Americans as country bumpkins was largely erased at the American exhibits at London's 1851 world's fair. After first seeing Cyrus McCormick's reaper, the *Times* of London described it as *"A cross between a flying machine, a wheelbarrow, and a chariot...An extravagant Yankee contrivance, huge, unwieldy, unsightly, and incomprehensible."* However, after seeing a demonstration of the reaper in action, the *Times* wrote *"The reaping machine from the United States is the most valuable contribution from abroad to the stock of our previous knowledge. . . It is worth the whole cost of the Exposition."* Another observer noted *"Americans were thought to be little more than amiable backwoodsmen not yet ready for unsupervised outings on the world stage. So when the displays were erected it came as something of a surprise that the American section was an outpost of wizardry and wonder. Nearly all the American machines did things that the world earnestly wished machines could do – stamp out nails, cut stone, mold candles – but with a neatness, dispatch and tireless reliability that left the other nations blinking. Cyrus McCormick displayed a reaper that could do the work of 40 men. Most exciting of all was Samuel Colt's repeating action revolver, which was not only marvelously lethal but made from interchangeable parts, a method of manufacture so distinctive that it became known as the American system."*

An American-made sewing machine was also displayed there. Isaac Singer then redesigned it, making it much more reliable and versatile. *"A shirt sewn by hand required more than fourteen hours to manufacture. With the new sewing machine, a seamstress could make one in only a little over an hour.* Although many clothing workers feared this new machine would destroy their livelihoods, the opposite happened. *"As the price of ready-made clothes plunged thanks to the sewing machine, the increased demand for them more than made up for the fall in price. This is the reason industrialization has greatly enriched, not impoverished, the world's workers, at least in the long term.*

Because there was no coal along the Atlantic Coast, using steam engines to power factories got off to a very slow start there. On the other hand, Pittsburgh, which is west of the Alleghany Mountains at the mouth of the Ohio River, had coal everywhere. By 1790, when it still had less than 400 residents, visitors were already complaining about coal smoke. Because of its abundant cheap coal, by 1817, it had already become a major manufacturing center with 6,000 residents and over 250 factories, led by glass and ironmaking. And it continued to grow. By contrast, even by 1830, there were only 250 factories in the rest of the USA, mostly in New England, and only four were powered by steam engines (and they burned wood). It was cheaper to ship coal to New England from Britain than to haul it east over the mountains from Pittsburgh. In fact, the cost of running a steam engine in New England, or even Philadelphia, was twice what it was in England, while steam in Pittsburgh was cheaper than in England. **Simply put, the cost of energy was then, and still is, a dominant factor in industrialization for any region or country.**

Again, stealing British ideas, the first horse-drawn railways began showing up in the USA in the late 1820s. They were also built with British industrial goods: locomotives, freight and passenger cars, rails, spikes, and bridge members. However, Americans soon began contributing to railway technology and production. The Baltimore and Ohio (B&O) Railroad began construction in 1828 with plans to use horse-drawn cars. Peter Cooper and two partners had built the Canton Iron works and desperately needed the railroad to make it a financial success. Horses were not enough. In six weeks, he cobbled together a steam boiler he already had with a railcar platform and even used sawed-off musket barrels for piping that could handle the heat and pressure to build a makeshift locomotive he named *Tom Thumb*. On its first run, it pulled a carriage with 40 people that went up to 18 miles per hour before breaking down. In that same timeframe, Robert Livingston Stevens developed the T-shaped rail in cross section, which is still used today. He also pioneered laying rail on wooden crossties with gravel between them as a roadbed for the rails. Railroad construction took off after that. By 1840, there were 3,200 miles of track (more than twice that in all of Europe), and 450 steam locomotives (and only 117 of those were imported from Britain) were running on them. President Andrew Jackson arrived for his inauguration in 1829 by horse and buggy. He left Washington in 1837 by train.

Railroads greatly accelerated the Industrial Revolution in the USA. They greatly stimulated mining, manufacturing, and travel, and created new industries in the manufacture of rails, locomotives, and rolling stock, while creating thousands of new jobs as engineers, firemen, brakemen, switchmen, conductors, and mechanics, further encouraging farmers and their children to move into other occupations. They promoted settlement and urban development at railheads. By the mid-1830s, the portion of the Nation's population that were city dwellers had risen to ten percent. As farmers continually moved west to settle new lands across the Midwest, railroads greatly increased the opportunities for farmers to ship their products to distant markets rather than relying on local consumption. This enabled them to focus more on cash crops rather than subsistence agriculture. The railroads also greatly expanded their opportunities as consumers by widening the choices of textiles, household goods, and farm equipment available at country stores. In 1844, Philip Hone, age 63, wrote:

This world is going too fast. Improvements, politics, reform, religion – all fly. Railroads, steamers, packets, race against time and beat it hollow...Oh, for the good old days of heavy post coaches and speed at the rate of six miles an hour!

This is the first recorded use of the phrase *good old days*. But then this was really the first time in human history that people would find that they were living like no generation before them had ever lived and realize that their children would probably be living in conditions not yet imagined. The rate of change from one generation to the next was quite staggering. In short, the USA was a vastly different place by the time of the Civil War than it had been just 50 years earlier during the War of 1812. Its technological expansion through steam riverboats, railroads, and factories not only altered daily life but was a major factor in the nation's geographic expansion. With the end of the Civil War in 1865, completing a transcontinental railroad became a priority. It was completed in 1869. And the USA was becoming an industrial powerhouse on the world stage.

1776 had been a truly remarkable year in human history. It was the year of the Declaration of Independence, which not only created the USA but laid out principles between the governed and their government that still reverberate around the world. It was the year that James Watt put his first steam engine into operation, creating the new source of energy that would power the Industrial Revolution. It was the year that Adam Smith, generally considered the world's first economist, published *The Wealth of Nations,* which laid out the argument that:

When an individual pursues his self-interest under conditions of justice, he unintentionally promotes the good of society. Self-interested competition in the free market would tend to benefit society as a whole by keeping prices low, while still building in an incentive for a wide variety of goods and services.

That is the basis for free enterprise. It also fostered innovation, new products, and new ideas like never before. And no country had ever been so open to new ideas, innovation, and change as the new USA. And it did so within an economic framework that enabled the Industrial Revolution to occur and continue to expand. That expansion resulted in what we now think of as *Capitalism.*

In earlier times, wealth and status were generally associated with land ownership. In Europe and many other parts of the world, there was generally a landed upper class, a merchant class, an artisan class who made things, a servant class, a labor class, and rural peasants. However, the new economic institution of banking freed up liquid financial resources (that had been tied up in property) well in advance of expected returns on a scale never before seen to build factories and railroads that vastly expanded the working class and the middle class. At the same time, it made a large array of manufactured goods available at much lower cost, from textiles to farm equipment and household items to that growing middle and working class, as well as rural farmers, that lifted the standard of living for them all.

THE TELEGRAPH – Timely transfer of information over long distances has always been valued. In fact, it is at least as important as the movement of people and things. Over two thousand years ago, Herodotus declared (the motto on the Postal Service headquarters):

Neither rain, nor snow, nor heat, nor gloom of night stays these couriers from the swift completion of their appointed rounds.

Pigeons have been used for centuries to send messages. Visible signals from ridgetop to ridgetop have long been used. Beginning in the 1790s, the French government established the fastest and most efficient communication system the world had ever seen, with a network of stations about six miles apart capable of relaying signals whenever visibility allowed. To describe these long-distance optical signals using symbols for written communications, the word *telegraph* was adopted into several European languages. By the 1820s, the Telegraph had become a popular name for newspapers in the USA.

As mentioned above, Benjamin Franklin was experimenting with electricity in the 1750s. Over the next 80 years, many inventors worked with electricity and its relation to magnetism while exploring possible uses. Some experimented with sending an electromagnetic pulse through a metal wire. However, Samuel Finley Morse (who had sent such a pulse through two miles of wire in 1838) mustered the political support for Congress to fund the construction of a wire strung on poles from Washington, D.C., to Baltimore in 1844. With help from others, he also developed an alphabet of dots and dashes (Morse code) and a paper tape machine that could receive messages by creating bumps in the paper in response to the electromagnetic pulses. The first message, *"WHAT HATH GOD WROUGHT,"* was sent by telegraph on May 24, 1844.

For the first time in human history, a message had been instantaneously sent and received over a long distance. Also, for the first time, a response could be given. A conversation could ensue. This, along with the expanding railroad system, contributed significantly to the belief that it really would be possible to successfully manage a single nation stretching from the Atlantic to the Pacific Ocean. Just three years earlier, in 1841, it had taken 110 days for the news of the death of President William Henry Harrison to reach Los Angeles. The telegraph changed perceptions of what was possible. *"It decoupled communication from transportation, sending a message from sending an object."* The next year, Texas was annexed. In 1850, California and Oregon became states, while 10,000 miles of telegraph wire had been strung within the USA. The first transcontinental telegraph line was completed in 1861. The Pony Express, which could make the trip from Missouri to Carson City, Nevada, in 10 to 16 days, had been operating for two years. It shut down two days after the first transcontinental telegraph message. Still, the telegraph was used primarily for commercial and news purposes, not individual social interactions. *"The electric telegraph from the outset was a long-distance medium that linked commercial centers."*

Further, the development of the telegraph began a significant shift in technological progress. *"The electric telegraph represented the first important invention based upon the application of advanced scientific knowledge rather than the know-how of skilled mechanics. The laboratory would begin to replace the machine shop as the site of technological innovation."* For centuries technological improvements had led to scientific discoveries. Here that process was reversed.

NEWSPAPERS – Various newspapers were being published in the Colonies by 1700. However, they had little resemblance to newspapers (or news websites) that we see today. Those early newspapers were largely the product of political factions, essentially editorial pages with a little news thrown in to support their positions (well, maybe not so different than many newspapers today – but today they don't admit it) and sell papers. Actual news only traveled by mail or word of mouth, so it didn't get to the newspaper any faster than it got to much of the public.

Then three things happened. First, in the 1830s, steam engines were connected to the newly invented rotary presses, so thousands of newspaper copies could be turned out overnight. Second, a Scottish immigrant, James

Gordon Bennett, began publishing the *New York Herald* on May 6, 1835. It was non-partisan and focused on trying to be first with actual news. It was intended for a mass audience and was the first to be sold by newsboys standing on street corners each morning for a penny a copy. It was the first to contain weather reports, sports news, business news, and stock prices. It played up local crime stories and sent out people to gather stories of public interest. It quickly became one of the city's most successful papers. He then signed up correspondents in Europe and Washington, D.C., to collect stories there. He had established a whole new concept of what a newspaper could be. Then third, with the invention and spread of the telegraph after 1844, newspapers had instant access to news from faraway places much faster than it would spread through other means (wire services like the *Associated Press* were born to distribute telegraphed news reports). These changes revolutionized advertising. Wide circulation newspaper advertising enabled the creation of the large department store with a wide variety of merchandise at fixed prices (and sometimes advertised sale prices to draw customers in) where people could browse without being constantly attended by a sales clerk. The newspaper revolution brought a consumer revolution.

THE RISE OF KING COAL – Unlike Britain, where any increase in population or urbanization put enormous pressure on Britain's dwindling forests and promoted the use of coal, the USA had plenty of trees. In fact, the entire USA east of the Mississippi River was really one huge forest. Timber was a major export of the colonies. So, not only did the initial steam engines in New England textile mills burn wood, but many of the initial railroad and riverboat steam engines also burned wood. Wood was also the primary fuel for domestic use, both in cities and rural areas, as America burned its way through its vast forests. The exception was Pittsburgh, where coal was so plentiful. And coal produces more heat than the same amount of wood.

However, five counties in eastern Pennsylvania contained most of the anthracite coal deposits on earth. Anthracite is coal that, through extended enormous pressure within the earth's crust, has had much of the oxygen and impurities squeezed out, leaving a much harder rock with a much higher carbon content, somewhat analogous to the metamorphic geological processes that turn shale into slate and limestone into marble. Anthracite is much harder to ignite than regular (bituminous) coal but burns much hotter and with very little smoke. It is also much better for producing iron and steel. In short, it is a much better fuel, both for residential and industrial use, than bituminous coal. And there were extensive deposits within a hundred miles of Philadelphia discovered before 1800. However, there were two problems: first, how to get it to Philadelphia from the deposits in those mountains, and second, teaching people how to get it to burn. When, in 1803, some entrepreneurs managed to get two loads there, no one would buy it. While the second problem was soon overcome, it wasn't until 1825, with the opening of the Schuylkill Canal, the USA's first successful commercial canal, that the first problem was solved. And what that canal carried to Philadelphia was anthracite. Over the next decade more canals were opened creating a network from various anthracite mine centers to New York and other ports. *"By the 1830s, the canals scraped across the landscape to bring coal into the cities formed the largest canal network in the nation, and America's first major inland transportation system."* However, canals froze over and couldn't go all the way to the mines in the mountains, so they soon gave way to railroads. Anthracite country has been called the cradle of American railroading. Coal companies began to build railroads, and railroad companies opened mines. Schuylkill County had far more tracks than any other area of comparable size in the USA. New anthracite furnaces making iron also sprang up in eastern Pennsylvania. There were 60 of them by 1850.

The use of coal gas to light city streets spread as coal became available in cities. By the 1830s, thanks to underground piping from gas works, after-dark activity increased markedly in cities as lighted streets replaced the dangerous gloom of prior centuries. By the 1850s, it was also being used for indoor lighting in some cities. *"For the first time in human history, interior illumination was cheap, so that it could be used in abundance, and people began to stay up later and read far more than previously. Books, magazines, and newspapers all increased sales markedly at this time, as did sheet music."* But it hissed and smelled bad. Central heating for many urban buildings and dwellings soon followed, which was another American original.

Within just a few years, two major bottlenecks to industrialization within the USA had been eliminated: the lack of cheap coal and the lack of cheap iron. Anthracite fueled the industrialization of the northeast, while bituminous coal was available to much of the rest of the country. This led to a huge rise in industrial mass production, primarily in the North. By the time of the Civil War, the North had ten times more factory production than the South, fifteen times more iron production, 32 times more firearms production, and 38 times more coal production. And the war only accelerated industrialization, needing more coal and iron.

On May 10, 1876, the USA launched its first centennial celebration in Philadelphia. In the words of Barbara Freese:

One of the most popular attractions was the behemoth of a coal-fired steam engine that powered the thousands of mechanical inventions set up in the exhibition's sprawling Machinery Hall. At the opening ceremony... before an exhilarated crowd of 100,000, President Ulysses S. Grant stepped up to the giant engine and pulled its control lever. With a hiss of steam, the engine's cross beam began to rock, its two enormous pistons began to churn, and eight miles of connecting shafts running through the hall began to rotate. A cheer rose from the crowd as fourteen acres of gleaming machinery simultaneously sprang to noisy life, spinning, sawing, sewing, pumping, and printing, trumpeting in unison the nation's arrival as an industrial power.

Historians have seen in the Centennial Exhibition a vivid symbol of the emerging industrial era in the United States, a showcase of the nation's optimism, its inventiveness, and its love of technology on a massive scale. Played out across the country, these same factors along with a flood of cheap labor and plenty of coal, would soon make the United States the world's leading industrial nation.

Coal, including a dependable and constant supply, became far more than an abstract political issue; it became an integral part of daily life for millions of Americans and fueled a huge change in domestic life.

Beginning in the 1830s, the first fully enclosed cast iron stoves started and then slowly spread throughout the USA over the rest of the century. Again, Barbara Freese:

In many American homes, the open fire, the flickering light that had been the focal point of our species' domestic life since before we were fully human, disappeared into a box. The move away from open fires brought another important change into the home as well: cooking, which since time immemorial had forced people to stoop over a fire, could finally be done standing up.

Wood was the primary fuel in rural areas, while coal use increased in urban areas. Two types of stoves evolved. The more common type had a flat top for cooking and would be used in the kitchen and houses with just one room. Most had an oven next to the firebox and were designed so that, with a damper, hot exhaust from the firebox could be forced around the oven to heat it evenly for baking before going up the stovepipe. The other kinds were cheaper, including the iconic *pot-bellied stove,* and were designed for heating the room. The benefits of stoves were dramatic. Besides being able to cook standing up and having an oven with a door, stoves were far more effective at keeping smoke out of the room, dramatically increasing indoor air quality. There were also two huge economic benefits to stoves. First, they were several times more efficient than fireplaces, thus requiring far less fuel, while doing a much better job of heating the whole room because they were out away from the wall. Second, because they could be installed with only a metal stovepipe going up through the roof, they were far cheaper and easier to install than a stone or brick fireplace and chimney. Thus, as pioneers moved west onto new land through the latter half of the nineteenth century and quickly built one-room log or sod houses to live in, a cheap stove could be installed on the first day. The 1897 Sears and Roebuck catalog showed several types of stoves priced from $5.97 for the simplest to $48.00 for the fanciest model.

The use of stoves would spread throughout the world, but it began in the USA. Britain was very slow to adopt stoves because Brits loved seeing the flame in an open hearth. I grew up with coal-burning stoves that heated our house and cooked our food until I went off to college. We always had both kinds because we had more than one room in the houses I grew up in. However, the bedrooms were still very cold in those Idaho winters because the other stove was in the living room.

By 1876, the nation was still getting twice as much of its energy from wood (primarily for home heating) as from coal. But that was changing fast as the vast eastern forest was being depleted. By 1900, 71% of the USA's energy came from coal and 21% from wood. The remaining 8% was scattered among waterwheels, windmills, oil, and natural gas. And the Second Industrial Revolution was just getting started.

9: THE DEVELOPMENT AND EXPANSION OF THE UNITED STATES

The development and expansion of European colonization of what is now the USA was distinctly different from how it happened in the Americas south of the Rio Grande River.

In Latin America and Brazile, the Europeans didn't come as farmers settling on the first arable land they came to, but as adventurers seeking riches to take home, which led them directly to Indian population centers wherever that might be. And because few women came, the social intermingling resulted in far more mixed-race descendants. However, there was generally a ruling European elite, along with distinct pockets of indigenous Indians that retained their own culture. Where agriculture was the goal, it was primarily sugar plantations, with the number of Africans brought in exceeding the number of Europeans who came to manage them by tenfold or more.

For the 13 British colonies, settlers came to stay, which meant farming. Even Jamestown, which didn't start that way, only succeeded because it turned to agriculture. We now often think of the western frontier as the area from the great plains to the Pacific coast, where white settlers moved in with wagon trains and fought with Indians in the process. However, in the eighteenth century, it ran the length of the Atlantic seaboard westward to the Appalachian Mountains. By 1800, the wild west stretched from the western slope of the Appalachian Mountains to the Mississippi. In short, for almost three centuries, the story of America was white Europeans moving ever further west across the continent from the Atlantic to the Pacific as they pushed aside the remnants of the original inhabitants that had survived disease epidemics. And most established farms.

With all that could be written here, I will focus on a few people, events, and forces that played a significant role in shaping the USA geographically and culturally into what is today. Indians are an essential part of this story because they were often an issue in the geographical expansion of the

USA. There was an overriding point of view of those white settlers moving west, as explained by historian H. W. Brands:

When Europeans, with their individualistic ideas of land ownership, entered Indian lands, unclaimed by any individual Indians, it was tempting for Europeans to assume that no one owned the land and that it was available for the taking.

While some of those Indian groups were farmers, the idea of individuals owning specific parcels of land was outside their frame of reference. Instead, they considered all lands within the control of their tribe as, collectively, their land. In varying degrees, colonial (and then state or federal) governments tried to control the expansion of settlers into Indian lands with, at best, limited success. H. W. Brands on how to get rich in the USA in the early nineteenth century:

The formula for western wealth was simple (and the same as it had been for generations and would be for generations more): get there early, acquire land cheap, wait for more settlers to arrive, and sell at a profit.

And land was an abundant resource. In the words of John Steele Gordon:

The growth of American agricultural production in the pre-Civil War era is without parallel in world economic history... However, because the supply of land seemed to be without end, the value placed on each unit was small. This is only common sense, at least in the short term (and, as Lord Keynes observed, in the long term, we are all dead). Caring for the land was an inescapable necessity in Europe, where there was no more to be had. But in America, new, unspoiled land nearly free for the taking was just over the next row of hills or river valleys, and settlers could always move on. For three hundred years, they did exactly that, with ever increasing speed.

THE NORTHWEST TERRITORY – As the Revolutionary War ended and the terms of the treaty ending the war were being finalized in 1783, Adams and Franklin insisted that all the land east of the Mississippi river and south of the Great Lakes be part of the new USA rather than part of Canada, which would remain under British control. That such a thing was even discussed between the new USA and Great Britain, demonstrated enormous hubris and ethnocentrism since the only English-speaking settlements in the entire area were a few along the western edge of the Appalachian Mountains. It was reminiscent of Spain and Portugal dividing up the entire Americas almost three centuries earlier. But, in the eyes of European nations, this treaty made that land part of the new USA. The longstanding Right of Conquest was in full effect between European nations, with little consideration given to the indigenous peoples who already lived there since they were presumed to lack the means to challenge European military dominance.

Then, In July 1787, at the same time the new Constitution was being debated and formulated in Philadelphia as discussed above, the existing Congress, which was meeting in New York City, passed "An Ordinance for the Government of the Territory of the United States, North-West of the River Ohio" that laid out a framework for governing settlements in the large area bordered by the Ohio River on the east and south, and the Mississippi River on the West, that now comprises the states of Ohio, Indiana, Illinois, Michigan, and Wisconsin. There was not yet a single settlement of Europeans in the entire area. The ordinance was patterned after the Massachusetts Constitution. Among its many provisions, it laid out three things of interest here: 1) *"utmost good faith shall always be observed towards the Indians; their lands and property shall never be taken from them without their consent...they shall never be invaded or disturbed, unless in just and lawful wars authorized by Congress"*, 2) *"There shall be neither slavery nor involuntary servitude in the said territory,"* and 3) freedom of religion.

These three provisions were not in the new national Constitution being drafted at the same time in Philadelphia. However, the third provision, freedom of religion, was included in the first amendment to the Constitution, which was passed two years later by the first Congress of the new USA under that new Constitution. On the second provision prohibiting slavery, the ordinance for the Northwest Territories was drafted and pushed by a group from Massachusetts, which had already completely abolished slavery four years before. When Ohio became a state in 1802, the state's new constitution retained, by the narrowest of margins in the state assembly, a prohibition on slavery. So, slavery has always been prohibited in the five states that arose from that Northwest Territory. The first provision, related to the treatment of Indians and taking their lands, proved to be a lost cause. Problems were inevitable and developed quickly.

After months of getting organized and collecting supplies, on December 31, 1787, an advance party of 48 men with an array of skills (surveyor, boat builder, carpenters, engineers, metal workers, etc.) and equipment set out on the 700-mile journey from Massachusetts, with the goal or arriving at their intended settlement site, where the Muskingum River flows into Ohio, in time to plant crops that spring. They arrived at a ferry on the Youghiogheny River, about 30 miles southeast of Pittsburgh, in mid-February. There they spent the next seven weeks building a roofed galley boat 45 feet long (which they named the Mayflower), a smaller flat boat, and three dugout canoes. From there, it took only five days to float down river through Pittsburgh and on to their destination, arriving on April 7, 1788. The Ohio River was a quarter mile wide during spring runoff, while the Muskingum was about 200 yards wide. The rivers were teaming with catfish, sturgeon, and pike, some over 50 pounds. In *the measureless forest, the gigantic trees of every kind – hickory, beech, sycamore, tulip, ash, buckeye, oaks six feet in diameter that reached fifty feet before breaking out in branches – were the dominant reality." "Wild turkeys and passenger pigeons were in unimaginable abundance. White-tailed deer, otter, elk, buffalo, beaver, wolves, and bears filled the forests in all directions. So plentiful were squirrels that hardly a day passed without a few hundred being killed."* About 70 Indians (men, women, and children) were also there to greet them that first day. The greeting was cordial, but the Indian chief was someone suspected of having tortured and killed an army officer before.

The settlers quickly cleared land, planted crops, and established a new settlement, the first in Ohio. They named it Marietta (in honor of Marie

Antoinette for her help in mustering French support during the Revolutionary War). More settlers arrived as the year wore on. By the end of the year, Marietta had a population of 132, including 15 families. However, they were only a small part of a mass western migration that was just getting underway. That first year, more than 900 boats (flatboats, rafts, barges, and keelboats) carrying 18,000 people floated past Marietta and headed further west down the Ohio River to establish and/or expand other new settlements.

Life in these new settlements was hard. While people came with a wide range of skills, no one was more essential than the blacksmith. *"The blacksmith was the gunsmith, farrier, coppersmith, millwright, machinist, and surgeon general to all broken tools and implements. His forge was a center of social as well as industrial activity. From soft bar iron, nails as well as horseshoes were forged as needed... Chains, reaping hooks, bullet molds, yoke rings, axes, bear and wolf traps, hoes, augers, bells, saws, and the metal parts of looms, spinning wheels, sausage grinders, presses, and agricultural implements were a few of the items either manufactured or repaired in his shop."* Life was hard for women and children. There was no loafing or days off. Besides cooking, cleaning, and washing, there were cows to milk, gardens to tend, candles and soap to be made, butter to churn, yarn to spin, fabric to weave, and clothes to make, mend, and patch.

Indians soon became very concerned about the large number of new arrivals. By the first fall, they began systematically killing off game in the area in an effort to starve out the settlers. They also began to steal from the settlers. In the summer of 1789, six soldiers were killed in an ambush a few miles outside Marietta. Other skirmishes followed as numerous settlements were established on the north side of the Ohio River, with some moving north from the river into the interior of Ohio. In the fall of 1790, *"a makeshift frontier army of almost 1,500 men, regulars and militia"* went out to teach the Indians a lesson. They encountered a much smaller force of Indians but were soundly defeated, with 183 dead or missing, while the Indians lost less than a dozen. In January 1791, Indians attacked a small settlement 30 miles up the Muskingum River from Marietta, killing 14 and taking three captives. Only two escaped. More killings on both sides followed. On May 3, 1791, Congress authorized a force of 2,000 to put down the Indian "rebellion." President Washington's parting words to the general in charge were:

Beware of surprise! You know how the Indians fight us.

Unfortunately, that general had never fought Indians and really knew nothing about them, so he had no idea what Washington meant.

The force finally got underway on October 4, 1791, with 1,700 troops and about 200 camp followers consisting of wives, washerwomen, mistresses, prostitutes, and children, as it headed overland into the center of Ohio. The force could only make one to three miles a day as it had to cut its way through the forest to get its wagons through, which were pulled by oxen. Some troops tried to desert. Two were caught and promptly hung. The few Indians they saw quickly ran away. Then, on a very cold morning on November 4, shortly after sunrise, as the troops were eating breakfast, they were attacked by about a thousand Indians from ten different tribes: Miami, Shawnee, Delaware, Wyandot, Ottawa, Kickapoo, Chippewa, Pottawatomie, Mohawk, and Creek. It was an overwhelming massacre, with the army soon driven into retreat. Army losses were 623 dead, including 39 officers. Over 200 more were wounded. Almost all the camp followers were killed. Only three women survived. The Indians lost less than two dozen men while acquiring 1,200 muskets, 163 axes, and eight cannons, along with baggage, wagons, oxen, and loads of camp equipment and ammunition left behind by the army.

What do we learn from all this? First, by 1791, Indian society in Ohio had already been transformed before white settlers even got there. Some, if not all, of these tribes had been farmers who had lived in stationary villages growing corn, beans, and squash. They were now apparently hunter/gatherer nomads. The settlers found no permanent Indian villages, open fields, or evidence of crops or annual burns. Instead, the woods had filled in with a tangled undergrowth that was difficult to cut through. There was now an overabundance of small game, particularly passenger pigeons, wild turkeys, and squirrels. Ten tribes speaking several different languages were now all in the same area. Some of these tribes were hundreds of miles from their original locations, now largely occupied by settlers. Second, unlike King Phillip's War, where friendly Indians assisted the pilgrims, this was a war where these ten tribes had buried whatever hostilities they had had with one another to unite against a common enemy, the settlers. This was a war between races and incompatible civilizations.

While the Indians won that battle very decisively, they ultimately and inevitably lost the war. Settlers won the next battle a year later. In 1802, Ohio became a state. The last 2,000 Indians in Ohio were expelled in 1830 under the Removal Act passed by Congress that year. They were put on steamboats at Cincinnati and shipped to reservations west of the Mississippi just 42 years after the first settlers arrived with the commitment that the Indians would be treated with "utmost good faith" and that their land would never be taken from them without their consent.

THE LOUSIANA PURCHASE AND THE LEWIS AND CLARK EXPEDITION – Since the Constitution leaves the method for selecting presidential electors up to the individual state legislatures. Initially, only about half the states held public elections where citizens could vote. Even there, voting was limited to males owning property and/or paying taxes in most states. Five states allowed free black males to vote as early as 1788. The presidential election of 1800 was a complicated mess as the incumbent, John Adams, a Federalist, ran for reelection. In the Electoral College, Thomas Jefferson and Aaron Burr, who ran on a joint ticket, each got 73 votes, while John Adam only got 65. Because no one got a majority, it went to the House of Representatives. However, under the Constitution, each state only gets one vote, and there were 16 states. After voting 35 times, the vote was still tied eight to eight between Aaron Burr and Thomas Jefferson. With John Adams out of the picture, Alexander Hamilton was the primary force within the Federalist Party, which had been backing Burr. Hamilton despised Jefferson's politics and his advocacy for an agrarian utopia with strong state governments and a weak federal government with little presidential power. Historian H.W. Brands has described their contrasting views of the role of the federal government (including regulating incursions by new settlers into Indian lands) this way:

Jefferson and his followers – many of whom had opposed ratification of the Constitution – signaled their continuing confidence in the people against the government, their preference for the principles of 1776 over those of 1787. They believed that people were naturally good and required only opportunity and encouragement to manifest their goodness. Less government was better than more, and the state governments were better than a central government. By contrast, Hamilton and his followers distrusted human nature and relied on the government to keep it in check. They supported the Constitution of 1787, which they conceived as a corrective to the libertarian excesses of 1776. They continued to try to strengthen the government against the people and the federal government against the states.

The split between Jefferson's crowd, who called themselves Republicans, and Hamilton's Federalists acquired economic and regional overtones. The Federalists were strong among the merchant and monied classes, especially in the Northeast. The Republicans looked to the landed folk, particularly the planters and farmers of the South and West. By the mid-1790s, Republicans and Federalists glared at each other across a widening gulf of ideology, economy, and section.

However, Hamilton deeply distrusted Aaron Burr because he felt Burr's only guiding principle was self-interest. Jefferson did envision his agrarian utopia as stretching across the continent all the way to the Pacific Ocean, while Burr was quite content with the idea that the area west of the Appalachian Mountains that drained into the Mississippi River should become a separate nation. So, Hamilton finally got involved and convinced enough Federalist House members in New York to switch their vote so that on the next ballot, New York voted for Jefferson, giving him the victory (Burr then became vice president and three years later bullied Hamilton in a duel where he killed Hamilton, who fired his shot into the air). Hamilton felt that Jefferson, once he became president, might discover that he actually liked presidential power. Sure enough, Jefferson, who became president in March 1801 by the narrowest of margins, did go on to exercise unprecedented presidential power.

At the time Jefferson became president, river travel was the primary means of inland long-distance transportation. And people believed that would always be true. With Tennessee already a state and Ohio becoming a state in 1802, access down the Mississippi to the Gulf was generally seen as critical to economic development and growth throughout the vast region between the Appalachian Mountains and the Mississippi. Therefore, Jefferson became quite alarmed when he learned that Spain and France (where Napoleon had recently taken charge) were about to finalize a deal that would transfer the New Orleans area to France. That would negate Spain's longstanding commitment to open access down the Mississippi through New Orleans to the Gulf. He was also alarmed to learn that a Canadian explorer had recently crossed over the western mountains and reached the Pacific Ocean at what is now Vancouver, B.C., cementing British interests in the Pacific Northwest. In response, Jefferson launched two initiatives: 1) to buy New Orleans, including access down the Mississippi to the Gulf, from France, and 2) to send an exploratory expedition to find a northwest passage to the Pacific and lay the groundwork for the USA's own claims to the area. On January 12, 1803, Jefferson submitted a bill to Congress asking for over nine million dollars to buy New Orleans. Six days later, he submitted another bill to Congress that included a request to fund an exploratory expedition to the Pacific. By then, planning for the expedition was already nearing completion.

By early April 1803, Jefferson had a team of negotiators in Paris, led by James Monroe, who were authorized to commit up to ten million dollars to buy New Orleans. They were shocked when, on April 11, France offered to sell all its interests in the North American continent, the entire western side of the Mississippi watershed, for fifteen million dollars. Napoleon had just lost his effort to retake Haiti, was about to begin a war with Britain, and knew he was in no position to defend New Orleans or their larger interests in central North America they were just acquiring from Spain. He decided it would be better to sell those interests now than lose them in war. He also saw other benefits to France in its struggles with Great Britain. He said:

The sale assures forever the power of the United States, and I have given England a rival who, sooner or later, will humble her pride.

Still, the negotiating team was afraid Napoleon might change his mind, so they signed a treaty making the purchase on April 30, without even having a chance to make Jefferson aware of the offer or weigh in on what they should do. Jefferson was pleased. The purchase treaty was publicly announced on July 4, 1803, with great fanfare. Lewis left Washington the next day and began his journey, taking him into the heart of this new land. The Senate ratified the treaty on October 20. With appropriate ceremonies that involved the lowering and raising of flags for each, on November 30, Spain officially conveyed ownership of New Orleans to France. Then, on December 20, ownership was officially conveyed to the USA. On March 9, 1804 (commemorated as Three Flags Day), ownership of St. Louis was conveyed From Spain to France to the USA. By then, Lewis and Clark had been camped across the river for three months as they made final preparations for their expedition. The Louisiana Purchase stands among the most consequential presidential decisions ever made. It roughly doubled the size of the United States in one stroke, though no one really knew just where the western edge of the Mississippi drainage even was (which was the new western boundary). Jefferson, *"from the beginning of the Revolution, thought of the United States as a nation stretching from sea to sea. More than any other man, he made that happen."* If Burr had become president, it would not have happened.

It had always been my understanding that the Louisiana Purchase led to the Lewis and Clark expedition. That is even what the Wikipedia page for the Louisiana Purchase still says (2024). However, that is false. Jefferson had long been interested in the entire expanse of North America to the Pacific. He had even been the instigator of three previous efforts, between 1783 and 1793, to send an expedition to the Pacific. However, none of them got further west than the Mississippi. In the summer of 1802, he learned details of British efforts in the Pacific Northwest. Since he was now president, he was able to respond forcefully. Jefferson and his personal secretary, 28-year-old Merriweather Lewis, immediately began to plan an official expedition on behalf of the USA. Lewis would lead it.

The expedition would go nowhere near New Orleans, the only area Jefferson was planning to buy from France. As they were planning, there were only two precise locations that were known (with latitude and longitude) west of St. Louis: 1) Canadian fur traders had pinpointed the Mandan villages on the Missouri River just north of what is now Bismarck, and 2) a British sea captain had named the Columbia River and pinpointed the location where the river's estuary enters the Pacific Ocean. The rest was a blank map. The expedition would go up the entire length of the Missouri River from where it enters the Mississippi just above St. Louis, find a passage to a river flowing west, follow it to the Ocean, and then return. Planning was a challenge since there would be no opportunity to resupply once they left St. Louis. What kind of boat? How big? How many men? What skills? How much would be needed in arms, ammunition, cooking pots, tools, rations, medicines, scientific instruments, and gifts for Indians? The list went on and on. Plans for the expedition became public in January 1803, with the request for funding from Congress. By the time Jefferson learned, much to his surprise and delight, that the USA had just bought the entire Missouri River drainage area, Lewis had already procured many of the supplies, settled on the boat design, contracted for its construction, and was being trained to use the scientific instruments he would take. The Louisiana Purchase only added to their excitement and goals for the expedition now that most of the journey, including all the Missouri River drainage, was within the new boundaries of the USA. Jefferson noted that the purchase "increased infinitely the interest we felt in the expedition." Now that they owned it, they just needed to tell the Indians already living there.

Jefferson thought of Indians as noble savages *"in body and mind equal to the white man"* who could be brought into the body politic as full citizens. He envisioned the land west of the Mississippi as a vast reservation for Indians, including those displaced from east of the Mississippi, where they could learn to farm, become "civilized," and ultimately integrate into the Nation's society. Therefore, for a few decades at least, white settlers would only settle east of the Mississippi on all the land still available on both sides of the Ohio River. However, as soon as the Louisiana Purchase had been announced, even more pioneers started heading west. As expressed by historian Stephen E. Ambrose:

This absurd notion showed how little Jefferson knew about Americans living west of the Appalachians. With the Purchase, or even without the Purchase, there was no force on earth that could stop the flow of American pioneers westward. The pioneers were the cutting edge of an irresistible force. Rough and wild though they were, they were the advance agents of millions of Europeans, mostly peasants or younger sons of small farmers, who constituted the greatest mass migration in history. Napoleon got it right: he might as well sell and get some money for the place, because the Americans were going to overrun it anyway.

That population explosion occurring in Europe, that was fueled by potatoes from the Andes, needed a place to expand into. And the place most often chosen was all the land drained by the Mississippi River, from the Appalachian Mountains to the Rockies.

The expedition was an amazing adventure saga taking over three years. The plan was to launch from Pittsburgh (where the boat was being built) in early July. However, the boat builder was drunk more than sober, so it was not finished until August 31, 1803. Three hours later, Lewis had the boat loaded and on its way. The keelboat was 55 feet long and eight feet wide with a shallow draft and a 30-foot mast for sails. Since they would be going upriver against the current for almost two thousand miles of the meandering Missouri River, the boat could be propelled four different ways: by sails, oars, pushing with poles shoved into the riverbed and then walking from front to back in the boat on each side, or pulling with ropes from the bank. Sometimes, they would end up employing all four means at the same time to make their way upriver.

On October 15, Lewis, now 29 years old, picked up his handpicked co-commander, 33-year-old Captain William Clark, at Louisville, Kentucky. The boat and crew reached St. Louis (population of about 1,000, largely French Canadians, still under Spanish control) in December. They camped for the winter along the Mississippi River across from its confluence with Missouri River. Lewis and Clark spent the winter filling out and training their crew and rounding up the last of their supplies from St. Louis. Among their first hires was George Drouillard, son of a French Canadian and a Shawnee Indian. He knew French, English, a few Indian languages, and Indian sign language. As gifts for Indians, Lewis loaded up on beads, brass buttons, tomahawks, axes, moccasin awls, scissors, mirrors, tobacco, face paint, fancy coats, and cloth.

The expedition was an official military operation titled The Corps of Discovery (Corps), with Captains Lewis and Clark in command. In addition to the captains, the main group consisted of Clark's personal black slave, York, three sergeants, and 22 privates, for a total of 29 men. There were also five additional troops and a corporal who would go as far at the Mandan Villages and then return to St. Louis with dispatches and specimens from the first leg of their trip, while the main group would head west from those villages up the rest of the Missouri River and then on to the Pacific. There were also a few co-travelers in canoes. Clark described the troops as:

in high Spirits – robust young Backwoodsmen of Character helthy hardy young men, recommended.

The Corps had four main assignments from Jefferson: 1) look for a passable land bridge between the Missouri River and a river, probably the Columbia, flowing west to the Pacific Ocean, 2) document natural conditions encountered, including soil conditions and new plants and animals, 3) map with latitude and longitude various notable points along the way, and 4) learn as much detail as possible about Indian tribes encountered while building positive relations with them, particularly the Sioux ("the most numerous and warlike tribe on the Missouri").

It was an exciting time. One sergeant wrote in his journal they are all of *"determined and resolute character that dispelled every emotion of fear"* even though they had been told that they were about *"to pass through a country possessed by numerous, powerful and warlike nations of savages, of gigantic stature, fierce, treacherous and cruel; and particularly hostile to white men."* Another wrote to his parents that *"I am So happy to be one of them pick'd Men. We expect to be gone 18 months or two years. We are to Receive a great Reward for this expedition, when we Return."*

As they traveled upriver, if they had the wind, they made good time. Otherwise, it was a struggle. Clark stayed with the boat while Lewis usually walked along taking samples of new plants and animals while looking for minerals and assessing soil conditions.

Discipline was harsh. They had taken about 120 gallons of whiskey with them. Each person got a very small daily ration. It was considered essential for troop morale, at least until they were far enough away that desertion would not be feasible. One night the man on guard duty decided to sneak a sip – and kept sipping. Another came along and joined him. By morning they were both drunk. A court martial was held. The first man got 100 lashes on his bare back. The second got 50 lashes. Two weeks later, and after they had begun to see signs of Indians (so guard duty was a matter of life and death), the man on guard duty fell asleep. He was sentenced to 100 hundred lashes *"well laid on"* at sundown for four consecutive evenings. Though harsh, lashings were effective and efficient since they strongly encouraged discipline and obedience to orders without removing the miscreant from the labor force (which is why slave masters also used whips). All hands were needed as they struggled upriver.

While the expedition was an incredible adventure, most of the rest of this discussion will focus on their interactions with Indians since, except for Oklahoma, northern plains Indians seemed to dominate much of the USA's policies toward Indians in the nineteenth century, as well as our current perceptions and attitudes towards Native Americans today.

The Corps didn't see an Indian for over 70 days. By then, they had passed where Omaha, Nebraska is now located. Life for all the Indian tribes they encountered throughout the expedition had changed dramatically over the past 150 years. Why? Horses! All had acquired horses and developed a horse culture, though some relied on horses more than others. While some tribes made saddles of some sort, others rode their horses bareback and without bridals. Guiding their horses with just their knees through intricate moves during hunting or fighting with each other, they could keep both hands free to use their bow and arrows or muskets. They all used horses for travel, hunting, and raids on other Indian tribes.

The tribes all along the Missouri River had also become dependent on European fur traders for various manufactured goods that they had come to value, including arms. Some, like the Mandan, Arikara, and Hidatsa, were still farmers living in permanent villages while growing primarily corn, beans, and squash, along with some pumpkins, tobacco and watermelons. Women did the farming. Men did the hunting and fighting. However, the Lakota Sioux, the tribe of most concern and interest to Jefferson, had changed far more. They, and the Cheyenne, were both originally from around Fargo and further east into Minnesota. However, as they acquired horses, they moved west onto the prairie where they fully adopted a horse culture, around 1700. They stopped farming and became buffalo hunting nomads living in easily movable teepee communities as they migrated further west to the Missouri River. Both tribes, like the Cherokee in North Carolina and northern Georgia, had developed a culture based on war with other tribes, and had become fierce warriors.

By 1750, the Cheyenne had moved all the way to the Black Hills and had taken them from the Kiowa, while the Sioux controlled the land east of the Missouri River. Around 1780, a smallpox epidemic swept through the northern plains devastating (killing about 80%) those farming tribes in permanent villages like the Arikara and Mandan, while having little effect on the nomadic Cheyenne and Lakota Sioux. Around that time the Lakota Sioux moved across the Missouri River and then on to the Black Hills, which they took from the Cheyenne. Some claim the smallpox epidemic was a major factor in the Sioux being able to move west across the Missouri, by clearing out the resistant tribes, so they could then move on to the Black Hills. Others claim the Sioux took the Black Hills before the smallpox epidemic. In any case, by the time the Corps arrived in 1804, the Sioux covered a wide swath reaching from east of the Missouri River to the Black Hills. The Cheyenne, after being kicked out of the Black Hills, moved further west into the Powder River Basin, pushing aside the Crow (also decimated by smallpox). The Lakota Sioux had become the ascendent tribe of the northern great plains, feared by the rest, even though, before horses, there had been no Lakota Sioux on those plains.

In the Corp's dealing with Indians *it would be impossible to say which side was more ignorant of the other.*" Lewis, in his stump speech to each tribe, promoted benefits of peace between the tribes and commerce with the USA, while also telling the Indians they were now a part of the USA. However, for the tribes, the idea of peace with other tribes was a nonstarter. Their primary occupations were hunting buffalo and raiding and fighting with other tribes. They felt that if they stopped raiding other tribes to steal horses and people, how would young warriors develop the skills and prestige needed to become chiefs as the current chiefs died off? They would be left leaderless. Instead, (much like the Pokanoket at Plymouth in 1621) they wanted the Corps' help defeating other tribes, or at least arms to aid in the fights. Even beyond the language barrier, there was a lot of misunderstanding and talking past each other so that neither side grasped how little was understood about the other.

Captain Lewis' efforts to make friends with the Sioux did not go well. They met a band of about 900 living in a hundred teepees (the first teepees seen by white Americans) that had just completed a raid on the Omaha in which they had killed 75 warriors and taken 48 women and children captive. Although things started out well, with Lewis being treated with great deference, the Sioux had no interest in the beads and shiny medals presented to them as gifts nor in making peace with the Omaha. They wanted whiskey and arms. Both Lewis and Clark were quick to get their back up at any perceived slight. With weapons drawn on both sides, Lewis barely managed to restrain himself enough to jump back into the boat and shove off before shots were fired. They had utterly failed in achieving Jefferson's goal of good relations with the Sioux.

Each tribe they met wanted help combating the Sioux, and each other. They all expected gifts; and were largely disappointed in what Lewis offered. They all expressed interest in friendship with President Jefferson as he was explained to them. Another wave of smallpox had gone through the region just a year or two before the Corps got there. They saw many abandoned villages with earth-lodge dwellings and crop fields, but no people. The once mighty Arikara (about 30,000 strong), that had been reduced by about 80% in the first wave of smallpox 25 years before, was further reduced down to just three villages in this second wave.

As the Corps camped with the Arikara, who had never seen a black person before, they were fascinated by York, Clark's black slave, who had a great time playing with Indian children. They called him *"the big Medicine."* The Arikara had an interesting belief, also held by the Mandan, that a man's strength and hunting prowess could be passed to another man through having sex with the same woman. Since the men of the Corps were seen as having great strength and power, young warriors brought their wives to the troops of the Corps. One sergeant noted that *"some of their women are very handsome and clean."* Whether or not the Indians got any power from these exchanges, STDs were soon rampant among the Corps.

When the Corps reached their destination for winter, the Mandan villages north of current Bismarck, they discovered that smallpox had reduced the Mandan to just two villages. However, these villages were still a hub of fur trading activity as many other tribes, as well as French Canadian and British fur traders, still came that fall. It was a busy place. There were also three Hidatsa villages nearby, so that there were about 4,000 Indian residents there, plus the visitors.

The Corps managed to establish excellent relations with the Mandan. They built a fort nearby and stayed for five months. *"The neighbors got along just fine. The chiefs and captains, warriors and men called on one another, went hunting together, traded extensively, enjoyed sexual relations with the same women on a regular basis, joked, and talked – as best they could through the language barrier – about what they knew."* Lewis and Clark learned all they could about what was to the west up the Missouri River and took careful notes. One of the soldiers was a skilled blacksmith. He was able to keep the whole company in corn throughout the winter as he made numerous repairs and fashioned new tools and weapons out of old hunks of iron for the Indians. It also contributed to very positive relationships with the Hidatsa as well as the Mandan, despite efforts by both tribes to undercut each other's relationship with the Corps.

In an odd twist, about 20 years later, the first battle against northern plains Indians by a unit of the USA army, with the aid of the Lakota Sioux, would be a crushing defeat of the Arikara. Not long thereafter, the Lakota Sioux would defeat and subjugate what remained of the Arikara, Mandan, and Hidatsa, so that they had sole control of all the upper Missouri River in what is now the Dakotas, and on into Montana.

Shortly after arriving at the Mandan villages, Lewis met a French trapper, Toussaint Charbonneou, a man in his mid-forties, who owned two teenage *"squaws"* (wives), who had been stolen from bands of Shoshone in the mountains west of the Missouri headwaters by a Hidatsa raiding party looking for horses and slaves. Charbonneou had won the two girls in a bet with the raiders who had captured them. Lewis signed up Charbonneou and one of his slave wives, Sacagawea, who was about fifteen years old and six months pregnant, to go with them. The two of them moved into the fort with the Corps. Lewis wanted Sacagawea because he needed someone who would be able to translate when they got to the Shoshone in those western mountains where they would need to buy horses to take them over the continental divide. Sacagawea spoke a little Hidatsa, as did her husband, who could then talk to Drouillard in French, who could translate into English. What could go wrong in those exchanges? There is apparently no record of how Charbonneou disposed of his other young slave wife. In February, Lewis, who also served as the expedition's doctor, helped deliver Sacagawea's baby, Jean Baptiste Charbonneou. He was nicknamed Pomp or Pompy by the crew.

Lewis had planned on sending a portion of the Corps back to St. Louis in the fall soon after they arrived at the Mandan villages. However, the river froze over before he could get things ready. So, on April 7, 1805, the expedition split with a party of seven headed downstream in the keelboat for St. Louis, while the rest headed upstream toward the Pacific Ocean.

On the keelboat, Lewis sent a 45,000-word handwritten report to President Jefferson describing all they had observed and done. He also sent 108 botanical specimens and 68 mineral samples, each with detailed written descriptions that included where they were found. Also included were skeletons, horns, and/or skins of numerous animals and birds that were new, along with detailed writeups on each. He also sent live magpies and prairie dogs. There were also many other letters and reports, along with a detailed map, prepared by Clark, showing all the area they had covered along the Missouri. It was a scientific expedition. He told Jefferson that they expected to make it to the Pacific Ocean and back to the Mandan villages by fall, and then return home.

His report to Jefferson included the following characterizations of the Mandan:

These are the most friendly, well disposed Indians inhabiting the Missouri. They are brave, humane, and hospitable.

His description of the Sioux was far different.

These are the vilest miscreants of a savage race, and must ever remain the pirates of the Missouri, until such measures are pursued by our government, as will make them feel a dependence on its will for their supply of merchandise.

However, due to disease and intertribal warfare with the Sioux, the Mandan were reduced from about 10,000 in 1750 to only about 150 by 1830, while the Sioux were on the rise.

Up out of the river channel, the open prairie seemed to extend forever without a single tree or shrub to be seen because the Indians set fire to the prairie every spring. In a letter to his mother, Lewis wrote the following about the land they were in.

This immence river so far as we have yet ascended, waters one of the farest portions of the globe, nor do I believe that there is in the universe a similar extent of country, equally fertile, well watered, and intersected by such a number of navigable streams. I had been led to believe that the open prarie contrey was barren, steril and sandy: but on the contrary I found it fertile to the extreem, the soil being from one to 20 feet in debth, consisting of a fine black loam with a luxuriant growth of grass and other vegitables.

Those going upstream with Lewis and Clark were in six dugout canoes (with three men with paddles in each) and two larger pirogues (with six oarsmen in each, along with most of the equipment and supplies). Lewis usually walked while Clark stayed with the boats. They had one teepee that they would set up each night. The two captains, Sacajawea, her baby, and her husband slept in the teepee, while the rest of the men slept in the open. Shortly after their departure upriver, Lewis wrote the following in his journal:

We are now about to penetrate a country at least two thousand miles in width, on which the foot of civillized man has never trodden; the good or evil it had in store for us was for experiment yet to determine, and these little vessells contained every article by which we were to expect to subsist or defend ourselves. However...Entering as I do the most confident hope of succeading in a voyage which had formed a darling project of mine for the last ten years, I could but esteem this moment of my departure as among the most happy of my life.

It is remarkable that, from the time they left the Mandan villages on April 7, 1805, until they reached the continental divide at Lemhi pass, along the Montana/Idaho border, on August 13, they had no contact with Indians. It had been a wild, treacherous, and exhausting trip through incredible country with grizzly bears and numerous huge herds of bison, but Indian contact had played no part in it. When they reached the area known as Three Forks, where three rivers joined to form the Missouri River, Sacagawea showed the Corps the place where her band had been attacked when she was stolen at age eleven. She said four men, four women, and several boys were killed, while four boys and the rest of the females were taken prisoner by the Hidatsa.

The chief of the band of Shoshone Indians they first encountered as they crossed the continental divide turned out to be Sacagawea's brother. She also met some others she knew and had a glorious reunion full of tears and hugs. Lewis described it this way:

Shortly after Capt. Clark arrived with the Intrepreter Charbono, and the Indian woman, who proved to be a sister of Chief Cameahwait. The meeting of those people was really affecting, particularly between Sah cah-gar-we-ah and an Indian woman, who had been taken prisoner at the same time with her, and who afterwards escaped from her captors and rejoined her nation.

Clark described it this way:

The Intertrepeter & Squar who were before me at Some distance danced for the joyful Sight, and She made signs to me that they were her nation.

That band was on its way down into the head waters of the Missouri River to hunt bison, despite the risks of clashes with the Blackfeet or Hidatsa, because there were no bison west of the continental divide. They were near starvation.

Lewis and Drouillard led a party of about 15 Indians, along with many horses, back to help haul the Corps equipment and supplies up the mountain and over the continental divide. Along the way Drouillard had gone ahead and killed a deer and proceeded to dress it by cutting it open and leaving a pile of entrails and organs on the ground as he hung up the deer. When the Indians arrived, they quickly fell on the organs and entrails and began to eat them raw. Lewis wrote:

Each had a piece of some description and all eating most ravenously. Some were eating the kidnies the spleen and liver and blood running from the corners of their mouths, others were in a similar situation with the paunch and guts... one of the last had provided himself with about nine feet of the small guts one end of which he was chewing on while with his hands he was squezzing the contents out at the other. I really did not untill now think that human nature ever presented in a shape so clearly allyed to brute creation. I viewed these poor starved divils with pity and compassion.

Drouillard killed another deer with the same result. Lewis gave the Indians all but one quarter of the meat from each dear. Instead of waiting for it to be cooked, they ate it all raw as well. Finally, after Drouillard killed a third deer, the Indians seemed to have satisfied their hunger.

As the Corps looked west from the Divide, much to their surprise and disappointment, there was an endless series of ridges. The Indians said the river just below them to the west (the Salmon River – later nicknamed the River of No Return), was impassible because of numerous rapids and falls. Clark went down and confirmed that was true. There was no easy passage from the Missouri River to the Columbia River draining to the west. They had just learned some very bad news for Jefferson. But they were yet to learn just how bad that crossing would be.

Only one of the Shoshone, Old Toby, had ever been through those mountains (the Bitterroot) to where the Nez Perce lived on the other side. However, they said there was a way because the Nez Perce also came over to hunt buffalo in the Missouri River drainage because there was very little game in the mountains. Old Toby agreed to be their guide. By the time they finally broke out of the mountains, starving and emaciated (they had eaten the last of their candles and were beginning to eat their horses even though they were essential to travel) and found the Nez Perce, it was September 22. It had been almost seven weeks since they first met the Shoshone.

The Nez Perce had horses by the hundreds, more than any other tribe in North America, and unlike most tribes, practiced selective breeding. But they would not eat them. They lived primarily on deer, elk, fish (mostly salmon) and roots, plus the annual trips of the most eastern bands into the Missouri drainage to hunt buffalo. They did not farm. Nor had they ever seen Europeans before. They were also rich in dogs, so Lewis often bought dogs to supplement their diet the entire time they were in the Columbia River drainage. However, Clark hated eating dogs. Lewis liked dog because it had more fat in it than elk. He thought elk meat was too lean.

The Nez Perce could have easily killed the Corps and taken everything they had. Instead, they nursed them back to health and helped them build canoes for the trip downriver. They even entertained them by torching sap-dripping fir trees that would then explode like Roman candles. The fact that the Corps had Sacagawea and her baby Pomp with them made all the difference. No war party would ever include a woman and her infant child, which convinced each Indian band they encountered of their peaceable intentions. The Nez Perce proved to be fast friends. They were scrupulously honest and honorable. The Corps stayed with them again for a month on the return trip the next spring (1806) while waiting for the snow in the mountains to melt enough for them to cross. After providing the Corps 60 horses to go east, the Nez Perce came and rescued them after Lewis, ignoring their warnings, left too early and got bogged down in deep snow. They then even provided guides all the way to the Missouri River.

As they had traveled west downriver toward the Pacific that fall (1805), all the Nez Perce bands they encountered along the Clearwater, Snake, and Columbia Rivers were also friendly and helpful. Then they left Nez Perce country and moved into the area of the Chinookan (who were at war with the Nez Perce) just above The Dalles, where the terrain transitioned from open plains to forest. The Chinookan would mill around and steal anything that was put down for an instant. There were villages all along the riverbank, so they had to remain ever vigilant. Still, they were constantly finding things missing. Only through enormous self-restraint did Lewis manage to keep himself, or any of the Corps, from firing on them. He and his men surely wanted to. But they knew it could start a fight they had little chance of winning. The Chinookan did not farm. However, thanks to all the fish in the river, they lived in permanent villages.

Once the Corps got to the Pacific Ocean, Clark described it as:

Ocian 4142 Miles from the Mouth of the Missouri R.

I am not sure just how he measured that so precisely. There they met the Clatsop Indians, a branch of the Chinookan, and found a place to settle in for the winter. It was in an area with good elk hunting and within reach of the coast where they could set up making salt from ocean water (they had long since run out). It was a long bleak winter.

On the return trip, Lewis, along with three of his men, had the Corps' only encounter with Blackfoot Indians, a fierce nomadic tribe. It happened well north of the Missouri River and was disastrous. They ended up killing two teenage boys and stealing a horse so they could escape and get back to the river as fast as possible. It was their only fatal encounter in the whole trip.

By the time the corps got back to the Mandan villages, where they dropped off Charbonneau and Sacagawea, Pomp was 18 months old. And Clark had become very fond of this little toddler. He offered to adopt him.

Clark did end up paying for Pomp's education and enabled him to spend a few of his young adult years in Europe.

From the perspective of the new USA, the Corps of Discovery was a colossal success. From the time they first headed up the Missouri River until they returned to St. Louis, it was almost two and a half years. From the time Lewis said goodbye to Jefferson until he returned to Washington to report to Jefferson in person, it was three and a half years. The entire crew were immediately celebrities and well compensated (except York who remained Clark's slave). The scientific aspects of the trip were hugely successful while the nation's imagination of stretching to the Pacific Ocean was the chatter of the day. The fact that nothing had been heard from the Corps since the keelboat returned over a year and a half before, and most people believed the expedition had been lost, only added to the enthusiasm of the nation upon their return.

Some, in the last few decades, have criticized Lewis, who grew up in a slave owning family and personally owned many slaves, for his bigotry towards Indians. However, comparing his views of Indians to his views of Africans, Stephen Ambrose describes Lewis this way:

When he talked about Indian "nations" he meant the word just as he applied it to European peoples. He was keenly aware of the differences between tribes, a subject he wrote about at length and with insight. He liked some Indians, admired others extravagantly, pitied some, despised a few. His response to native Americans was based on what he saw and was completely different from his response to African Americans. With regard to blacks, he made no distinctions between them, made no study of them, had no thought that they could be of benefit to America in any capacity other than slave labor.

One reason for including so much here about the Corps of Discovery is that, while we often lump Native Americans into a homogenous group, they were not. There was at least as much diversity within North American Indians as within Europeans, from Greece to Norway, from Portugal to the Ural Mountains. Indians spoke many more different languages. And, just like Europeans, some tribes fought each other while being friends with others. The Crow supported the U.S. army in its wars with the Cheyenne and Sioux. Why? Because experience had taught them it was in their self-interest to do so: that they had less to fear from white settlers and the army than they did from the Cheyenne and Sioux. Also, we see that, thanks to horses and disease, life for all these Indian tribes had been dramatically altered by European contact with America (even those who had never yet seen a European) long before they ever encountered Lewis and Clark.

This probably the best place to point out the irony of various claims to the Black Hills. In 1868, in an effort to protect white settlers on the Oregon Trail and to end intertribal warfare, The U.S. government entered into the Fort Laramie Treaty, which created the Great Sioux Reservation that included the Black Hills, protecting them *"forever"* from white settlement. In 1874, just six years later, gold was discovered in the Black Hills by Custer's army while on its way to getting wiped out at Little Big Horn. For a year the government tried to keep white miners from moving in, then gave up to the inevitable rush. To make a long story short, the USA retook control of the Black Hills in 1876 during a new war against the Sioux and Cheyenne. Over a century later, in 1980, the Supreme Court held that the government violated the 1868 treaty when they took back the Black Hills just eight years after granting it to the Sioux nation forever. It ordered remuneration to the tribe of over 100 million dollars. The Sioux nation refused to accept payment and is holding out for the return of the Black Hills. That payment account, which continues to accrue interest now has over a billion dollars in it. Yet, the Lakota Sioux had taken the Black Hills by force, kicking out the residents that were already there, in the late 1770s – at the same time the thirteen British Colonies were fighting the Revolutionary War. The Sioux colonized this area based on the same Right of Conquest principle (might makes right) used by various peoples around the world for millennia, including Europe's colonization of the rest of the world. The Sioux then occupied the Black Hills for less than a hundred years before they were removed. But for Columbus, followed by Spanish horses, the Lakota Sioux would have still been in the Red River Valley around Fargo growing beans and corn, and would have never seen the Black Hills, which they now claim as eternal sacred ground. History takes strange twists.

PRESIDENT ANDREW JACKSON – The presidential election of 1828 was the first where virtually all adult white males in all the states were eligible to vote. Limitations tied to property ownership or paying taxes had been eliminated. While restrictions had changed over the years, there were still several northern states that allowed free black males to vote. In that election, Andrew Jackson handily defeated the incumbent John Quincy Adams to become the seventh president of the USA. It had been 40 years since Washington was first elected. Jackson was the first person to become president who was neither a wealthy Virginia planter nor a Harvard educated Adams: the first common man to do so. He was living proof that force of personality could be enough to elevate someone to the presidency regardless of the circumstances of family or birth, even if opposed by powerful people. In fact, like many in the ruling class, Thomas Jefferson's reaction to the idea of Jackson becoming president was:

I feel much alarmed at the prospect of seeing General Jackson President. He is one of the most unfit men I know of for such a place. He has very little respect for law or constitutions... He is a dangerous man.

But the common people loved him. He was elected two years after Jefferson's death and was our first populist president. He detested inherited privilege and believed in pushing the locus of power down the social scale. He not only ushered in and shaped today's Democratic Party but what would become known as Jacksonian Democracy as well. He had been born very poor and had no intention of dying poor. And he did not.

So, what were his roots? King James, who was king of both England and Scotland, planted a colony, predominated by lowlander Scots, in the north of Ireland shortly after becoming King in 1603. His goal was to subdue the unruly Irish, who were considered savages by the English. These lowlander Scots were battle-hardened through centuries of conflict with the highlanders and the English. However, in Ireland, they found themselves battling for land that was hardly better than what they had left in Scotland. After a century, some began to leave for America, where they became known as Scotch-Irish. Because they were poor, fiercely individualistic, and disliked government, they largely settled in or near the Appalachian Mountains where the sloping land was cheap (or they could just move in as squatters and begin clearing forest) and the colonial governments had little reach. Since they had been battling Irish and highlanders for generations, they had little fear of Indians as they moved in.

Andrew Jackson left Ireland with his wife and two young sons in 1765 and settled near his wife's sisters in the Waxhaw area along the North Carolina-South Carolina border. In early 1767, Andrew died from an injury he received while clearing land for his family farm. A couple of months later his wife gave birth to their third son. She named him Andrew, in honor of his dead father. So young Andrew was fatherless from the day he was born. His mother moved her young family in with one of her sisters. Life was hard. And they worked hard to compensate for their support by her sister's family. Andrew *"was a wild child, with an almost unimaginable will and a defiant temper."* Andrew's mother sent him for a few years to a local common school where he learned his letters and numbers and was even exposed to a little Greek and Latin.

The Revolutionary War came to the Jacksons in 1780, when young Andrew was thirteen. The Carolinas were deeply divided by the war with the coastal areas full of Tories while the west was dominated by patriots (rebels). The infamous Tarleton, with his green coated Tory dragoons, stormed through the Waxhaw district destroying everyone and everything in their path. Andrew's family managed to escape but lived in hiding for months before returning to their destroyed homestead. His oldest brother had joined the patriot forces and was soon killed. With that, though only thirteen, Andrew began serving as a scout and courier for the patriots. At fourteen, he began riding with them as an irregular soldier. Then he and his remaining brother were captured and sent to a horrendous prison camp while the patriot forces were suffering terrible losses. Smallpox soon ravaged their prison camp.

His mother managed to find where her two remaining boys had been taken and to arrange a prisoner swap to free them. His brother died of smallpox two days after his mother got them home, while Andrew became gravely ill. Though he overcame the fevers, delirium, and pustules that racked his body for a time, he was incapacitated for several months. After he began to improve, his mother left to try to rescue from a prison camp two nephews she had raised almost as her own. On the way, she contracted cholera and died within days. So, Andrew, at fourteen, with his parents and two brothers all dead, was alone in the world. Before his mother left to find her nephews, she had said the following to Andrew, her only remaining son:

Andrew, if I should not see you again, I wish you to remember and treasure up some things I have already said to you: In this world you will always have to make your own way. To do that you must have friends. You can make friends by being honest, and you can keep them by being steadfast. You must keep in mind that friends worth having will in the long run expect as much from you as they give to you. To forget an obligation or be ungrateful for a kindness is a base crime – not merely a fault or a sin, but an actual crime. Men guilty of it sooner or later must suffer the penalty. In personal conduct be polite, but never obsequious. No one will respect you more than you esteem yourself. Avoid quarrels as long as you can without yielding to imposition. But sustain your manhood always. Never bring a suit at law for assault and battery or for defamation. The law affords no remedy for such outrages that can satisfy the feelings of a true man. Never wound the feelings of others. Never brook wanton outrage upon your own feelings. If you ever have to vindicate your feelings or defend your honor, do it calmly. If angry, first wait till your wrath cools before you proceed.

Whether or not she actually said all that just that way, that was the way he remembered it. And it is what guided his life. He later said of this message from his mother:

Gentlemen, her last words have been the law of my life. I might about as well have been penniless, as I was already homeless and friendless.

The memory of my mother and her teachings were, after all, the only capital I had to start in life, and on that capital, I have made my way.

Just what the law was in this new nation was rather problematic. Most of the colonies' lawyers had been Tories, with many leaving after independence. Further, each state was writing a constitution, which created a whole new framework of laws while English common law, which formed much of the day-to-day framework for lawyers, had to be reinterpreted in light of the new constitutions. So, the law was whatever lawyers could convince judges to say it was. After apprenticing with two different attorneys, beginning when he was seventeen, Jackson stood before two judges of the North Carolina Superior Court of Law and Enquiry and passed his examination to become a licensed attorney at the age of twenty, the same year a new constitution for the USA was under development. That was two years before North Carolina ratified that new federal constitution and joined the new USA under that constitution.

For a few years after the revolution, North Carolina lost interest in trying to manage the settlers and settlements that had moved west of the mountains into the Tennessee River Valley. Then, in 1788, as the new Constitution was being ratified by some states, North Carolina decided to assert jurisdiction west of the mountains again and sent 21-year-old Andrew Jackson west to be its prosecutor there. He settled into the Nashville area in 1789. In addition to his legal duties for the state, he speculated in land and merchandise, including slaves. He participated in the 1796 constitutional convention for the new state of Tennessee (he suggested naming it after the river) and became the first to represent the new state in the House of Representatives later that year. In 1797, he was elevated to the Senate. However, he resigned after three months. Again, in the words of H. W. Brands:

After three months in the House and another three in the Senate, Jackson discovered he wasn't cut out for politics, at least not legislative politics. His was an executive temperament. He could make decisions far more easily than he could make compromises. He had much greater confidence in his own judgement than in that of others. Action came naturally, patience harder. He believed a single honest man more likely to find truth than a committee. He was a born leader and couldn't make himself into a follower.

Jackson was a hard man. He participated in at least three duels, including one with the governor of Tennessee. There would have been more had the other party not backed out. In one, he killed his opponent, who had fired first and wounded Jackson, who still stood his ground and got off the kill shot despite his own chest wound. Jackson was also severely wounded in an 1813 hotel gunfight. He carried that bullet in his shoulder for the rest of his life. He was totally devoted throughout his life to his wife, who happened to be another man's teenage wife when he first met her. That caused issues since he would not tolerate any comments disparaging her.

In 1812, he became major general of the Tennessee militia. Under orders, he took his untrained recruits downriver from Nashville to Natchez, 500 miles on their first deployment. Once there, he drilled his men into a fighting force in the middle of winter while they awaited further orders. Then Jackson received orders from the War Department saying they were no longer needed there and that they should immediately disband, return all government equipment and arms, and make their own way home. Jackson was furious. And disobeyed the order since it would leave all his troops stranded there, 500 miles from home. Instead, he pledged his own resources, if necessary, to supply and feed the troops and pay them as they marched home as a unit. *"His pledge of his personal resources on behalf of his men won him their love and admiration as nothing else could have. He might be cashiered, might lose his home and farm, but he would get them home safely. Now they saw in him a toughness, a resilience on which they could rely. Someone compared him to a hickory branch: thin but impossible to break."* He was given the nickname Old Hickory. The Nashville newspaper wrote: *"Long will the General live in the memory of the volunteers of West Tennessee for his benevolent, humane, and fatherly treatment to his soldiers. If gratitude and love can reward him, General Jackson has them."*

Many Indian tribes along the western frontier, from the Great Lakes to the Gulf Coast, saw the War of 1812 as an opportunity to push back against the western movement of the USA by siding with the British in this war. Among these was a branch of Creek Indians that called themselves the Red Sticks. They were led by a chief who was more white than Indian (3/4 Scotch) as they went to war with all settlers along the southern frontier as well as starting a civil war with the rest of the Creeks. Many terrified settlers had gathered at a ramshackle fort northeast of Mobile that was poorly defended in the late summer of 1813. There, they were attacked by over a thousand Red Sticks. As one survivor described it: *"There were 553 citizens and soldiers and among the number about 453 women and children...Only 13 escaped."* The army major who was sent to bury the dead described it this way: *"Indians, negroes, white men, women, and children lay in promiscuous ruin. All were scalped, and the females of every age were butchered in a manner which neither decency nor language will permit me to describe. The main building was burned to ashes, which were filled with bones. The plains and the woods around were covered with dead bodies."*

With that, President James Madison called the Tennessee volunteers, led by Jackson, back into service to deal with the Indian problem. And deal with it, he did. To make a long story short, he eliminated the Red Sticks over the next eight months in three major battles. In the first, while destroying a Creek Indian town, 176 were killed, and 80 were taken prisoner while Jackson picked up one young Indian boy and took him home for his wife, Rachel, to raise. In the second, 300 Red Sticks were killed while losing only 17 of his men. As they continued to seek out the Red Sticks, he executed one of his soldiers, a 17-year-old recruit, for getting belligerent with one of his officers at breakfast after a long, cold night on guard duty. There were no more disciplinary issues among his troops. And in the final battle, in March 1814, over 800 Red Sticks were killed. It was, and still remains, the bloodiest battle ever fought in the Nation's history between armies of the USA and Indian tribes. In the last two battles, Jackson's troops had received considerable and essential help from friendly Creek Indians who were also battling the Red Sticks. Yet, in the peace settlement that followed, Jackson treated those Indians who had fought with him no better than those who had not. They all lost land.

With that, President Madison made him a general in the regular army. He would go on to take his troops into Spanish Florida, against direct orders from the President, under the thin pretext of chasing escaping Indians. He would also win the Battle of New Orleans, as it turned out, after the peace treaty had already been signed in London. And his popularity continued to grow as he burnished his reputation as a fierce Indian fighter.

Jackson had always hated banks, banknotes, and paper money. He believed in hard currency. And he hated debt, including the National Debt. When he was elected president in the landslide election of 1828, he was finally in a position to do something about both. And he did. He held up popular projects to pay off the debt. In fact, the last years of his administration are the only ones in the entire history of the USA that the country has been debt-free. And he killed the Bank of the United States which was first put in place by Alexander Hamilton to oversee and stabilize private financial institutions. It had lapsed in 1811, resulting in financial turmoil. So, Congress granted a 20-year charter to the Second Bank of the United States in 1816. In 1832, Jackson vetoed a 20-year Congressional extension of that Bank's charter. Then, in 1833, he withdrew all federal funds from the bank and let its charter expire in 1836. With that, boom and bust cycles with numerous private bank failings *"was to become as American as apple pie."*

Jackson also had a serious conflict with the Supreme Court. The Cherokee tribe had settled in northern Georgia in accordance with treaties that had been approved by the Senate. As they did so, they took on many white ways. They had *"devised a written version of the Cherokee language, and they produced a newspaper, books, and other accouterments of what the whites called civilization. They prospered alongside their white neighbors, engaging in agriculture and commerce."* Their white neighbors became increasingly jealous and coveted their land. So, Georgia passed a series of laws blatantly designed to make life miserable for the Cherokee in an effort to get them to move west across the Mississippi as other tribes in the area had done. The Cherokee had learned enough white ways that, instead of going to war, they took Georgia to court on the claim that they were an independent nation beyond the jurisdiction of Georgia laws.

By the time the case reached the Supreme Court in 1832, John Marshal had been Chief Justice for 31 years. In that time, he had firmly established the Supreme Court as a co-equal branch of government with the authority to interpret the Nation's laws and even negate laws that it determined were in conflict with the Constitution. The Court, with Marshal writing, ruled against the tribe. In doing so it declared that Indian tribes are *"dependent domestic nations,"* the term that still dominates Indian law today. In response, the tribe went back to court; this time arguing that Georgia's laws were invalid because they conflicted with Federal treaties ratified by the Senate governing relations with the tribe. On those grounds, with Marshal writing, they won.

President Jackson not only refused to take any action against Georgia in response to this decision saying Georgia was in conflict with Federal law and treaties, but he also actively encouraged Georgia in their efforts against the Cherokee and told the tribe they needed to move west. He simply was not convinced that *"the decisions of the courts bound the executive branch."* And he felt strongly that it was in the best interests for the Cherokee to move west or they would face *"utter annihilation."* H.W. Brands put it this way:

> *The harsh fact of the matter was that Georgia was determined to expel the Cherokees and take their land. Jackson knew this, and he refused to prevent it.*

The result was the infamous trail of tears as the Cherokee were forced to move to Oklahoma. When John Marshal died in 1835, after serving as Chief Justice of the Supreme Court for 34 years, Jackson appointed Roger Taney to that position. Taney would remain chief justice until his death in 1864 and would author the infamous Dred Scott decision.

FLORIDA – Though there were no permanent settlements there until St. Augustine in 1565, Spain had claimed Florida for 250 years before trading it to Britain in exchange for the return of Cuba (which Britain had recently captured), at the end of the Seven Years War (the French and Indian War in North America) in 1763. The British gave it back to Spain 20 years later as part of the 1783 Paris Treaty, ending the Revolutionary War and creating the USA.

Although there were other scattered settlements, including Indians and escaped black slaves from South Carolina and Georgia, the primary settlements were St. Augustine on the east coast of the Florida peninsula, and Pensacola and Mobile on the Gulf Coast. The boundary between Florida and Georgia had always been ambiguous and contested. In addition to minor incursions, The USA invaded Spanish Florida twice. In the first, during the War of 1812, the USA took control of Mobile and never gave it back. In 1817, General Andrew Jackson chased Seminole Indians deep into Florida. By then Spain was dealing with revolts in South America.

At that point, John Quincy Adams, who was serving as Secretary of State under President Monroe, made his mark as a statesman. He negotiated with Spain what became known as the Adams-Onis Treaty in 1819, that 1) gave all of Florida to the USA, 2) extended Louisiana west to the Sabine River, 3) Established the Red River and Arkansas River as new fixed boundaries between The USA Missouri Territory and Spanish Mexico, and 4) established the 42nd parallel as the northern boundary between Spanish California and the Oregon Territory which the USA and Britain jointly claimed. These boundaries had all been very vague until then (The year before, 1818, a treaty with Britain fixed the boundary between the USA and Canada west from Lake of the Woods to the Oregon Territory as the 49th parallel). With that, Florida was now a new territory within the USA. In 1823, the Monroe Doctrine, which was largely developed by John Quincy Adams as Secretary of State, was announced to the world. It announced the USA's position against European or Asian interference in the Americas.

With General Andrew Jackson as the first military governor of the Florida territory, several groups of escaped black slaves fled to Cuba or other Caribbean islands. Three Indian wars with the Seminoles occurred over the next 20 years as more and more were forced to relocate west of the Mississippi, while a few continued to hide out in the Everglades as white settlers moved in and established sugar and cotton plantations. During the wars in the 1830s, while Jackson was president, he put Zachary Taylor in charge of the fight and gave him the following advice:

The commanding general ought to find where their women are, and with his combined forces by forced marches reach and capture them. This done, they will at once surrender.

Apparently, it worked. When Florida was admitted as the 27th state in 1845, there were very few Indians left. By then, cotton and sugar plantations dominated the economy, while almost half of Florida's total population were black slaves.

TEXAS – For over three centuries, Spain claimed Texas, though France did poke around a little in that time. Yet, throughout the eighteenth century, the dominant force in Texas was the Comanche. The ink was barely dry on the 1819 Adams-Onis treaty, clearly defining the boundary between Spanish and American interests from the Gulf to the Pacific, when Mexico won its independence from Spain in 1821.

The 1824 constitution of Mexico liberalized immigration law. By then, new immigrants from the USA had begun arriving. They were mostly from the southern states and brought black slaves with them. By 1825, there were 443 black slaves in East Texas. In 1829, Mexico issued a national edict outlawing slavery with a one-year grace period for slaves to be freed. Slave owners got around that by making them indentured servants for life. In 1830, Mexico outlawed immigration from the USA. Still, by 1836, there were 5,000 black slaves in Texas. That year, the war for Texas independence broke out, with its most famous battle occurring at the Alamo in San Antonio. Independence was soon won. However, the boundary between Texas and Mexico remained in dispute, with Texas claiming an area along its western edge, beginning with the area between the Nueces and Rio Grande Rivers along the Gulf Coast (from Corpus Cristi to Brownsville) and stretching north. While Mexico didn't really recognize independence at all, it certainly still claimed all that disputed land on the west side of Texas, where virtually all the European inhabitants had come up from Mexico and spoke Spanish.

Texans immediately convened the first Congress of the Republic of Texas, which overturned the prohibition on slavery, outlawed the freeing of slaves, and barred free blacks from living in Texas. More immigrants from the USA began to pour in and bring their slaves with them. In that same time period of the late 1830s, thousands of German immigrants poured into North Texas. By the presidential election of 1844, annexation of Texas had become a national issue. James K. Polk campaigned on a platform of annexing Texas and resolving the dispute with the British over Oregon in favor of the USA. In March 1845, just after Polk's inauguration as President, Congress narrowly approved the annexation of Texas and granted it statehood if Texas agreed. Then Texas approved a constitution and voted to become part of the USA. So, Texas became a state on the same day it was annexed. One of the primary reasons Texas wanted annexation was that it had huge debts, and Congress had agreed to assume much of that debt if it joined the USA.

PRESIDENT JAMES K. POLK AND "MANIFEST DESTINY" –
The term Manifest Destiny first appeared in the press to promote the USA's westward expansion to the Pacific shortly after Polk was inaugurated in 1845. While the nation had been pressing ever further west from its beginning, the invention of the Telegraph the previous year suddenly made the concept of one nation stretching from sea to shining sea seem a realistic (and inevitable?) possibility. Ever since the conflicts between Hamilton and Jefferson in the late eighteenth century, there had been two competing views of the future of the USA. The view of Jefferson, as carried on by Jackson and the Democratic party he created, was that of an agrarian society stretching ever further west. The party was strongest in the South, which had industrialized very little compared to the North by the 1840s. The view of Hamilton, which was still carried on by the Whig party, saw the growth of the USA much more in terms of qualitative economic improvement than quantitative expansion of territory. The party's strength was in the Northeast. Most Whigs had opposed the annexation of Texas and had little interest in further western expansion.

As one Whig put it: *"The United States ought to provide its less fortunate sister republics with support and assume the role of a sublime moral empire, with the mission to diffuse freedom by manifesting its fruits, not to plunder, crush, and destroy."* Slavery, an agrarian institution, was important to most Democrats and opposed by most Whigs. While the population of northern states were still predominantly farmers, they had smaller family farms that they worked with their own hands.

When the constitution was written in 1787, one of the compromises was that three-fifths of the number of slaves would be used in apportioning seats in the House of Representatives even though they could not vote. That gave the South a substantial advantage by giving it more representatives in Congress, and more presidential electoral votes, per voter. For 48 of the first 60 years of the USA, the president was a slave owner from the South. James K. Polk was one of them. And even one of those who was not, Martin Van Buren, was a democrat handpicked by Jackson. The only others were one term each for John Adams and then his son John Quincy Adams 24 years later. In short, there had been strong support from the Nation's President for slavery and western expansion throughout most of the first half of the nineteenth century.

The disputed Oregon territory, claimed by both Britain and the USA for decades, stretched west from the Continental Divide to Pacific Ocean from California (42nd parallel) on the south to Russian Alaska (54 degrees, 40 minutes) on the north. The British Hudson Bay Company had been working throughout the area trading furs with Indians and had established a trading post on north shore the Columbia River, across from the mouth of the Willamette River and named it Vancouver. By 1844, that post had been there for over 20 years while the company had about 700 employees spread across the Oregon territory. However, they were there on temporary assignments rather than as permanent settlers. The Oregon Trail, from Independence, Missouri to the Willamette Valley south of the Vancouver trading post (now Portland), opened around 1840, so that, by 1844, there were 5,000 immigrants from the USA (mostly from Missouri) there. They were a rowdy, aggressive bunch that was quite willing to fight with both the British fur traders and the local Indians. In the 1844 presidential campaign, Polk's democratic party platform argued for all of Oregon, with the slogan *"Fifty-Four, Forty or Fight!"* and was supported by both southern and northern democrats. After Polk won, the Hudson Bay Company abandoned its Vancouver trading post on the Columbia and retreated to Victoria, on Vancouver Island.

California, on the other hand, had very few settlers from the USA. As the Spanish moved up the Pacific coast of Mexico, they initially thought California was a huge island as they sailed across the Gulf of California to settle in Baja. The Spanish named cities in California were settled by friars establishing missions within just a few years, beginning with San Diego in 1769 and ending with the San Francisco in 1776. Thus, almost all Europeans in California were Spanish speaking Mexicans. Mexico had banned the sale of land to Americans in 1842.

When James K. Polk won the 1844 election, he was 49 years old, making him the USA's youngest president to that point. Yet, he was a very accomplished politician who had already been Speaker of the House of Representatives (at age 40) and Governor of Tennessee. He turned out to be an extraordinarily successful and consequential president as well.

Mexico had long said that annexation of Texas would lead to war. Upon the USA annexing Texas in 1845, Polk's first year in office, Mexico broke diplomatic relations with the USA, while expressing a willingness to negotiate. Taking Texas into the USA meant its boundary dispute with Mexico over all the land between the Rio Grande and the Nueces River, and stretching north into southern Wyoming, was now a dispute between Mexico and the USA. However, there were virtually no English-speaking settlers in the disputed area, while there were over 50,000 Mexicans. The Texas claim, now assumed by the USA, was dubious at best.

Although feelings were running high in Congress that the USA should have all of Oregon, Polk privately coveted California far more than the Pacific northwest (acquisition of California was one of his four personal goals from the start, but he never publicly announced that). As the annexation of Texas was being finalized, he sent a delegation to negotiate with Mexico to resolve disputes. They were to insist on the Rio Grande as the boundary and offer to buy New Mexico and California. Yet, the delegation was labeled such that to receive them, Mexico would have to renew diplomatic relations with the USA, making it extremely difficult for

Mexico to even let them in the door without losing face. On the Oregon question, Polk's strategy with Britain was the opposite. In the words of Daniel Walker Howe:

Polk's strategy toward Mexico was precisely the converse of his strategy toward Britain. On Oregon, he wished to appear uncompromising but achieve a compromise. Regarding the issues with Mexico, however, he wished to seem reasonable and open to discussion while pressing uncompromising demands that would probably lead to war.

He succeeded on both counts while juggling the timing. By early 1846, The American public was very nervous about a war with Britain over Oregon as Polk sent his delegation to Mexico. Polk had secretly offered Britain a compromise on Oregon that would split the disputed territory along the 49th parallel (extending to the Pacific Ocean, the current boundary between the two countries in the Great Plains) and throwing in Vancouver Island to sweeten the pot. However, he insisted that, if acceptable, Britain would make the offer public as if it were coming from them. When the delegation to Mexico failed, as expected, Polk sent a small expeditionary patrol across the Nueces River and on down to the Rio Grande. Mexican calvary attacked the patrol, killing 16. Both nations then declared war. Again, in the words of Howe:

Depending on how the Oregon issue was playing out at any given moment, he slowed down or speeded up the confrontation with Mexico. In the end, the timing worked out just right for him. The British offered the Oregon compromise before learning of the fighting in the Rio Grande; Congress voted for war against Mexico before the Democratic expansionists had been disillusioned by the partition of Oregon.

So, the northern boundary of the USA was now set, from the Atlantic to the Pacific, while the USA went to war with Mexico, a fellow republic in North America, over a swath of disputed land along the Texas-Mexico border wherein the current population all spoke Spanish and considered themselves Mexicans. And the USA took the fight to Mexico, from the Gulf to the Pacific, and finally to Mexico City. Its capture ended the war less than two years after it began.

What did the USA gain from this war that began in April 1846 and ended in February 1848? All of California, Nevada, and Utah, two thirds of Colorado (the entire western and southern borders), almost all of New Mexico, the Oklahoma panhandle, and most of Arizona (north of the Gila River), in addition to the disputed area between the Rio Grande and Nueces Rivers within current Texas that was the primary justification for going to war. That is a lot of land. While much of it is desert, it also includes a beautiful coast, incredibly productive farmland, vast mountains and forests, extensive natural resources, and some of the most remarkable scenery in the world. Almost all of the entire area's current European inhabitants had come up from Mexico and spoke Spanish.

Was the war with Mexico justified? That is highly questionable. But it was an incredibly effective land grab! In short, this war epitomized the Right of Conquest principle in action. President Polk had, in less than three years, overseen the expansion of the USA to include all the areas from Houston to San Diego to Seattle to Salt Lake City and back to Houston, and more. Polk had two other significant accomplishments, both in 1846. Tariffs were significantly lowered, making the USA more of a player in international markets. Also, the Independent Treasury was established to help manage the nation's money supply independently of banking and financial systems. This helped ease the chaos created by the loss of the Bank of the United States a decade before thanks to President Jackson. It functioned until the creation of the Federal Reserve in 1913. In 1848, having accomplished all four of the big things he had set out for himself, President Polk honored the commitment he had made during his first campaign and did not seek reelection. In just one term, he had made an indelible mark upon the nation.

However, Texas still struggled with debt. In an 1850 compromise, Texas agreed to give up a large part of its claimed territory, comprising what is now parts of Colorado, Kansas, Oklahoma, New Mexico, and Wyoming for ten million dollars. That reduced Texas to its current boundaries.

In 1853, the USA and Mexico agreed to the Gadsden Purchase, which firmed up the boundary between the two nations and moved it further south, enlarging Arizona and New Mexico. That brought Yuma and Tucson into the USA, which was looking for a southern route for a transcontinental railroad now that California was a state. Many felt that the best possible route was to go through this area. Thus, the USA's current boundary for the contiguous 48 states had been achieved, and its geographical expansion from coast to coast had run its course. In just 50 years, between 1803 and 1853, the USA had obtained Florida, the Gulf Coast, and all the land west of the Mississippi to the Pacific Coast, so that it stretched from sea to shining sea.

The acquisition of California proved to be transformative for the USA since gold was discovered there just as the war was concluding. At the time of the war, there were about 8,000 Mexicans, 150,000 Indians, and only a few hundred English speaking Americans living in California. By 1849, the Gold Rush was on. And it had worldwide reach. California was admitted to the Union as a state in 1850 and included in the 1850 census (the records for San Francisco were lost in a fire, so it was not included). That census showed a total population of 92,597 (92.5% male), with only 8% having been born there. Two-thirds of the population came from other parts of the USA, and over 96% of them were male. The other 25% of the population (94% male) had been born in other countries, with many coming from China. Indians were not counted in the census. The census took another count of San Francisco in 1852. Thanks to the Gold Rush, San Francisco rapidly grew from a few hundred in 1846 to over 36,000 just six years later, while San Diego and Los Angeles remained small Spanish villages.

So, let's review what the USA consisted of in 1860 as the Civil War approached. The USA stretched from the Atlantic to the Pacific. California and Oregon had been states for a decade. As listed in the 1860 census, the nation consisted of 36 states (Kansas, Nebraska, and Nevada had been added since the 1850 census), and six territories, including Washington, D.C. The total population was 31,443,321 people. The three largest states were New York (3.88 million), Pennsylvania (2.91 million) and Ohio (2.34 million). The population included 4,441,830 *"colored"* people (14% of the total population), 89% of which were slaves. Of the 488,070 free blacks, the states where the most lived were Maryland (83,942), Virginia (58,642) and Pennsylvania (56,949). Washington, D.C., had a population of 75,080, including 11,131 free blacks and 3,185 slaves. Those slaves in D.C. were freed in 1862 by an act of Congress and their owners were compensated from federal funds for that loss of property.

From Texas to California, Hispanics were included in the "*white*" count, so we don't know how many there were. There were 34,933 Chinese, all living in California (9% of the population there). There were also 44,021 "*taxed Indians*" (those living among the general population) who were enumerated in the nationwide census (included in the total population count), with 40% of them living in California (5% of its population) and 14% in Michigan (1% of its population). There were also an estimated 295,400 "*Indians not taxed*" (those "*living on reservations under the care of Government agents, or roaming, individually or in bands, over unsettled tracts of country*") that were not included in the nation's population totals. So, the total number of Indians living in the USA in 1860 was equivalent to only about 1.1% of the total population and was even less than the number of free blacks (who accounted for 1.6% of the USA population). Of the over 50,000 Indians (Choctaw, Cherokee, Creek, Chickasaw, and Seminole previously moved west) living in what is now Oklahoma, over a thousand owned slaves. Black slaves owned by Indians in this territory totaled 7,369 (about 12% of the local population). So, these black slaves were included in the USA's population count, but their Indian owners were not.

10: THE CIVIL WAR – BEFORE, DURING, AND AFTER

In April 1861, the USA went to war with itself. The Civil War is the centerpiece of American history. All that went before seemed to lead to it. All that has come after has been affected by it. Ken Burns' 1997 documentary film, *The Civil War,* began with the following characterization of the reach, magnitude, and brutality of the Civil War:

The Civil War was fought in 10,000 places, from Valverde, New Mexico and Tullahoma, Tennessee to St. Albans, Vermont and Fernandina on the Florida coast. More than three million Americans fought in it and over 600,000 men, two percent of the population, died in it.

American homes became headquarters. American churches and schools sheltered the dying. Huge foraging armies swept across American farms and burned American towns. Americans slaughtered one another wholesale, here, in America, in their own cornfields and peach orchards, along familiar roads, and by waters with old American names.

In two days, at Shiloh, on the banks of the Tennessee, more American men fell than in all previous American wars combined. At Cold Harbor, 7,000 Americans fell in 20 minutes.

Most of the officers on both sides had served in the Mexican/American War 15 years before. They knew each other. They had fought together. Many on both sides were West Point graduates. Some had been classmates. Officers who had been friends were now enemies.

So, what was the cause of this terrible war? One word: *slavery.* It is worth stating again: *"While there were some people who spoke against slavery before the Revolutionary War, it was never a major public issue. After the Revolution, there was never a time when it wasn't a major public issue."* Therefore, among the war's causes were compromises made in

Philadelphia in 1887 in order to gain acceptance of all the 13 colonies that were now states. Without those compromises, one nation comprising all 13 colonies would not have been possible. However, those compromises then festered, so more compromises followed. Finally, the American people spoke through a presidential election, and the South's bluster was called with the election of Abraham Lincoln in 1860. The USA became the only nation in the history of mankind to fight a brutal civil war between factions of its dominant race to end the enslavement of a different race.

FREDERICK DOUGLAS – Frederick Douglas was the most photographed American of the nineteenth century. It is also likely that more Americans heard him speak than any other public figure of his time. He also traveled far more widely than most. He supported himself and his family by giving speeches. Although he also ran a printshop, it was more of a financial drain than a profit center and was also supported by his speeches. And he became the conscience of the USA when it came to race and slavery. Biographer David W. Blight described him this way:

He was brilliant, courageous, and possessed a truly uncommon endurance. He wrote many words that will last forever. His literary genius ranks with that of many of America's greatest writers of his century. But he was also vain, arrogant at times, and hypersensitive to slights. He liked being on a pedestal and did not intend to get knocked off. He was thoroughly and beautifully human. Spoken and written language was the only major weapon of protest, persuasion, or power that he ever possessed.

Frederick Douglas, a slave at birth, was born Frederick Augustus Washington Bailey (Fred Bailey) in Talbot County, Maryland (on its eastern shore), in February 1818 to Harriet Bailey, a slave, according to handwritten records of her owner, Aaron Anthony. There is no record of who his father was, though, based on Fred's complexion, his father was obviously white. It was most likely Mr. Anthony, though he did have two sons, ages 21 and 18 when Fred was born, which are also possibilities. Fred's grandmother, Betsy Bailey, was a slave married to a free black man.

Since she belonged to Mr. Anthony, under slave law, so did her ten children. Her five daughters, including Harriet, Fred's mother, produced at least 20 more children, all belonging to Mr. Anthony. Harriet had seven children, with Fred being somewhere in the middle. However, young Fred hardly even knew his mother and rarely saw her from the time he was born because Mr. Anthony kept leasing her out to others. So, she was only allowed to see him on infrequent short visits. He last saw his mother when he was seven. She died a year later.

Fred was raised by his grandmother, Betsy, along with several other young cousins in her cabin. He loved her dearly. However, when he was six, she walked with him twelve miles to the Wye House and delivered him to Mr. Anthony. There, he joined a group of about a dozen slave children under the tyrannical rule of Aunt Katy, who ran the kitchen. It turned out that three of the other children there were his older siblings and six more were cousins, but he had never met any of them before. He did not become close to them. Douglas later wrote at various times of his parents and siblings:

My poor mother, like many other slave women, had many children, but NO FAMILY!
Of my father I know nothing.
He is shrouded in a mystery I have never been able to penetrate.
I say nothing of ***father****...Slavery does away with fathers as it does away with families. The order of civilization is reversed here.*
Brothers and sisters we were in blood, but slavery had made us strangers.

Mr. Anthony lived in the Wye House, along with his family, including his two adult sons and a daughter, Lucretia, married to Hugh Auld. Mr. Anthony was the head overseer of the Wye plantation, which consisted of 13 farms totaling about 10,000 acres and over 500 slaves. Its primary cash crop had recently shifted to wheat. It also produced lots of corn and pork. There were large herds of sheep. The stables were full of horses, including racehorses. There was a private deer park. Edward Lloyd V owned the Wye plantation and was possibly the richest man in Maryland. He served as Maryland's governor three times. Mr. Lloyd and his family lived in the elegant part of the cavernous Wye House, where they had 15 attendant slaves, who also dressed in the finest silks and fashions as they took care of the Lloyds and their guests. The only thing they had in common with the rest of the slaves was skin color.

There were no beds or blankets for the slave children Aunt Katy managed. They all ate cornmeal mush out of a large wooden trough with an oyster shell as their only utensil. Young Fred never really bonded with the other slave children. Instead, he became close to the twelve-year-old son of Mr. Lloyd, *"who treated Frederick as both servant and playmate. They shared secrets and explored the estate together."* Lucretia Auld also took an immediate liking to this little six-year-old brown boy who seemed so alone. She treated his wounds when he was hurt and occasionally gave him bread and talked to him. When he was extra hungry, he would hang around her backyard window and start to sing. And she would give him a piece of bread.

Over the next two years there were six events that were seared into his memory and that he would often retell in vivid prose for the rest of his life. Shortly after arriving there, screams awakened him from sleep in his usual place on the floor of a closet off the kitchen. He looked out through cracks and saw that his 15-year-old aunt had her hands tied over her head to a rafter and pulled tight so that her toes barely touched the bench she was standing on. She had been stripped to the waist, and Mr. Anthony, age 57, was lashing her across the back and shoulders with a whip while cursing as blood ran down her back and onto her clothes. Her crime? She had been seeing a teenage slave boy and then rejected Mr. Anthony's advances.

Old Barney, the head groom, and stableman, had to endure much abuse if the horses didn't look just right when any of the Lloyds would come out to ride. One day, Mr. Lloyd himself gave Old Barney 30 lashes across his bare back because of the appearance of his favorite horse.

One day, he saw a strong, tall slave woman begin to fight back as one of the overseers was beating her. He finally dragged her to a tree, tied her there, and beat her to a bloody pulp in front of her five children and anyone else who was watching. Her crime? Impudence!

Another young slave man was receiving a lashing from an overseer for some offense. After a few lashes, the slave got up and jumped in the creek, where he stayed up to his neck in water. The overseer stood on the bank with a shotgun and told him to get out of the water. Then, after counting to three, he blew his head open with the shotgun blast.

There was one old crippled slave, Uncle Isaac, who liked to take a switch to the slave children. Douglas would later write:

Everybody in the South wants the privilege of whipping somebody else. Uncle Isaac shared the common passion of his country.

And finally, each month designated slaves from all over the plantation would come to receive their allotted provisions for the month. As they came, they would sing. Douglas wrote:

While on their way, they would make the dense old woods, for miles around, reverberate with their wild songs, revealing at once the highest joy and deepest sadness.
Sorrow and desolation have their songs, as well as joy and peace. Slaves sing more to make themselves happy, than to express their happiness.

When young Fred was eight, thanks to Lucretia, he was sent to Baltimore to be a companion to her husband's brother's son, who was the same age. That single event is what made the rest of his life possible. Again, in the words of David Blight:

But at this juncture, no one could imagine how the history of the Chesapeake region, as well as that of the entire nation, would change in no small measure because this fresh-faced orphan slave boy rode a boat to Baltimore that day in 1826.

At that point, Baltimore was a city of 80,000, and was growing rapidly with European immigrants, primarily from Ireland and Germany. About

75% of the population was white, while 80% of the black population was free. So, only about 5% of the city's residents were black slaves.

Mrs. Sophia Auld had never been a slave master before young Fred Bailey arrived. She treated this eight-year-old more as a mother than a slaveholding mistress. He got his first pair of real pants and began eating with a spoon and fork instead of an oyster shell. When she taught her son to read and write, she taught Fred too. She read the Bible to them. Fred loved the book of Job.

After Fred had been in Baltimore for 18 months, they learned that his owner, Aaron Anthony, had died. So, Fred had to be taken back to Wye House to be disposed of with the rest of Anthony's property. Sophia Auld and her son both wept bitterly as they shipped him off. Mr. Anthony had died without leaving a will. That meant that all his property would be divided equally among his three children. However, since his daughter, Lucretia, had died a few months before, her share would go to her husband, Hugh Auld. Mr. Anthony had 29 slaves, ranging from toddlers to Grandma Betsy, almost all related. They all anxiously lined up in a row to be appraised by the court appointed appraisers – to have a dollar value attached to them like animals in a stockyard. They were then divided into three groups of supposedly equal dollar value. Luckily, Fred was placed in the group that was given to Lucretia's husband. And he promptly sent Fred back to his brother's wife and son. So, Fred was back in Baltimore under the tender care of Sophia Auld.

Then, when he was eleven, Mr. Auld found out that his wife had been teaching Fred, right along with their own son, to read and write. He tore into her, oblivious of Fred being right there listening as he angrily went on and on along the following vein:

Learning would do him no good, but probably a great deal of harm – making him disconsolate and unhappy. It will make him unfit for the duties of a slave.

To eleven-year-old Fred Bailey, it felt like his eyes were being opened for the first time to the condition of slavery. He would later describe his feelings as:

Awakening for the first time to the white man's power to perpetuate the enslavement of the black man. If knowledge unfits a child to be a slave, I had found my path to freedom. That which he most loved I most hated, and the very determination which he expressed to keep me in ignorance, only rendered me the more resolute in seeking intelligence. In learning to read and write, therefore, I am not sure that I do not owe quite as much to the opposition of my master, as to the kindly assistance of my amiable mistress.
Education and slavery are incompatible with each other.

It was a challenge for the kind, compliant Sophia to switch from friendly caregiver to her son's companion into a hardnosed slave mistress trying to keep him from reading. But she tried, to her moral ruin. She got angry whenever she found Fred with books. But it was too late. The train had left the station. By that point, young Fred could already read and write well enough to continue his education. Douglas would later write:

She lacked the depravity indispensable to shutting her slave boy up in mental darkness. She needed a great deal of training in forgetting my human nature and treating me as a thing destitute of a moral or intellectual nature.
Nature had made us friends. Slavery made us enemies.

He then pursued knowledge and things to read as never before. He went out into the streets and developed friendships with immigrant white boys and relished the challenge of interacting with and learning from people unlike any he had ever met before – boys who had never been exposed to slavery. One of them showed him a book *The Columbian Orator* by Caleb Bingham. He loved it and managed to get a secondhand copy that he kept for the rest of his life.

When Fred was 15, a dispute arose between the Auld brothers that led to Hugh, his owner, demanding Fred's return to him on the Eastern Shore. By then, Hugh had remarried and was operating a store in town. He had four slaves, all related: Fred, his 17-year-old sister, his aunt, and a cousin who had been seriously burned in a fire and left too crippled to work. Hugh frequently beat her until blood ran. For the first time in many years, Fred was suddenly exposed to what life was really like for a slave. As a small child he had observed it. Now, at 15, he lived it. Indian cornmeal was about the only food given to the slaves, and Fred was constantly hungry. He stole food every chance he got. Hugh was a weak, mean, and inconsistent slave master. And this impudent, smart, difficult young teenager drove him crazy. After several months, and shortly before Fred turned 16, Hugh leased him out for a year to a farmer with a reputation for breaking the spirit of slaves. Over the next eight months, Fred earned all the lash scars on his back that he would occasionally display for the rest of his life. Then, one day, he fought back. And wrestled his tormentor to the ground. He could have been hung for this offense. However, the man was apparently concerned that acknowledging the event would damage his reputation. He did not whip Fred again during the last few months he was there. Fred was leased out over the next two years to a farmer who was much more laid back. Fred taught reading classes to a dozen or more other slaves each Sunday. During the second year, he and three others planned an escape. However, they were betrayed and arrested before they even began the attempt. The most likely outcome was that he would be sold and shipped south. However, after two weeks in jail, Hugh Auld finally came and got him and sent him back to his brother in Baltimore instead.

Now, a young man at 18, and 6'1", he was put to work in the shipyards learning to be a caulker, with Mr. Auld getting his wages. Two years later, he escaped north, went to New England, changed his last name to Douglas (since he was now a runaway slave he needed a new identity), and began using his entire first name, Frederick. He soon became involved in the abolition movement. Fred Bailey, the slave, thus became Frederick Douglas, the abolitionist, telling and retelling the story of slavery from a firsthand perspective of a slave in a way that rocked the Nation and the world. And the rest, as they say, is history.

David W. Blight summed up his long and very public life this way:

He was a radical thinker and a proponent of classic nineteenth-century political liberalism; at different times he hated and loved his country;

he was a ferocious critic of the United States and all its hypocrisies, but also, after emancipation, became a government bureaucrat, a diplomat, and a voice for territorial expansion... Douglas was a serious constitutional thinker, and few Americans have ever analyzed race with more poignancy and nuance than this mostly self-taught genius with words. He was a radical editor, writer, and activist, informed by a hard-earned pragmatism. Douglas was Jim-Crowed more times than he could count, but loved the Declaration of Independence, the natural-rights tradition, and especially the reinvented US Constitution fashioned in Reconstruction.

WHITE CULTURE IN THE SOUTH – The South was different. *"From early in American history, foreign visitors and domestic travelers alike were struck by cultural contrasts between the white population of the South and that of the rest of the country in general – and New England in particular."* Frederick Laws Olmstead is considered the father of landscape architecture and was the co-designer of Central Park on the island of Manhattan. He was also a journalist who traveled extensively in the South between 1852 and 1857 and wrote of his travels for a New York City newspaper.

The citizens of the cotton states, as a whole, are poor. They work little, and at that little, badly; they earn little, they sell little; they buy little, and they have little – very little – of the common comforts and consolations of civilized life. Their destitution is not material only; it is intellectual and it is moral. They were neither generous nor hospitable and their talk was not that of evenly courageous men.

The differences between Southern whites and those living in northern states were manifest in several ways: *"an aversion to work, proneness to violence, neglect of education, sexual promiscuity, improvidence, drunkenness, lack of entrepreneurship, reckless searches for excitement, lively music and dance, and a style of religious oratory marked by strident rhetoric, unbridled emotions, and flamboyant imagery."* They were far more inclined to rely on fights, duels, and vigilante justice than the rule of law. One historian noted, *"Of southern statesmen who rose to prominence after 1790, hardly one can be mentioned who was not involved in a duel."* Another noted: *"Editors of Southern newspapers became involved in duels so often that cartoonists depicted them with a pen in one hand and a dueling pistol in the other. Most duels arose not over substantive issues but over words considered insulting."* As explained by Malcom Gladwell:

> *The violence wasn't for economic gain. It was **personal.** You fought for your honor.*

This was thought of as the Honor Culture, where the slightest insult was grounds for a fight, if not a duel. After one such hand-to-hand fight, the cheering crowd lifted the maimed and bleeding winner on their shoulders while the loser lay in the dirt with his nose bitten off, both rears ripped off, and both eyes gouged out. Risks were taken. *"Even where there was no conflict or hostility involved, Southerners often showed a reckless disregard for human life, including their own."*

And then there was economic activity. One contemporary stated many white southerners are *"too poor to keep slaves and too proud to work."* South Carolina Senator John C. Calhoun said:

> *Not even the poorest or the lowest, will under any circumstances perform menial labor. He has too much pride for that.*

General Robert E. Lee declared:

> *Our people are opposed to work. Our troops officers community & press. All ridicule and resist it.*

A Richmond, Virginia newspaper *"attributed the success of Northern farmers where Southerners had failed to the social nature of the latter, which led them to gather around the courthouse and country stores to smoke, chew, talk politics, and, in general, to waste time."* Many Southern businessmen often failed to pay their bills or deliver goods and services when promised.

Southern whites "*loved dancing, fighting, hunting, and other physical activities, so sloth was not the real issue.*" Yet, when Olmstead found "*work done efficiently, promptly, and well during his travels through the South – when he found well-run businesses, good libraries, impressive churches, and efficiently functioning institutions in general – he almost invariably found them to be run by Northerners, foreigners, or Jews. Nearly all of the Old South's successful storekeepers were either Yankees or Yankee-trained Southerners.*" Southerners would also ford rivers and streams rather than build bridges over them. "*No Northern farmer would neglect to build a bridge over a stream that crossed his property; indeed, two 'live Yankees' would complete the work in a single day, but the Southern planter will ford the creek lying between his house & stable a whole lifetime.*"

In colonial Virginia, almost half of white men were so illiterate that they could not sign their name while 75% of women were illiterate. Even by 1850, according to the census, over 20% of Southern white adults were illiterate, while less than one percent of New England adults were illiterate. The North had four times as many schools and four times as many pupils. Patents were rarely issued to Southerners since they rarely innovated or invented anything. Ely Whitney, from New England, had been in the South for less than a month when he invented the cotton gin. Thomas Jefferson complained that there was not a single bookstore in Charlottesville. In short, schooling and intellectual activity were simply not priorities for most Southern whites.

Sexual norms were also different. In Massachusetts, the average age for women getting married was over twenty, while pregnancy before marriage was very rare. Rape was a hanging offense. In the South, most white girls were married by seventeen. One missionary stated that for over 90% of the backcountry marriages he performed, the bride was already pregnant. Rape was more likely to be addressed by vigilante justice handed out by the family than by law enforcement. In colonial times, sexual exploitation of white indentured servant girls was common in the South before the slave population was large enough for white servants to be replaced by black slaves.

Religious practices also differed in the white South. Many services were held outdoors. Whether inside or outside, the preachers were louder and more dramatic, while the congregations were much rowdier and nosier. Speech patterns were also quite different for Southern whites, while many words had distinctly different pronunciations.

But why was the white culture in the antebellum South so different from the North, particularly New England? Olmstead and de Tocqueville blamed it on slavery. While it is easy to believe slavery helped these cultural attributes flourish, it is unlikely that they originated with slavery since it was also practiced in the North until it was phased out after the Revolutionary War.

Historians are still debating the origin of this Southern culture since it has potentially explosive relevance to current racial issues. Grady McWhiney, a prominent and influential twentieth-century historian and man of the South, published *Cracker Culture* in 1988. In it, he laid out these cultural differences and traced them to immigrants from the warlike borderlands (with Celtic origins) of the British Isles, in contrast to the Anglo-Saxon origins of colonists in the Northern colonies. Critics of McWhiney have pointed out that he doesn't account for the fact that many who went to southern colonies were poor indentured servants from southern England. Almost simultaneously (January 1, 1989), historian David Hackett Fischer published *Albion's Seed: Four British Folkways in America,* which describes migrations from four different areas of the British Isles with distinct cultural differences into four different parts of the American colonies. However, he says little about who came to the coastal colonies below Virginia. Instead, he points out that those settling in Appalachia (extending down into northern Georgia) in colonial times were Scotch-Irish, Scotts, and those from the lawless borderlands of England, where these cultural traits dominated. One writer characterized the different groups of immigrants this way: *"When English arrived, they built a church. When Germans arrived, they built a barn. When Scotch-Irish arrived, they built a whiskey still."* There seems to be general agreement that these cultural attributes found in the south were evident in seventeenth-century Scotland, the Scotch-Irish from Northern Ireland, and England's largely lawless northern borderlands where most of the immigrants to Appalachia came from. By the early 1800s (a century after Scotland merged with England to form Great Britain), Scotland was transforming into having among the highest literacy rates in Europe, and the rule of law was becoming well ingrained throughout Great Britain. However, the immigrants populating Appalachia were long gone by then. And those cultural traits they brought with them survived here long after they had disappeared back home.

Historians can continue to debate how these cultural attributes so apparent in seventeenth-century British borderlands and then in the Appalachian Mountains, also came to be found throughout the South in the nineteenth century. However, there is little doubt that this culture was dominant throughout the South. In short, it is more likely than not that ancestry was more responsible than slavery for the cultural differences between Southern and Northern whites.

This Southern white culture was what most slaves were exposed to. By 1860, the importation of slaves had been outlawed for over 50 years, so almost all slaves in the USA were born here. And they had lost not only the languages and religions of their ancestors in Africa, but they had also lost much of their culture. But they picked up the language, religion, and culture of the whites around them who controlled their daily lives. The consequences of that will be discussed later.

CONGRESS LEADING UP TO THE CIVIL WAR – We hear and voice concerns about how dysfunctional Congress is today. Many think there is too much partisan bickering and that little gets done. However, 200 years ago, and for the next 40 years until the Civil War, things were much worse. Or, at least, much different. *"There seemed to be so much violence in the House and Senate chambers in the 1830s, 1840s, and 1850s. Shoving. Punching. Pistols. Bowie knives. Congressmen brawling in bunches while colleagues stood on chairs to get a good look. At least once, a gun was fired on the House floor."* And most of that fighting was over slavery. Those in Congress seemed to fall into one of three categories: 1) fighting men, almost all from the South; 2) non-combatants, almost all from the North; and 3) compromisers, mostly from the border states between North and South. In the South, a Code of Honor was ingrained.

To directly insult a man was to challenge him to a duel. To be deliberately insulted and not demand a duel was to be no man at all. The last words of Andrew Jackson's mother to him regarding protecting his manhood were still in full sway across the South and the western frontier. As a result, *"All in all, many southerners considered dueling an unfortunate but necessary civilizing force."* It helped restrain intemperate speech and actions. Further, as Jackson had shown, an inclination to violence didn't hurt a politician's popularity. One house member from North Carolina castrated two men he claimed committed adultery with his wife. After being released from prison, he won reelection. A man from Alabama was elected to the House and then the Senate after *"killing an unarmed man by shooting him in the chest, pistol-whipping his head, and stabbing him with a sward cane."* Many southern members were armed with a knife, gun, or both, while on the floors of Congress.

Northern culture by this time, was totally against dueling. Instead, northerners would look to authorities to help resolve heated disputes. Plus, most of them were far less familiar with guns and the whole culture of dueling. Many southern Congressmen were quick to take advantage of this by simply, and frequently, bullying their northern colleagues. Most newspapermen of the era were blatant partisans. They often launched verbal attacks on Congressmen, or the opposing party in general. The Honor Code of dueling only applied to those of equal status. Thus, a congressman could ignore the taunts of the press without considering his manhood challenged unless that taunt was presented to him personally or directly.

In February 1838, this strange culture of honor led to the only fatal duel between two sitting members of the House of Representatives. And they didn't even dislike each other. Jonathan Cilley, age 35, a Democrat from Maine, had made some charges about improper banking activities in New York. The editor of a Whig paper came down to Washington ready for a fight. He wrote a letter to Cilley and casually asked a Whig House member, William Graves, age 33, from Kentucky, a friendly acquaintance who was not even aware of his current dispute with Cilley, to deliver a letter to Cilley for him. When Graves told Cilley who the letter was from, Cilley refused to accept it. Not accepting a letter, presumed to be insulting, that was coming from a newspaperman was a matter of honor to Cilley. Delivering a letter he had agreed to deliver was a matter of honor to Graves. After three days of negotiations involving at least a dozen other House members, they went to a dueling ground outside of D.C. (They even had to ask a local if they were outside the District yet). There, they dueled with rifles at 80 yards. They both stood sideways to narrow the target. Cilley was near-sighted and hadn't touched a rifle in five years. Graves wasn't very experienced, either. The man in charge would shout *"FIRE"* and then count to four. Each dueler was to fire before he got to four or not fire at all. Cilley fired before he got his rifle raised. Was Graves satisfied? Could they shake hands and go home? Their representatives debated this while the duelers remained in place. No. So, they reloaded and faced off again. This time, Graves misfired before his rifle was fully raised. Satisfied? No. On the third go, Cilley was hit in the abdomen and died within minutes.

Beginning in the 1820s, Indian tribes from east of the Mississippi were being relocated into a large Indian territory that included Oklahoma (except the western panhandle) and extended north to include the eastern two-thirds of Kansas and Nebraska. The Missouri Compromise of 1820 prohibited slavery in all territories north of Missouri's southern border as it extended westward. The Kansas-Nebraska Act of 1854 created the Kansas and Nebraska territories, removed them from Indian territory, and, in a partial repeal of the Missouri Compromise, left whether they would be slave states or free states up to the vote of the residents there. The result was both slave owners and abolitionists poured into Kansas as settlers in an effort to sway the vote. And they fought with each other, sometimes killing each other, so that it became known as *Bloody Kansas.*

In May 1856, Congressman Preston Brooks, from South Carolina, walked into the Senate chamber and proceeded to beat Senator Charles Sumner from Massachusetts with his cane while Sumner sat at his desk. He hit him at least twelve times (until his cane broke) while another house member, holding a gun, kept anyone from coming to Sumner's assistance. By the time the beating ended, Sumner was lying on the floor, nearly unconscious. His crime? Sumner was an outspoken abolitionist who opposed Kansas becoming a slave state. Brooks then resigned and left his fate to the voters. His district quickly reelected him in a special election.

THE REPUBLICAN PARTY IS FORMED – In order to retain its southern members, the Whig party had avoided becoming an antislavery party even though a majority of its members opposed slavery. However, after its heavy losses in the 1852 election, the Whig party began to fall apart. With the passage of the Kansas-Nebraska Act, which opened both territories to slavery and would allow them to become slave states, an antislavery group in Wisconsin met, decided to form a new party, chose the name Republican for their new party, and selected a slate of statewide candidates for the upcoming election. Soon, other Midwest states started doing the same. The new Republican party *"envisioned modernizing the United States, emphasizing expanded banking, more railroads and factories, and giving free western land to farmers ('free soil') as opposed to letting slave owners buy up the best properties. It vigorously argued that free market labor was superior to slavery and was the very foundation of civic virtue and true republicanism; this was the 'Free Soil, Free Labor, Free Men' ideology."*

In February 1856, the new republican party held its first national organizing convention in Pittsburgh. It selected national officers for the party and passed resolutions opposing various aspects of slavery. It was first and foremost, an antislavery party. It met again in June in Philadelphia and nominated John C. Fremont for president behind the slogan: *"Free soil, free silver, free men, Fremont and victory!* Fremont lost, but the party dominated state elections in New England, New York, and the northern Midwest.

Then, in 1857, Chief Justice Taney, appointed by Andrew Jackson over 20 years before, authored the Supreme Court's infamous Dred Scott decision. It held: 1) that Dred Scott, despite having lived freely in a free state, was still a slave because he had returned to Missouri where he had been a slave, 2) that the Constitution barred Congress from prohibiting slavery anywhere, including US territories, 3) that the *Missouri Compromise,* which barred slavery in some territories, was unconstitutional, and 4) that free blacks were not, and could not be, citizens of the USA because they were part of an inferior race.

His goal was to end the national debate over slavery and blacks once and for all by providing definitive answers to issues around slavery from the Nation's highest court. The result was the opposite. One Supreme Court justice resigned in protest. It also bolstered the popularity of the new anti-slavery republican party, which did well in the 1858 congressional elections. Then, in 1860, the party nominated Abraham Lincoln for president. He won, and the USA went to war with itself. Taney died in 1864, just as his home state of Maryland abolished slavery.

THE CIVIL WAR – Lincoln was elected president with less than 40% of the popular vote. His name didn't even appear on the ballot in most southern states. He carried every northern state but New Jersey. Even before he took office, seven southern states seceded from the USA and seized control of Federal forts, arsenals, and other Federal property in the process. A fourth of the USA army was stationed in Texas and soon surrendered. In February, delegates from these states met and formed the Confederacy. In his inaugural address on March 4, 1861, Lincoln argued that the Constitution was a binding contract and called secession *"legally void."* He said he had no intention to invade the South nor to end slavery where it existed but that he would use force to maintain possession of Federal property, including that already seized by the Confederacy. Then, on April 12, South Carolina attacked Fort Sumter, located on an island in Charleston harbor. In response, Lincoln issued a call for 75,000 volunteers. Four more states then seceded. The eleven states that had seceded included 5.45 million whites (20.2% of the nation's white population) and 3.65 million blacks (82.3% of the nation's black population), with 96.4% of those being slaves. There were still about 433,000 slaves and 355,000 free blacks living in those states (and in Washington, D.C.) that remained within the Union.

War is expensive. And this war was very expensive. In April 1861, when the war started, the Federal government was spending about $172,000 a day. Just nine months later, it was spending $1.5 million a day, a ninefold increase. By the time the war was ending in 1865, it was spending over $3.5 million a day, more than 20 times the daily expenditures before the war started. There are three ways for a government to raise money: 1) taxes, 2) borrowing it, and 3) printing it. Both sides used all three but in very different ways. With southern congressmen having all resigned and gone home, the reduced Congress was suddenly able to get all kinds of things done that had been impossible before. It immediately passed an income tax, along with many other taxes. The Union raised 21% of its revenues during the war through taxes. It needed to borrow but was hampered by no longer having a central bank of its own to negotiate with foreign interests. So, it mainly borrowed from its own citizens by inventing war bonds. At that time few people had bank accounts, while most kept their savings under the mattress. War bonds were marketed with the message that it was patriotic to buy them. And it worked. Suddenly, all that money that had been sitting idle under mattresses was in circulation, fueling the economy and helping to pay for the war. The national debt rose from $0.93 per person before the war to $75 per person after the war, with much of that debt owed to citizens holding war bonds. And the Union printed money, mostly new *greenbacks,* that did remarkably well at holding their value. Before the War, there had been over 50 different kinds of money in circulation, most of it various private banknotes. After the war, gold, silver, and federal greenbacks were the only forms of money available. Though deeply in debt by the end of the war, the Union had become an industrial and economic powerhouse.

Beginning in 1866, after the war ended, the USA went 28 straight years in which government income exceeded expenditures so that the national debt was reduced to a third of what it had been at the end of the war in total dollars. Compared to GDP, the drop in debt went down from 50% to less than 10%. In 1872 the income tax was eliminated.

The Confederacy also tried all three, but it had far less liquid capital to tax or borrow (most of the South's assets were tied up in land and slaves while cotton exports collapsed), so it had limited success with the first two, and mostly printed money. And the value of that money kept going down and down. And down. By the end of the war, the South was in financial ruin.

It was a year and half into the war, September 22, 1862, before the bedrock issue at the heart of the conflict was finally faced head-on with the issuance of a preliminary Emancipation Proclamation to become effective January 1, 1863. President Lincoln then issued it in final form on that date, effective immediately. I had always been troubled over why Lincoln issued a proclamation that only freed slaves in states that had left the Union and were no longer under his control – so it would be ignored there – but did not free slaves in the slave states that were still part of the Union: Delaware, Maryland, Kentucky, and Missouri. Further, if the goal was just a feel-good gesture, why was it written in such dense, dull legalese rather than using beautiful rhetoric as we know Lincoln was capable of? I may be the only one who didn't already know this, but recently I finally found out why he did it the way he did. Lincoln did not issue it as head of state. Instead, he issued the Proclamation *"by virtue of the power in me vested as Commander-in-Chief, of the Army and Navy of the United States in time of actual armed rebellion against authority and government of the United States."* He did it that way because, unlike actions he might take as head of the civilian government that would be within the jurisdiction of the Supreme Court where Chief Justice Taney still presided, the Supreme Court had no jurisdiction over military actions by the Commander-in-Chief within areas that were in complete armed rebellion and conflict against the United States and its military forces. Lincoln didn't want this Proclamation tainted by an unfavorable review by the Supreme Court. So, it was written under authority that would preclude court review. And he did so, despite its dense verbiage and limited immediate benefit to those enslaved since it only applied to slaves in states already in rebellion, because just issuing the Proclamation made it obvious to all, for the first time, that this war was not just a fight to reunite the Union, but to end slavery within the USA once and for all. It gave the war a new cause.

A few more points on the war. Because Washington, D.C., was like an island cut out of the southern boundary of Maryland, it was critical that Maryland stay in the Union. Otherwise, the Nation's capital would be in enemy territory cut off from the remaining USA it was supposed to govern. Maryland voted to close its rail lines to prevent them from being used to move Union troops and supplies. Lincoln responded by declaring martial law, suspending *habeas corpus,* arresting a third of the state's general assembly, and holding them without trial in order to prevent them from being able to assemble and vote to leave the Union. When the Supreme Court, still led by Chief Justice Taney, ruled these actions violated the Constitution, Lincoln ignored the Court's ruling and kept legislators jailed. Lincoln also jailed a prominent newspaper editor in Baltimore for speaking out against these actions. He felt desperate times called for desperate measures, so he tromped on the Constitution's *Bill of Rights* to preserve the Union. It worked. Maryland, along with the slave states of Delaware, Kentucky and Missouri, stayed in the Union.

By 1861, the USA was still just a collection of states in the minds of many, if not most, of its citizens. People tended to identify themselves more with their state than their country. Most famously, for Robert E. Lee, being a Virginian mattered more to him than being a citizen of the USA. So, when President Lincoln offered him the opportunity to head the Union Army, he turned down the president and went with his state to the Confederacy.

Some states were divided against themselves. For instance, there were many unionists in Texas, particularly Mexicans still there and German immigrants in north Texas. The governor of Texas, Sam Houston, refused to take an oath of allegiance to the Confederacy, so he was deposed. In Cook County, 150 suspected unionists were arrested, 25 were lynched without trial, and 40 more were hung after a summary trial. Draft resistance was widespread among German and Mexican communities, with Germans going into hiding and many Mexicans fleeing to Mexico. In August 1862, Confederate troops executed 34 pro-union German Texans. Virginia did split with the formation of West Virginia in 1863, which was immediately accepted as a new state into the Union. That left a smaller Virginia as part of the Confederacy.

Home turf matters. Most of the war was fought within the eleven states that had left the Union. They felt they were defending their homes and their way of life as they fought off an invasion. Thus, they were far more invested. The South had far fewer deserters. Further, Lincoln had a terrible time getting his generals to fight, particularly in Virginia. And when they did engage, they would retreat after one day's battle. They were uncomfortable being invaders.

After two years of repeated successes, General Lee lost focus on his strategic advantage and decided to take the battle into the Union and finish the war. It wasn't until Gettysburg, where General Meade, a Pennsylvanian, was battling an invasion of his home state in July 1863, that Union troops were kept in the battle for days. And finally won one. But when Lee retreated to Virginia, Meade would not chase him and continue the fight. For all his vaunted military expertise, Lee had failed to grasp the huge strategic advantage of fighting on his home turf. And it cost him dearly while giving the Union a critical victory.

Only Lincoln and Ulysses S. Grant (and it took Lincoln three years to discover Grant was his man) seemed to grasp the reality that (like the problem the British faced in the Revolutionary War) all the Confederacy had to do to win the war was avoid losing it until the Union's population got tired of this fight and quit supporting it. On the other hand, for the Union to win, they could not simply win a few battles or defend territory. The Union could only win by going into the South and destroying the Confederacy militarily, structurally, and politically, before the Union population got tired of an endless war far from home over an issue (slavery) that did not affect their daily lives. Grant later explained what both Lincoln and Grant understood:

There had to be an end to slavery...Then we were fighting an enemy with whom we could not make peace. We had to destroy him.

ULYSSES S. GRANT – Lincoln was the President and Commander in Chief, but Grant won the war, and they both knew it. And the whole nation, both North and South, knew it. Who was he?

Born Hiram Ulysses Grant on April 22, 1822, Grant preferred being called Ulysses, though kids at school sometimes called him Useless. His family were staunch abolitionists living near Cincinnati. His father was an overbearing opinionated, loudmouth braggart who was always dreaming up some new scheme. His mother was prim, kind, refined, straitlaced, proper, and quiet. She did not express affection either verbally or physically. His father never stopped talking, while his mother never started. Ulysses never seemed to quite please either of them, but he modeled himself after his mother. *"He was self-contained, as if he had trained his face to mask emotions and keep his inner life secret."* He was very earnest and *"had more determination than any boy I ever saw."* He was also incapable of guile and generally failed to see it in others, which became a serious problem when he became president. When, at age 8, he was sent by his father to bargain for a horse, he blurted straight out to the farmer:

Papa says I may offer you twenty dollars for the colt, but if you won't take that, I am to offer twenty-two and a half, and if you won't take that, I am to give you twenty-five.

That story dogged him throughout his life. He never swore. He honored women and *"spent a lifetime avoiding the coarse jokes and bawdy anecdotes that were commonplace in the military."* Said a cousin: *"He revered women and thought such stories demeaned the female sex. I have seen him freeze up a man instantly with a look when a vulgar story was told in his presence."* Because he was reserved and refused to promote himself, his father was always frustrated and pushing him forward. He developed a deeply entrenched modesty. Through connections with a senator, his father finally got him recommended to West Point. When his father told him about West Point, Ulysses said he wouldn't go. His father insisted. He went. Before going, he went across the street to the Bailey's, where Mrs. Bailey and her daughters cried as they said goodbye to him. Grant was shocked at the tears and said:

*Why you **must** be sorry I am going. They didn't cry at our house.*

At age 17, Grant arrived at West Point, standing 5'2" and weighing 117 pounds. When he went to sign in, he learned that his letter of recommendation had misstated his name as Ulysses S. Grant. The army refused to change it, so that became his name for the rest of his life. When the other cadets saw *U.S. Grant* on his assigned locker, they immediately called him *Uncle Sam.* He then became *Sam Grant* to the rest of the cadets for his entire time at West Point.

Throughout his life, Grant had a truly unique relationship with horses. They just seemed to understand each other. By the time he was five, he would ride a galloping horse, standing on one foot on the horse's back. At West Point, he was not only the best horseman but accomplished feats on horseback that were talked about for years. When he graduated, he hoped to be assigned to the Cavalry. But the army, being the army, assigned him to an infantry unit near St. Louis. By then, he was 5' 8" and had graduated in the middle of his class. He excelled in math, engineering, and map drawing but was mediocre in military classes, where he showed little interest. Yet one classmate predicted: "*Well sir, if a great emergency arises in this country during our lifetime, Sam Grant will be the man to meet it.*

While stationed at St. Louis, he met Julia Dent, his West Point roommate's little sister. Her father, a domineering man, owned a plantation with many slaves south of St. Louis. Julia was swept away by Grant.

I thought he was a knight from one of the romances I used to read...He entirely enchanted me... He was handsome, kind, honest, brave, he was scarcely real to a little girl like myself.

And Grant immediately loved her. "*They formed the deep bond craved by bashful men who need the unconditional devotion of one loving, loyal woman. She believed in him more than he believed in himself, and was more ambitious for him as well. She bolstered his confidence, soothed his wounds, and pierced through his shyness until he learned to count on her constant strength.*" Her mother also saw greatness in Grant. However, her father blocked the marriage for several years because he didn't think Grant was good enough or rich enough for his daughter.

Grant ended up being assigned to the unit in Texas that was sent down to the Rio Grande, where it got into the skirmish with Mexican forces that precipitated the Mexican-American War. Three days after his 24th birthday, he got his first taste of battle and discovered that, unlike most of us, he felt a clear-eyed, calm detachment in battle. The gut-wrenching gore and chaotic scenes surrounding him seemed to have no effect until the battle was over. For a time, he was assigned quartermaster duties and learned the importance and means of logistics and supply lines. He was appalled by how the victorious sometimes abused the defeated. He was also exposed to the politics of war as successful generals were replaced because their success might make them political rivals. Later, he was part of the invading forces that were moved by ship to Vera Crus and went on to take Mexico City. Late in his life, he would write of the Rio Grande incursion and the war that followed:

> *Texas had no claim beyond the Nueces River, and yet we pushed on to the Rio Grande and crossed it. I am always ashamed of my country when I think of that invasion.*
> *For myself, I was bitterly opposed to the measure, and to this day regard the war, which resulted, as one of the most unjust ever waged by a stronger against a weaker nation.*

Over the next several years, as Grant moved through a series of lonely military posts, primarily in Northern California, that required extended separations from Julia, he became a serious drinker while they were separated. In short, he became an alcoholic. He finally resigned from the Army, at the rank of Captain, under somewhat of a cloud, in 1854, at the age of 32. There was nothing official in the record, but rumors abounded.

Caught in a war between Ulysses' abolitionist tyrannical father, who detested Julia and her family, and Julia's slave-owning tyrannical father, who had little use for his son-in-law and detested his family, the couple spent the next four years trying to farm near the Dent plantation in Missouri. Julia had slave servants who kept her household during that period. After four years of farming with little to show for it, Grant moved his family to St. Louis in 1858, where he failed as a businessman. He was too much of a soft touch for anyone with a hard luck story. While there, he took the slave his father-in-law had given him, and that he had worked side by side with (to the disgust of his neighbors) for a few years on the farm, and signed the papers setting him forever free even though Grant was desperate for money and slaves were still bringing a high price. Then, in 1859, thanks to an olive branch from his father, Grant moved his family to Galena, Illinois, where he worked as a shopkeeper with his older brother in a leather shop owned by his father. He was now 37 and had four children. Through these hard times, Julia managed to keep Grant sober. It was a role she handled well throughout their marriage, whenever they were able to be together, despite serious financial setbacks. He adored her. Just her presence was enough to conquer his demons. And, because she couldn't bring slaves into Illinois, Julia learned to get by without slaves taking care of household duties.

As the Union began to raise troops in April 1861, Grant wanted back in as his passion for the Union cause grew. Since the government had spent money training him and giving him combat experience, he felt he owed it to the nation to play a part now. However, Julia said Ulysses:

could no more resist the sound of a fife and a drum or a chance to fire a gun than a woman can resist bonnets.

But then, she was still quite sympathetic to the southern cause to which her father, whom she always adored, was totally committed. She always tended to see the world through rose-colored glasses and still viewed her childhood as idyllic. Even late in her life, she remembered all their slaves as loving her and her mother and father. She wrote that their slaves were all:

very happy. At least they were in Mamma's time, though the young ones became somewhat demoralized about the beginning of the Rebellion, when all the comforts of slavery passed away forever.

Grant's first assignments back in the military were maddening desk assignments in the recruitment process. That discouraged him. Then, out of the blue, the governor assigned him to replace an incompetent colonel and command the Twenty-First Illinois Regiment. And his rise began. Shortly after his first venture back in combat, he was promoted to brigadier general. He quickly realized that his lack of attention to paperwork could be a problem and managed to get a lawyer from Galena he had worked with before, John Rawlins, assigned as his chief-of-staff. Before accepting the post, Rawlins, who had his own issues with alcohol, got a commitment from Grant that he would not take a drink of alcohol until the war was over. He then vigorously assumed the role Julia had played for years. If Julia wasn't there, he watched over Grant like a hawk to protect him from alcohol throughout the war. While many rumors were spread, often by those eager to undercut him, only three or four had any substance. The few problems that did occur were within the first few days after a major victory when Grant was constantly being offered a drink in congratulations.

Over the next two years, Grant went from victory to victory to victory as his responsibilities and fame grew. Some battles were extremely bloody multiday affairs where he kept the fight going until he persevered. And he would accept nothing less than unconditional surrender. In fact, people began to say that U. S. Grant stood for *Unconditional Surrender* Grant. And some accused him of having no concern for the cost of human lives. Yet, the siege that finally brought down Vicksburg on July 4, 1863, was hailed (and still is) as both a huge strategic success because it opened the entire Mississippi River to Union Control and split the Confederacy into two disconnected halves, and as a tactical masterpiece for the way he did it. Grant had not only won a huge victory, but he had also removed an entire army of 43,000 Confederate soldiers from the fight. Grant's soldiers *"stared in respectful silence"* as beleaguered Confederate soldiers laid down their arms and, paroled by Grant, quietly headed home. One aid said of Grant *"Nothing pleased him more than to reduce the enemy's strength by capture than by slaughter."* This grand victory at Vicksburg *"retired all residual doubts about Grant's skill as a general. Whether dealing with the overall strategy or tactical minutiae he had excelled. Vicksburg was a comeuppance for skeptics who had derided him."*

President Lincoln, and Congress, and the public, took notice. *"Until Vicksburg, the western theater had been something of a sideshow. Now Ulysses S. Grant, an uncomplaining man of proven competence, found a place in Lincoln's affection."* Lincoln said:

He isn't shrieking for reinforcements all the time. He takes what troops we can safely give him and does the best he can with what he has got. Grant is my man, and I am his for the rest of the war.

On July 7, 1863, Grant was named major general in the regular army. *"For a man drummed out of the regular army in disgrace a decade earlier, the move completed the spectacular transformation of his life."*

In orders Grant received on October 17, 1863, President Lincoln created a new *Military Division of the Mississippi* that consolidated the three existing Armies of *the Ohio*, *the Cumberland*, and *the Tennessee*, and placed Grant in charge of this new unit with his headquarters in the field. At the time, the Army of the Ohio was trying to hang on to Knoxville while the Army of the Cumberland had just been driven back into Chattanooga after a devastating loss, where its 45,000 troops were essentially surrounded and running low on supplies (nearly 10,000 horses and mules had already died of starvation while the troops were living on half-rations and about to run out). So, Grant headed for Chattanooga. And he had to cover the last 60 miles on horseback after dark, in the most harrowing ride of his life over a destroyed up and down road littered with broken wagons and dead horses and mules, that was the only way open into the city. To make a very long story short, over the next six weeks, Grant managed to bring in supplies and more troops, defeat the surrounding Confederate force, and drive what remained of it into Georgia, while Knoxville was also secured. During the chase into Georgia, one new aid described Grant: *"We rode for half a mile in the face of the enemy, under an incessant fire of cannon and musketry. Not once do I believe did it enter the general's mind that he was in danger. He requires no escort beyond his staff. Roads are almost useless to him, for he takes short cuts through fields and woods, and will swim his horse through almost any stream that obstructs his way. He will ride from breakfast until one or two in the morning, and that too without eating."*

Following these victories, one contemporary historian wrote: *"So far as I can understand the subject, Ulysses Grant is **at least** equal to any general now living in any part of the world, and by far the first that our war has produced on either side."* Newspapers sounded similar praise. The war suddenly looked winnable. Congress began debating a bill that would create the position of Lieutenant General for Grant. The debate noted that Grant had *"won seventeen battles and taken one hundred* *thousand prisoners and five hundred artillery pieces."* The bill passed on February 26, 1864. Lincoln signed it on February 29 and named Grant to the position. The Senate confirmed Grant's appointment and on March 3, Grant received a telegram summoning him to Washington to receive his new commission from Lincoln. To that point, they had never met.

When Grant arrived in Washington, he took his teenage son with him to the Willard Hotel, Washington's finest. *"When Grant, short and shabby, entered the lobby of this haven of the city's power brokers, he brought into its elegant precincts the rough garb of the western theater of war. He was known only by his rank and reputation, and few capital denizens had ever seen him in the flesh. Hence, he and Fred created no stir as they slipped unnoticed into the hotel. Grant was an easy man for easterners to patronize, and the desk clerk treated him with casual contempt, telling him a small top-floor room might be available. Unfazed, Grant said that would do and signed the register 'U. S. Grant and son, Galena, Ill.' When the clerk spun around the register and saw Grant's name, he changed on the spot from haughty to fawning, giving him Parlor 6, the most luxurious suite, where Lincoln had stayed prior to his inauguration."* Wherever he went, it was never-ending adulation. Grant had made it plain from the beginning that he would be a field general and would not sit behind a desk in Washington. Now, he couldn't wait to get out of town. Lincoln's secretary asked him what he thought of Grant:

Well, Stoddard, I hardly know what to think of him altogether. I never saw him myself until he came here to take command. He's the quietest little fellow you ever saw... makes the least fuss of any man you ever knew. I believe, two or three times, he has been in this room a minute or so before I knew he was here ... The only evidence you have that he's in any place is that he makes things git! Wherever he is, things move! Grant is the first general I've had. He's a general! You know how it has been with all the rest. As soon as I put a man in command of the army, he'd come to me with a plan of a campaign and about as much as say, "Now I don't believe I can do it, but if you say so, I'll try it on" and so put the responsibility of the success or failure on me. They all wanted me to be the general. It isn't so with Grant. He hasn't told me what his plans are. I don't know, and I don't want to know. I am glad to find a man who can go ahead without me.

Grant was now in charge of over half a million battle-ready troops and all the support that went with them. He *"was as absolutely supreme, as free to dictate its every movement as any general who ever took the field."* He laid out a strategy reaching across the entire South to bring the war to an end. Thanks to the telegraph and the thousands of troops keeping the lines up-to-date and protected as each part of his vast armies moved, he was able to stay constantly informed and maintain control across the entire South. *"It had never happened before in the history of war that one man directed so completely four distinct armies, separated by thousands of miles, ordering the operations of each for the same day, and receiving at night reports from each that his orders had been obeyed."* Thus, the final campaign began that spring.

Grant had a hard job. Both he and Lincoln fully understood that the only way to win the war was to destroy both Lee's army and General Johnson's army in Georgia, along with the infrastructure that supported them, while all the Confederacy had to do to win the war was avoid letting its armies be destroyed until the northern public got tired of supporting this war over an issue that didn't affect them. Beginning in May, over a four-week period of intense fighting with General Lee in northern Virginia, the Union lost 65,000 troops, dead, wounded, or missing, while Lee lost 35,000. Why the disparity? Because the Union had to attack entrenched positions while Lee was just defending them. Still, Lee had lost an irreplaceable 40% of his army (the Confederacy had, by then, conscripted all white males between the ages of 17 and 50 for military duty), while Union replacements were plentiful. Still, after his one-sided loss at Cold Harbor, Grant halted frontal attacks and moved south toward Richmond, which forced Lee to take his reduced army into Richmond to defend the capital of the Confederacy. The siege of Richmond had begun with Grant and Lee entrenching against each other while General Sherman moved toward Atlanta against General Johnson, and General Sheridan proceeded to wreak havoc in the Shenandoah Valley, which was the breadbasket for Richmond and General Lee's Army.

The magnitude of the human slaughter in those first four weeks of battle shocked the northern public. And there was a presidential election coming in November. The democrats nominated General McClellan, whom Lincoln had fired two years before because of his unwillingness to push the fight. The war was the only significant issue in the campaign. McClellan's platform was to end the war, strike a deal, and let the Confederacy go as a separate slave nation.

It looked like Lincoln would lose. Unless the tide turned in the war, Lincoln expected to lose. Then, on September 1, just two months before the election, Atlanta fell to General Sherman. A month later he would start his march to the sea. The war again looked winnable, with the end in sight. Lincoln won in an electoral landslide. However, he only got 55% of the popular vote. For the first time, those in the military were allowed to vote with Lincoln getting 80% of the vote of the troops. So, he only got 53% of the civilian vote, which means 47% of the northern public was willing to let the South go its separate way as a slave nation. The nation was tired of war.

After a long siege of Richmond, General Lee finally fled with his starving army with Grant's well-fed army in hot pursuit. General Robert E. Lee, age 58, surrendered his Confederate Army of Northern Virginia to General Ulysses S. Grant, age 42, at Appomattox Court House, Virginia, on April 9, 1865, effectively bringing to close the Civil War. After some discussion between the two generals, with Lee looking splendid in his finest full-dress grey uniform and gold-hilted sward while Grant was in mud-splattered boots and a dirty, well-worn field uniform, Grant quickly wrote out in pencil the terms of surrender. Lee then reviewed them and said:

Yes, I am bound to be satisfied with anything you offer. It is more than I expected.

Grant then called in his staff officers and asked one to write out the terms in ink for signature. However, the man was so nervous that his hand shook, so Grant called Ely Parker, another staff officer, to do the writing. Parker was a full-blooded Seneca Indian from upstate New York who had been on Grant's personal staff for a year and a half. When Grant introduced Parker to Lee, Lee *"blushed deeply, eyeing tensely his complexion."* One observer noted, *"What was passing in his mind no one knew, but the natural surmise was that he at first mistook Parker for a negro, and was struck with astonishment to find that the commander of the Union armies had one of that race on his personal staff."* Another onlooker figured Lee believed *"a mulatto had been called on to do the writing as a gratuitous affront."* However, Lee soon realized Parker was an Indian. As he shook Parker's hand, Lee said:

I am glad to see one real American here.

Ely Parker then replied:

We are all Americans.

So, the Civil War came to an end. Along with its huge monetary costs, it had cost one life for every six slaves freed. And thousands more were permanently maimed.

Then came the hard work of trying to rebuild a single unified nation. Although I have heard the term *Reconstruction* all my life in relation to the first few years after the Civil War, I had little understanding of what it meant. It just seemed to be glossed over. At the same time, all I remember learning about Grant, in school or otherwise, was that he was a drunken butcher as a general and a corrupt president who was only elected because he was a war hero. Today, we do not appreciate what a beloved figure Grant was during his lifetime or his stature in the world. Over a half million people filled the streets of New York City for his funeral. His memoir, 336,000 words, was written out in longhand with virtually no markups in the final year of his life as he was dying in agony of throat cancer (he died just one week after finishing it). He wrote it to provide financial support for his wife after his death. It sold over 300,000 copies, an astounding number for a memoir in that period. It *"widely viewed as a masterpiece, is probably the foremost military memoir in the English language, written in a clear supple style that transcends the torment of its composition."* I have come to believe that these historical oversights of Grant and reconstruction for more than a century are linked, as I learned that Grant was the central figure in reconstruction. I can only speculate as to how or why these oversights began, but they continue today. In his 2018 biography of Frederick Douglas, David W. Blight barely mentions Grant's name in passing and does not discuss him at all, let alone his relationship with Douglas, while covering extensively the links between Lincoln and Douglas. Yet, Douglas was a staunch defender of Grant and even campaigned for him. Douglas wrote:

Abraham Lincoln made the negro a free man, and Gen. Ulysses S. Grant made him a citizen.

Grant stretched federal power as far as he could to make reconstruction work, but it all collapsed the day he left office. And, as described by Ron Chernow, the result was disastrous:

Once Reconstruction collapsed, it left southern blacks for eighty years at the mercy of Jim Crow segregation, lynchings, poll taxes, literacy tests, and other tactics designed to segregate them from the whites and deny them the vote. Black sharecroppers would be degraded to the level of debt-ridden serfs, bound to their former plantation owners. After 1877, the black community in the South steadily lost ground until a rigid apartheid separated the races completely, a terrible state of affairs that would not be fixed until the rise of the civil rights movement after World War II.

Historian Richard N. Current saw Grant as the most underrated American president and wrote:

By backing Radical Reconstruction as best he could, he made a greater effort to secure the constitutional rights of blacks than did any other President between Lincoln and Lindon B. Johnson.

RECONSTRUCTION – The plot was to kill both Grant and Lincoln that night of April 14, 1865, at Ford's Theater, just five days after General Lee's surrender. However, Mrs. Lincoln had somehow offended Julia Grant earlier in the day, causing Julia, at the last minute, to insist that Ulysses take her out of town before nightfall. That saved Grant's life. When Abraham Lincoln ran for reelection in 1864, he wasn't expecting to be shot and killed just 40 days after the inauguration, or he would have picked a different running mate for vice president. Andrew Johnson, a former slave owner, had been a senator from Tennessee. As the country came apart in 1861, he did not support secession by southern states and was the only senator from a state that seceded from the Union that did not resign. After the Union had gained control of most of Tennessee in 1863, Lincoln appointed him the governor of Tennessee. So, asking Johnson to be on the ticket as candidate for vice president seemed like a canny political choice that would help unite a deeply divided country when the war finally ended. However, Johnson was still a southerner who considered blacks seriously inferior and sympathized with the plight of white southerners as the war was ending. Meanwhile, Radical Republicans (as they called themselves) now controlled congress and had very different views of the South.

The South, with its unique white culture, one-crop economy, and little industrialization, had always been much poorer than the North despite the plantation owners living well. Now, it was in ruins structurally and financially. Plus, it now had millions of rural free blacks that were essentially illiterate, broke, and homeless. Further, while slavery had finally ended, the virulent racism that had developed with it over more than two centuries had not ended. To the contrary, resentment among white southerners over the war and black freedom only heightened racist feelings. Arguably, this intensified racial bigotry and prejudice after the war is as great, if not a greater, a stain on the USA as slavery itself. Slavery was a common and accepted practice elsewhere in the Americas and around the world in 1776. But the insidious and toxic racism that dominated the southern states of the USA in and after 1865 may well have been as intense as that of the Afrikaners in South Africa.

Eleven states had left the Union. Now, they needed to be brought back in. Hmmm, how to do that? And just what was the legal status of those newly freed? Those were the two issues for *Reconstruction*. Politically, it was as turbulent as the lead-up to the war or as the war itself. The nation was on a knife's edge. So, it is difficult to summarize in a few pages, but here goes.

Congress, with encouragement from Lincoln, had passed the 13th Amendment banning slavery in January 1865, and sent it to the states for ratification. The *Freedmen's Bureau* was created in March 1865 by Lincoln with the mandate to *"feed, clothe, and educate former slaves, providing them with medical supplies and legal protection and relocating them on more than 850,000 acres of land the federal government had come to control during the war."* This fostered the idea that newly freed slaves would get *"forty acres and a mule,"* as thousands of young new agents for this new bureau began to swarm into the south where they were labeled *carpetbaggers* by southerners. With Congress out of session for the rest of the year, President Johnson, on August 16, issued an order that enabled southern whites to recapture land confiscated during the war, which made him a hero to southern whites while dashing the hopes of rural free blacks, particularly those who had already begun to work the 40 acres they thought would be theirs. It turned them into powerless sharecroppers.

By the end of 1865, a new caste system was already emerging in the south, where freed blacks worked as indentured servants under contracts that subjected them to arrest if they left their assigned land. In Florida, blacks who showed disrespect to their bosses or rode conveyances reserved for whites could be whipped. In Mississippi, they could not hunt or fish. Further, blacks began to be killed at will across the South since they were no longer valuable property to be cared for. No sheriff or policeman (all white) would arrest a white man for harming or killing a black man. Nor would a white judge try them, nor a white jury convict them. White supremacy was quickly being reestablished across the south.

The 13th Amendment was ratified and went into effect in December 1865. That same month Congress came back into session. And the battle over reconstruction began. Congress made clear that they would not accept, as members of Congress, any Representatives or Senators sent from a state that had left the Union and joined the Confederacy until that state had complied with criteria acceptable to the sitting Congress. And this became the standard for southern states full readmission to the Union. President Johnson fumed. The army was still spread throughout much of the South where they were the only protection for blacks and for white agents of the Freedmen's Bureau. And Grant was still over the army. In January 1866, he finally began to realize the level of oppression being imposed on freed slaves and issued a general order that protected *"colored persons from prosecutions if charged with offences for which white persons are not prosecuted or punished in the same manner and degree."*

In February, Johnson vetoed renewal of the Freedmen's' Bureau. In response, Congress passed a civil rights bill that nullified Black Codes in southern states that prevented freedmen from owning property, making contracts, and filing lawsuits. The bill also made the federal government, not the states, the guarantor of basic liberties and citizenship rights. Johnson vetoed it. Congress promptly overrode the veto, making it law. Grant saw his job as following the law, despite opposition from his boss, the president. His commanders in the south proceeded to abolish state Black Codes that had different laws for blacks than whites. Race riots continued across the south with blacks being slaughtered. In June Congress passed the 14th Amendment that defined citizenship and guaranteed due process and equal protection under the law to all citizens in a way that included all blacks but still excluded Indian tribes. Although it was denounced by President Johnson, it was sent to the states for ratification.

Both sides of this reconstruction fight (between President Johnson and the Radical Republicans in Congress) were still trying to curry favor with Grant who was still trying to keep the military out of politics while complying with the law. So, in July, the President proposed, and Congress quickly passed, a new law creating a position with the simple one-word title of *General* specifically for Grant at more than double the salary of his current position. It was a title no one had held since Washington. And it made Grant, easily the most popular person in the nation, politically untouchable by the President.

While trying to appear neutral and remain apolitical, as he felt the army should in the disputes between Congress and the president, Grant was increasingly imposing martial law in portions of the South to protect blacks and federal agents, something Johnson strongly opposed. Unable to sway Grant, Johnson wanted him out of the way. Finally, in a fiery cabinet meeting, Johnson ordered Grant to go to Mexico to address a political conflict there. Grant refused to take the assignment. Johnson flew into a rage at his insubordination. Grant jumped up and replied:

I am an officer of the army, and bound to obey your military orders. But this is a civil office, a purely diplomatic duty that you offer me, and I cannot be compelled to undertake it.

And then Grant left the room. He knew Johnson could not afford to fire him, and he was not about to yield control of the military at this critical time in the South. In this same timeframe, Confederate veterans in Tennessee formed the Ku Klux Klan, which then spread across the South with former soldiers working under their former commanders in a secret society against blacks.

Johnson did everything he could to keep states from ratifying the 14th Amendment. However, Grant felt it should be a condition of acceptance back into the Union. The Radical Republicans in Congress gained more seats in the 1866 elections. Then, in March 1867, they (in consultation with Grant) passed the First Reconstruction Act. It divided up ten southern states (Tennessee had ratified the 14th amendment, so they were excluded) into five military districts with enormous power for district commanders to oversee conventions to draft new state constitutions, along with requiring states to ratify the 14th amendment and grant voting rights to blacks before readmittance to the Union. Johnson promptly vetoed it. Congress promptly overrode the veto.

This elevated things to a whole new level. Many who had supported abolishing slavery had not really thought through the next step of granting them citizenship and the right to vote. Oh! My! Grant, however, immediately proceeded to implement this new law with the view that it provided military governments for the rebel states and that present state governments should be considered provisional (giving district commanders power to remove elected state and local officials). Then, a few weeks later, Congress passed the Second Reconstruction Act, which basically gave military leaders control over elections and the power to register voters. Johnson raged at this bill as he vetoed it. As did whites across the South. The idea of their slaves not only being free but now voting? No! Congress promptly overrode the veto. In July, Congress passed the Third Reconstruction Act that confirmed the power of military district commanders to fire civilian officials and expanded their supreme power over voting rights and elections. The president vetoed it, and Congress overrode the veto. Grant then enthusiastically enforced the new law.

Across the South, conventions began to meet to draw up new constitutions, many with a majority of black delegates. They formalized civil rights for all. Blacks registered to vote in incredible numbers. New elections brought in black sheriffs, school board members, state legislatures, and congressmen. While Grant considered Reconstruction a noble experiment and was pleased with the progress being made, he was uncomfortable with military rule and hoped to end it as soon as possible without sacrificing the gains made. On the other hand, for the Southern whites, finding their former slaves in these positions of power and with the right to vote, all sustained by an invading federal army, was a world turned upside down. Fury kept building.

Still, In June 1868, six states qualified for readmission to the Union. The next month, the 14th Amendment was ratified, guaranteeing black citizenship. That summer, the Republicans nominated Grant as their candidate for President of the United States on the expectation that he would accept the nomination even though he had never said whether he would accept it or not. After being notified of his nomination, Grant went home to Galena, Illinois, until the election. He did not campaign. As the 1868 election approached, The Klan became increasingly active in a guerilla campaign of murder and arson against blacks.

Grant won an electoral vote landslide and won the popular vote by five points. He carried all the southern states but Georgia and Louisiana, where Klan violence was the worst. He probably lost a majority of the nationwide white vote. Some northern states did not yet allow blacks to vote. At age 46, he was the youngest man elected as president to that point. Since he had not campaigned, he had no campaign promises to fill. People were not sure what they would get.

A few weeks before Grant took office, Congress passed the 15th Amendment, which states in part:

The right of citizens of the United States to vote shall not be denied or abridged by the United States or by any state on account of race, color, or previous conditions of servitude.

This amendment, which also gave Congress the power to enforce this right by appropriate legislation, was then sent to the states for ratification. Grant had strongly supported this amendment and urged its ratification in his inaugural address. When Grant took office in March 1869, three states, Virginia, Mississippi, and Texas, had not yet been readmitted to the Union. He asked Congress to authorize elections to ratify new state constitutions while insisting that those constitutions secure the civil rights of both black and whites within their borders. They were each readmitted within a year.

This was before the days of a career civil service, so every government job was political patronage. *"Grant made extraordinary strides in naming blacks, Jews, and Native Americans to federal positions."* Blacks dined at the White House and for the first time, ordinary blacks visiting the White House were allowed in the front door. He appointed black diplomats for Haiti and some African countries. He appointed Jews. He named Ely Parker, his Seneca Indian aid during the war, as Commissioner of Indian Affairs, the first Native American to hold the position and the first non-white to hold any such high-level government position. Together, Grant and Parker tried to clean up the corrupt and very lucrative network of licensed government traders (previously selected through congressional patronage) who routinely cheated Indians on supplies (food, clothing, shelter) they were contracted to provide them. Grant replaced many of these traders with Quakers, known for their pacifism and integrity. Unfortunately, he also replaced some with army officers who were far from pacifists.

Grant raised human rights issues abroad, particularly for Russian and Romanian Jews. He also pushed to annex the Dominican Republic and make it a state as had happened with Texas 25 years before, but he could never muster sufficient congressional support.

The 15th Amendment was ratified on February 3, 1870. While blacks only made up 13% of the total population, they accounted for 36% of the population in the South. They were in the majority in South Carolina and Mississippi. Southern whites were outraged. Throughout 1870, Grant was receiving pleas from southern governors for help combating the Klan and other quasi-military secret groups. Witnesses were too terrified to testify against Klan members (five were murdered in Mississippi) and juries were afraid to convict. In May 1870, Congress passed, and Grant signed, the first Enforcement Act, which banned the use of force or intimidation to abridge the right to vote because of race. Grant pushed for and signed the bill creating the *Department of Justice* that June (previously the Attorney General only had a small personal staff) and gave it the immediate task of ensuring compliance with the 13th, 14th, and 15th Amendments in the southern states. Grant also sent additional federal troops to the south. However, Republican advocacy for black voting rights was suddenly costing them white votes all across the nation. In the 1870 elections that November, Democrats won easily in several states while the Republican majorities in Congress shrank drastically. Still, six black congressmen were elected in the deep South, with four of them having been born as slaves. However, thanks to Klan intimidation, Democrats regained control in Georgia, Florida, and Alabama. In Mississippi, dozens of black churches and schools were burned without prosecutions.

Grant and Congress were undeterred. The 1870 voting irregularities in several southern states triggered the second Enforcement Act, which Grant signed in February 1871. It enabled federal judges to appoint election officials to supervise elections and certify results. At the same time, Grant sent army officers into South Carolina with the authority to arrest Klan members while having U.S. attorneys from the Justice Department prosecute the cases and Federal judges hear the cases. It was the first time the federal government, instead of state or local government, was used to punish private criminal acts.

He also called Congress back into session in March (they weren't scheduled to meet again until December) to provide further federal measures to combat the Klan and enforce the new amendments. Democrats were apoplectic. One congressman complained, "*It seems to me that this will virtually empower the President to abolish State Governments.*" Grant was referred to as "*Kaiser Grant, a dictator, a despot.*" Still, on April 20, 1871, Grant was able to sign the third Enforcement Act that became known as the *Ku Klux Klan Act.* It laid down criminal penalties for depriving citizens of their right to hold office, sit on a jury, or vote. It authorized the federal government to prosecute such crimes if states refused to act. It also expressly empowered the president to suspend habeas corpus, declare martial law, and send troops. It made it illegal to go in disguise on a public highway to deprive any person of equal protection under the law or to conspire with others to do so. To further its reach, Grant issued a General Order allowing troops to arrest violators of the Act and to break up and disperse "*bands of disguised marauders.*" Armed with all this, Grant went to war against the Klan. Amos Akerman, the Attorney General charged with leading this war, said this about the Klan:

I doubt whether from the beginning of the world until now, a community, nominally civilized, has been so fully under the domination of systematic and organized depravity.
The Klan is the most atrocious organization that the civilized part of the world has ever known.

By the end of the year (1871), over 3,000 had been arrested and over a thousand convicted. Those numbers went up even more in 1872 as the election that fall approached. During Grant's reelection bid in 1872, against Democrat Horace Greely, Frederick Douglas would be among his most ardent supporters and campaigners. Douglas tried to add up all the black employees scattered throughout the federal bureaucracy "*and was simply staggered by their numbers.*"

During the campaign, Douglas said of Grant:

To Grant more than any other man the Negro owes his enfranchisement.
I have called upon him often... and have always found him to be easily
accessible, gentlemanly, and cordial.
If as a class we are slighted by the Republican Party, we are as a class
murdered by the Democratic Party.

Grant won overwhelmingly in the Electoral College and got 56% of the popular vote. He got almost all the black vote. Republicans also gained comfortable majorities in Congress. However, there were a few problems. Grant got zero votes in three Georgia counties with majority black populations. In Louisiana, Republican votes dropped by half, and there were claims of over 2,000 being killed or injured leading up to the election. Further, in Louisiana, both the Republican and Democrat candidates for governor claimed victory, as did their candidates for the state legislature. Each party then proceeded to place their people in office. Chaos.

Through 1873 and 1874, still more thousands of Klan members were arrested, tried by Federal prosecutors, and convicted in federal courts as people began to feel it was safe to testify against Klan members. As the 1874 mid-term elections approached, the Klan had been broken. And the Department of Justice had made its reputation. However, efforts to intimidate blacks continued.

Southern white feelings against blacks intensified along with resentment of the military and federal law enforcement. Meanwhile, those in the northern states were getting weary of military occupation of southern states, while many weren't all that keen on black voting rights anyway. Further, concern about corruption in Grant's administration was growing. The problem for Grant was that while he was incapable of placing self-interest above the public interest as he discharged his public duties, he thought that was true for most other people as well. It is not. He placed some untrustworthy people in high positions of public trust because he mistakenly trusted them. And then would not listen when stories of corruption began to surface. It cost him dearly in terms of public trust. Plus, the nation was suddenly in a recession.

Thus, the 1874 elections were disastrous for the Republican Party. Republicans lost control of the House, where they had had a sizable majority, for the first time since the war. Democrats won in New York, New Jersey, Massachusetts, Pennsylvania, Ohio, Missouri, and Illinois. Half the house committee chairmanships were taken over by southerners who were committed to blocking any further racial progress by Grant. They launched investigations into the new Department of Justice and imposed steep cuts in funding for enforcing Reconstruction. Also, *"The northern public, beset by economic troubles, soured on Reconstruction."*

The 1874 elections were also disastrous for blacks in the South. The old white elite Democrats regained control of Alabama. In Mississippi, the elections were quiet because blacks had already been intimidated. White supremacists in Vicksburg simply evicted the elected black sheriff from the courthouse. When a black militia group came to support him, whites declared martial law and went on a murderous rampage killing blacks. As explained by Ron Chernow:

White Democrats had demonstrated that without the protection of federal troops, they could resurrect the prewar power structure. The Vicksburg vote showed the fundamental weakness of a political revolution that had relied heavily on force applied by outsiders in Washington – something that couldn't be maintained indefinitely. The lesson was well learned by armed White League and White Line militia in Mississippi, Louisiana, Arkansas, Alabama, and South Carolina, who mobilized to retake control of their states.

The Presidential election of 1876 was the most contentious in the history of the USA. Grant did not seek reelection. The Republican nominee was Rutherford B. Hayes, governor of Ohio. The Democrats nominated Samuel J. Tilden, governor of New York. Despite credible allegations of fraud, violence at the polls, disenfranchisement, and intimidation, it remains the highest voter turnout in American history, with 82% of the eligible voting-age population voting. Tilden won the popular vote, but the electoral vote was indecisive. With 185 votes needed to win, Tilden had 184, while Hayes had 165. In three states (Florida, Louisiana, and South Carolina), with a total of 19 electoral votes, both the Democrats and Republicans claimed victory and sent electors to Washington to cast their ballots in the Electoral College. So, neither set of electors were counted. In Oregon, one elector was declared illegal and was replaced, so that vote was contested. What to do? In a compromise, the Democrats conceded all 20 contested votes to Hayes, and, in return, the Republicans agreed to withdraw all federal troops from the South. So, Hayes won in the Electoral College 185 to 184. And Reconstruction was over.

THE POST CIVIL WAR SOUTH – White southerners again had unconstrained power, and Jim Crow segregation basically ruled for the next 80 years. Since the newly freed blacks were now fully counted in the census (rather than just 60%), the South had increased its representation in Congress while still blocking blacks from voting. Thus, southern white voters had even more influence in Congress per voter than before the war compared to voters in the rest of the nation.

Among the first things evident among newly freed blacks in the South were desperate attempts to find family members who had been separated during slavery. Then, a new form of agrarian economy formed in the South with the end of slavery after the war. Former slaves, almost all from plantations or farms, were free, but landless, broke, illiterate, and largely without skills. Thus, a sharecropper system evolved that would dominate southern agriculture for almost a century. *"The South retained the essential attributes of what today is called a Third World country: ownership of means of production by a small, privileged elite; desperate poverty and grinding toil for most of the population; and an economy based on agriculture and extractive industries rather than manufacturing and services. . . For eighty years after its catastrophically failed attempt to achieve independence, the South would remain a Third World country, inside one that would develop the largest and most dynamic First World economy on earth."*

Frederick Douglas had learned as a child that education and slavery were incompatible. Slave owners had worked hard to keep their slaves illiterate. Yet, by 1866, just one year after the war ended, there were about 1,400 Northern white teachers who moved to the South and began teaching black children in 975 new Southern schools. By 1870, those numbers had risen to over 2,500 Northern white teachers in over 2,000 new Southern black schools, mostly one-room schools. Although New England only had about a sixth of the North's white population, about half of those teachers came directly from New England, while most of the rest were born there. In short, this was a New England crusade to educate black children, which was not without personal peril for these teachers in those early chaotic years of reconstruction. *"The missionaries from New England who founded the first schools for Negroes in the South left the imprint of their Puritan background upon Negro education. In addition to strict morality, these missionaries promoted the Yankee virtues of industry and thrift."* This was deliberately done in an effort to supplant the Southern culture that dominated among both whites and their newly freed slaves. *"First, students were taught to speak English correctly and thus avoid the ungrammatical speech and dialect of the masses. They were expected to be courteous, speak softly, and never exhibit spontaneous boisterousness."*

Because these educators were trying to supplant culture as well as educate, some boarding schools were established, which gave teachers around-the-clock control over students' lives. In 1871, an official board of evaluators attended exams at a new black school in Atlanta. One board member, an ex-slaveowner, expected it would confirm blacks' inferiority. Instead, as described in an Atlanta newspaper, the board could hardly *"believe what we witnessed. To see colored boys and girls fourteen to eighteen years of age, reading in Greek and Latin, and demonstrating correctly problems in Algebra and Geometry."* A substantial share of future black leaders were educated in the black schools and colleges in the South established by New Englanders after the war, including Thurgood Marshall and Martin Luther King Jr.

While the Ku Klux Klan would not resurface again until the end of the nineteenth century, it then rose and became the enforcement arm of white supremacy across the South for the first half of the twentieth century. And some of our leaders were just fine with that. For example, Woodrow Wilson who, after serving as president of Princeton University, was elected President of the USA in 1912 and again in 1916, stated that it was laudable for:

white men of the South to rid themselves, by fair means or foul, of the intolerable burden of governments sustained by the votes of ignorant Negroes.

And he wasn't alone. As mentioned earlier, ethnocentrism, including racism, is a near universal human trait. While white racism in the South was particularly virulent, bigotry based on race, culture, and religion still extended throughout the USA – and the world. Further, in the early twentieth century, *Eugenics* was the latest rage among progressive thinkers, in the West and around the world, including Wilson and Margaret Sanger (the founder of Planned Parenthood). This was, at least in part, spurred on by Darwin's ideas on evolution and *survival of the fittest*. The idea that reproduction in the "inferior" races should at least be limited (Planned Parenthood is still the largest provider of abortions in black neighborhoods in the USA, though the rationale has been changed to a woman's right to choose) was held by many progressives as many blacks were unknowingly sterilized. Outright extermination was only advocated by a few. However, Hitler cited these promoters of eugenic ideas as he developed his approach to Jews.

The South, both white and black, retained much of the Southern culture described earlier. The Honor Culture was particularly evident in Appalachia. Malcom Gladwell cites Fischer as he explains that family feuds, such as the Hatfield's & McCoy's, were the rule rather than the exception in southern Appalachia because of the culture the first settlers brought with them from British borderlands. He tells of one feud between families that started over accusations of cheating in a poker game. Over the coming days, as various family members were killed, one young man, Will Turner, stumbled home howling in pain after being shot in a gunfight at the courthouse with the Howards. His mother snapped at him: "*Stop that! Die like a man, like your brother did.*" So, "*Will Turner shut his mouth, and he died.*" Gladwell cites another incident involving white Southerners around 1930 to demonstrate that the Honor culture still continued. "*The case before the jury involved an irascible gentleman who lived next door to a filling station. For several months he had been the butt of various jokes played by the attendants and the miscellaneous loafers who hung around the station, despite his warnings and his notorious short temper. One morning, he emptied both barrels of his shotgun at his tormenters, killing one, maiming another permanently, and wounding a third."* Only one member of the jury voted to convict him. Another jury member said: *"He wouldn't of been much of a man if he hadn't shot them fellows."*

Gladwell then cites a 1990s study at the University of Michigan where male students' responses to various insults were measured (even adrenaline levels). The researchers found that the deciding factor in how students reacted *"wasn't how emotionally secure they were, or whether they were intellectuals or jocks, or whether they were physically imposing or not. It was where they were from."* Those from the South were soon ready to fight. The rest were not. And these weren't poor kids from the mountains of Kentucky. They were from upscale families living in places such as the Atlanta suburbs. While current mobility within the USA is certainly diluting it, 130 years after the Civil War, remnants of that Southern *Cracker* Culture were still evident. Even in this century, southern whites dominate the infantry and other frontline fighting troops in our current all volunteer military.

WOMEN'S SUFFERAGE – The first presidential election, where the right to vote was extended across all the states to virtually all adult white men, regardless of property ownership, was the 1828 election of Andrew Jackson. And with it came *Jacksonian democracy*. While women had been allowed to vote in a few places on certain things before the Civil War, the broad understanding was that voting was for men only. Susan B. Anthony was an early advocate in the women's suffrage movement. She was also an abolitionist and an ally of Frederick Douglas. So, she was disappointed when he did not support her efforts to have women included in the 15th Amendment that granted blacks the right to vote. However, Douglas, while generally supporting the right of women to vote, was not about to see the idea of black voting rights get sidelined by tying it to another highly controversial issue.

The Wyoming Territory, in 1869, was the first jurisdiction to grant women the right to vote in all elections, followed by the Utah Territory in

1870 and the Washington Territory in 1873. Susan B. Anthony registered to vote in Rochester, New York, in 1872 and then voted for Grant. She was arrested, jailed for a short time, and convicted for casting a fraudulent ballot. But she never paid the $100 fine levied against her. From that point on, women's right to vote became a hot political issue, with people organizing on both sides. Wyoming retained that right when it became a state in 1890 and was the first state to allow women to vote in all elections. Utah restored that right when it became a state in 1896 (that right in Utah had been removed by Congress in 1887).

Over the next two decades, various states debated the issue, with some states granting full voting rights to women and other states granting women the right to vote in some elections but not others, ranging from only school board elections to only presidential elections. By the time the 19th Amendment was finally ratified in August 1920, granting the right to vote to all citizens, regardless of sex, 15 states had already granted that right. They included ten western states (all but New Mexico), along with South Dakota, Kansas, and Oklahoma in the Great Plains. Michigan and New York had also granted full voting rights to women. Only seven states had not granted any voting rights to women by then: Pennsylvania, Maryland, West Virginia, Virginia, North Carolina, South Carolina, and Alabama. The remaining 26 states had a wide range of hodgepodge rights in some elections.

THE ABOLITION OF LEGAL SLAVERY IN THE WORLD – A strong movement under the banner of *Social Justice,* has developed in the twenty-first century, particularly among progressives and the younger generation, that divides humanity into two groups: oppressed and oppressors, and then uses colonization by white Europeans since Columbus to define which is which. Thus, regardless of economic status, all whites are privileged oppressors, and all non-whites, except for some Asians, are oppressed. If only the history of humans was that simple. Among those pushing this view is black activist Nova Reid, who, while apparently claiming to speak for all black people, wrote in 2021:

We have been rescuing ourselves and revolting against the oppressor throughout history. Contrary to the popular belief that only great white men rescued us from slavery, it was the Haitian Revolution from 1791 to 1804, the only successful slave revolt in history, that instigated the global abolishment of slavery.

She then goes on to claim that what happened in Haiti triggered other slave revolts in the British West Indies that caused Britain to reconsider whether enslaving blacks was sustainable because:

there was a huge fear (still present to this day) that Black folk would want to seek revenge and go on a murderous killing spree of white Europeans.

She is correct that the Haitian Revolution was the only slave revolt in history that managed to create a new nation led by former slaves. It is also true that Britain got out of the international slave trade in 1807 and that the USA got out of the international slave trade in 1808, just a few years after the Haiti revolt ended. However, her claims about the reasons for that are fiction.

There are at least four problems in her statement. First, *"the oppressor throughout history"* has often been black. Black Africans had been enslaving other black Africans in Africa for centuries, maybe millennia before black African slaves began serving white European masters on the Island of Madeira in 1450. *"Even at the peak of the Atlantic slave trade, Africans retained more slaves for themselves than they sent to the Western Hemisphere."* As much as a third or more of the population in several West African kingdoms were slaves. Black Africans continued to enslave other black Africans by the millions in Africa for decades after the last black slave serving a white master in Europe or the Americas was freed. Legal slavery was not abolished in Sierra Leone until 1928.

Second, she ignores the fact that Islam enslaved as many black Africans as white European Christians. Islam had been shipping millions of black African slaves east and north before any black slaves went to Madeira, or the Americas, to serve white Europeans. And they continued to do so after the Atlantic slave trade ended. Eyewitness accounts document the horrendous conditions of Islamic caravans of black slaves going north across the Sahara 40 years after the last white (Portuguese) owned ship carried black slaves to the Americas (Brazil). British ships, at considerable expense of blood and treasure, continued to patrol the East Coast of Africa in the second half of the nineteenth century, intercepting Islamic slave ships. While these British ships were able to rescue tens of thousands from slavery, some slave ship crews would throw their cargo of slaves overboard to drown rather than be captured with slaves on board.

One African king, upset by Britain's efforts to end the African export of slaves, said: *"We think the trade must go on. That is the verdict of our oracle and the priests. They say your country, however great, can never stop a trade ordained by God himself."* It was only due to British pressure that the Ottoman Empire and Egypt finally abolished slavery late in the nineteenth century. Slavery was not abolished in Saudi Arabia until 1962.

Third, the idea that Britain (in 1807) or the USA (in 1808) banned participation in the international slave trade, or that Britain banned slavery throughout all its colonies in 1833, or that all the northern USA states that had abolished slavery, did so because they were afraid of being killed in murderous slave revolts is simply ludicrous. Neither the British parliament nor the legislatures of northern USA states had anything to fear from slave revolts because there were few if any, slaves there to revolt. The northern states abolished slavery because of ideals contained in the Declaration of Independence, and since only a few owned slaves, there was little economic or political penalty for doing so. On the other hand, southern states had millions of slaves, and their owners were certainly nervous about slave revolts. But that only led to more harsh and repressive treatment of slaves rather than the abolition of slavery there.

While black abolitionists like Frederick Douglas certainly had an impact, it was with words impacting the conscience of the dominant white majority. Beginning in 1845, Douglas spent almost two years traveling the British Isles (Ireland, Scotland, and England), giving speeches, selling his autobiography, and raising money for the abolitionist movement in the USA. British abolitionist groups raised the money ($712) to purchase his freedom from Mr. Auld so that he was able to return to the USA in 1847 as a free man rather than an escaped slave.

It was the Civil War, fought between white southerners and primarily white northerners, and three constitutional amendments between 1865 and 1870 passed by a white national congress and then ratified by white state legislatures that freed black slaves in the USA, made them citizens, and gave them the right to vote (although it took another century before that white majority gained the will to enforce the commitments contained in those amendments). European countries abolished slavery throughout their colonial territories, including the Caribbean, because of pressure from the population at home rather than in response to the fear of slave revolts of local whites living in those territories. Nor did fear of slave revolts drive the rest of the Americas to free slaves. Mexico banned slavery (in 1829) just eight years after gaining independence because slavery was not a significant part of their economy, and they wanted to limit the immigration of slave owners coming into Texas from the USA with their slaves.

When Abraham Lincoln expressed the view that slavery was morally wrong *"It was a belief less than a century old in the West and still virtually non-existent outside the West."* As expressed by Thomas Sowell:

It was the rise of modern free societies and their accompanying ideologies in the West which made slavery stand out in stark contrast, and it was the emergence of a general questioning of institutions and beliefs in the eighteenth century – also in the West – that brought slavery into question.

That such an institution could last so long unchallenged, on every inhabited continent, is a chilling example of what can happen when people simply do not think.

Finally, moral objections to slavery began before the Haitian Revolution. The Protestant Reformation of Christianity in Europe was based upon questioning historical practices, and that extended to include the morality of slavery. In the eighteenth century, *"Quakers were the first religious group to find slavery morally intolerable – a threat to their own eternal salvation, rather than simply a temporal misfortune of others."* In 1772, nineteen years before the slave rebellion in Haiti even began, a British court ruled that a slave could not be exported against his will. Vermont, in its initial state constitution in 1777, banned slavery. The first abolitionist organization in Britain, led by William Wilberforce, was organized in 1787. Legal slavery had been officially abolished in several European countries (and on Madeira – where enslaving Africans by Europeans all started) before the Haitian slave revolt began in 1791. Six northern states (a phase out in some states) in the USA had abolished slavery by then. The 1787 charter for the Northwest Territory prohibited slavery, while anti-slavery societies had been created in Europe and U.S. states (the first in Philadelphia in 1775). In short, the move by European nations and many states in the USA to abolish slavery was led by Christian moral opposition to the practice and was already well underway before the Haitian slave revolt began in 1791.

Still earlier, the Catholic Church began opposing Christians enslaving other Christians about a thousand years ago. There were a couple of Papal decrees stating that it was okay for Christians to enslave heretic Islam (who were enslaving Christians for a thousand years), which was the rationale (not race) for taking black African slaves to Madeira. Slavery had essentially ended in the British Isles by 1200. As a practical matter, both serfdom and slavery in Western Europe had largely ended by 1500. While the transatlantic slave trade brought Europe back into the slave business for a few centuries, including a few thousand brought directly into Europe, moral opposition slowly began to build as the idea of free societies began to spread in association with the Protestant Reformation and really got rolling in the last half of the eighteenth century with the American Revolution. The claim that Africans, beyond Haiti, freed themselves is a convenient fiction. As is the idea that other Africans played no role in their enslavement.

In short, *"On the issue of slavery, it was essentially Western Civilization against the world. At the time, Western Civilization had the power to prevail against all other civilizations. That is how and why slavery was destroyed as an institution in almost the whole world."* Like the Industrial Revolution, *"While Britain spearheaded the anti-slavery movement in the world, the nineteenth century saw anti-slavery feelings spread until they became common throughout Western Civilization – and only in Western Civilization."* Which then pushed it on the world.

Economics also played a role. By 1850, in the USA, slavery had become an agrarian institution tied to plantation agriculture. Even in southern cities, where bigotry was still in fashion, the percentage of free blacks rose since slavery made little economic sense in urban settings. Then, as mechanization linked to the Industrial Revolution spread to agriculture across the USA, the need for year-round unskilled farm labor dropped, and the economic case for slavery was gone.

In conclusion, the horrors of slavery as an institution need to be acknowledged and taught. Further, the chattel slave system of black Africans serving white European masters, as practiced in much of the Americas for almost 400 years, was slavery at its worst. While it began as Christians enslaving Islam, it fostered repulsive racial bigotry that still persists. In fact, the Civil War and the Reconstruction that followed only exacerbated that bigotry in the South, which is as great a blot on this nation as slavery itself. Jim Crow apartheid and the KKK were a national disgrace. And bigotry, in some forms, extended far beyond the South in the USA, and the world.

THE END OF THE AMERICAN FRONTIER – While the first half of the nineteenth century saw the massive expansion of the boundaries of the USA to the Pacific Ocean, it was in the rest of the nineteenth century that much that land west of the Mississippi filled with settlers. And it was a terrible time for Indians. Almost all *Western* novels, movies, and TV shows have been set in that period. It is the era of cowboys and Indians, wagon trains and Indians, settlers and Indians, cavalry and Indians, cowpunchers and sodbusters, cattlemen and sheepmen, cattle drives from Texas to railheads in Kansas, mining boomtowns, and an opulent Chyenne, Wyoming as the cattle country boom attracted European royalty, and railroads extending into the west.

By 1860, $500 million in gold had been extracted in California (sixteen times the then national debt). However, most miners went bust. The surest way to get rich in California was to open a business selling supplies or services to miners. Levi Strauss brought blue denim to San Francisco and got rich, making pants for miners. By 1860, the easy gold was gone, and California's population was 380,000. By then, most miners were paid laborers working for mining companies with substantial capital investment.

In the 1860s, Seattle became a coal mining boomtown shipping coal to a burgeoning San Francisco. By 1870, the Indian population in California had been reduced by 80%. While many died of disease, California killed more Indians than any other state by far. At least two California municipalities openly placed a small bounty to be paid for any Indian scalps or heads brought in. The 1848 treaty ending the war guaranteed full citizenship and property rights to the Spanish already living there. However, by 1860, most had been pushed aside as squatters moved onto and into their property without consequence. Tens of thousands of Chinese came seeking gold. And they were not welcomed. Because they worked harder and were more disciplined, they often succeeded on mining claims whites from the East had given up on. The State imposed taxes applicable only to Chinese that generated half of all state revenues in at least one year in the 1850s. In short, California began as a wild, undisciplined place.

Beginning in 1850, some effort was made to identify and count Indians in the census. During the census counts in the first few decades after the Civil War, Indians were divided into two categories in accordance with the Constitution. Per the 1880 census taker instructions: *"Indians not in tribal relations, whether full-bloods or half-breeds, who are found mingled with the white population, residing with white families, engaged as servants or laborers, or living in huts or wigwams on the outskirts of towns or settlements are to be regarded as a part of the ordinary population of the country for the constitutional purpose of the apportionment of the Representatives among the States, and are to be embraced in the enumeration."* Indians thus counted were included in the total count of the USA population and were listed in the census summary tables as *"civilized Indians."* They totaled 44,021 in 1860, 25,731 in 1870, and 66,407 in 1880. All remaining Indians were considered *"Indians not taxed"*. The report stated: *"By the phrase "Indians not taxed" is meant Indians living on reservations under the care of Government agents, or roaming individually, or in bands, over unsettled tracts of country."*

Only an estimate was made for the number of these Indians, and they were not included in the total population of the USA. Thus, they were clearly not considered citizens. Their numbers showed a steady decline from 295,400 in 1860 down to 240,136 by 1880.

In 1887, Congress passed the Dawes Act, which began the allotment of tracts of Indian reservation lands to individual Indians in an attempt to convert them into property-owning farmers. This went on, tribe by tribe, for over two decades and was largely a failure. Trying to track ownership of those allotted lands has turned into a disaster since, over a century later, each of these allotments now has dozens to hundreds of owners of an undivided interest in those tracts, with the government still holding the title in trust for them. Since many of those trust allotments have produced substantial revenues from oil, gas, coal, or other mineral leases, distribution of those revenues to the individual descendants of the original allotees turned into multibillion-dollar litigation that drug on for decades, extending into this century.

Also, beginning around 1890, Indian schools were opened on many reservations, some of them boarding schools, where children were taught English as part of an effort to integrate them into the general society of the country (to *"civilize"* them). This effort continued well into the 1960s, when the general attitude toward Indians began to change across the country with a broad acceptance of the right of Indian tribes to maintain their culture and languages.

In the 1890 census, the Census Bureau declared that the *"frontier"* had ceased to exist. *"Up to and including 1880 the country had a frontier of settlement, but at present the unsettled area has been so broken into by isolated bodies of settlement that there can hardly be said to be a frontier line. In the discussion of its extent, its westward movement, etc., it cannot, therefore, any longer have a place in the census reports."*

With that, the census stopped tracking the westward movement of settlers. 1890 was also the year of the massacre at Wounded Knee, the last major battle of the Indian wars. In it, about 300 Lakota Sioux were killed (men, women, and children) along with 31 federal cavalry troops. Today, it seems shocking that the Congressional Medal of Honor was awarded to 20 of the cavalry troops. By then, all Indian tribes had been confined to reservations, and there were no longer any free roaming Indian bands. The number of bison, which had roamed the Great Plains by the millions, had been reduced to about 500 animals.

It was not until 1924 that Congress finally passed a law granting birthright citizenship to all Indians. Still, it took a few more decades before every state granted Indians the right to vote.

11: THE SECOND INDUSTRIAL REVOLUTION

The First Industrial Revolution had given us the factory system that manufactured a wide range of products far more efficiently, along with a revolution in transportation, through railroads and steam ships, that moved things and people farther, faster, and more efficiently than had ever been thought possible. Human productivity for each hour worked had soared to unimaginable heights while a wide variety of goods from faraway places were now available at affordable prices. While a few industrialists and financiers had become unimaginably wealthy, it had also vastly increased the standard of living for millions of people while expanding the middle class. It also increased urbanization and multiplied the number of working-class jobs. Although many paid low wages and had poor working conditions, young people from farms, as well as immigrants, still poured into the factories eager to take those jobs.

So, what was life really like in the USA in 1870, as the Second Industrial Revolution was about to begin? The boundaries of the continental USA were set. The USA had 60,000 miles of railroad tracks. The population was nearing 40 million, ten times higher than it had been in that first 1790 census just 80 years before. Around 75% still lived on farms (now less than 2%). About 60% of the population was under 25 (compared to 34% in 2010). About 14% were foreign born, mostly European (in 2010, about 12% of the population were foreign born, most from Latin America or Asia). Blacks accounted for 12.6% of the population (still the same in 2010), while 87% were white (now 60%). Most adults were married and were having lots of babies. The fertility rate was 4.6 babies per white woman (2.1 in 2010) and 7.7 babies per black woman (2.2 in 2010). Rarely were households headed by single adults, male or female. The average household size was five people (now 2.5). Income per-capita had risen to 74% of British and 128% of German per-capita income. *"Living conditions for a substantial share of Americans living in small towns and rural areas were actually much better than in Europe."* Yet, older men often worked until they dropped. The concept of retirement was yet to come.

By 1870, many more products and tools were available and affordable than could have been found in 1776. However, half the family budget was still spent on food. With the invention of the Mason jar in 1859, home preservation of food had begun to extend beyond salting pork to include canning garden produce and fruit. However, other than stoves making their way into some houses, living conditions hadn't changed that much. As described by Robert J. Gordon:

We are so used to the essential comforts of everyday life, of being clean and warm, that we can easily forget how recently those comforts were achieved. In 1870, farm and working-class family members bathed in a large tub in the kitchen, often the only heated room in the home, after carrying cold water in in pails from the outside and warming it over the open-hearth fireplace. All that carrying and heating of water was such a nuisance that baths were not a daily or even weekly event; some people bathed as seldom as once a month. Similarly, heat in every room was a distant dream.
The greatest curse of the rural and urban housewife was the need to carry fresh water into the house and dirty water out of the house.

Often the same bath water was used for multiple family members. And all that was still true by 1890, except most homes had a stove by then so cooking could be done standing up. As late as 1893, most city dwellers, even in the nation's largest cities (88% in Baltimore), only had access to an outside privy. Clothes were still washed with a washboard. By 1870, shoes began to distinguish between right and left feet and the treadle sewing machine was just becoming available which *"held out the impossible promise that one the great drudge pastimes of domestic life could actually be made exciting and fun."* Again, by Robert J. Gordon:

In 1870, except for the upper-class women who could afford to hire a dressmaker or buy designer fashions, most women made their own clothes, as well as a substantial fraction of their children's garments and at least some of their husband's clothes. Each woman was expected to sew; indeed, such skills were indispensable throughout most of the nineteenth century.

In 1870, the railroads were the primary means of moving people and things around the country, which made the railroad companies a powerful force in national policy, which is what led to four time zones being established in the USA. It wasn't always that way. In fact, for the first century of this nation, most cities had their own time, based upon the position of the sun at noon. So, Boston was several minutes ahead of New York City, which was a few minutes ahead of Washington, D.C., and on across the nation. However, this played havoc with railroad schedules. So, railroad executives got together and devised the four time zones and imposed them on the nation, effective November 18, 1883, for all train schedules. While there were many complaints that the country should operate on *"God's time – not Vanderbilt's,"* within a few years, people and cities had fallen in line and the railroads' standard time became the nation's standard time without the involvement of the federal or state governments.

In the five decades between the Civil War and the beginning of World War I, *"the American economy changed more profoundly, grew more quickly, and became more diverse than in any earlier fifty-year period in the nation's history."* Thus, the Second Industrial Revolution, which was largely a product of the USA, would have an enormous impact on daily life for virtually everyone. Some have adopted the *special century* approach to describing its life changing impact; *"holding that economic growth witnessed a singular interval of rapid growth that will not be repeated – the designation of the century between 1870 and 1970 as the special epoch applies only to the United States, the nation which has carved out the technological frontier for all the developed nations since the Civil War.* As explained by John Steele Gordon:

One of the underappreciated aspects of a free-market economy is how it deals so efficiently with shortages. As demand outstrips supply prices rise. The price, in turn, causes both increased conservation of the scarce resource and an intensified search for additional supplies or substitutes in order to convert the high prices into profit.

And in no other place on earth were people as willing to innovate or try new things as in the USA. Gordon then goes on to quote another writer who noted: *"the impetuous energy with which the American mind takes up any branch of industry that promises to pay well."*

The result was the Second Industrial Revolution, which magnified economic growth and improved living standards in the USA (making almost all people vastly richer) and around the world, even for inventions that occurred in other countries. This revolution involved several life changing inventions, mostly between 1875 and World War I, primarily in the USA. Most were by individual inventors rather than a large corporation. Each was a one-time event that often took years, or even decades, for its impact to spread through society. *"Many inventions are one-time only events subject to a long succession of subsequent incremental improvements."* The positive impacts of these inventions on society can be measured to some extent in standard economic terms like national GDP. However, despite initial growing pains, they also had enormous intangible benefits to the quality of life, including the decrease in the physical difficulty and discomforts in the nature of work, the increase in free time as household work was simplified, and productivity increases enabled the workweek to drop from 60 hours to 40 hours, the elimination of child labor, greater home comforts, improved schooling, improved health through safer food and control of infections and disease, greater cleanliness, new travel options, and increased recreation and entertainment options. However, it often took decades for the full benefits to spread as additional improvements were made across society at large. These benefits are taken for granted today, but they had never before been available or even thought of in human history. The Second Industrial Revolution gave us most of what we have come to think of as modern society.

It was also a time of enormous political and financial change. No industrial business was listed on the New York Stock Exchange in 1865. Yet, by the turn of the century, the USA had the largest and most modern industrial economy on earth, led by giant corporations unimaginable 35 years earlier. As this industrial explosion began, nothing characterized

American politics and its economy more than corruption. *"Ulysses S. Grant, himself personally honest to a fault, would go down in history as presiding over the most corrupt administration in the nation's history."* Capitalism needs enforceable rules applicable to both government officials and industry to make it stable and fair. And the USA was just beginning to figure out how to do that. Decades later, Herbert Hoover would write:

The trouble with capitalism is capitalists. They're too damn greedy!

And politicians in positions of power can be greedy too. The process of figuring out new rules and institutions that would allow this new economy to flourish, while assuring that it would operate within rules that would benefit all segments of society, would dominate American politics for the next century. But, to a large extent, the nation did learn how to govern a highly dynamic industrial economy while keeping both industrialists and politicians somewhat honest, by relying on the *"insights of the founding fathers: that men are not angels, that they are driven by self-interest, and that that self-interest can be exploited to the general good by an interlocking system of divided powers."* Now, on to the Second Industrial Revolution.

Of all the new inventions occurring between 1875 and World War I, the two that most shaped and characterized the Second Industrial Revolution occurred within ten weeks of each other in late 1879: one in New Jersey, the other in Germany. Each would be associated with a totally new form of energy that led to dramatic changes in daily life as they spread around the world. Over time, each of those two new forms of energy would be every bit as impactful on the course of human history as the Watt steam engine had been a century before.

THE ELECTRIC LIGHT BULB AND THE DAWN OF THE ELECTRIC AGE – The first of these two major new inventions was Thomas Edison's creation of a viable electric light bulb. Up to that time, throughout human history, the only way to have light after dark was with a flame. Indoor fires always produce some degree of odor and smoke.

Throughout human history, the worst air quality that humans had encountered had been within human dwellings. Not only did humans spend much of their time inside their dwellings, but the air quality there was often much worse than the worst outdoor urban air quality we complain about today.

For generations, the source of indoor light for Europeans had been candles. Around 1800, coal gas was discovered, which gave excellent light in urban settings for outdoor streetlights and indoor light for large buildings like factories, office buildings, and apartments. However, because the gas had to be distributed through pipes, it was considered impractical for most residences. By 1800, whale oil lamps were becoming popular in homes because they gave more light with less flame. However, as whale populations declined, whale oil had become very expensive by 1850, when kerosene was first distilled from coal tar (coal tar is the goop left over after extracting coal gas from coal). Kerosene was cheaper, burned brighter, and safer than whale oil. By the late 1850s, one plant in New York City was producing 5,000 gallons per day of kerosene from coal tar. In the last half of the nineteenth century, other commercial products would also come from coal tar, including aniline dyes (which destroyed the market for vegetable dyes like indigo) insecticides, paints, medicines, and plastic.

Still, each candle or kerosine lamp had to be individually lit and extinguished. Thomas Edison was committed to finding a way to make light from electricity. One late night in September 1879, his laboratory was focused on finding a lasting filament for an electric light.

"At 1:30 in the morning, Batchelor and Jehl watched as Edison began on the ninth fiber, a plain carbonized cotton-thread filament... set up in a vacuum glass bulb. They attached the batteries, and the bulb's soft incandescent glow lit up the ark laboratory, the bottles lining the shelves reflecting its gleam. As had many another experimental models, the bulb glowed bright. But this time, the lamp still shone hour after hour through that night. The morning came and went, and still the cotton-thread filament radiated its incandescent light. Lunch time passed and the carbonized cotton fiber still glowed. At 4:00 pm the glass bulb cracked and the light went out. Fourteen and a half hours!"

Not only did Edison develop a practical and viable electric light bulb, but shortly thereafter, he also built an electric generating station and a distribution system to go with it. His Pearl Street generating station opened in New York City in 1882. With that, the world began to change forever. Now, there were electric lights that not only were clean because they had no flame, but they could be turned on and off with the flick of a switch, even several at one time. *"No more lighting and snuffing."* Instead, *"light was contained in a glass vacuum and need never again be linked with flame or coaxed forth and adjusted; light that did not waver, tip, drip, stink, or consume oxygen and would not spontaneously ignite cloth, dust in factories, or hay in the mow. A child could be left alone with it."* What a miracle! The role of electric lights in developing our modern world was underway and is quite apparent. Enough said about lights.

With a distribution system for electricity for lights came more possibilities. Various inventors had been experimenting with electric motors. By the 1880s, they had reached the point where they were becoming viable for powering machines. Oh, the possibilities! From small motors that could power hand tools in the kitchen or workshop, greatly easing drudgery and increasing productivity, to large motors that could power machines in factories and trolleys on city streets.

While trains powered by steam locomotives were great for intercity and cross-country travel, they were too cumbersome and smoky to be practical for intracity travel. Yet, within cities, people and things were constantly on the move. By 1880, city streets across the country had thousands of horses pulling carts, wagons, carriages, and trolleys everywhere. And they left all the refuse on those streets that goes with thousands of horses constantly on the move. In New York City, the streets were foul because *"Much of the muck followed from the still unavoidable reliance on horses – forty thousand of them, who each working day generated some four hundred tons of manure, twenty thousand gallons of urine, and almost two hundred carcasses."* Electric trolleys and trams revolutionized city travel and cleaned up the streets. *"The transition from horse-drawn streetcars to electrified streetcars was fully complete in the United States between 1890 and 1902."* Then, there were subways, with the New York City system opening in 1904.

Electric lights and motors transformed America. As described by Robert J. Gordon:

When electricity made it possible to create light with the flick of a switch instead of the strike of a match, the process of creating light was changed forever. When the electric elevator allowed buildings to extend vertically instead of horizontally, the very nature of land use was changed, and urban density created. When small electric machines attached to the floor or held in the hand replaced huge and heavy steam boilers that transmitted power by leather or rubber belts, the scope for replacing human labor with machines broadened beyond recognition.

However, electricity can't just be pulled out of the air. This new form of energy that was coming into widespread use for many things, must be generated somehow. Like steam, it doesn't just happen. It must be made. Steam is made by burning fuel to boil water, which creates steam, which can then turn a wheel. Until recently, electricity could only be generated by turning a wheel: waterwheels (at dams or waterfalls), heat (from coal, oil, natural gas, or nuclear reactors), or windmills. An electric motor is the reverse of the same process: using electricity to turn a wheel and power a machine. Now, sunlight, using photovoltaic cells, can generate electricity.

The 1893 Chicago World's Fair, which attracted 26 million visitors, was an incredibly successful showcase to the world of American industrialism and the dawning electric age, not only with all its lights but all the things that electric motors, along with other inventions, were making possible and practical. Among the things first introduced to the world at that fair that we can hardly imagine living without today were zippers, spray paint, and dishwashers. The whole idea of commercially processed foods that could be shipped to faraway markets was just beginning. At that fair, new food products were introduced to the world, such as crackerjacks, cream of wheat, and shredded wheat. William Wrigley, just 31 years old and with an underfinanced tiny new company, used the fair to introduce his first chewing gum, *Juicy Fruit*. It was an immediate sensation. He soon followed that with spearmint-flavored gum. Americans began chewing gum.

THE INTERNAL COMBUSTION ENGINE – Carl Benz, working in Germany in December 1879, is generally credited with building the first operating internal combustion engine. He wrote:

My heart was pounding. I turned the crank. The engine started to go "put put put", and the music of the future sounded with regular rhythm. We listened to it run for a full hour, fascinated, never tiring of the single sound of its song. The longer it played its note, the more sorrow and anxiety it conjured away from the heart.

At the time he had no idea of all the cars, motorcycles, trucks, and airplanes that would follow. In fact, it wasn't until 1885 that Benz first mounted an engine, of a much-improved design on a three wheeled carriage chassis; the first horseless carriage, a self-propelled *automobile*. Over the next 15 years, Benz and other Germans continued to experiment and make improvements. These included such things as moving the engine from under the seat to the front of the carriage so it could be larger, along with spark plugs, carburetors, and transmissions. The 1890s was also the decade when bicycles began to be mass produced and the solutions for many bicycle problems were then applied to early automobiles. The first *diesel* engine prototype, developed by Rudolf Diesel, another German, was successfully operated in 1893. However, the practical application of diesel engines took much longer than Benz's sparkplug engines. American engineers didn't begin serious consideration of the automobile and its internal combustion engine until 1895. Then, the development and use of the automobile in America soon far outstripped European efforts.

In 1900, there were only 8,000 registered automobiles in the USA. By 1905, the number of registered cars had risen to 78,000. A 1906 survey in Minneapolis of a section of road for 24 hours recorded 2,722 horse drawn vehicles, three horse riders, 786 bicycles, and only 183 automobiles, a ratio of 15 to 1 for horse drawn vehicles to automobiles. Two separate 1916 surveys found a ratio of two automobiles for each horse drawn vehicle in Pittsburgh and a ratio of five automobiles for each horse drawn vehicle in an Illinois town. By 1927, the ratio was fifty to one. The number of registered cars in the country had risen from 468,000 in 1910 to nine million in 1920, to 23 million in 1929. By 1910, the total power generated by motor vehicles already exceeded that of all farm animals. As expressed by Robert J. Gordon:

A basic difference between the railroad and motor vehicle, viewed as fundamental inventions in the history of transportation, is that the railroad did not replace the horse but rather raised the demand for horses by extending civilization into hitherto unreachable parts of the country, whereas the motor vehicle replaced the horse and led to its disappearance as a prime mover.

Internal combustion engines – cars, trucks, and farm tractors – had taken over the country, both in the city and in rural America. Although technical improvements have continued, with the addition of air conditioning around 1970, travel by car had, by then, achieved all the speed and comfortable ride on an expanding interstate highway system that we experience today.

Henry Ford played a role in making cars available to the middle- and working-class, which would extend throughout manufacturing across the USA. He created the Ford Motor Company in 1903, one of 57 car manufacturing companies created that year in the USA (27 promptly went bankrupt), and it was moderately successful. His first Model T went on sale in 1908 for $850, a fraction of what most cars cost at the time. It was designed to endure the awful roads then in existence. He sold 10,607 Model Ts that year. After visiting a meat packing plant and seeing how animals were disassembled as they moved down a line, he decided cars could be assembled moving down a line. He introduced the first assembly line in 1913. That year, it took only 93 minutes to assemble a Model T. The price was down to $360. By 1920, the Ford Motor Company was producing fully half of the cars made in the world. Thanks to his ever-improving assembly line methods, a new, improved Model T sold for only $269 in 1923 despite those improvements and intervening inflation. *"The result of Henry Ford's relentless drive to lower costs in manufacturing the Model T was one of the most astonishing economic success stories in world history."* From 1908 to 1927, Ford manufactured 15 million Model Ts, and had $700 million in undistributed profits on hand. Ford's new Model A, introduced in 1928, sold for $480.

However, in his drive to efficiently produce low-cost cars for the public, Ford forgot to pay attention to the changing wants or increasing wealth of his customers. All 15 million of those Model Ts were painted black (black paint was cheaper) and had hand cranks even though electric starters had been invented by 1915. By 1927, General Motors was producing five different models ranging from the cheap Chevrolet, through the nicer Pontiac, the sporty Oldsmobile, the comfortable Buick, and on to the luxurious Cadillac. They all came with electric starters in a variety of colors. By 1927, General Motors was selling more cars than Ford, and had become the world's largest automobile manufacturer. And it maintained that lead decade after decade.

Powered flight, also using internal combustion engines, would begin in America in 1903. By World War II, airplanes had become a major weapon in war, in addition to moving people and things. The need for bombers that could haul heavy payloads long distances quickly revolutionized the design and construction techniques for large aircraft. After the war, this new accumulated knowledge was soon transferred to passenger planes and air travel. Much of the development of jet engines was done by the Germans. By the end of the War, they had started building jet fighters but lacked the rare metals needed to make long-lasting engines. Without the internal combustion engine (also invented by a German over 60 years before) that powered all the planes flying around, the jet engine would have never been thought of. After the War, the USA studied the German designs intensely and was producing jet fighters in time for the Korean War. In 1958, the first Boing 707 jet passenger plane went into service. Suddenly, a trip from New York to Los Angeles dropped from three days to five hours, while a trip to London dropped from a week to seven hours. With that, long distance passenger trains in the USA and passenger ships on the Atlantic Ocean were on the road to extinction. The world had suddenly shrunk. With the first passenger flight in January 1970 of the Boeing 747, commercial air travel had achieved all the speed, size, distance, and physical comfort that we now experience over 50 years later.

During the war, the Germans developed unmanned rockets that could deliver one ton of explosives two hundred miles and began to use them against Britain in 1944. After the War, both the USA and the USSR scrambled to get the remaining rockets and the German engineers and scientists who had developed them. And poured millions into expanding the technology. Following the USSR's successful rocket launch of Sputnik, a man-made satellite, in October 1957, the space race was on. The USA created NASA in 1958. The first seven American *astronauts* were picked in 1959. In 1961, President Kennedy set a fixed goal:

before this decade is out, of placing a man on the moon and returning him safely to the earth.

America sent its first astronaut into space in May 1961, one month after the USSR had done so. Neil Armstrong was the first to circle the Earth in orbit in February 1962. By 1965, the USSR had put eleven men into space to our seven. However, from that point on, it was no contest, despite the death of three astronauts during a launch pad test in January 1967. An astronaut first circled the moon in 1968. The successful moon landing occurred on July 20, 1969. It was on live TV, from the takeoff to the lunar landing and moonwalks, to the successful landing in the ocean back home. It was an eight-day trip for the astronauts.

"One small step for man, one giant leap for mankind." It was only 65 years and seven months from the time of the Wright brothers' first flight and less than 12 years after the USSR first put Sputnik into orbit around the earth. It capped an era in which anything seemed possible. And that would never have happened without that first internal combustion engine just 90 years before. Rockets also led to ICBMs that could send nuclear warheads halfway around the planet and to communication satellites that would lead a revolution in communications. By the late 60s, thanks to satellites, live TV events could be broadcast around the world, and the cost of intercontinental phone calls plummeted. The number of such calls exploded from one million in 1950 to 200 million by 1980 and 6.3 billion by 2001. And that made financial markets instantly global.

Thanks to electric trams and subways in the cities, cars and trucks throughout the country, and the airplanes that would follow: *"no longer did society have to allocate a quarter of its agricultural land to support the feeding of horses or maintain a sizable labor force for removing their waste. Transportation among all the great inventions is noteworthy for achieving 100% of its potential increase in speed in a little more than a century, from the first primitive railroads replacing the stagecoach in the 1830s to the Boing 707 flying near the speed of sound in 1958."*

STEEL – An alloy of iron and carbon, and sometimes other metals such as chromium, surpasses cast iron's hardness and strength while retaining wrought iron's flexibility. It is also much less prone to rust. Humans had been making steel for over 2,000 years. However, making steel was very labor intensive and done only in small quantities, so its uses were primarily limited to swords and knives. The Bessimer process for mass-producing steel from iron was invented in Britain in the mid-1850s. Yet, little steel was being produced in the USA by 1870.

Andrew Carnegie was born in Scotland in 1835. His father, like his grandfather, was a weaver who made intricately patterned damask cloth with his handloom. However, the Industrial Revolution destroyed his livelihood since he couldn't match the price of cloth from the huge new mills. While his father sank into despair, his realistic mother took charge and moved the family to the USA, where they settled in Pittsburgh near her sister in 1847. Andrew immediately got his first job, at the age of twelve, as a bobbin boy in the same cotton mill where his father began working. Andrew worked twelve-hour days six days a week for $1.20 per week. After two years, at 14, he got a job as a telegraph messenger boy, making $2.50 a week. This gave him the opportunity to visit business establishments across the city, and he made the most of those contacts. This was just seven years after the first telegraph transmission, so the telegraph was rapidly expanding across the country, and hundreds of miles of new lines were being strung every year. He soon learned to operate the telegraph himself and could even interpret incoming messages by ear, writing down the words directly as he heard the dots and dashes coming from the machine. By the time he was 17, he was making $25.00 per month. Then, the head of the Pennsylvania Railroad, who frequently visited the telegraph office, decided he needed his own telegraph operator, so he hired young Andrew. Both the railroads and the telegraph were rapidly expanding. By the time Andrew was 33 in 1868, he was making $50,000 a year (about $3 million a year in 2024).

Then, in 1872, he visited a Bessimer steel plant in Britain. And decided to bring the Bessimer process to the USA. His new steel mill opened in 1875. When that plant opened, it *"started the growth of the United States as a major world steel producer,"* while the price of steel rails for railroad tracks was suddenly cut in half as steel replaced iron in railroad track construction. By the 1890s, the price of steel had dropped another two-thirds, and production continued to soar as steel replaced iron as the primary structural material in the USA for the Second Industrial Revolution that was just getting underway. And Andrew Carnegie became one of the richest men in the world in the process of providing all that cheap steel. Not bad for a kid who started working 72 hours a week at age 12, at less than two cents per hour.

After the Civil War, the USA became a major exporter not only of steel, but also of manufactured goods made from steel and iron. While the nation's exports of iron goods were only worth $6 million in 1860, by 1900, the nation was exporting $122 million worth of locomotives, rails, machinery, wire, pipes, boilers, and even sewing machines and typewriters, a 20 fold increase.

RUBBER – It is difficult to imagine how different our modern way of life would be without those strange trees from the Amazon rainforest that produce rubber. As UCLA professor H. B. Hecht explained:

Three fundamental materials were required for the Industrial Revolution, steel, fossil fuels, and rubber.

The first major use of rubber in the USA began in 1825 with the importation of rubber shoes from Brazil. They were supposedly great in wet, sloshy conditions. In just a few years, hundreds of thousands were sold. At first blush, they seemed great. However, they turned brittle when cold and melted when hot. Rubber shoes put away in the closet in the spring would be a stinky black puddle by fall. The rubber shoe market collapsed within ten years.

Just before that market collapse, a frequently bankrupt entrepreneur, Charles Goodyear, became obsessed with rubber. He was determined to find a way to make rubber stable over a wide range of temperatures. Lacking any understanding of rubber or chemistry in general, he spent years randomly trying everything. One day, while trying to mix sulfur with rubber, he accidentally dropped some of the goop on a hot stove. To his surprise, it didn't melt. While it burned a little crust on the outside, the inside of his glob turned into a new kind of rubber that retained its shape and elasticity at both high and low temperatures. He never understood why it worked. But, through numerous trial and error attempts, he and others did figure out how to get the process to work consistently. It became known as *vulcanization*. And vulcanized rubber became indispensable in a changing world.

Rubber molecules have an incredibly long backbone chain of carbon atoms that curl up like a bowl of cooked spaghetti. If a rubber molecule was as thick as spaghetti, it would be over 100 yards long but all curled up on itself. When stretched, it uncurls and then returns to its original clump when tension is removed. Somehow, the sulfur stabilizes those molecules so that vulcanized rubber retains its unstressed shape at various temperatures while retaining flexibility.

Inflatable tires are the most obvious contribution of rubber to the Second Industrial Revolution. They were first tried on bicycles. In just the seven years between 1887 and 1894, 24 USA patents were issued related to solving the problems of putting rubber tires on metal wheel rims. Benz, almost from the beginning, was putting rubber tires on his automobiles. By the time Americans began to seriously look at automobiles, putting rubber tires on them was standard practice. That practice led to paved roads, which enabled higher speeds. If cars had only ever had metal wheel surfaces, they would never have been able to go very fast as they clanged over rough dirt roads. Paved roads would never have been developed because metal tires would have torn them up. If automobiles had stayed on rails, it would have drastically limited mobility and where they could go. In short, without rubber tires, our world dominated by cars and trucks moving people and things over superhighways and paved streets would have never happened.

While the Wright brothers' first airplane didn't have wheels, by 1910, all those building planes were using wheels with inflatable rubber tires. Rubber tires were absolutely essential in enabling planes to get up sufficient speed to take off and in enabling them to land at sufficient speeds to land safely. Without rubber, airplanes would have remained small experimental toys launched from towers like that first Wright airplane. They would probably have never even developed to the point where they could take off and land on water. In short, without rubber, there would be no cars, buses, trucks, or airplanes hauling people and things around. We would all still be traveling and moving things by train, steamship, and horse drawn vehicles.

Rubber also has other endless uses. In the words of Charles C. Mann:

The impact of vulcanization was profound, the inflatable rubber tire – key to the adoption of both the bicycle and the automobile – being the most celebrated example. But rubber also made electrification possible: try to imagine a modern building without insulation on its wiring. Or imagine dishwashers, washing machines, and clothe dryers without the belts that transmit the motions of their engines to the appliance itself. Equally important but less visible, every internal combustion engine contains many pipes and valves that channel, usually under pressure, water, oil, gasoline, and exhaust vapor. Unless parts are manufactured perfectly, engine vibrations will cause liquids or gases to vent dangerously from joints. Flexible rubber gaskets, washers, and O-rings almost invisibly fill the gaps. Without them every home furnace would be at constant risk of leaking natural gas, heating oil, or coal exhaust – a potential death trap.

We should note here that by World War II, organic chemists had figured out how to produce artificial rubber from petroleum. However, because the artificially created molecules are much shorter, artificial rubber has less strength or flexibility than natural rubber. Because natural rubber was in short supply during the war, artificial rubber was used extensively for tires. This continued after the war as the USA continued to use bias ply tires for at least two more decades. However, tire life was only about 10,000 to 15,000 miles, and retreading tires was common. On the other hand, Europe had gone to radial tires made of natural rubber because they provided a smoother ride and lasted much longer. By 1970, radial tires were becoming common in the USA. Soon, bias ply tires made of artificial rubber disappeared in the USA as well. As one rubber chemist put it: *"I would not want to be on a Boing 747 that was about to land on tires made of artificial rubber."*

Add to all that the critical role of rubber in medical gloves and equipment, as well as rain gear, toys, and sports footwear. Is it any wonder that ever-increasing vast areas of Southeast Asia are covered in nothing but rubber trees? We should not forget how critical those rubber tree forests are to our modern world and the USA's economy.

PETROLEUM – Rock oil (*petroleum* in Latin) had been found in a few locations around the world for over a thousand years, but no one had ever thought of a use for it (although it was sometimes peddled as a cure-all medicine). In 1853, George Bissell was visiting an old professor at Dartmouth, where he saw a bottle of rock oil in his office. He knew it burned and was struck by the idea that it might be used for light. He asked Benjamin Silliman Jr., a chemist at Yale, to see if there was anything in rock oil that might be burned in lamps. Silliman discovered that kerosene could be extracted by heating it. However, the supply of rock oil was very limited. Later, in New York City, Bissell saw an advertisement for a patent medicine made from rock oil that showed derricks of the kind that were used to bore for salt. The advertisement said that the medicine came from rock oil, which was a byproduct of salt drilling. He wondered if that technology could be used to drill for rock oil. He found some investors and formed a company with Silliman. They sent Edward Drake to Titusville, Pennsylvania (where surface seeps of rock oil were known to occur) to locate some drillers willing to drill for rock oil. While everyone thought it was a stupid idea, Drake finally found one crew who was willing to drill for anything if they got paid for it. On August 27, 1859, the world's first attempted oil well struck rock oil (petroleum) at a depth of 69 feet. They then set up a refinery to extract kerosene. With that, the worldwide oil industry was born. As one contemporary writer put it *"The discovery of petroleum in Pennsylvania gave kerosene to the world, and life to the few remaining whales."*

Carl Benz used coal distillates in his first engines. What we now call gasoline (Brits call it petrol) had been isolated from petroleum as a byproduct of refining for kerosene in that first refinery. It is highly volatile and burns with explosive force. However, it was just thrown away until it was finally tried as fuel for an internal combustion engine around 1890. The first automobile with an internal combustion engine burning gasoline was built in 1892. The first gasoline-powered automobile patent in the USA was issued in 1895. In 1913, the process for *cracking* the heavier oils found in petroleum into gasoline was developed. This greatly expanded the amount of gasoline that could be obtained from a barrel of petroleum. Other products followed, such as diesel oil, jet fuel, heating oil, motor oil, tar, etc. Refineries now produce about 19-20 gallons of gasoline, 11-13 gallons of diesel fuel, and 3-4 gallons of jet fuel from each barrel of petroleum (42 gallons). The residue from refining Petroleum soon replaced coal tar as the feedstock for numerous other products in wide use today, including all kinds of plastics, pharmaceuticals, paints, and synthetic fabrics such as nylon. The heaviest residue is used in asphalt to pave roads. Thus, petroleum is much more than just the new source of energy unleashed through the internal combustion engine. Petroleum not only powers cars, trucks, and planes but also lubricates them. By the 1950s, diesel had replaced coal as the fuel for trains and ships, while fuel oil began heating homes in the northeast. Around the world, petroleum now moves everything: on land, on water, and in the air. Coal has been reduced to being a principal energy source for generating electricity and for making cement for the ever-expanding demand for concrete. Fuel oil has been the principal fuel for generating electricity for islands such as Hawaii and Puerto Rico for decades. That makes electricity much more expensive there than in the mainland USA. The use of wind turbines and solar panels to generate electricity has only begun to make a dent in the use of fuel oil on those islands in the twenty-first century.

GERMS AND PUBLIC HEALTH – James A. Garfield, after winning the 1880 election, was inaugurated President of the USA on March 4, 1881. He was 49 years old and in excellent health. Four months later, on July 2, he was shot twice at close range on a railway platform in Washington, D.C., by a dilutional office seeker who had failed in his efforts to get an appointment to a government job. One bullet grazed Garfield's arm, and the other struck him in the back. However, that bullet in his back is not what killed him. He died 79 agonizing days later from massive infections caused by his doctors' repeatedly probing the bullet wound with unwashed fingers looking for the bullet. At autopsy, his body was full of infection, including huge puss pockets and infected tissue, while the bullet was found, far from where the doctors thought it was, encased in a protective shield of tissue that had grown around it to wall it off.

A method for inoculating against smallpox had been developed in China about 500 years ago and arrived in Europe and America in the eighteenth century. The modern smallpox vaccine was introduced in 1796. However, no one understood how or why it worked. The idea that infections of wounds (causing inflammation and puss), diseases, and fermentation were due to tiny organisms too small to see (the *germ* theory) began in France with Louis Pasteur around 1860. He developed the idea of heating milk and other liquids (now called *pasteurization*) to kill any such organisms so they could not pass on diseases. Although broad acceptance of these dramatically new ideas came quite slowly, British doctor and surgeon Joseph Lister was intrigued by the concepts and pondered how they might apply to surgery and treating wounds. In 1865, after repairing a boy's compound fracture of his leg, Lister placed a bandage dipped in carbolic acid over the wound. He was amazed when he removed the bandage a few days later and found there was no inflammation or puss. He then began wiping all instruments to be used in surgeries with carbolic acid. Just as Pasteur is considered the father of bacteriology and microbiology, Lister is viewed as the father of antiseptic surgery and treatment of wounds.

However, these ideas had not crossed the Atlantic Ocean to America. When Lister presented his ideas and methods at a conference in Philadelphia in 1876, they were roundly rejected. One prominent doctor has been quoted as saying: *"Little if any faith is placed by any enlightened or experienced surgeon on this side of the Atlantic in the so-called carbolic acid treatment of Professor Lister."* President Garfield suffered the consequences of that rejection in open view of the entire nation. By 1890, antiseptic surgery was widely practiced across the USA. The value of washing hands and the importance of soap also began to be widely understood and promoted.

In 1878, an epidemic of yellow fever killed 10% of the population of Memphis. *"Victims literally turned yellow and died in agony."* This was more than a decade before anyone knew that yellow fever was transmitted by mosquitoes. Although window screens were first advertised by a Detroit company in 1874, they were not widely used until the role of mosquitos and flies in spreading disease began to be widely understood. By 1900, window screens were coming into common use.

The last two decades of the nineteenth century saw new vaccines for a range of infectious diseases begin to be developed while the use of antiseptic practices began to spread throughout the field of medicine. The first use of anesthetics to control pain during surgeries was in the 1890s. Before that, laudanum or drinking alcohol were about the only things available for pain. The German company Bayer developed aspirin in 1899. Yet, by 1900, over 37% of all deaths in the USA were still caused by infectious diseases. That dropped to 5% by 1950 and is now less than 2%. The last case of smallpox anywhere in the world was in the 1970s. In 1979, a commission of scientists solemnly declared that smallpox is now extinct. On the other hand, in the USA in 1900, deaths from cancer, heart disease, and strokes accounted for only one in 14 deaths. Now, they account for over two out of every three deaths. In 1900, few people were living long enough to need to worry about cancer, heart disease, or a stroke.

A major consequence of the public health revolution as it has spread around the world is a population explosion. The world population has been increasing for at least the last thousand years. It was probably around 300 million in the year 1000. By 1500, it was around 500 million. With the spread of American crops to Europe, Africa, and Asia, by 1870, the world population had reached 1.3 billion as the understanding of germs began. It reached two billion around 1925. Then, despite precipitous drops in birthrates across the developed world in the last 40 years, the world population reached eight billion in 2022, a four-fold increase in less than a century.

CONNECTED HOMES – In 1870, few urban dwellings and no rural houses were connected to any services anywhere in the world. While a few cities had developed some primitive water supply systems early in the century, they usually preceded any kind of sewer system. As a result, getting rid of dirty water was an issue. This had become so serious in Boston that, in 1844, the city passed an ordinance that prohibited taking a bath without a doctor's order. In the USA, as sewer systems were added, for those cities on rivers or lakes (most cities), almost all dumped raw sewage into the same water body that provided their water supply. Even then, many dwellings were not connected. Municipal sewer and water systems, as well as indoor bathrooms, began to proliferate in cities and towns across the country after 1890. However, treatment to purify water supplies and any treatment of raw sewage before discharge did not begin until after 1900.

The availability to individual dwellings of fresh water from a tap connected to a water supply, and a connection to a sewer system to drain away dirty water, expanded rapidly after 1900. The only plumbing fixtures offered in the 1897 Sears catalog were sinks. By 1908, the Sears catalog listed several full sets of bathroom equipment, including a clawfoot bathtub, a porcelain-enameled sink, and a toilet with a golden oak tank and seat, all for $43.80, equal to about three weeks of working-class income. By then, the use of water heaters had also started to spread. This was all a great equalizer between rich and poor. In the previous century, when water had to be hauled in, heated, and dirty water hauled back out, or chamber pots emptied, the rich had servants to heat the water and do all the hauling, while middle- and working-class people had to do it themselves. With these changes, both rich and working class alike just turned a tap, pulled a plug, and pushed a flush handle.

It is noteworthy that the sharp decline in mortality rates, in both children and adults, between 1900 and 1940 had little, if anything, to do with drugs, doctors, or hospitals. Even by 1950, spending on medical care was still a very small part of the family budget. Instead, improved health was attributable to clean water piped under pressure into dwellings, adequate sewer systems, cleaning up the food supply sold to the public, refrigeration, window screens, increased cleanliness, and distributing newly developed vaccines for a wide range of diseases through nurses going to public schools. Clean water technologies have been considered the *"most important public health intervention of the twentieth century."* Regulations cleaning up the food supply, particularly milk and meat, which I haven't discussed here, would be a close second. Sinclair Lewis' 1906 novel, *The Jungle,* set in the awful health and working conditions of the Chicago stockyards, was a prime mover of the public outrage that led to change. Then came penicillin in the 1930s, in time for World War II. Other antibiotics followed. The polio vaccine was developed in 1955. However, there were serious ethical issues in how blacks were used or unknowingly experimented on in the development of new medical knowledge.

By 1900, houses in urban areas were also being connected to electricity, giving them access to electric lights and an ever-increasing number of electric appliances and tools. By 1930, this was largely complete in cities and even in small towns. Electricity came to Heber, Utah, my father's family, about 1910, and to my mother's family farm at Ioka in the 1920s. However, it didn't reach the farm community of Randlett, where my family had lived for 19 years, until 1949, two years after we had moved to a small farm near Idaho Falls, Idaho.

There were four major electrical appliances invented by 1920 that spread rapidly in the following two decades. The electric kitchen range enabled food preparation without the burden of building a fire (plus all the heat that came with it in the summer) as it replaced the coal or wood-burning kitchen stove. The water heater made hot water available without using the stove. The washing machine, with an agitator in the tub and a wringer (two heavy rubbery rolls that squished the water out of clothes), greatly reduced the time and effort of washday. The refrigerator (the first refrigerator for home use went on sale in 1927) enabled meat, milk, leftovers, and anything else to be kept cool, which extended their useful life by preventing spoilage. So, by 1940, electricity had transformed living conditions for most Americans, rich and working-class alike, in unimaginable ways. Further, by 1910, large department stores such as Macy's had opened in large cities and were selling all kinds of clothes and household items. For the first time, women had access to readymade clothes just as electric sewing machines began to replace treadle machines.

Alexander Graham Bell, a Scottish immigrant, invented the telephone in 1876. By 1893, there were 250,000 phones in use in the USA. By 1907 that had grown to more than six million and they could be found in many individual residences. By 1930, almost all urban houses were connected to public services in four ways: municipal water and sewer systems were connected by pipes, while electricity and telephones were connected by wires. These were dramatic changes that could only happen once and would not be duplicated. Human society and daily life were being irreversibly transformed, even for the working class, in ways that were unimaginable, even for the rich, just 50 years before. And these things all began to spread to the rest of the world.

By 1940, another connection was underway as natural gas (a byproduct of drilling for petroleum) pipes began to be connected to individual residences. Central heating with furnaces, fueled by crushed coal or heating oil, had already been placed in many homes. But with natural gas, the burden of shoveling coal or getting the fuel oil tank refilled was gone. And the entire house was now comfortably warm. Gas could also fuel kitchen ranges. This was the fifth connection for American homes. Then cable television came in the 1970s, vastly expanding available channels.

After World War II, three more major electric appliances became available in homes: automatic washing machines that eliminated the need for wringers – just drop the clothes and soap in and later take out clean damp clothes; clothes dryers that eliminated the need for clotheslines and all the effort of hanging out the wash; and freezers that could keep food and ice cream frozen until needed. These came with an amazing array of small appliances, from eggbeaters to toasters, can openers, and alarm clocks. Yet clotheslines for hanging the wash out to dry were still common in many backyards until the 1970s. Whole house air conditioning began to spread in the 1960s and became common in most homes by the 1970s. That led to a population explosion in the American South and Southwest, from Las Vegas and Phoenix to Atlanta and Miami, as Americans began to move south in much greater numbers. This is evident in the shift in the number of seats in the House of Representatives from each state as adjusted after each census. Between 1950 and 2020, the number of seats for New York dropped from 45 to 26 and for Ohio from 24 to 15, while the number of seats for Arizona went up from 2 to 9, for Texas from 22 to 38, and for Florida from 8 to 28. That would never have happened without air conditioning.

BUNGALOWS – The idea of small tract homes, bungalows, began around Los Angeles but had spread to Chicago by 1910, where 80,000 were built over the next 20 years. Chicago came to personify bungalow neighborhoods. These neighborhoods *"represented the first stage of a multistep process by which the pre-1900 working class became the broad middle class of the 1950s and beyond."* The typical bungalow in Chicago had a first floor of 1,000 to 1,200 square feet, with most having a second floor of about 400 square feet for extra bedrooms. They had *"generous"* windows, a full basement, indoor plumbing, electric service, and central heat. Each was built on a narrow lot on parallel streets with a detached garage in the back. Every block was bisected with an alley behind the houses that provided access to the garages on each side. Electric and telephone lines were along the alley so they could not be seen from the street. There was a parkway between the sidewalks and the street's curb and gutter (another new concept in residential areas) where trees and grass were planted. Rather than being built with local materials by expert craftsmen as had been standard practice in the nineteenth century, these bungalows were the first to be built with thin-cut lumber in standard sizes with evenly spaced studs and joists that set the pattern we still see in houses today (sometimes called balloon construction). They gave us the ubiquitous 2x4. Builders found ways to vary the street appearance with different windows and external finishings. These homes typically had hardwood floors, built-in cabinets, bookcases, window seats, china closets, breakfast benches, fireplaces, mantels, and radiator enclosures. They could be bought with bank loans paid back in monthly installment payments spread over many years (another new concept – the home mortgage).

Bungalows quickly spread to many other cities. The entire house with all its furnishings could be bought from the Sears catalog and shipped to any address. The buyer just needed to have a lot with a foundation installed along with available hookups for water, sewer, and electricity. In 1918, Sears was offering all the pre-cut components of a Chicago style bungalow for between $750 and $2,000 with the claim that it could be assembled in 352 carpenter-hours. Individual home ownership for the urban middle- and working-class exploded. As expressed by Gordon:

The revolution that remade the American dwelling and the American standard of living occurred during a relatively small slice of human history. Viewed from the perspective of millennia of economic stagnation, the networked modern conveniences arrived in a rush, from virtual invisibility in 1910 urban America to near pervasiveness in 1940.

DAMS – For millennia, people have been diverting water from streams and rivers for irrigation of crops. As waterwheels developed, small dams were used sometimes to create enough fall to power the waterwheel. However, large dams on rivers are a product of the 20th Century. And it began in the United States. In the late 1800s, Congress passed several laws designed to encourage diversions and canals in the West to promote irrigation and settlement. Then, in 1902, under the direction of President Theodore Roosevelt, the Federal Government began to get directly involved in the dam-building business in the West. Among the largest of the early projects was the Roosevelt Dam on the Salt River in Arizona. Built between 1905 and 1911, it was 280 feet high and formed the largest manmade lake in the world at that time. Hoover Dam, built from 1930 to 1936 (during the heart of the Great Depression) stands 726 feet high, backs up a lake 120 miles long, and was an engineering marvel that repeatedly broke new technological ground in its construction. Over 150 workers died during its construction. By 1936, five of the largest structures on Earth, all dams, were simultaneously under construction in the Western United States: Hoover on the Colorado, Shasta on the Sacramento, Bonneville and Grand Coulee on the Columbia, and Fort Peck on the Missouri. Grand Coulee Dam, still the largest manmade structure on Earth, is 550 feet high, a mile long, and backs up a reservoir 150 miles long. At the time it opened it was capable of generating a third of the Nation's total electric output. The Tennessee Valley Authority, which included 42 dams on the Tennessee River, was also started during this period. By 1980, there were over 75,000 dams on the Nation's waterways, including 19 on the Mississippi and 36 on the Columbia. And they serve many purposes: water supply and storage for cities, irrigation, recreation, flood control, and electric power generation. Electricity generation from dams is limited by the amount of water available to pass through its turbines and turn the generators. Dams now provide less than 10% of the USA's electricity. Large dams now exist throughout the world. They also create problems that require considering tradeoffs. Most notable is their impact on migrating fish. Prior to any of these dams, the Columbia River was home to the largest Salmon population on earth. That population has been decimated.

ENTERTAINMENT AND COMMUNICATIONS – The telephone, discussed above because it required a wire connection to the dwelling, was only one of the new means of communication. In 1877, Thomas Edison developed the first *phonograph* that could both record and play back sound. It was strictly a mechanical acoustic apparatus that did not involve electricity. The sound went in (and back out) a large cone that, at the narrow end, channeled that sound to a pointed stylus that left tiny marks on a rotating cylinder covered with a hard, waxy substance. Then, running it again, the stylus would go over those tiny marks, and the sound would come back out. It was used primarily to record music. The only way to make a copy was to have another phonograph recording, as the first was playing back, which reduced the quality of the copy. Or multiple phonographs could record the live session. It was another 25 years (1902) before someone figured out how to stamp out a duplicate of the original record with comparable quality, which made mass production possible.

Over the next two decades, various competing approaches came and went, finally settling on dinner plate-sized discs rotating at 78 revolutions per minute (RPM) on inexpensive windup phonographs that were only capable of playback. The record and music recording industry was underway.

Then came the radio. People had been playing with radio waves for decades. By 1910, two-way radios were a common way for ships at sea to communicate. After rescue efforts to help the Titanic were complicated by the mass of unregulated radio signals in the area that impacted other nearby ships' ability to receive the message, Congress passed the Radio Signal Act in 1912 which began the licensing and assigning wave frequencies for radio signal broadcasts.

George Westinghouse, whose electronics firm was in Pittsburgh, was always looking for some new electric appliance to market to the public. He decided to build and market an inexpensive mass-market radio that would only receive radio signals but not broadcast. He would also build a large broadcasting station that could send signals throughout the surrounding region to create a mass market for his receiver radios. He got his broadcast station licensed, with a frequency assigned, in October 1920. However, his new radios were not quite ready to go on the market. He decided to broadcast anyway. So, on Tuesday, November 2, 1920, the night Warren G. Harding was elected president of the USA, Westinghouse broadcast the election returns live, the first radio broadcast on the world's first commercial radio station, KDKA (still the only station east of the Mississippi that begins with a K). His radios went on the market a few weeks later. By 1923, broadcast radio stations had sprung up all across the nation (KSL radio in Salt Lake City was licensed to broadcast in April 1922 – just 17 months after Westinghouse's first broadcast – while a radio station first came to Idaho Falls in December 1928) as radios were sweeping into households everywhere there was electricity and a station. They broadcast news, weather, music, comedy shows, everything. A whole new world of communication and entertainment was opening up as families across the nation would spend their evenings gathered around the radio. The radio industry continued to improve the quality of the sound being broadcast, the quality of the programming, and the ability of the home radio to produce quality sound. Several vaudeville stars made their way to radio as vaudeville began to collapse.

Then, in 1925, someone thought of bringing this new electronics expertise to the phonograph. Electronic microphones went into the recording studio instead of singing into a cone. Electronics helped improve the quality of the recording itself as the record was being cut. And loudspeakers and amplifiers greatly enhanced the quality of the sound coming from the phonograph. With these improvements, playing records on the radio increased, music was available to everyone as never before, and the world of popular music and artists in various genres was born. The Grand Ole Opry was first broadcast from a Nashville radio station in November 1925. And sales of phonograph records made popular through radio broadcasts soared. The combination of radio and recorded music was like a match made in heaven.

Television followed (thanks to a long string of inventors with Philo Farnsworth being the most prominent), and reached commercial broadcast possibilities by World War II. However, the war then delayed further progress. By 1947, there were 40 million radios in the USA but only 44 thousand TV sets, with most of those in New York City. Stations spread rapidly over the next few years. KSL in Salt Lake City began broadcasting TV on June 1, 1949, while TV came to Idaho Falls, where we were then living, on December 20, 1953 (I was in the sixth grade). Many radio programs, from daytime soap operas to weekly comedies and dramas, moved from radio to TV as families across America now gathered in front of the TV rather than around the radio in the evenings. However, by 1960, there were still only three channels, with only one or two available in many areas. Color TV came in the 1960s, and then HD TV, with flat screens and a wider format, began to spread after 2000.

The Germans developed the use of magnetic tape to record sound so realistic it was basically indistinguishable from a live broadcast in the 1930s. But it was not shared with the world. During World War II, the allies became aware of German broadcasts, which they thought must be pre-recorded, but the quality was so good that they sounded just like live broadcasts. As the war was ending, John Mullin, an audio engineer with the U.S. Army signal corps, went into German broadcast studios to investigate. He brought home two suitcase-sized tape recorders and 50 reels of recording tape.

He worked with these over the next two years to make refinements. In 1947, he went to Hollywood to promote this new technology. Bing Crosby hated doing live radio broadcasts. He wanted to prerecord in the studio. However, NBC refused because of the poorer quality of records. So, he had dropped out of live radio for a year. When he heard of Mullin's new technology, he gave it a try. It was an immediate hit. *"The taped Bing Crosby radio shows were painstakingly edited through tape-splicing, to give them a pace and flow that was wholly unprecedented in radio."* They even added canned laughter. Magnetic tape recordings went on to revolutionize the music recording industry, both through the quality of the recordings, the elimination of time limits on the length of songs, and the ability to add and mix sounds.

Cameras were developed in Europe, with the first picture taken in 1825. Years were spent trying to refine the process with various substances to record the images and develop the final pictures. Cameras had arrived in America by 1850. Until 1888, taking pictures, which were recorded on plates, was strictly the work of professionals with complicated equipment. That year, George Eastman, an American, began selling a simple inexpensive camera, which he named *Kodak*, for use by the general public. It was equipped with film on a roll that could be advanced for the next picture. Amateur picture takers could then take the film to a professional shop to have the film developed and pictures printed. The following year he began using celluloid for the film. Could taking a series of pictures to capture motion be far behind?

While many worked on the issue on both sides of the Atlantic, credit for inventing motion pictures is generally given to Thomas Edison, who, in the early 1890s, first demonstrated a motion picture he had produced. The history of motion pictures, or *movies*, is too long and well-known to repeat here. Let's just say, the impact and influence of movies on the USA and the world is colossal in terms of culture, documenting history, and disseminating information, knowledge, and ideas, all while entertaining us.

In sum, in the century beginning in 1870, the Second Industrial Revolution totally transformed daily life throughout the USA, with much of that change occurring between 1910 and 1940. People had much more free time and far more options for spending that free time, including entertainment, recreation, and travel options, which were unimaginable to even the wealthiest in 1870. In addition, living conditions were far more comfortable; a smaller share of income had to be spent on food while diets were far less monotonous, and less time and effort was spent preparing that food; and occupational opportunities were far greater, more enjoyable, and less dangerous. And death was no longer a constant companion among family and friends. By 1950, most people grew old before dying as child mortality had dropped by orders of magnitude. And the middle class was born. And these changes had begun to spread throughout the world.

THE AGRICULTURAL REVOLUTION – While volumes could be written about the details, let's just hit the highlights. The agricultural revolution that enables the world to now feed eight billion people began around 1840 with guano from islands off the coast of Peru. It has continued to accelerate and expand ever since as it extends its reach around the world. *"The key is producing more food on less land. While the amount of land used for agriculture has increased by 8 percent since 1961, the amount of food produced has grown by an astounding 300 percent."*

The Agricultural Revolution has spread simultaneously with the public health revolution, and has enabled food production to match the population explosion. The Agricultural Revolution that is now capable of feeding eight billion people on this earth consists of seven main elements. First, the development and use of commercial fertilizers. Second, the development and use of insecticides and other pest control measures. Third, the refinement of crops, exemplified by hybrid varieties of corn to increase yields, to seedless watermelons and grapes, and a dozen new varieties of apples. Fourth, the spread of irrigation to vast areas (including much of the American West with water from those huge dams that were built) where there is insufficient rainfall to sustain crop production, along with improvements in irrigation efficiency. Fifth, replacing draft animals (horses, mules, etc.) with tractors and combine harvesters in developed nations has eliminated the need to dedicate substantial amounts of farmland to feeding those animals (in the USA, this amounted to 25% of the land used for agriculture). Hundreds of millions of draft animals are still being used on farms in Asia, Africa, and Latin America, and if they are replaced by machines, they will free up vast areas of farmland for other uses, including environmental conservation efforts. Sixth, huge improvements in mechanization and technology have enabled far fewer farmers to get far more done, and to do it more efficiently and with little manual labor. And finally, factory (feedlot and fish) farms for livestock and fish that produce far more eggs, chicken, turkey, pork, dairy products, beef, fish, etc., on far less land or impact on marine life and rivers than would otherwise be possible. There is simply not enough arable land in the world for us all to eat grass-fed beef and free-range chicken and eggs in the quantities we eat them, while fish farms help preserve ocean life. Just since 2000, there has been a worldwide drop in pastureland of 4.5%, while milk production has increased 19%, and beef production has increased 38%. We are now beginning to see stacked farm factories producing fresh vegetables.

By 2020, there were only about a fourth as many people living on farms in the USA as there were in 1870, while the total population is almost ten times higher than it was then. In Short, in 1870, it took 75% of the population working on farms to feed us all while in 2020, only 2% of the population still worked on farms to feed the rest of us. And the USA still exports far more food than it imports. That is a staggering increase in productivity. Just in the 30 years since 1990, the share of humans worldwide who are malnourished has dropped from 20% to 11%.

Again, thanks to the Agricultural Revolution, humans have been able to feed its population explosion, thus closing the Malthusian trap. Famines have been largely eliminated as the population exploded, and now, they only result from political problems that prevent food from getting where it needs to go, not from a lack of enough human food in the world.

All this efficiency in agriculture has not been without environmental costs, tradeoffs, and controversy. But at least we can have full tummies while we argue about the issues.

SCIENTIFIC KNOWLEDGE – Simultaneous with, and to a large part dependent on, the Industrial Revolution came a dramatic expansion of scientific and technical knowledge and understanding. Compared to what was known in 1776, or even 1870, about chemistry, biology, geology, physics, medicine, pharmaceuticals, nuclear energy, and the creation of new materials like plastics and synthetic fabrics, the mass of mankind's accumulated knowledge by 1976 (when the Third Industrial Revolution began to take over) about the world and the universe in which we live, multiplied to unimaginable heights. Then add in the creation and expansion of the social sciences. It was an amazing century from the 1870s to the 1970s. And that growth in scientific knowledge continues at an accelerating rate.

12: WORLD WARS I & II AND THEIR LEGACY

With all that could be said about these two world wars and the depression that came between them (and volumes have been written), just a few points here as they relate to human progress and the development of the USA.

WORLD WAR I – The first World War began with the assassination of a Duke in Yugoslavia, a region racked by ethnic conflict for centuries. It quickly spiraled out of control because of various alliances between nations across Europe. And it solved nothing. For Germany and France, about 80% of males between the ages of 15 and 49 fought in the war. About nine million soldiers died in combat. Much of the fighting occurred in northern France, which left the area devastated, while there was little impact on the German countryside. Much of the War was fought with nineteenth century tactics using twentieth century weapons. The deep timber reinforced trenches that characterized the war were first used around Richmond during the Civil War as Grant put Richmond under siege. World War I ended in an armistice that left each side imbittered and the Islamic Ottoman Empire in ashes. Led by Winston Churchill, new national boundaries were drawn that often ignored existing ethnic boundaries. Some conflicting ethnic groups were stuffed into the same country while some groups were split so that they were not a majority in any country. While this was often intentional, it created conflicts that are still evident.

As the war ended, the American economy was booming from having geared up to sustain the war effort. Germany was saddled with huge reparation payments owed to France and Britain, which were saddled with huge loans from the USA they needed to repay. Congress then rejected having the USA join the League of Nations that President Wilson worked hard to try to form.

THE GREAT DEPRESSION – World War I was followed by the roaring twenties as daily life was being transformed across the USA thanks to a boundless stream of new products (from cars to radios to refrigerators) moving into most households. That fueled the economy, as did massive exports of food and manufactured goods. Then came the Great Depression, which lasted for a decade. And that decade-long depression did more to change the nature of the relationship between the citizens of the USA and their government than any other single event in the 235 years since the Constitution was ratified. As late as the depression during the 1890s, when some people came to President Grover Cleveland seeking some form of public aid, his answer was:

The people should support the government, not the government support the people.

How things have changed! And that change began in the 1930s with the Great Depression that not only dramatically altered the course of society in the USA, but also the West, and the world. But what caused the Great Depression? Why was it so severe? Why did it last so long? What was it like for real people? Answers to these questions have been extensively debated. And few of us have any idea of what it was like to live through it. Here is my best shot at the answers.

The initial cause was twofold. First, the stock market crash was due to out-of-control herd-mentality speculation that sent stock prices well beyond reasonable value. Borrowing money to buy stocks is never a good idea. And many people lost their shirts. And their pants. The second cause went beyond our shores. Exports were a major factor driving the USA economy. And Europe could no longer afford to continue to both make its war debt payments to the USA and still buy our exports. So, as exports declined, the economy began to shrink.

The reason the depression was so severe and lasted so long was due primarily to government policies and human herd mentality, although a drought across portions of the country in the early 1930s also had a severe impact on those regions. Since the USA refused to grant debt relief, Europe could no longer buy our goods. In response, the USA raised tariffs (the worst possible response), further reducing foreign trade. After the stock market crash in October 1929, unemployment peaked at 9% by

Christmas. Then the economy began to pick up some and unemployment then began to drop. By June 1930, it was down to 6.3%. That is when the government took its first major intervention into the economy by raising tariffs. By November, unemployment had reached 11.6%. And, thanks to a series of further government interventions over the next several years, unemployment stayed in double digits for the rest of the decade.

As the economy shrank, people began to panic, which led to runs on banks. In response, the government tightened monetary policy (again, the worst possible response), causing further runs on the banks. As expressed by Nobel Prize-winning economist Milton Friedman:

The fact is the Great Depression, like most other periods of severe unemployment, was produced by government mismanagement rather than by the inherent instability of the private economy. A government established agency – the Federal Reserve System – had been assigned responsibility for monetary policy. In 1930 and 1931, it exercised this responsibility so ineptly as to convert what otherwise would have been a moderate contraction into a major catastrophe.

As hundreds of banks closed and loan foreclosures escalated, the money in those accounts and loans evaporated into thin air. Between October 1929 and March 1933 (when Franklin D. Roosevelt was inaugurated), the money supply in the USA was reduced by a third. As Copernicus had taught us 400 years earlier, when the money supply shrinks, prices must go down because there is less money in circulation to buy things. Again, Milton Freidman:

I know of no severe depression in any country or any time that was not accompanied by a sharp decline in the stock of money and equally of no sharp decline in the stock of money that was not accompanied by a severe depression.

That is a simple straightforward truth. Remember, way back in the beginning we said that money is a commodity like every other commodity, but that it is also the catalyst that makes the exchange of goods flow.

Therefore, when there is a shortage of money, it slows down the exchange of goods – economic activity – as people begin bartering (trading apples for oranges) with each other because they lack money. Further, prices must also decline since there is less money circulating to buy anything. But somehow those in power, inside the Federal government with the responsibility to respond, did not understand these simple facts about money.

A story of government help under President Hoover and its impact on real people. My parents were married in 1925. In late 1927, they bought a farm in the small farming community of Randlett in the southwest corner of Uintah County, Utah. The farm was still 90% sagebrush that had never been plowed. It had no improvements (the farm was within a portion of an Indian reservation that had been opened to white settlers in 1912 but the initial owner had only plowed a few acres and had added no buildings, fences, or ditches). In May 1928, my father built a one room cabin with logs he brought down out of the Uintah Mountains. They then moved in and began to cultivate the rest of the farm. By 1932, my parents had four kids under six (I was not yet born) and had added a corral and sheds for livestock, along with fences and irrigation ditches. Yet, despite these improvements, because of the Depression, the farm was only worth about 10% of what they had paid for it five years before. They had no well, so they had to haul water for household use from irrigation canals or wherever else they could find it. In the winter they stored blocks of ice from the river on the north side of the house they then melted for household water.

In 1929, my father was made bishop of the local congregation of the Church of Jesus Christ of Latter-day Saints. So, almost everyone, members or not, called upon him to arbitrate/resolve various disputes (property, inheritance, etc.) because he didn't charge anything, and they couldn't afford to get lawyers and/or go to court, which was several hours away in Vernal. In short, he was the *de facto* community leader. One day, a neighbor came back from Vernal and told my father that the government was giving away grain and flour. From a 1973 recorded interview:

A few days later a man came from Vernal who told me about the program and asked if I would accept the responsibility of distributing the grain and flour in our community. I told him I would. I didn't have room to store it, so I went up to Randlett to Willy Stevens, who owned a big old building that had been the boys' dormitory when it was an Indian school. He had a little store in part of it, and lived in part of it, but had several empty rooms. I asked him if he would let me store the stuff there and then when people came and asked for help, I'd give them an order that they could bring to him and then he would give them the flour or grain or whatever it was. As I was explaining it to him, there was a man standing there, a local man, who listened and then said "You couldn't run fast enough to give me a sack of that flour." I can remember that very distinctly.

Later on, people came to me wanting help. I would give them orders for so many sacks of flour and so many sacks of grain to be distributed out as the stuff kept coming in. Periodically, they would send a new shipment over and I tried to help people out who needed it. We had had a hard winter in 1932. The snow was still on the ground late in March and our feed was all gone. We just turned our stock loose out in the snow and let them find what they could in the brush, because we had no feed for them. Others were in the same situation. So this feed was very welcome. We didn't take any of the flour. We used some of the grain for the cattle. Our neighbors all had some help that way.

In the late summer, the daughter of this man I had talked to at the store came to the house. The girl said "I'd rather take a beating than ask for help." But then she told me what her father needed. I gave her an order to get so many sacks of flour and feed just like I did for everybody else. She accepted it.

In the fall I heard that this man was pretty riled up at me. He was saying a lot of things, so I went to see him and find out what it was all about. He saw me when I drove into his yard and came to talk to me. When I asked what the problem was, he was so mad he could hardly talk. He was just frothing at the mouth. He said "I didn't get my share of that feed and flour." That illustrates the change in attitude in just a few months' time when you start just giving to people. They feel entitled.

Why did the Depression last so long? At least partly because of the government's continued failure to increase the money supply. As expressed by David Stockman:

Hoover landed a haymaker on the requisites for a recovery of the American export-dependent economy and FDR finished the job – no gold, no trade, no capital flows, and no cancellation of destructive war debts.

His simplistic belief was that the Great Depression was due to low prices, and that the key to restarting the nation's economic engines was a Washingtom-initiated "reflation" of cotton, wheat, hog, and steel prices.

Roosevelt tried a wide range of things to address the depression. *"Some economists, including John Maynard Keynes, saw the uncertainties about the future generated by the experimental policies of the New Deal administration in the 1930s as tending to discourage investment that was much needed to get out of the Great Depression."* However, Roosevelt did not understand that low prices were caused by a shortage of money. The first thing he did was order that gold, including government-minted coins, could no longer be used as money. He ordered the confiscation of all privately held gold (except jewelry) in the country for the government established face value, which was well below the current market value for gold. This further shrunk the money supply. Then, because prices continued to fall, he undertook efforts to raise prices artificially. My father described one of those efforts in that same interview:

With the drought in 1934 added to already falling prices, I guess the economy in our area sort of hit bottom, like it did in other areas. In 1934, the government had a program of giving relief to the drought areas by buying up livestock. They sent a group, two or three fellows came out from Salt Lake, who were authorized to buy up any stock the people wanted to sell in order to get a little money out of them. They paid from $12 to $20 a head according to their condition. For calves, *they paid $6 per head. If one was fit to butcher, they permitted you to take the calf home and butcher it. But for all the cows, they just drove the whole herd of them up on the side hill, away from where anybody would be bothered by the smell, and shot them. They must have shot 30-40 head there in our little community. We sold quite a number of our cows, I don't remember just how many. I think our check was somewhere around $200. We just took it up to the bank and applied it on our note, paying off some of the 1928 loan that we used to buy those same cows for $90 a head six years before. We got $12 to $16 each.*

My parents had used their farm as collateral to obtain that 1928 loan. So, by 1934, they were at risk of losing their farm. However, the bank did not want to foreclose on a farm it could not resell for the amount due. So, by then, for every dollar paid against the loan, the bank reduced the remaining debt by two dollars. Such occasional adjustments to the terms of their bank loans probably did more to help my parents survive the Depression than government policies did.

As my mother watched those government agents sprinkle lime over the cows they had just shot to make sure no one could salvage any meat from them, she, despite being a farm girl with only an eighth-grade education (there was no high school available to her childhood community), had enough common sense to know that this was an unconscionable waste. And it was terrible public policy. The goal was to drive up prices (because they were perceived as being too low), while helping the poor in the process. If you want to help the destitute while improving the national economy, you don't destroy the primary cash generating asset of those poor in exchange for a desperately needed pittance. The problem wasn't an oversupply of beef, cream, milk, butter, and cheese (or anything else). Nor is an economy ever helped by destroying the means of production owned by the poorest. That is the worst possible approach. The real problem was that most people had no money to buy anything. In short, the nation had an inadequate money supply. Destroying a $90 asset that produces income in return for $12 of desperately needed immediate cash does, in the long run, more harm than good for the those most in need, and spreads poverty, not wealth. Yet, Roosevelt did little to increase the money supply.

And without money, bartering became commonplace. In 1939, my parents obtained a used gasoline-powered home electric generator system with batteries to provide electric lights in the house. By then my mother was 37 years old and had six sons, and they had added another room as a bedroom for the boys. It had a dirt floor. They traded a horse, a milk cow, and two calves to get that generator, including delivery and installation, from a family in a community that had recently been attached to the electric grid. Commercial electricity did not come to Randlett, where we lived, until after we had moved away in 1947 (because our 1946 effort to get a well to provide water for household use ended up being a dry hole). My mother would later write:

> To press a button and have such bright lights seemed like a wonderful miracle to me. I had never had electric lights before.

Roosevelt established job programs, built roads and dams, etc., to reduce unemployment. However, for most of those programs, one had to claim they were utterly destitute to get one of those jobs. It didn't matter if you were broke or not, you just had to sign your name claiming you were. That is lousy public policy that impacts one's sense of independence, integrity, and self-worth. Again, my father, in that 1973 interview:

> In order to get a job on one of the government programs like the WPA or the FERA, you had to sign a paper that was nicknamed the "pauper's oath", which stated your financial condition. You didn't have this, and this, and this. I don't remember what all there was to it, but the man that was in charge of a little road project that came along told me to come to work, along with all the neighbors around, on his project. Of course, everybody wanted work. He asked me to bring a plow and to trail a road grader that was set up on a neighbor's place. I went over and got the grader and pulled it up there. I was an hour or so getting there. The others were all at work when I got there, so I just unhitched off that grader, unloaded my plow, and went to work. I worked till noon.

*When noon came, he came around with this paper to sign. I wasn't in the habit of signing things I hadn't read without reading them first. When I read it, I told him I couldn't sign it. I desperately needed this work, but I wasn't that bad off. I don't remember now all that it said; just how poor you were, on and on to the point you were destitute. I just couldn't sign it. I just wasn't **that** bad off. I told him I couldn't sign it. He tried to persuade me. He said you can't work unless you do. That was the "pauper's oath." He didn't call it that; that was just the nickname that was given to it. So I just hooked up my team and went home instead of going to work in the afternoon. Well, all of the men needed work and the money, a few of them even more than I did, but I knew them all and there weren't very many of them that I really felt were in a position where they could honestly sign that paper. At least I couldn't, I didn't sign it. I think many of them resented the fact I didn't sign it and I didn't get to work, while they signed and worked on that project.*

Later that next winter this same man who was in charge of welfare for the county gave me an order one day. He just gave me a piece of paper in the presence of several other people. I didn't really know what it was he was handing me. He just told me to take it so I put it in my pocket. When I got home, I read it and realized what it was. Loreen [my mother] was there too and she saw what it was. We both knew how badly we needed it. We could sure use it. It was for about eight dollars. After quite a little persuasion and arguing about it, I finally consented to go. One day we hitched up the team and drove up to Wong Sing's store up at Fort Duchesne. That would be about 11 miles. We went in and picked out a few things. I was watching the prices so I knew about just what this would cover; some things for the kids and some overshoes for me. I handed him the order. He just said "Oh, on the county." That just got me. I said "Give me that order, will you." He handed it back to me. I walked over and dropped it in the stove and said to Loreen "Come on. Let's go." She followed me out. And we went home without.

The government relief programs may have provided some short-term relief, but I feel it did long-term damage to the people. . . My feeling was that most of these programs really pushed people into them because they hired case workers. In every area they had somebody hired as a case worker. I don't know what they got paid, but they would go to every home and just try to persuade people to accept help. Most people got to the point where they were happy to take all they could get. But I felt like people were pushed into taking, accepting charity, more than they really would have needed to do. It is now to the point that people feel the government owes you a living.

There is no doubt, the Great Depression dramatically altered the relationship between the general population and the federal government. For the first time, the federal government took on the role of creating jobs, of guarantying bank deposits in approved banks, and of creating the first steps of a government social safety net for those who are destitute. Child labor outside the family business became illegal while Social Security was created to provide minimal federal pensions. New rules strengthened unions in their battles with corporate management. In 1936, the federal government began providing financing to take commercial electricity to rural America. All this direct interjection of the federal government in peoples' lives was welcomed by many and despised by some. For better or worse, these *New Deal* programs led to dramatic changes to human society in the USA. Many new programs were challenged in court and tossed out by the Supreme Court as unconstitutional. In 1937 and 1938, Roosevelt made a concerted effort to expand the Supreme Court with additional judges. While that effort failed, the Court had changed enough that it began to decide that the *Commerce Clause* that authorizes Congress to "*regulate interstate commerce*" was elastic enough to authorize almost any economic program the government tried.

World War II brought the Great Depression to an end as Franklin D. Roosevelt became the first and only president to seek, and be elected to, more than two terms. He won four elections, but died in April 1945, just one month after his fourth inauguration, so that he served 12 years and one month. In 1951, the 23rd amendment was ratified, which limits a president to two terms.

WORLD WAR II – This war was the greatest calamity to befall the human race in recorded history, and is thus, a pivotal point in human history. It changed everything. The purpose of combat in a war is generally threefold: kill people, break things, and control territory. And, as with everything else, the Industrial Revolution had magnified many times over human efficiency and productivity in making war. Thanks to tanks, airplanes, larger ships, submarines, bigger guns, better explosives, and finally nuclear bombs, humanity's ability to kill one another and break things had reached unimaginable proportions. It made the whole idea of future all out wars between major powers unthinkable. Despite its troops being engaged in several limited conflicts since World War II, the USA, through Congress, has not formally declared war on another nation since declaring war on Romania, in 1943, in the middle of its involvement in World War II.

Estimates of the number killed by the war range from 40 to 80 million with the variation due to differences in which civilian deaths to include. The following summary is based on about 50 million deaths. That would be between two and three percent of the world's total population. Of those killed, about 20 million were military. The countries with the most military deaths were, in descending order, the Soviet Union, Germany, China, and Japan. The countries with the most civilian deaths were China, the Soviet Union, Poland, Indonesia, and Germany (note that despite extensive firebombing and two atomic bombs being dropped on Japan's cities, it doesn't make that list). The countries with the most deaths (both military and civilian) as a percent of the total national population were Poland at 18%, the Soviet Union, Lithuania, Latvia, and then Germany at 11%. In Short, Northeastern Europe was particularly devastated. East Prussia, a German-speaking country sandwiched between Poland and Lithuania along the Baltic Coast, disappeared from the map as boundaries were redrawn after the war. Ruta Sepetys on the War's impact:

There are many important stories of World War II. Much has been documented about combat, politics, guilt, and responsibility. Suffering emerged as the victor, touching all sides, sparing no nation involved. I am haunted by thoughts of the helpless children and teenagers –

innocent victims of border shifts, ethnic cleansings, and vengeful regimes. Hundreds of thousands of children were orphaned during World War II. Abandoned or separated from their families, they were forced to battle the beast of war on their own, left with an inheritance of heartache and responsibility for events they had no role in causing. Many experienced unspeakable atrocities, some miraculous acts of kindness by complete strangers. For many, war redefined the meaning of home.

The extermination of six million European Jews fueled the creation of the state of Israel in 1947.

World War II was waged because of Hitler fanatically promoting Germans as a super race entitled to rule Europe and beyond while a fanatically ethnocentric Japan pursued imperialism across Asia and beyond. In short, Both Japan and Germany considered themselves superior, both as peoples and nations, and entitled to rule. Thus, this war (like the Civil War) could not, and did not, end in an armistice or political settlement. The war ended with the unconditional surrender and complete destruction of the ruling governments of both Germany and Japan. The victors then occupied and ruled both countries for years before either was allowed to reestablish its own government under supervision by the victors in the War. The result was a remarkable cultural change in both countries.

Further, the United Nations was soon formed while *imperialism, colonialism, racism,* and *eugenics* were discredited and lost appeal worldwide. All four became socially unacceptable as European nations gave up what remained of their colonial empires over the next few decades. The Cold War, based upon the concept of Mutual Assured Destruction (MAD) between the West and the Soviet Bloc, dominated international relations for 50 years.

THE POST-WAR ERA – The War, in the USA, demonstrated that the government can be very efficient and effective managers of industrial output when they get to decide what that output will be. But, like Henry Ford by 1927, governments are not good at anticipating what consumers will want. Only a free market can do that. If you want to pay more for everything and have far fewer choices available to buy, have the government manage production and distribution. And so the private sector quickly regained control of the economy in the USA after the war.

As the war was ending, there was considerable fear that the USA would fall back into depression when all the soldiers returned home and began looking for jobs. So, the government enacted the GI Bill of Rights that would pay much of the cost for returning veterans to go to college. Its primary purpose was to keep many of them out of the job market for a few years. In one of the most remarkable twists of unintended consequences, over eight million veterans obtained more education in college or technical schools than they otherwise could have afforded. And they constituted an enormous addition to the human capital that fueled the postwar economy. It also powered a social revolution by opening well-paying jobs to segments of the population that had never dreamed of such jobs before (three of my parents' first four sons among them), thereby greatly expanding and diversifying the nation's economic upward mobility. The GI Bill also revolutionized housing through low-cost VA mortgages that vastly expanded home ownership to many who had not even dreamed of such a possibility. In the process, it created a housing boom.

The problem after the War was not a lack of jobs but inflation caused by high demand for everything. During the war, no cars, washing machines, stoves, or anything else had been made because the entire industrial capacity of the nation had moved to building the tools of war. Now, all those things made before the war were wearing out, and it took a while to retool all the factories. When demand exceeds supply, prices go up. And it took a while to restore balance.

Race relations began to change in the USA after the war. President Truman, who 15 years before had taken steps to join the KKK before changing his mind (in the early 1930s, in Missouri and across the South, membership in the KKK was sometimes seen as beneficial in democratic party politics), integrated the military in 1947. That same year, Jackie Robinson joined the Brooklyn Dodgers and became the first black player in Major League Baseball (the last team to begin using black players was the Boston Red Sox in 1959, twelve years later). In 1954, the Supreme Court overturned a 56-year-old precedent and held that segregated public schools were unconstitutional. Then came the civil rights movement of the 50s and 60s. The Civil Rights Act was passed in 1964 to end Jim Crow segregation in the South. In the Senate, 82% of republicans and 63% of democrats voted for the bill, while in the House, 80% of republicans and 61% of democrats voted for the bill. Most of the no votes by democrats were from the solidly democratic South. However, President Johnson, from Texas, pushed for and signed the bill into law, while the republican nominee for President that year, Barry Goldwater, opposed it. With that, black support for the democratic party rose dramatically and has remained there ever since, while the South has shifted from being solidly democratic to predominantly republican.

The Voting Rights Act was passed in 1965 to ensure blacks could vote in the South. While there was plenty of noise and controversy with some violence in the South related to these new laws, compared to what happened during reconstruction a century before, violence was minimal. Instead, the worst race riot was the 1965 Watts riot in Los Angeles, which lasted six days and killed 34 people. Detroit and other northern cities also had race riots. By 1970, to be labeled a racist in the USA or anywhere else in the West had become socially unacceptable, and a new order had been established. The KKK had not only shrunk but had to go underground. Segregation in public schools and spaces had been eliminated, and blatant racism (toward blacks, Indians, or any other ethnic group) had largely become socially unacceptable. The racism and imperialism that had driven Germany and Japan into causing World War II only succeeded in bringing both ideas into worldwide disrepute (at least publicly) in a much more integrated world.

The movement of rural southerners to northern and upper mid-western industrial cities greatly accelerated after the war. And they were not all well received. *"These people are creating a terrible problem in our cities. They can't or won't hold a job, they flout the law constantly and neglect their children, they drink too much and their moral standards would shame an alley cat. For some reason or other, they absolutely refuse to accommodate themselves to any kind of decent, civilized life."* That was written in Indianapolis in 1956, not about blacks, but about poor southern whites who had come into the city after the war. In a 1951 survey in

Detroit, more residents considered southern whites *"undesirable"* than they did blacks. A southern accent was enough to be told that a job or apartment was no longer available. One Chicago plant manager said, *"I told the guard at the plant gate to tell the hillbillies that there were no openings."*

Thomas Sowell lays out the case that this *cracker* or *redneck* culture of southern whites, which likely had its origins in the British borderlands of the seventeenth century, is the culture that was largely adopted by black slaves in the South as the languages, religion, and cultures of their African roots were stripped away. Thus, that cracker culture of southern whites is the origin of the inner-city black culture we see today with its disdain for education, its own form of English (Ebonics), its sensitivity to the slights or insults, and its casual regard for regular employment, marriage, the rule of law, or human life – even one's own. It is deeply ironic and tragic that, in today's urban black culture, to study hard in school or hold a steady job is seen disdainfully as *acting white* (when it is really just acting American), while they have already unwittingly adopted a culture taken from those whites who enslaved blacks for centuries and then imposed Jim Crow, and the KKK to enforce it ruthlessly, for another century. In short, inner-city African Americans have now largely adopted the cracker culture of those whites who enslaved and then persecuted them while rejecting the American culture of those whites who fought a war to end slavery, amended the constitution to make blacks free citizens with the right to vote, and then passed laws during the 1960s to end Jim Crow. It is noteworthy that neither black African immigrants nor those black immigrants from the Caribbean whose ancestors were also enslaved demonstrate this inner-city black culture. And, in general, both groups are faring far better economically in the USA than those blacks descended from slaves in the American South.

VIETNAM AND THE SIXTIES – It is impossible to overstate just how much the culture of the USA changed, even beyond the civil rights movement, in just a decade. It isn't always simple to distinguish between the causes and the effects, but there are a few clear driving forces for the changes wrought during the sixties. Probably the single most significant factor was the Vietnam War and the nation's reaction to it, led by the generation that was being drafted to fight it. As the Nation's involvement increased over time, so did the anti-war movement. While there were numerous large and small demonstrations on college campuses against the Vietnam War across the nation for several years, the best known and the one that most clearly exposed the severe split in the country in a disastrous way was the one held at Kent State University on May 4, 1970. On April 30, President Nixon had announced the extension of the War into Cambodia. Demonstrations increased over the next day or two at Kent State and other campuses across the country. The Governor of Ohio called out the National Guard to help maintain order at Kent State. For reasons that have never become clear, at some point, one group of National Guard troops (young men about the same age as the student protesters) opened fire on the unarmed demonstrators during the May 4 demonstration. In a span of 13 seconds, 67 rounds were fired. Four students were killed and another nine were injured, one permanently paralyzed. Of those killed, two girls and two boys, two were 19 and two were 20. Three of them were well over 100 yards from the Guardsmen. Two weren't even part of the demonstration. They were just walking across campus between classes. Over four million high school and college students boycotted school over the next day or two across the country.

That war was a disaster for the USA. But it was an even bigger disaster for Vietnam. And neither side understood why the other side was even fighting. The USA was fighting to limit the spread of communism in Asia, while North Vietnam and the Vietcong, were fighting to keep the USA from replacing the French as an imperial power ruling Vietnam. While over 58,000 thousand American soldiers died in the course of that conflict, 300,000 South Vietnam soldiers died, while over a million Vietcong and North Vietnam soldiers died. In addition to the soldiers killed, about two million Vietnamese civilians were also killed. By the mid-sixties, the measure the U.S. military used to report success in war for the nightly national news broadcasts was not land taken, but the body count of enemy killed. What gets measured gets done. Sure enough, some deaths were counted that by any reasonable measure would have been considered civilian deaths that should never have happened. The USA won virtually every battle it was in but lost the war. It is impossible for a democracy to win a long drown out war far from home where the enemy is willing to lose 20 soldiers and 40 civilians to kill one American. Like the British in the Revolutionary War, and almost like the Union in the Civil War, the American public got tired of this war, so we came home. The USA completed its pullout in 1973. The South Vietnamese government the USA had been backing was then defeated within a year. With that, many of those Vietnamese who had allied with the USA began a traumatic mass exodus to escape reprisals. Tens of thousands died at sea in unstable crafts, while about one and a half million eventually made it to other countries, with about half a million reaching the USA. The unified communist Vietnam soon collectivized agriculture and nationalized industry throughout the country, which then became an economic basket case for decades. Vietnam was soon at war with its neighbors in Cambodia and China, generating another million Vietnamese refugees.

Among the lasting impacts on the USA of the War were the end of the compulsory draft (the current all-volunteer military), the end of mandatory ROTC for male students at state universities, and the 26th amendment to the Constitution, lowering the voting age from 21 to 18.

The environmental movement really got rolling with *The Silent Spring* by Rachel Carson in 1962. The Wilderness Act was passed in 1964. By 1969, Congress was passing other federal environmental laws. The Environmental Protection Agency (EPA) came into existence in 1970. The first Earth Day was held on April 22, 1970, with various events across the Nation.

Drug use, including marijuana and synthetics like LSD, simply exploded. The terms Hippies and Flower Children and the phrases *Sex, Drugs, and Rock and Roll* seemed to characterize the times. In August 1969, the four-day *Love and Piece* rock festival at a rural farm near Woodstock, NY, drew 400,000 young people without any apparent publicity to promote it.

Abortion was also a growing issue in the sixties. In 1967, Colorado became the first state to legalize abortions in certain very limited circumstances, while Hawaii, in 1970, became the first state to legalize abortion on demand. By the time of the Supreme Court's 1973 Roe v.

Wade decision legalizing abortion across the country, 20 states had already legalized some abortions.

Beginning with its 1954 decision outlawing segregated public schools, the Supreme Court continued to reshape the nation's laws. It struck down prayer at public schools (at the time, it was one of the most unpopular decisions the court has ever issued – 49 governors expressed opposition to it), recognized a "right to privacy" as part of the 1st amendment even though it is unstated, and substantially increased the rights of criminal defendants by imposing stricter rules and limits on police and prosecutors regarding evidence and testimony. Both oral argument questions and written opinions often focused as much or more on the impact of the decision on individual people than the underlying legal issues. The Court's direction led President Eisenhower to lament that the worst decision of his Presidency was to nominate Earl Warren as Chief Justice of the Supreme Court. Justice William Douglas, who sat on the court from 1939 to 1975 (the longest any justice has ever served) and was labeled by *Time* magazine as *"the most doctrinaire and committed civil libertarian ever to sit on the court"* was in his heyday with the Court during the sixties. He and Warren often seemed far more concerned with what they saw as fair and right than what the Constitution or laws on the books said. Douglas proclaimed:

I would rather set a precedent than follow one.

13: THE THIRD INDUSTRIAL REVOLUTION

The Third Industrial Revolution is the Digital Revolution – the Information Age – that shifted from mechanical technology and analog electronics to digital electronics, leading to machines that don't need a wheel or have any moving parts as electronic pulses fly around in microprocessors. Unlike the Second Industrial Revolution, which *"covered virtually the entire span of human wants and needs, including food, clothing, housing, transportation, entertainment, communication, information, health, medicine, and working conditions,"* the Third Industrial Revolution has a more limited reach, particularly effecting entertainment, communications, information, and working conditions – the nature of work. Since we are all still living through this revolution, I will only note a few things here.

It began with punch cards. The 1880 census was the last tabulated by hand. It took seven years to complete. For the 1890 census, a young engineer and statistician, Herman Hollerith, developed a punch card machine based on a weaving machine that made complicated patterns that used an electric circuit to count needle holes in a card. With it, the 1990 census was tabulated in just six months, and the digital age was born. Hollerith's company, in 1924, merged with two other companies to form the International Business Machine Company (IBM). During World War II, there was an enormous need to quickly calculate the trajectory of artillery shells and decrypt codes, which led to the first computers that could do more than just count but also do calculations. And the race to build a digital world was on.

The World's first general use computer was built at the University of Pennsylvania. It took three years to build, was completed in 1946, and was the size of a bus. It used as much electricity as a small town, and by today's standards was glacially slow. It had to be manned constantly to replace burned out vacuum tubes and remove the occasional insects that would fly into the system, thus the phrase *debugging*. Then came the invention of transistors in 1947, which were much smaller and more durable than vacuum tubes. Portable transistor radios with batteries became common in the late 1950s. Then came the integrated circuit in 1959. With that, universities would have one or two mainframe computers capable of complex work in the 1960s, with data stored on magnetic tapes rotating back and forth. The first microprocessor was produced in 1971. With it came handheld electronic calculators (machines without wheels) that made the slide rule and the adding machine obsolete.

By 1980, word processors were replacing typewriters with personal desktop computers soon to follow. By 1990, recorded music had gone digital with CDs. During the 1990s, the internet spread. The World Wide Web (www.) went online in 1992, while TV broadcasts and movies went digital, and laptop computers began to spread. Then, after 2000, came digital cameras, GPS, DVRs, and flatscreen HDTVs. Then came iPods, smartphones, and social media. We can now ask Siri or Alexa almost anything and get an immediate answer. Almost all of these dramatic changes were first invented and developed in the USA, even though most mass manufacturing then shifted offshore to Asian nations. Even home appliances like refrigerators and washing machines now have computers in them.

Since 1970, as the digital revolution's effects first began to show up in daily life with the handheld calculator, our economy began a trade revolution in which American manufacturing has been increasingly replaced by imported goods, with a corresponding loss of well-paying blue-collar jobs. The US economy has become largely a service economy, with the principal services being restaurants, travel, and health care, while most manufactured goods are now imported. As explained by John Steele Gordon in 2004:

Computing power that cost a thousand dollars in the 1950s costs a fraction of a cent today. The computer, like the steam engine, produced an economic revolution, and for precisely the same reason: it caused a collapse in the price of a fundamental input into the economic system. The steam engine brought down the price of work-doing energy: the computer brought down the price of storing, retrieving, and manipulating information.

And that trend has only accelerated in the two decades since that statement. Like the Second Industrial Revolution a century before, the digital revolution has been led by a few individuals who have made unimaginably massive fortunes, like Bill Gates, Steve Jobs, and Jeff Bezos, while delivering incredible products to the masses in the USA and around the world. And, as always in the American economy, most of the richest were self-made. Of the 400 wealthiest Americans in 2000, 263 created their own fortunes from scratch. Only 19% of those making that *Forbes* list inherited enough money to qualify. The rest made their own fortunes.

Another important factor of the Third Industrial Revolution (one that is rarely acknowledged or mentioned) is its impact on the speed of economic activity throughout the world, and thus the growth of wealth. As previously mentioned, money is a commodity. It is also the catalyst that speeds up economic activity. The creation of banks greatly facilitated the function of money by making it no longer necessary to haul around gold, silver, or other precious materials. Instead, paper receipts could be used as money. Banks also freed up the capital tied up in property to fund the First Industrial Revolution. Then, after World War I, the use of checks drawn on individual bank accounts began to explode. With that, companies no longer needed to take the expense and risk associated with providing huge amounts of cash to hand out on payday. Instead, they could issue a paper check. And individuals could buy things (or pay a bill by mail) with a personal bank check rather than hauling around cash. By the end of World War II, almost all adults had a bank checking account and a checkbook. Then, with the Third Industrial Revolution came instantaneous electronic money transfers with bank credit or debit cards, ATMs, and online transfers. Barcodes greatly simplified retail sales and inventory management for stores. These all not only substantially reduced the cost of money transfers but also dramatically increased their speed. And that increased speed enabled a huge increase in worldwide economic activity.

Some have stated that we are now entering a Fourth Industrial Revolution, the age of *Artificial Intelligence* (AI), which has the potential for another massive boost in productivity (getting more done with fewer people in less time). In any case, the demand for rechargeable batteries has skyrocketed as the number of smartphones and laptop computers proliferate, and electric cars are now becoming a significant part of the market, as are self-driving cars.

14: THE PRESENT AND THE FUTURE

Enough history. It is time to sum up where we humans currently are. And see if there are any lessons to be learned from how we got here. We also need to consider where we may be going. Let's start with what Harvard's Steven Pinker had to say about worldwide poverty until 1800:

> *The average income was equivalent to that in the poorest countries in Africa today (about $500 a year in international dollars), and almost 95% of the world lived in what counts today as extreme poverty.*

That matches an earlier quote from an economics commentator who had this to say about the human condition throughout history until 1800: *"Almost everyone lived on the modern equivalent of $400 to $600 a year, just above the subsistence level. . . Then – just a couple of hundred years ago – people started getting richer. And richer and richer still."*

How rich? Unquestionably, almost all of us in the USA, and much of the world, now have far better living conditions, more free time, more options in how to spend that free time, and more resources to spend as we chose among those options, than ever before in human history. Even the wealthiest elites and rulers from previous eras lacked most of these living conditions and options.

Pinker called the Industrial Revolution the *"Great Escape"* from poverty. And that great escape continues. Just since 1980, the share of the worldwide human population living in extreme poverty has dropped from 44% to 10% as industrialization continues to spread around the world.

Economic comparisons between the present and the past are often made in dollars, or inflation adjusted dollars. Marian L. Tupy and Gale L. Pouley recently used an ingenious method for comparing past and present: *time price*. That is, by factoring in wages earned per hour worked, it is possible to calculate how long a person had to work to buy a specific commodity then and now. They found that for the time worked by an unskilled worker in the USA to buy a single pound of rice in 1850, that same amount of time worked in 2018 would buy 53 pounds of rice. Phrased another way, in

1850, an unskilled person had to work a long week (53 hours) to buy the same amount of rice that could be bought with one hour's wages in 2018. That is a time price drop of over 98%. They looked at several other commodities and found that the purchasing power of an hour worked had increased from 1850 to 2018 for every item they checked, almost all by more than twenty times (more than a 95% drop in time price). The smallest time price drop was 70% for beef. They then looked worldwide between 1960 and 2018. Time prices had fallen 84% worldwide in just 58 years. That is, a person could buy more than six times as much stuff with the wages earned in the same length of time worked in 2018 as they could have bought in 1960. Not only that, but the work done was less strenuous and less dangerous, and often more enjoyable, than most unskilled work was in those previous eras. Plus, the share of the workforce employed in unskilled positions in 2018 was far less than in the USA in 1850, or worldwide in 1960 when I graduated from high school. And that was looking at 2018, before the huge jump in wages for low skill jobs that has occurred since COVID hit in 2020 as *help wanted* signs were everywhere in the USA and teenagers began getting over $15/hour for work at fast food places.

In short, throughout history, we humans have never had it so good. The rise of our modern world has not been a zero-sum game in which for everyone who wins, someone else loses. Instead, while some have won far more than others, virtually everyone has won. In the USA, and much of the world, almost everyone is vastly wealthier and has far better living conditions and life options than their ancestors had in 1023, 1776, 1870, or even 1960. However, there are concerns that the wealth gap is growing in the USA as it shifts from a production to a service economy.

So, what sustains our modern way of life in the USA? Our complex modern society (which now extends to much of the world) is able to function and continue to innovate for two basic reasons: 1) its ability to produce things and move things with incredible efficiency (most things we buy have traveled over a thousand miles from where they were produced), and 2) it operates largely within a free market system (controlled by supply and demand) within a framework of rules and expectations (primarily voluntary compliance with the rule of law). The USA has led the way in building and sustaining our modern way of life.

All this increase in wealth, free time, and life options has also enabled a vast increase in the number of people (no longer confined to the drudgery of trying to keep themselves and their family fed and sheltered) who can now sit around and debate the meaning of life and dream up concepts like *modernity, postmodernism,* and *nihilism. "Our prosperity is made possible by using energy and machines so fewer and fewer of us have to produce food, energy, and consumer products, and more and more of us can do work that requires greater use of our minds and that even offers meaning and purpose to our lives."* Personally, not having had them as a child, I would hate to now have to give up clean hot and cold running water, indoor bathrooms with toilets, central heating and air conditioning with a thermostat, a TV, a cellphone, recorded music, a home computer, the internet, shopping centers, a good mattress, medical care, jet air travel, the wide variety of ethnic and seasonal foods now readily and constantly accessible, etc. and etc., that were not available to even the wealthiest and most powerful anywhere on earth 150 years ago. In short, I like modern life and would like it to continue for my great-grandchildren.

The USA has led the way in wealth growth for at least the last 150 years. About twenty years ago, as a new century was beginning, John Steele Gordon characterized the USA as follows:

Today the United Sates possesses only 6% of the world's land area and 6% of its people – virtually all of whom regard themselves as Americans and speak English...It has close to 30% of the world's gross domestic product.

Its economy is not only the largest in the world, it is the most dynamic and innovative as well. Virtually every major development in technology in the twentieth century – which was far and away the most important century in the history of technology – originated in the United States or was principally industrialized and turned into consumer products here. Its culture, therefore, from blue jeans to Hollywood movies to Coca-Cola to rock and roll to SUVs to computer chat rooms, pervades the rest of the planet.

The Internet, the most powerful means of communication ever devised, is largely an American invention, and English is the language of more than 80% of the four billion websites now in existence.

The ultimate power of the United States, then, lies not in its military – potent as that military is, to be sure – but in its wealth, the wide distribution of that wealth among its population, its capacity to create more wealth, and its seemingly bottomless imagination in developing new ways to use that wealth productively...Others [nations] want what we have and are willing, often eager, to adopt our ways in order to have them too.

While getting richer, the demographics of populations in the USA and around the world have also changed thanks largely to the public health revolution that controlled infectious diseases. For the first time in human history, most new babies live to see adulthood, even in poor countries. Further, far more people are living past 80, or even 90. In 1945, the first comprehensive effort to predict world population growth was undertaken because of concerns that food production would not be able to keep pace (the Malthusian trap). The world population at the time was a little over two billion. The Office of Population Research at Princeton estimated that the world population would reach 3.3 billion by the year 2000. Instead, the world population reached six billion by 2000, and has added another two billion since.

And the population now is vastly older. And will continue to get older still. That means fewer people will be working to support older adults who are no longer working. That means productivity must continue to increase to avoid a drop in living standards. Meanwhile, birth rates across Europe and much of Asia are below replacement rates. The number of children is going down as the number of elderly is expanding rapidly. One study projects that, by 2100, worldwide, the number of children under five will drop to less than 60% of what it is today, while the number of people over 80 will be six times higher than today. The highest birthrates are in the poorest countries, primarily in Central Africa. China held to a one-child policy for 40 years, which was finally lifted in the last decade. It now has a population almost devoid of siblings, aunts, uncles, cousins, nieces, and nephews. The entire family circle is one child with two parents and no extended family. For a culture that had been dominated by family relationships for centuries, that shift is colossal. It is now a nation of disconnected individuals. Further, because sons were preferred over daughters, China now has tens of millions more young men than young women, which can only further destabilize society. Because of falling birthrates worldwide, the world population is expected to peak before 2100 and then begin to fall in the next century.

In the USA, the percentage of households having just one person has more than doubled (now 27%) since 1960. In 1990, one in ten women remained childless. Now it is one is six. In 1960, the mean age for a woman's first marriage was 20.4. Now it is 28.6. Parents with children under age 18 fell from 40% in 1970 to less than 18% in 2021. The percentage of adults who are not married has skyrocketed. Despite the huge population increase with many more living in cities, loneliness is now more prevalent than ever as people feel disconnected even in crowded cities. These are huge demographic shifts in human populations, never before seen in world history that need to be factored in as we look ahead.

So, what about the Future? Will the rapid rise in living standards in the USA and the world continue? Or will it all come tumbling down? There are now worldwide conferences to address concerns that the environmental costs associated with all that increase in wealth and comfort are making the earth unlivable. Industrialization is seen as the culprit in the Climate Change debate that is sweeping the world. At the November 2021 multination climate change conference in Glasgow, Scotland, Greta Thunberg, the well-known young environmental activist from Sweden, denounced the British as *"climate villains"* responsible for the horrors of climate change since it all:

started in the UK where the Industrial Revolution started, where we started to burn coal.

Even Boris Johnson, the Prime Minister of Great Britain at the time, got in on blaming his own country when he acknowledged that his nation was where the steam engine *"produced by burning coal"* was invented. It was referred to as *"the doomsday machine"* that led the world into burning fossil fuels However, England actually began burning coal seven centuries before that.

Not acknowledged at that conference (where many of the participants arrived on private jets) was that *but for* the industrial revolution, daily life would still be much like it was around the world in 1776. And most of us would have never been born. The world would still be struggling to feed a vastly smaller population, with over 90% often being hungry while living in poverty. That is not to say that human caused climate change isn't real. The problem is that most solutions being pushed to address it by activists and national and world leaders are far more dangerous to the world's human population **and** the natural environment than climate change itself. In short, the *Cure* they are pushing is worse than the disease. But it may not ever be fully implemented. As one commentator put it: *"The transition to renewables is doomed because modern industrial people, no matter how romantic they are, do not want to return to pre-modern life."* Still, as we look to the future, powerful forces are committed to undercutting the pillars that sustain modern life with little understanding of the unintended consequences of their goals. As Yogi Berra put it:

It is difficult to make predictions, especially about the future.

We now have advocates, politicians, and even scientists armed with computer models, giving dire predictions of what the world will be like in 2100. However, in the words of Prominent scientist Steven E. Koonin:

Despite the certainty with which projections are reported as facts, estimating human influences is a highly uncertain business. Imagine being back in 1900 and trying to project what civilization would be like in the year 2000. At the time, the first powered flight and the first mass-produced automobile were yet to come, radio had just been invented and X-rays just discovered, and antibiotics weren't even imagined. Even the most prescient prognosticator back then would have missed most of what transpired in the subsequent century as the global population quadrupled and the global economy grew by a factor of 40!

They'd be amazed at the scale and rapidity with which people, goods, and information now move around the globe, at how we manufacture, and at our advances in agriculture and medicine.

Just 24 years ago (at the turn of the century and millennium in 2000), there were no flat-screen HD TVs. There were no DVRs. There were no TV or audio streaming services. There were no smart phones or social media. Amazon was a new company that only sold books online and had yet to make a profit. There were no electric cars. Fracking for oil and gas (which vastly expanded the USA's energy reserves and production) was yet to come. Over 50% of our electricity was generated by burning coal. Windmills for electricity were just beginning. The newest or latest rages were DVD players and the internet (with dial-up connections). No one had GPS, digital cameras, or wireless home routers. Home speakers and theater systems were all hard-wired. Home computers were as big as a small suitcase. There were no iPads. Though iPods were yet to come, they are now already obsolete. Self-driving cars were a Syfy pipedream.

No one can see 76 years into the future or begin to know what 2100 will be like. But we do know that the future is not yet fixed. Absent divine intervention (which many believe will come), human civilization and conditions of the earth could go off in a wide range of different directions between now and then. Decisions being made now will affect that future. But not necessarily in the ways intended. Unintended consequences are apt to far exceed intended consequences. Why? Because of ignorance, often willful ignorance, of two things. First, what got us, as humans, to where we are today – our history, as discussed above. And second, what actually enables our modern way of life – the essential pillars that sustain how we live. In fact, these two things are often being willfully distorted to promote an agenda with little understanding of the consequences that agenda will bring far beyond what is intended.

So, here is my take on what history teaches us about what has enabled our modern world. It is basically one thing that has made it all possible – and that is ever-increasing *productivity*. Ever-improving technology, primarily over the last 250 years, has enabled massive and sustained increases in productivity: getting more done in less time by fewer people while continually creating new stuff and moving things around faster and more efficiently. And what has enabled all that? It is sustained by six essential pillars. The first three were brought up in the above discussion of early civilizations, namely: 1) Materials, 2) Energy, and 3) Accumulated Knowledge. Then, the next three come into focus as we look at history. They are: 4) Culture, 5) Institutions, and 6) Optimism and Hope. Each of these are discussed below.

MATERIALS – Materials make up all the structures around us and all the things we use. If we stopped using any materials, we would all be naked, living in caves (or sleeping on the ground or in trees), and eating plants and animals raw that we tore apart with our own hands. In short, even the most primitive hunter/gatherer societies used materials. Even beavers and birds use materials. Creating and maintaining a fire takes materials. Building a shelter takes materials. Making wraps, clothes, tools, machines, containers, and anything else takes materials. Our extensive use of materials is what takes human living conditions beyond that of beavers and birds.

And where do we get materials? From animals. From plants. And from the earth. And how do we get materials from the earth? By mining and drilling. If we stopped all mining and drilling, all structures, tools, clothes, containers, anything, would have to come from plants or animals. All metals come from the earth, as do many building materials like granite, marble, slate, limestone, sandstone, and the components of concrete. Stone aggregate for roads, along with clay for bricks, ceramics, and porcelain, come from the earth, as do the sands used to make glass. All of these are obtained by mining. If we were to stop all mining and drilling, electricity would soon disappear since metals, essential to its generation, transmission, storage, and use, can only be obtained by mining. Plastics and synthetic fabrics would disappear, along with most chemicals and pharmaceuticals. Living conditions would soon be no better than they were a thousand years ago. And the world population would rapidly drop by 95% (in "you first" chaos) to bring us down to a sustainable level with almost all living in extreme poverty. Yet, many supposedly bright people in the USA and much of the West oppose all mining and drilling. And consider it a moral issue. Many of them are at universities. For all their brilliance, learning, and influence on society, they are largely focused on group rights and are completely ignorant of how modern society functions and what sustains it. And that is incredibly dangerous since it puts civilization, including all those social issues they hold so dear, at risk.

Some raw materials are abundant, and some are rare. Some are concentrated in a few places, while others are widespread. The USA has been uniquely blessed with an abundance of a wide variety of natural resources. However, there are some critically important materials we don't have at all, while there is strong opposition to the domestic production of others. Many materials essential to both national defense and daily life, such as rubber, must be imported.

The First Industrial Revolution, led by Britain and the USA, was made possible by iron and coal. The three principal materials of the Second Industrial Revolution, led by the USA, were steel (made from iron), fossil fuels (as petroleum and natural gas were added to coal), and rubber. Aluminum became increasingly important after World War II. Now, in the Third Industrial Revolution, we are seeing increasing demand for rare earth metals, mostly produced by China, for complex electronics. About 90% of the world's advanced processing chips are produced in Taiwan. The most complex components in each iPhone are made only in Taiwan, while almost all final *Apple* products are glued together in China. No wonder China wants control of Taiwan. Most *Samsung* products are assembled in Vietnam. In fact, Vietnam recently passed Britain in terms of trade volume with the USA. Many tech companies manufacture in India.

Lithium and cobalt are essential in meeting the rapidly increasing demand for lithium-ion rechargeable batteries, including large batteries for electric cars and huge batteries for electric utility companies. However, the USA produces very little lithium or cobalt. Over 90% of lithium imported to the USA comes from Argentina and Chili. Worldwide, Australia and China are also major producers. There are also extensive reserves in the Congo. As electric cars increase their share of the market and electric utilities try to increase their storage capacity as they shift to renewable energy sources like wind turbines and solar panels, which only produce electricity some of the time, the demand for lithium and cobalt could well increase by as much as 50 times just in the next decade (more on this in the energy discussion that follows).

Meanwhile, efforts to open a new lithium mine in Nevada are being challenged in court by green energy advocates. Also, in January 2023, the government announced a ban on mining covering almost a quarter of a million acres in Minnesota's Iron Belt, our primary source of iron, copper, nickel, and other metals. Yet, there is no other country on earth where mining will occur that would do it with less environmental degradation than the USA.

Cobalt, a metal generally found in conjunction with nickel and copper, is also an essential component of most lithium-ion rechargeable batteries. The price has fluctuated wildly (from $20,000 to $90,000 per ton) over the last five years. About two-thirds of the world's cobalt production currently comes from the Congo (more than ten times the production of any other country), where it has historically been mined by hand in deplorable conditions, sometimes with child labor, and is the focus of human rights groups. The Congo's share of the world market is only expected to increase because it contains an overwhelming share of world reserves.

Petroleum is not only a fuel, but also an essential feedstock for many synthetic materials, including plastics, synthetic fabrics, and chemicals. We will still have a continuing need for petroleum long after the last internal combustion engine has gone to the scrap heap. Yet, the USA has recently taken several actions to limit domestic oil and natural gas production.

And there is another important point to be made here regarding *synthetic* or *artificial* materials – materials not found in the natural world but that are created by humans. Some, including many environmentalists, are opposed to the use of such materials simply because they are not natural. But that is biting off their nose to spite their face. Some examples.

Because the material is beautiful and malleable, the shells of hawksbill sea turtles have been used by humans around the world for thousands of years to make jewelry, hair combs, and other items. For over a hundred years (still in fashion when I was a kid), tortoiseshell frames for eyeglasses were the rage. An international tortoiseshell trade developed in the 1840s and lasted for 150 years until Japan finally agreed to join the international ban on sea turtles in 1992. *"Scientists estimate that since 1844, humans have killed nine million hawksbill turtles, or about sixty thousand each year. Humans killed so many hawksbill that the dramatic reduction in the species altered the function of coral reef and seagrass ecosystems around the world."* And brought those turtles to the edge of extinction. However, plastic began to replace tortoiseshells for many uses even before the ban went into effect. Almost all combs and many eyeglass frames around the world are now made of plastic, which can be made to replicate the marbled pattern found in tortoiseshells. While plastic straws have killed a few sea turtles, in the larger picture, plastic is playing a central and essential role in saving sea Turtles from extinction.

Ivory has been used for centuries in many ways. During the nineteenth century, elephants were being killed by the thousands for their tusks. An 1866 New York Times report stated that 22,000 elephants were being killed each year just *"to supply the cutlery establishments of Sheffield, England, with the handles for the knives and other cutlery made there."* The primary use of ivory in the USA was for piano keys (a practice that lasted until the 1970s) and billiard balls. In the 1860s, A billiard ball maker offered a reward of $10,000 to anyone who could make a suitable substitute for ivory. Within a couple of decades, plastic had replaced ivory in the manufacture of billiard balls and for many other uses. *"The best ivory has no grain and looks just like plastic."*

Yet, there is now a strong pushback against the use of any plastic. California banned plastic bags. However, because much more energy and materials are needed to make a paper bag, it needs to be reused 43 times to have a smaller impact on the environment than a single plastic bag properly disposed of in a landfill. Further, producing a glass bottle has about three times more impact on the environment than making a comparable plastic bottle. There are strong concerns about plastic degradation of the world's oceans and a push to reduce the use of plastic in the USA. Yet, 90% of the plastic flowing into the oceans comes from 10 rivers: eight of them are in Asia and two in Africa. The USA contributes only about one percent of the plastic found at sea.

Further, plastic properly disposed of in a landfill is sequestered carbon. When you place plastic waste in the recycle bin, you have no idea where it will end up. It may well be shipped to China and end up in the Ocean. If you put it with regular garbage, you know it is going to a landfill where it will safely sequester carbon. Do the environment a favor and send it to the landfill.

Some advocate the use of bioplastics – that is, plastics made from sugar or other plant materials. However, they all don't necessarily degrade faster. And those that do emit methane, a powerful greenhouse gas. Further, since bioplastics are made from crops, the USA would need to increase farmland by about ten percent to produce bioplastics to replace plastic from petroleum residue. *"We must overcome the instinct to see natural products as superior to artificial ones... The good news is that, to some extent, this is already happening. In many developed nations, consumers condemn the consumption of natural products, like products made from ivory, fur, coral, or tortoiseshells. Humankind is thus well-prepared to understand an important paradoxical truth: it is only by embracing the artificial that we can save what is natural.*

In short, opposition to all domestic drilling or mining is to promote national suicide. Such opposition worldwide also promotes the end of the modern world and the return to living conditions that are worse than they were a thousand years ago while harming natural systems.

ENERGY – The Industrial Revolution forever changed how humans use energy. In fact, it was driven by new sources of cheap energy that magnified productivity to unimaginable levels. As previously noted, for millennia, the primary source of energy for human endeavors was muscle power (human and domestic animals) and fire, augmented in some cultures by wind (sails and windmills) and water wheels. The steam engine, which uses heat to turn a wheel and power a machine, followed by the internal combustion engine and electricity, changed everything. In fact, electricity has transformed virtually every aspect of daily life, particularly urban life. It is the sole reason we now have buildings over six stories high and subway systems. It would be inconceivable to previous generations that humans would ever spend as much time and money as is now spent on fitness centers and exercise machines, as well as playing games requiring physical excursion, because the most physically taxing work most of us do regularly is hitting keys on a keypad, opening a can or package in the kitchen, or loading the dishwasher.

Abundant, reliable, and inexpensive energy is the lifeblood of the modern world. *"Globally, the history of human evolution and development is one of converting ever-larger amounts of energy into wealth and power in ways that allow human societies to grow more complex. How wealthy we are is thus reflected in the amount of energy we consume."* Even though evolving technologies continue to improve energy efficiency, cheap energy is still the bedrock of the economy in the USA or any other developed country. As was on glaring display in 2021 and 2022, when the cost of energy goes up, the cost of everything else must go up. And the people get poorer. **That is the simple truth**. Period.

So, what kinds of energy do we now use in the USA? According to the federal Energy Information Administration, in 2020, the sources of energy used in the USA (as measured in BTUs – British thermal units) were petroleum 37%, natural gas 33%, coal 10%, nuclear 8%, wind turbines and solar panels 7%, dams 3%, and liquid biofuels (primarily corn ethanol) 2%. In short, 80% of our energy still comes from fossil fuels. That has been largely true for at least two decades, as a dramatic rise in natural gas use was offset by a drop in coal use by more than half.

And what is all that energy used for? In 2020, generating electricity consumed 38%, while 28% went for transportation (petroleum products used by cars, trucks, trains, barges, airplanes, and ships that move people and things across the country and in and out of ocean ports), 22% for industrial purposes (making things), and 12% for commercial and residential purposes.

That brings us to a second truth. Cities concentrate energy use in small areas. Modern cities even more so. The amount of energy required to keep Manhattan functioning is enormous compared to the space it covers. Most people in the USA now live in cities. To sustain all those cities, minimizing the area necessary to provide all that energy is a critical consideration. In discussions about energy policy, this is referred to as *surface power density*. It turns out that renewable energy sources (solar, wind, biomass, dams) require 100 to 1,000 times more land than fossil or nuclear energy sources to generate the same amount of energy. And that has enormous consequences for land use, including agriculture and the preservation of natural areas.

But how does all that energy get moved around to where it is needed? There are basically three ways to move energy. First, wires. While this only works for electricity, it is highly efficient in terms of cost and energy consumed for long-distance shipment through high voltage transmission lines and local distribution to individual residences and businesses. However, locating and constructing new high voltage transmission lines is intensely controversial. Second, pipes. While pipes only work for petroleum, liquid petroleum products, and natural gas, they are, again, extremely efficient in terms of operating cost and energy consumed. This is also true for local distribution to residential houses and businesses for natural gas. However, locating and constructing new large, long-distance pipelines is also intensely controversial. Third, bulk transport by truck, train, barge, or ship (in ascending order of efficiency). This is the only way to move coal and solid biofuels (mostly wood). However, it is far less efficient than pipes or wires, both in terms of cost and the energy consumed during transport. It is also more hazardous to people and the environment. That is why, in the 1970s and 80s, many coal fired generating stations were built in remote locations near large coal deposits across the country (mine-mouth power plants). Shipping electricity through wires is far cheaper and more efficient than shipping coal to power plants near cities. Bulk transport is also often used for petroleum, petroleum products, liquified natural gas (and propane), and biofuels. However, pipes are far preferable for large volumes and long distances because they are safer, cleaner, cheaper, and use less energy.

Since 80% of the energy used in the USA is fossil fuels, where does it all come from? While the petroleum share has remained about the same for the last 20 years, where it comes from has changed dramatically. From 2000 to 2008, the USA was producing less than half of the petroleum it was using with production continuing to fall. The rest was imported. Then, as the new technology of *fracking* began to spread, production began to climb and passed consumption in 2019 for the first time in over half a century. Fracking was the reason for that increase (and the corresponding drop in price), with more than four-fold production increases in West

Texas and along the Gulf Coast, accounting for much of the nation's production increases. Since virtually all of the natural gas and coal used in the USA is produced here, the rise in natural gas consumption is a direct result of the rise in production associated with fracking and has enabled the dramatic drop in coal use. And since natural gas plants emit far less CO_2 to generate the same amount of electricity when compared to coal, it has enabled the USA to reduce its CO_2 emissions significantly.

The burning of fossil fuels invariably involves emissions of CO_2 into the atmosphere. Rising levels of CO_2 are seen as the primary culprit in the climate change debate that has been going on for over 40 years (discussed further under Accumulated Knowledge below). Suffice it to say here that this has led to an ongoing intense effort across the developed world to reduce carbon emissions. As being pushed by various national and international organizations and interest groups, the general goal is to reach net zero CO_2 emissions by 2050, with some groups pushing to shorten that to 2035 (the Green New Deal). The issue then is how to meet our ever-increasing energy needs while reducing CO_2. So, it is important to point out that, based solely on CO_2 emissions for the same amount of energy produced, burning wood (or other biomass) is the worst. Coal is better than wood. Petroleum is better than coal. Natural gas is better than petroleum. And nuclear energy, wind turbines, and solar panels are better than Natural gas because they have zero emissions. We have largely eliminated burning wood for fuel in the USA. Coal use has already been drastically cut, and we can expect that to continue. So, let's look further at petroleum and natural gas, which account for 70% of our current energy supply.

A government can do a few things to reduce the use of these two fossil fuels. First, do things that will improve fuel efficiency. In response to the 1974 oil shortages, the USA imposed a nationwide speed limit of 55 mph to reduce gas consumption, with increased traffic safety considered as a worthwhile side benefit. That national speed limit was increased to 65 mph in 1986 and then eliminated in 1995 because of its continued unpopularity. And no one wants it back. The USA also imposed more restrictive milage standards on new cars sold to reduce gas consumption. This has been effective in leading to increasingly efficient engines, as well as reductions in car size and in car weight by replacing metal with plastic where possible.

Second, reduce demand by making fossil fuels more expensive by taxing it. The USA has debated a tax on carbon for decades but hasn't done it. Nor has it raised gas taxes. The American public does not like high gas prices. Which leads us to a **third truth**: people are disinclined to accept something that has an immediate, measurable personal negative impact but only offers a subjective potential future public benefit. And that is even more true when a significant portion of the public loses confidence and trust in its government. Europe has successfully used much higher taxes on gasoline to limit consumption for years. However, the European lifestyle is more closely linked to public benefits and transportation, and is not as dependent on individual cars as life in the USA. Further, cars are generally much smaller there.

Third, find alternatives to fossil fuels that can replace their critical role in daily life for much of the population. The obvious answer here is nuclear power to generate electricity. However, nuclear power began to lose favor with the public in much of the world over 40 years ago. In 1996, the share of the world's electricity generated by nuclear plants peaked at 18%. By 2018 it was down to 10% and continues to drop. The push this century has been *renewables,* wind turbines, biofuels, and solar panels. Despite new laws and enormous government investments to promote new technologies along with a range of tax incentives, wind and solar still provide less than 10% of the USA's energy needs. Europe has invested even more with similar results.

Fourth, limit supply. The USA has debated a *cap & trade* system for decades that would limit the amount of carbon used. But is that a good idea? Daniel Turner compared gas to the pencil example I cited at the beginning of the section on the First Industrial Revolution.

In the spirit of "I, Pencil," I similarly marvel at the fossil fuel industry. Gas is as ordinary as a pencil. We fill up our tanks every day, or jump in a ride share, hop on a plane, jet ski around a lake, without taking any notice of the miracle of this fuel. Gas is the result of the labor of innumerable individual contributions, from geologists to tanker drivers; it begins miles underground and ends at the local filling station, yet it is cheaper than bottled water.

Pencils and gas are both marvels of free market capitalism, as are countless petrochemical products, from plastics and rubber to laundry detergent and cosmetics. The only non-market force capable of disrupting this well-oiled machine is government.

In 2021, the federal government took other steps to limit supply in its push to shift transportation (28% of our energy consumption) from using petroleum to using electricity. As a part of that, it canceled the completion of the nearly finished Keystone pipeline that would have provided easy access to petroleum from Canada, our closest ally geographically and politically. It not only meant that whatever oil comes from those oil fields to the USA would have to continue coming by train tanker cars (costing more and consuming more energy in transport while creating greater hazards), but it limited the ability to increase the amount of oil coming from that source (it will still be produced but go elsewhere with more energy being consumed to ship it there). At the same time, the government began limiting access to new federal oil reserves while railing against fossil fuels, which has reduced investment. The immediate result of limiting the supply of an essential commodity will always be an increase in its price. And a price hike in transportation costs inevitably increases the price of everything. By 2022, after gas and diesel prices inevitably skyrocketed, the USA sought more oil from Saudi Arabia, Venezuela, and others who are not allies (oil that would have to be shipped in bulk tankers burning diesel) while tapping the strategic petroleum reserve. Then came the war in Ukraine, which brought an energy crisis and inflation to Europe, which had been pursuing similar policies.

Unfortunately, the government launched its effort to have everything powered by electricity at a time when the electric grid itself was already becoming less reliable and more expensive. Further, it did so without a viable plan for meeting current electric needs, let alone the vast increase in demand that would be associated with a huge growth in electric vehicles.

Since the federal government is now engaged in an enormous push to promote electric vehicles, including financial incentives and a huge expansion in the number of charging stations, a few things should be clarified about electricity. First, where do we get our electricity in the USA? According to the Energy Information Administration, in 2021, 39% came from natural gas power plants (up from 25% in 2011 and 20% in 2001). Combined cycle natural gas plants are 55-60% efficient, while simple gas plants are 45% efficient. That is, for all the energy in natural gas consumed by the plant, only 45% to 60% comes out of the plant as electricity. Coal now provides 22% of our electricity (down from 42% in 2011 and 52% in 2001). Coal plants are, at best, about 40% efficient. Nuclear power plants provide 19% (19% in 2011 and 20% in 2001). They are only about 33% efficient. The rest of the energy is lost as waste heat. That is why we associate nuclear plants with the giant parabolic cooling towers that dominate the skyline around them. These towers are essentially radiators to disperse waste heat. The only thing coming out of them is water vapor. They emit no CO2, pollutants, or radiation. Wind turbines now provide about 11% (up from 5% in 2011 and near zero in 2001) of our electricity. Hydroelectric dams provide 6% (down from 8% in 2011 and 10% in 2001 – apparently recent droughts have limited the water behind these dams). Solar panels now provide about 3% (none in earlier decades).

Thus, 61% of our electricity still comes from fossil fuels (down from 67% in 2011 and 72% in 2001). We only use petroleum to generate electricity on islands (Hawaii, Puerto Rico, and other U.S. territories), where it is the primary source. That makes electricity much more expensive on those islands, which makes it much harder to attract industry or other economic development beyond tourism. In 1972, the government in Puerto Rico scrapped efforts to complete the construction of a nuclear power plant on its south coast due to intense opposition from environmentalists. And switched to an oil-burning plant at that site instead. Two years later, the worldwide oil embargo by OPEC hit and the price of oil more than doubled. What a difference it would have made to the Puerto Rico economy over the last 50 years if they had had access to inexpensive electricity. The island is now an economic basket case.

Electricity put into any electric network must always exceed the amount of electricity being used across the network. If demand exceeds supply, the system will crash, causing enormous damage to its infrastructure. So, system networks have a range of switches that can be triggered to cut off demand (creating power outages) to keep the system functional. Unfortunately, the demand for electricity fluctuates widely, not only at different times of the year but also at different times of the day (driven by such things as lighting, heating, industrial demand during working hours, or air conditioning). Historically, electric utilities have looked for two kinds of generation. Baseload plants, usually nuclear and coal fired powerplants, are expensive to build but cheap to operate and slow to start up or shut down. Nuclear plants only account for less than 10% of the USA's generating capacity but produce 19% of our electricity because they are kept running flat-out almost all the time to provide baseload. Peaking plants, often natural gas plants, are cheaper to build but more expensive to operate and can be started up or shut down much more quickly. However, they are now also being used for baseload as the use of coal has diminished. Dams are also excellent for handling peak loads because they all have more generating capacity than they have water behind the dam to keep the generators going all the time. Plus, all that is needed to start them up or shut them down is to open or close the huge valves that send water to the turbines. Electric utilities are constantly monitoring their systems to ensure supply always exceeds demand while limiting the excess as much as safely possible because it is wasted.

Wind turbines and solar panels create a whole new ballgame. Wind turbines only generate electricity when the wind blows. And some completely froze up during a 2021 cold snap and ice storm in Texas. Solar panels only generate electricity during daylight hours. Even then, output can be sharply reduced by clouds, dust, or when covered by snow. As their share of total generation increases, the ability to manage generation to match demand fluctuations decreases. This brings us to massive storage of electricity in batteries for when it is needed to keep the lights on and electricity flowing from the wall sockets at home.

That leads us to a **Fourth truth** as exemplified by Germany and California. *"Renewables make electricity more costly everywhere they are* *deployed at scale."* And less reliable. Among the most damaging lies ever told by an American politician (President Biden) was that wind and solar are cheaper and more reliable than coal. Whatever their comparative benefits, wind, and solar are never cheaper or more reliable than coal. California has gone further than any other state in shifting its electric grid to renewables. Now, as a result, it has the most expensive and least reliable electricity in the continental USA. Then, in August 2022, California announced that it would ban all gasoline-powered vehicles beginning in 2030. Five days later, California's largest electric utility urged residents not to charge their electric vehicles between 4 and 9 pm in order to prevent blackouts. In short, California is unprepared and has no plan to deal with the consequences of the ban it just announced that will seriously exacerbate the problem.

In just the last few years, some efforts have begun to build batteries large enough to help sustain the nation's electric grid. However, it will take an incredibly massive buildup of battery capacity to even out supply and demand imbalances created if that supply is ever primarily from wind turbines and solar panels. Estimates are that, in northern cities, because of the low angle of the sun and fluctuating weather conditions, a two-month supply of electricity would need to be stored in batteries. The idea of having batteries big enough to keep apartments, hotels, and offices warm; and the subway, taxis, buses, and private electric cars all moving; and all the lights on at Times Square and throughout the city on a cold, windless New Year's Eve in Manhattan boggles the mind. I doubt it will ever happen. New Year's Eve at Times Square will never be the same if the city is ever totally dependent on wind and solar energy.

A **fifth truth** about energy is the need to keep energy output as electricity high when compared to the energy input needed to build and operate the system in order to maintain modern living standards. A study in Germany found that a nuclear plant will produce about 75 times the amount of energy input required to build it. For fossil fuels, the energy output is about 30 times the input to build it. For wind, it is 3.9 times, while for solar, the energy output is only about 1.6 times the energy consumed to make the system. And that translates to much higher dollar costs per energy output. As summarized by Michael Shellenberger in comparing France and Germany, two adjacent and similar economies:

France spends a little more than half as much for electricity that produces one-tenth of the carbon emissions of German electricity. The difference is that Germany is phasing out nuclear and phasing in renewables, while France is keeping most of its nuclear plants online. Had Germany invested $580 billion into new nuclear power plants instead of renewables like solar and wind farms, it would be generating 100% of its electricity from zero emission sources and have sufficient zero-carbon electricity to power all its cars and light trucks as well.

Instead, Germany, like Austria and the Netherlands, now has had to reopen some of its old coal-fired generating plants just to keep the lights on and keep homes warm in winter.

In Sri Lanka, the president recently adopted a get-to-Net-Zero policy and banned the importation and use of nitrogen-based fertilizer (which requires lots of CO_2 producing energy to make). In 2022, food production dropped 40% while prices rose 80%. He was ousted and that policy has been abandoned. The same issue arose among farmers in Holland, with comparable results.

Within the USA, in 2019, San Antonio, one of the most impoverished large metropolitan areas in the country, adopted a policy to reduce CO_2 emissions in its electric generation. That policy was expected to raise utility bills by $1,000 a year per household when fully implemented. In January 2023, the city abandoned that plan and replaced it with a plan to use more natural gas. The mayor said: "*People want to make sure that we can affordably keep the lights on in San Antonio.*" In California, Huntington Beach and Orange County also recently abandoned plans to move to 100% renewable energy with the claim that: "*the authority failed to inform the public that their electricity bills were increasing.*" The public needs to know the truth about costs.

Lithium-ion rechargeable batteries have skyrocketed since 2000 with the proliferation of portable electronic devices like cell phones and laptop computers. Electric cars (EVs) are now pushed and subsidized by the government. They are extremely quiet, accelerate quicker, and are almost impossible to tip over because the battery (for the average sized car it weighs about 1,000 pounds) is beneath the passengers, so the car is much heavier and has an extremely low center of gravity. They seem great for local travel since they can be plugged in at home overnight to recharge them. However, since the CO_2 footprint of building an electric car is much higher than that of a gas-burning car, it takes a few years of normal driving – 30,000 to 70,000 miles, depending on the source of the electricity it uses – before an electric car begins to contribute to a reduction in CO_2 emissions. Further, on a trip, electric cars can only go three to four hours before needing to stop for an hour to recharge. Then comes winter. Cold temperatures significantly reduce the capacity of electric batteries. Plus, lights and heat inside the car must all come from the battery. I wouldn't want to be dependent on an electric car in Green Bay in January.

In 2022 the government mandated that EVs must make up a substantial portion of new cars sold by 2030. However, despite government subsidies, EVs are accumulating unsold on car lots, while the demand for hybrids exceeds supply. In Short, the government has mandated the *sale* of a product the public isn't buying. That is terrible public policy and a waste of resources.

Air travel is another problem. While electric motors can certainly turn a propeller, weight in airplanes is a critical factor. The size of batteries for any long flights would dramatically reduce the amount of payload or passengers that could be hauled. And then there are jet planes, which make up the vast majority of current air travel. There is no way to replace a jet engine with an electric engine. The very basis of a jet engine is combustion. As long as people and things continue to move around the world through the air at more than 400 miles an hour, we must have petroleum. Then, there are rockets used by the military and to launch communication satellites.

While electric delivery trucks and buses may be viable for local use, using electric freight trucks (18 wheelers) for long-distance hauling is problematic. The batteries would have to be huge (8,000 lbs.+), substantially reducing freight capacity while needing to stop every 4-5 hours for a few hours to recharge. This would dramatically increase transportation costs, and the final purchase price, for virtually everything we buy. And because the batteries are so heavy, these vehicles will have far more impact on roads and highways. There is already concern that many parking garages may not be strong enough to support full capacity if all cars are electric.

And then there is farming. America's farms run on diesel. And that use is often intense during short cycles in the growing season making battery charge delays problematic. And barge traffic on the nation's rivers is extremely efficient and extensively used for bulk transport. And there are the Nation's freight trains. The disparity in the time required to fill a diesel tank when compared to recharging sufficient batteries for any of these uses is enormous. And time is expensive. And so are the batteries. And then there is international shipping on the oceans. I see nothing on the horizon that could replace diesel fuel for all the shipping going on around the world. I can't imagine batteries large enough to power a cargo ship across the Pacific Ocean. We have used small nuclear power plants for naval submarines and aircraft carriers for over half a century. However, their cost is prohibitive for commercial tankers and cargo ships.

In January 2023, word got out that the government was considering a ban on new natural gas stoves. California has already banned the extension of natural gas lines into some new developments, while some cities are considering similar bans. It doesn't get any more wrong-headed than that. Because a gas kitchen stove (and furnace and water heater) is close to 100% efficient in generating heat, while generating electricity with gas is, at best, 60% efficient, and over 60% of our electricity still comes from fossil fuels, cooking dinner and heating your home and water with natural gas emits less CO_2 than using an electric stove, furnace, or water heater unless you have your own solar panels. This new proposed ban is also being justified by claims it will reduce in-home air pollution. Since humans first began using fire, they have had fires in their homes. And natural gas is the cleanest fuel humans have ever had to burn in their homes.

What about biofuels – wood, biomass, corn ethanol, etc.? Because biofuels have been labeled *renewable,* their use as an energy source is being promoted over fossil fuels to combat climate change. The rationale is that the earth's *carbon cycle* is a closed system in which the carbon in CO2 is removed from the air by plants through photosynthesis to make up plant material, some of which is eaten by animals. Then, these plants and animals decompose releasing CO2 back into the atmosphere. *Viola!* A natural closed cycle. Therefore, biofuels are good because burning them is just part of that cycle of carbon, while burning fossil fuels is bad because that adds more carbon to the system (that had long ago been taken out of the system and isolated for millions of years), thus disrupting the natural order while increasing CO2 in the atmosphere. There are serious flaws in this argument.

First, the greenhouse effect of emitting CO2 is the same, whether that CO2 comes from burning fossil fuels or burning biofuels. Neither the atmosphere nor the plants extracting CO2 from the air can tell the difference. Further, to get the same amount of energy, burning biofuels emit more CO2, as well as other air pollutants, than burning coal, the worst of fossil fuels because biofuels have substantially lower energy content. Second, much of that carbon taken up by plants in those biofuels would have been tied up there for decades, if not centuries, as wood. Burning that wood shortens one side of the carbon cycle while increasing the amount of carbon in the atmosphere, thus disrupting both sides of the cycle.

Third, the carbon cycle is not really a closed system, so the whole idea collapses. Carbon is constantly being removed from the atmosphere by ocean absorption and from the ocean through coral formation, shells, and sediments that might one day become limestone. Carbon is a major component of limestone, dolomite, marble, chalk, and other minerals that are major components of the earth's crust. Volcanoes emit CO2. In summary, the line between organic and inorganic carbon in the earth's crust is not absolute. And finally, the earth's forests are critical to healthy natural environments as they remove CO2 from the atmosphere through photosynthesis and provide diverse habitats for much of the life on Earth. While forest management can reduce the severity of forest fires (emitting massive amounts of CO2), it is far better to use cleared material to keep that carbon locked up than to burn it as fuel.

In short, the idea behind biofuels as an answer to climate change is also wrongheaded and based on willful ignorance. Adding CO2 to the atmosphere has the same effect, whether it comes from biofuels or fossil fuels. The world's forests are already under enough pressure without promoting wood over fossil fuels. In the USA, promoting biofuels is just a sop for Midwest corn farmers to increase the demand for corn.

Solar panels and wind turbines drive up the cost of materials also used in other industries, further contributing to making everything more expensive. They use three times more copper and seven times more rare earth elements per unit of energy generated than fossil fuels. Wind, solar, and batteries require 10 times more steel, concrete, and glass, 19 times more nickel, 25 times more graphite, and 42 times more lithium than fossil fuels to produce the same amount of energy. And worldwide, that means comparable increases in mining, with all the disturbance and loss of agricultural and natural lands that would be involved.

Then there are the environmental hazards and land use problems associated with the wind turbines and solar panels themselves. Wind turbines (their tips are moving at well over 100 miles per hour) are constantly killing bats (which eat flying insects) and birds. Of particular concern are raptors, with many, like eagles, being federally protected species. In just the last few months, there has also been concern that the sharp increase in dead whales washing up along New Jersey shores are related to developing offshore wind turbines there. Environmental groups focused on the preservation of marine life are now battling with those groups focused on climate change.

Both wind turbines and utility scale solar panels take up massive amounts of land for the energy produced. The area taken up by oil and gas development on remote federal lands, which environmental groups have complained about for years, is miniscule compared to wind turbines and solar panels for the same amount of energy produced. In Alaska, I have flown over both the Prudhoe Bay oil fields and the north slope portion of the Artic National Wildlife Refuge (ANWR) in a small high-wing plane at an elevation of a few hundred feet. I have seen the caribou and caribou trails wandering among the oil wells of Prudhoe Bay. With new horizontal drilling techniques, the surface space required for development in the Refuge would be far less intrusive than at Prudhoe Bay, where the caribou are doing fine. In Short, there is no valid environmental reason supporting the USA's halting oil development in ANWR.

Then there is a **sixth truth** about energy. Those areas and countries in the world that do not yet have access to reliable abundant, cheap energy want it. They also resent any efforts by developed nations that might restrict their access to it. Energy use in the world is only going to go up.

The undeveloped portions of the world today are in a comparable position to what was happening in England 500 years ago as burgeoning populations (the world's highest birthrates are in the poorest countries) are placing enormous strains on forests and wildlife. Worldwide, humans are burning more wood than ever before in history.

Meanwhile, world populations of wild mammals, birds, fish, reptiles, and amphibious animals declined by about half in the 40 years between 1970 and 2010. The decline was over 80% in Latin America and two-thirds in Southeast Asia. In the Congo, wood still provides 90% of domestic energy. Its use places enormous strains on forests, endangered gorillas, and other wildlife there. The primary home fuel for much of rural India has been dried cow dung for decades. Many areas that were still jungle roamed by tigers in 1947 have long since been reduced to scrubland by the burgeoning population having stripped the forests. Europe and the USA saved their forests by switching to coal, followed by other fossil fuels and some nuclear power. Worldwide, wood still provided 50% of energy needs in 1850. That is now down to 7% even though more wood than ever is now being burned because energy consumption has soared.

For any undeveloped society or third world country to begin to modernize and improve daily life while relieving pressure on natural ecosystems, they need to stop burning wood or other biomass. But they desperately need cheap, reliable energy, which means fossil fuels or nuclear energy, with a hydroelectric dam thrown in here or there. Only as that energy starts to flow can they do the two things most needed to join the modern world. First, modernize farming. Worldwide "*the key is producing more food on less land. While the amount of land used for agriculture has increased by 8% since 1961, the amount of food produced has grown by an astounding 300%.*" Land dedicated to agriculture peaked worldwide in the 1990s and has declined slightly since while productivity continues to increase. In the USA, replacing horses and mules with tractors and harvesters in the twentieth century eliminated the need to produce animal feed and reduced the amount of land needed for agriculture by 25%. *"Today, hundreds of millions of horses, cattle, oxen, and other animals are still being used as draft animals for farming in Asia, Africa, and Latin America. Not having to grow food to feed them could free up significant amounts of land for endangered species, just as it did in Europe and North America."*

Second, start making things. *"For more than 250 years, the combination of manufacturing and the rising productivity of farming have been the engine of economic growth for nations around the world. Factory workers spend their money buying food, clothing, and other consumer products and services, resulting in a workforce and society that is wealthier and engaged in a greater variety of jobs. The declining number of workers required for food and energy production, thanks to the use of modern energy and machinery, increases productivity, grows the economy, and diversifies the workforce. Almost every country in the world, from Britain and the United States to Japan to South Korea and China, has transformed its economy with factories."* Factories are labor-intensive and can absorb a large number of unskilled farmers. As Harvard economist Dani Rodrik put it:

> *You could start with very poor initial conditions, get a few things right to stimulate the domestic production of a narrow range of labor-intensive manufactures – and viola! You have a growth engine going. It is fairly easy to turn a rice farmer into a garment factory worker.*

Because labor is cheaper in developing countries, we like to call them *sweatshops*. But, thanks to international monitoring, most are far better than Manchester was 200 years ago when rural British peasants were pouring into those first steam-driven mills. Young adults across the developing world are grateful to escape the farm and obtain a factory job that enables them to buy a TV and maybe even a motor scooter. In short, if you want to help the poor in developing countries (which drives our immigration problems), buy products made in those countries.

Now, a **seventh truth** about energy. Most of the noise and clamor pushing for huge reductions in CO2 emissions remains focused on the USA and Europe. Yet, greenhouse gas emissions in the USA in 2020 were already 22% below what they were in 2005. However much the USA does to further reduce use of fossil fuels, it will have negligible effect on worldwide CO2 emissions or future atmospheric CO2 concentrations. The USA's climate envoy, John Kerry, was assuring the UN at Glasgow in 2022 that by 2030 the USA will have stopped using coal. However, in 2020, 350 new coal-fired electric generating plants were under construction worldwide: 184 in China, 52 in India, 13 in Japan, and seven in South Korea. None were in the USA, Canada, or Western Europe. The USA hasn't opened a new large coal-fired electric generating station in this century. The country that consumes the most coal per capita is Australia. Five of the next six are in Eastern Europe. India gets 75% of its electricity from coal, and that percentage is only going to go up as the total demand for electricity increases by 5% each year. Pakistan has recently announced plans to quadruple its use of coal to generate electricity and not build more gas-fired plants. Worldwide coal use is at an all-time high and will continue to climb. Asian countries are expected to be using half of the world's electricity by 2025. Currently, more than half of the world's urban greenhouse gas emissions already come from 25 large cities. Twenty-three of them are in China. None are in the USA. While China has 19% of the world's population, it already emits 28% of worldwide greenhouse gases. Yet, climate change activists' focus remains on the USA and Europe. Whatever the USA does, it will have far more impact on our economy than on climate change. *Issues & Insights,* an online news service, in a recent editorial gave one explanation for why the focus is still on the West and not China with all its new coal plants: *"The climate scare is more about pulling down capitalism, weakening the U.S. and other developed nations, cranking out international transfers of wealth, and advancing socialism than it is about saving the world. It's no coincidence that the countries that are constantly mugged by the alarmists are those whose economic systems are the furthest removed from socialism on the political spectrum. There's no reason for them to denounce China because it's already laboring under the system they want to inflict on the world."*

The view that *Green is the new Red* has been around for decades. That is, those who were pushing socialism decades ago are now pushing climate change because they see it as an effective surreptitious way to achieve their desired social reforms. True? I don't discount it.

And now to the **final truth** about energy. Until some new technology is discovered (nuclear fusion?), the only way to maintain modern life in the developed world to expand it to those hundreds of millions who do not yet have the benefits of clean water, electricity, and adequate shelter and to save more of the natural world and open spaces, including endangered species; while reducing atmospheric CO_2 and any associated climate change, is nuclear power. If the world would shift to investing as much in nuclear power as it is now spending on wind turbines, solar panels, biomass, and fossil fuel plants, the future of our modern way of life would be far more secure as would the preservation of more of the natural world.

Many are now pushing hydrogen as the answer. However, it takes more energy (electricity) to generate the hydrogen gas to be burned than will then be created by burning it (a loose, loose situation). Apparently, the goal is to overcome that problem with solar panels. But they have their own problems. This seems like an inefficient way to get electricity from solar at night. Unless the laws of physics are changed (and Congress can't do that), hydrogen is not viable.

However, don't discount human ingenuity. There will be new ways of doing things developed over the remainder of the century we have not yet even conceived of, just as occurred in the last century. I doubt we will be relying on windmills, solar panels, or hydrogen. But who knows?

ACCUMULATED KNOWLEDGE – Continually adding to and disseminating Accumulated Knowledge is the basis of human progress. Being open to new ideas and challenging the status quo define science. As stated by Robert Oppenheimer, the father of the atomic bomb:

> *There is no place for dogma in science. The scientist is free, and must be free to ask any question, to doubt any assertion, to seek for any evidence, to correct any errors.*

Why? Because science is the search for truth. And truth is what it is, no matter how many people may believe otherwise, or how few may accept it. However, new ideas need to be tested since any idea, old or new, needs to be verifiable and able to withstand critical challenges to be of value. So, debate must be allowed. That even applies to debates about climate change, medicine, history, race, gender, and culture. Allowing skepticism is key to individual freedom of thought, which is essential to progress. Implicit in freedom of speech is freedom of thought.

We now live in a worldwide information age. The amount of recorded human knowledge that now exists is unbelievably vast, readily available, and continues to expand rapidly. There is now an endless number of scholastic disciplines, each with its own body of detailed information and discipline-specific journals where credentialed experts debate the frontiers of the discipline.

It is impossible for any of us to know everything that is known. What each of us doesn't know would fill volumes. Donald Rumsfeld often talked about the things we don't know as falling into two categories: 1) what we know we don't know, and 2) what we don't know we don't know. The second kind of ignorance is far more dangerous. There are now many, including students and professors at elite universities, that are so unaware of how much they don't know they don't know that they actually think they are well informed. And are quite self-righteous about it – to the point of belligerence – with minds closed to opposing ideas. That is dangerous. And antithetical to the very concept of what a university is supposed to be. Skepticism and critique are essential to scientific progress. Yet, there is a growing tendency in universities to now suppress ideas and research that challenge current politically correct narratives. Thomas Sowell:

In a democracy we have always had to worry about the ignorance of the uneducated. Today we have to worry about the ignorance of people with degrees.

Some of the biggest cases of mistaken identity are among intellectuals who have trouble remembering that they are not God.

Sowell was born in North Carolina in 1930 to poor black parents, but was raised in Harlem after age eight. While a teenager, he dropped out of high school and became a Marxist. He remained a Marxist through a stint in the Marine Corp, attending Howard University, earning a BA from Harvard, and an MA from Columbia. While earning a PhD from the University of Chicago, he abandoned Marxism after working as an intern in the Federal government where he realized that the career bureaucrats he was working with were primarily interested in their own careers and continued expansion of the programs they were working on. They had no interest in evaluating whether those programs did any good or were even run in a cost-effective way. He later wrote:

In retrospect, even my misfortunes were in some ways fortunate, for they taught me things that would be hard to understand otherwise, and they presented reality from an angle not given to those, among intellectuals especially, whose careers have followed a more strait-line path in familiar grooves. I have lived through experiences which they can only theorize about. I had daily contact with people who were neither well-educated nor particularly genteel, but who had practical wisdom far beyond what I had. It gave me a lasting respect for the common sense of ordinary people, a factor routinely ignored by the intellectuals among whom I would later make my career. This was a blind spot in much of their social analysis which I did not have to contend with.

And speaking of skepticism, we all need to remember that it is human nature for self-interest to prevail over public interest. A few have overcome that tendency, but most of us have not. So, follow the money. If you are a scientist at an academic institution today and want to study climate science, grant money is all on one side of the issue. And so are the panels that will review your work for publication after completing any research.

Patrick T. Brown acknowledged in September 2023 that he left out any discussion of the role of forest management practices on forest fires in an article published in *Nature* magazine. He:

knew that it would detract from the clean narrative centered on the negative impact of climate change and thus decrease the odds that the paper would pass muster with Nature's editors and reviewers.

The editors of these journals have made it abundantly clear, both by what they publish and what they reject, that they want climate papers that support certain preapproved narratives – even when those narratives come at the expense of broader knowledge for society.

While that misinforms the public and makes practical solutions more difficult to achieve, identifying and focusing on problems rather than studying the effectiveness of solutions makes for more compelling abstracts that can be turned into headlines, but it is a major reason why high-profile research is not as useful to society as it could be.

And this shading of scientific and technical publications is also true if you are a social scientist, economist, or biologist. If you do research that seems benign but produces results that contradict current politically correct notions of truth, be prepared for a tsunami of pushback. Harvard has recently undercut one of its own, a tenured black economics professor, Roland Fryer. In doing so, while the punishment was updated to twenty-first century standards, Harvard assumed the same role the Inquisition played against Galileo 400 years ago. Then, in the summer of 2023, the dean, Claudine Gay, who chaired that inquisition against Fryer became Harvard's new president.

Fryer, as a teenager, was selling contraband from his bedroom with a pistol in his lap. Then he went to college on an athletic scholarship, where he fell in love with economics. And his star quickly rose. As a tenured Harvard professor, he was just trying to help other poor black kids who are headed nowhere. Some peers have called him the greatest economist of his generation, but he was put in Harvard's doghouse devoid of funding or staff (his lab with a staff of 100 was closed, and he was suspended from teaching for two years) after he uncovered and published information about education and policing in the USA that cut against accepted narratives. Some colleagues urged him not to publish. He then asked if the results had come out the other way, should he publish them? Yes. With that, he knew he had to publish what he had found. So, based on a dubious sexual harassment claim (a few off-color jokes?) that even the reviewing office that handles such complaints said warranted only a few hours of training, Harvard shut him down.

Now, with anyone being able to put anything on the internet and many, particularly younger people, getting most of their news from social media, there is a great deal of public concern about *disinformation*. This concern has been heightened by controversies from climate change to race, gender, elections, COVID, wars, and even Hunter Biden's laptop. These controversies have all made clear that today, to paraphrase Thomas Sowell: ***the basic question is not what is true and what is disinformation, but who gets to decide what is true and what is disinformation***?

And that should never be government, academic administrators, social media companies, editors, or students. Truth is found in the open market of ideas. For much of this century, college student protests have been shutting down speakers with disfavored political views. Many prominent leaders and thinkers have been canceled. Even Ayaan Hirsi Ali was canceled at a few universities for speaking out against the abuse of women and girls within Islamic communities in the West because her views are considered anti-Islam. Such cancelling has now spread to social media and has recently been labeled *Woke*. The Woke hate haters. The problem is that, in doing so, the Woke have become a hate group themselves. Some have compared this new Woke trend to religion. Being Woke *"is powerful because it has emerged as the alternative religion for supposedly secular people, providing many of the same psychological benefits as traditional faith. It offers a purpose and casts them as heroes. And it provides a way for them to find meaning in their lives – while retaining the illusion that they are people of science and reason, not superstition and fantasy."* So, they defend their faith with righteous fervor against the unbelievers. Thus, the Woke are modern-day xenophobic Puritans who demand safe spaces from any idea, thought, fact, or people that might upset their tender psyches. Its active arm is *Cancel Culture,* the modern-day Inquisition against all heretical ideas and people. After all, tolerance of evil is intolerable. A March 2023 survey found that, in the USA, those who consider *tolerance for others* as a very important value has dropped from 80% to 58% in just the last four years. It is much lower among those under

30. The Holy Trinity for the Woke are climate change, race, and gender, with anti-capitalism at the core of all three.

The *1619 Project* essays trash capitalism, as does Ibram X. Kendi, a Boston University professor and prime advocate of Critical Race Theory (CRT) and Diversity, Equity, and Inclusion (DEI):

In order to be truly antiracist, you also have to be truly anti-capitalist.

Is capitalism racist? Or is the charge of racism, along with climate change, being used as a strawman to fight capitalism? In any case, social media platforms are using algorithms, as well as direct human intervention, to promote favored ideas, information, and people, while minimizing or blocking disfavored ideas, information and people. And this stifling of debate by censoring views or information by social media companies, news outlets, politicians, universities, or even government officials, if it conflicts with politically correct narratives, is a dark cloud that hangs over truth and the continuing expansion of objective Accumulated Knowledge in today's society. So, let's look at four areas where society's ability to maintain and expand objective Accumulated Knowledge (truth) and utilize it effectively are being hampered because pushing favored narratives is now taking precedence over facts and the search for truth.

CLIMATE CHANGE is currently a dominant force in public policy debates in the USA and the world. Here, again, we constantly hear that *The Science* is settled. Yet, *"Climate science is a lively field. Thousands of researchers supported by billions of dollars work to observe the climate, understand it, and project its future. They report their results in scientific journal articles, publishing more than ten thousand each year."* If The Science is already settled, why are we doing that? Three reasons. Because there really is still a lot of uncertainty in climate projections. Because the answer is important to the future of humanity and the earth as we know it. And last but not least, because there is a lot of money to be made doing these studies.

While the results of these studies are found in dense scientific literature, projections are also released to the public. As one researcher, the late Stephen Schneider, put it clear back in 1989:

We are not just scientists but human beings as well. And like most people we'd like to see the world a better place, which in this context translates into our working to reduce the risk of potentially disastrous climactic change. To do that we need to get some broad based support, to capture the public's imagination. That, of course, entails getting loads of media coverage. So we have to offer up scary scenarios, make simplified, dramatic statements, and make little mention of any doubts we might have.

Thus, we get outlandish predictions like this one (only one of many) from Mostafa Tolba in 1982, when he was executive director of the United Nations Environment Program:

Inaction will cause, by the turn of the century [2000], an ecological catastrophe which will witness devastation as complete, as irreversible as any nuclear holocaust.

Yet, despite inaction, no such devastation happened before the end of the century. And that was 24 years ago. Then there are the activists. Paul Watson, the cofounder of Greenpeace, said:

It doesn't matter what is true, it only matters what people believe is true.

And then Timothy Wirth, former U.S. Senator and President of the UN Foundation:

We've got to ride this global warming issue. Even if the theory of global warming is wrong, we will be doing the right thing in terms of economic and environmental policy.

Note his economic policy reference: green is the new red. Over the last three decades, climate change research has been summarized in periodic government assessment reports prepared by official international and USA groups. From these reports summaries are prepared by people far distant from the original scientific literature and provided to the media, who then pull out what will be sensational and thus attract attention from their readers and viewers. In the USA, the federal government prepares a National Climate Assessment every four years. After the 1918 report, the American Association for the Advancement of Science put out a report titled *"How We Respond"* that begins with the following high-level summary of *The Science* as laid out in that 2018 National Climate Assessment:

Our nation, our states, our cities and our towns face an urgent problem: climate change. Americans are already feeling its effects and will continue to do so in the coming decades. Rising temperatures will impact farmers in their fields and transit riders in cities. Across the country, extreme weather events such as hurricanes, floods, wild-fires and drought are occurring with greater frequency and intensity. While these problems pose numerous risks to society and the planet, undoubtedly the biggest risk is to do nothing. Science tells us that the sooner we respond to climate change, the lower the risks and the costs will be in the future.

Now for a few facts. Worldwide, in the decade beginning in 1920, 5.4 million people died from natural disasters. In the decade beginning in 2010, only 0.4 million people died from natural disasters, even though the world population had quadrupled. As a share of the population, that is 98% drop in mortality due to natural disasters over the past century. In the five-year period ending in 2020 fewer people died in natural disasters than in any other five-year period since 1900. In short, humans are far better at coping with natural disasters than they were a century ago. A hurricane that just killed thousands in Haiti can strike Florida with the same force without killing a single person. Why? Because rich nations are more resilient. That is also true for earthquakes and other natural disasters.

Which means we need to help poor nations become richer. Future food production, particularly in poor nations like those in Central Africa, will depend far more on access to technology, irrigation, and infrastructure than climate change. Denying them access to electricity, fossil fuels, dams, and fertilizer is what will doom them to war, drought, death from natural disasters, and continued poverty, not climate change. Rich nations are far better equipped to deal with a changing climate than poor nations.

Steven E. Koonin is a physicist with impeccable credentials going back decades. He is a life-long democrat who, during the Obama administration, was Deputy Secretary for Science in the Department of Energy. He has conducted climate science research and studied reports, including that 2018 National Climate Assessment Report as well as international reports. He has been a member of the American Association for the Advancement of Science for almost 50 years, and a Fellow within it for many years. He states the above opening statement from the Association's report was never sent to its members or Fellows for comment or concurrence. In other words, that Association statement, supposedly issued on behalf of its member scientists, had no input from those scientists. Koonin has written that, if he had been asked, he would have summarized that assessment report and the other literature on climate change quite differently:

The earth has warmed during the past century, partly because of natural phenomena and partly in response to growing human influences. These human influences (most importantly the accumulation of CO_2 from burning fossil fuels) exert a physically small effect on the complex climate system. Unfortunately, our limited observations and understanding are insufficient to usefully quantify either how the climate will respond to human influences or how it varies naturally. However, even as human influences have increased almost fivefold since 1950 and the globe has warmed modestly, most severe weather phenomena remain within past variability. Projections of future climate and weather events rely on models demonstrably unfit for the purpose.

I have no doubt that CO2 is a greenhouse gas that can trap heat, that the level of CO2 in the atmosphere is increasing, that the primary cause of that increase is the burning of fossil fuels, and that reducing the amount of CO2 being added to the atmosphere is a good idea. But I have no confidence in the computer-generated projections of what the future climate will be like. In short, I am fully on board with Koonin's above summary, and I love his last sentence.

I have long felt that the climate computer model projections touted by the press are worse than useless because none of them can match up with or account for known variations in the historical data. There are simply too many unknown variables and questionable data in those models. As part of earning a PhD in Biology in 1971, I had to develop a multiple regression computer model to predict what would happen under conditions not studied and then test that model. Any computer model that cannot account for past variations is of no value in trying to predict future results. In short: garbage in – garbage out.

Nor do I have confidence in the solutions to potential climate change now being pushed in the USA and around the world. Instead, I am convinced that the solutions being pushed are far more dangerous to both human society *and* the natural environment than climate change itself.

So, I will close out this part with quotes from Michael Shellenberger (emphasis in originals):

Some people will, when they read this, imagine that I'm some anti-environmentalist. I'm not. I became an environmentalist at 16 when I threw a fundraiser for Rainforest Action Network. At 17 I lived in Nicaragua to show solidarity with the Sandinista socialist revolution. At 23, I raised money for Guatemalan women's cooperatives. In my early 20s I lived in the semi-Amazon doing research with small farmers fighting land invasions. At 26 I helped expose poor conditions at Niki factories in Asia. At 27 I helped save the last unprotected ancient redwoods in California. In my 30s I advocated for renewables and successfully helped persuade the Obama administration to invest $90 billion into them. Some facts:

- *Climate change is **not** making natural disasters worse*

- *Fires have **declined** 25% around the world since 2003*
- *The amount of land we use for meat – humankind's biggest use of land – has **declined by an area nearly as large as Alaska***
- *The build-up of wood fuel and more houses near forests, **not** climate change, explain why there are more, and more dangerous, fires in Australia and California*
- *Netherlands became rich not poor while adapting to life below sea level*
- *We produce 25% more food than we need, and food surpluses will continue to rise as the world gets hotter*
- *Habitat loss and the direct killing of wild animals are bigger threats to species than climate change*
- *Wood fuel is far worse for people and wildlife than fossil fuels*
- *Preventing future pandemics requires more, not less "industrial" agriculture*
- *Factories and modern farming are the keys to human liberation and environmental progress*
- *100% renewable energy would require increasing the land used for energy from today's 0.5% to 50%*
- *Greenpeace did not save the whales, switching from whale oil to petroleum and palm oil did*
- *"Free-range" beef would require 20 times more land and produce 300% more emissions*
- *Greenpeace dogmatism worsened forest fragmentation in the Amazon*

The alarmism is working: few people have a realistic understanding of climate change. Few consider whether, at its current rates, it might be less dangerous than efforts to mitigate it.

GENDER is a hot topic now in the USA, Europe, and some other parts of the world under the banner LGBTQ+. Of all that could be said here on either side of this hot issue, I will just note that when, at the end of a muddled exchange on gender issues, Supreme Court nominee Ketanji

Brown Jackson was finally asked at her Senate confirmation hearing to define *woman*. She said she could not because she is not a biologist.

For someone who is now sitting on the Supreme Court of the USA, that is simply a terrible answer. First, the word *woman* is contained in some of the nation's laws that she will be in a position to rule on. Second, if she is going to defer to biologists (*The Science*), the answer is simple. A *woman* is an *adult female human* (those three words in any order). Or an adult human without a *y* chromosome in the cells of her body. There are a few humans with rare genetic anomalies that need to be treated with dignity and respect. Whatever the merits of thinking gender is a choice, or somehow being psychologically hardwired in personality independent of the presence of a *y* chromosome, it falls within the fluid world of the social sciences, not biology.

COVID hit the world like a tsunami in March 2020. From the beginning, Dr. Anthony Fauci wrapped himself in the cloak of *The Science* on all things related to COVID. To disagree with him was to deny science. Despite the fact that, from the beginning, fatality rates were strongly linked to the elderly and/or those with co-morbidities like diabetes and obesity, Fauci, with the full support of news media, social media, and the government, pushed broad lockdowns, social distancing (six feet apart), school closings, universal masking (after first saying masks didn't help), and then the pushing of universal vaccinations without any consideration of natural immunity from being previously infected. The Fauci mob did their best to shut down and cancel out any dissenting voices. Fauci also immediately shut down any discussion of the virus originating from a nearby virology laboratory in China (where he had helped provide funding for bat virus research) and claimed that the virus was unquestionably of natural origin. Social media sites then blocked any contrary views for more than a year.

In February 2023, the Department of Energy determined that it is more likely than not that the virus originated in a laboratory. The FBI had already come to that conclusion. The U.S. Intelligence community continues to support the view that it originated in nature. Natural immunity is now recognized. It is also recognized that the vaccines were only somewhat effective. Most masks didn't help that much. The virus is probably not transmitted by surface contact, so all that mandatory wiping down of everything made little difference. Fauci recently acknowledged that no scientific support existed for six-feet apart social distancing. Closing schools has done serious damage to children, both in terms of being behind in learning, and in socializing. And there is finally some recognition that, for healthy children and adults under 50, COVID is often no worse than the flu. Much of this is coming from studies in other countries because the Center for Disease Control in the USA did little in the way of controlled studies or data analysis related to COVID-19. In short, the USA's response to COVID is a case study of how **not** to pursue the expansion of accurate Accumulated Knowledge or how to use it. Instead, it shows the impact of implementing public policy based on half-baked information while stifling debate of legitimate factual disputes. Sweden got it right far more than the USA did.

HISTORY is a critical part of Accumulated Knowledge. How it is taught is what tells any society who they are and how they got to where they are, whether that history is written down or consists of oral stories and legends passed on from generation to generation. Accurate history and analysis can guide us if we let it and own it.

Each July fourth, we celebrate Independence Day. We have been doing that for almost two and a half centuries because most Americans have felt a strong sense of pride in, and gratitude for, our country and its history as we learned it at home and school. But that seems to be changing.

In 1997, Ayaan Hirsi Ali, a refugee from Somalia, was granted Dutch citizenship after living in Holland for five years. Her university friends held a party for her.

I told them "I'm Dutch!" Nobody snickered exactly, but they looked at me strangely. It wasn't that I was black and claiming Dutchness: that was fine. It was because being Dutch meant absolutely nothing to these people. If anything, my Dutch friends seemed uncomfortable with the symbols of Dutchness: The flag and the monarchy...They saw nationalism as almost the same thing as racism. Nobody was proud of being Dutch.

That same attitude now exists for many within the USA. Growing concerns over issues like race, culture, religion, gender, abortion, history, immigration, energy, climate change, law enforcement, and economic policies are now challenging the perspective that the USA, including its founding and development, has been, and is, a positive force in the World. A 2018 Gallup survey found that, for the first time, less than half (47%) of Americans were *"extremely proud"* of their country. For those adults under 30, it was only 33%. In a series of Wall Street Journal surveys, 70% said that patriotism was very important to them in 1998, 61% in 2019, and, in March 2023, only 39% said patriotism was very important. For those under 30, only 23% said so.

How we each feel about the USA seems to depend in large part on how we each view our nation's founding and development – our history. Even when looking at the same historical facts, there are now opposing views of what those facts tell us. These strongly held views are now becoming so disparate that they are creating tribalism, based on political or social views, that is tearing at the social fabric and civility of the nation. We each view these things through our own biases, knowingly or unknowingly, like filters on a camera lens that accentuate what matches our biases and minimize or filters out what doesn't fit with them. Unfortunately, for most of us, whatever we see, we think is the clear-eyed *correct* view, and those who see things differently are, at best, wrong, and, at worst, evil. Almost all of us consider our own view as *superior*, and we prefer to associate with other like-minded people who also see things *correctly.*

One reason for these divergent views of history is the growing trend, even among historians, to view history *"through the prism of contemporary social justice issues – race, gender, sexuality, nationalism, capitalism."* James H. Sweet, the president of the American Historical Association, wrote an editorial in the Association's monthly magazine in August 2022 in which he expressed his concern about this growing inclination to use *Presentism* (looking at the past through the values of the present) as we look at history. That editorial included the following statement after citing two recent examples that he felt ignored accurate history: the *1619 Project,* and Justice Alito's 2022 opinion overturning *Roe vs Wade* on abortion.

> *Doing history with integrity requires us to interpret elements of the past not through the optics of the present but within the worlds of our historical actors. Historical questions often emanate out of present concerns, but the past interrupts, challenges, and contradicts the present in unpredictable ways. History is... a way to study the messy, uneven process of change over time. When we foreshorten or shape history to justify rather than inform contemporary political positions, we not only undermine the discipline but threaten its very integrity.* (Underline in the original)

However, even within the professional historian community, he was vociferously attacked for writing that. And, in the next issue – he apologized! Yet, documentary filmmaker, Ken Burns, was expressing the same thought when he said:

You can't understand the past until you walk a mile in its shoes.

It is certainly true that using presentism to judge those who lived in the past makes it very easy for us living now to feel superior to them. The problem with presentism is that it presupposes that had we been living in their time, facing what they faced, with the value systems that had been inculcated in them, we would have behaved any differently. And that is absolutely unknowable. To suppose we would have behaved any better in their shoes only reflects our ignorant arrogance. Shame on us. What we can do is try to learn from the consequences, good and bad, of what they did and then try to do better: to improve things. Donna Brazile wrote:

Give educators and students the gift of facts.

Can we at least agree on some basic facts? Apparently not. As previously noted, an open challenge to the longstanding view of our

Nation's founding was elevated in a major way in August 2019 when the New York Times Magazine published ten essays under the banner *"The 1619 Project"*, so named because that is the year black Africans were first brought into what would become the USA. The banner headline on the first essay, written by Nicole Hannah-Jones, is *"Our democracy's founding ideals were false when they were written."* The headline on the second essay is *"If you want to understand the brutality of American Capitalism, you have to start with the plantation."* The third headline: *"Myths about physical racial differences were used to justify slavery – and are still believed by doctors today."* The remaining seven essays went on from there. The 1619 Project is a strong indictment of the USA, particularly on the issues of race and capitalism. It received a Pulitzer Prize in the spring of 2020 and is being adopted by many public school districts as curriculum material for teaching American history despite strong pushback by several historians on the accuracy of some of its claims.

Then, amid the months of protests, riots, and destruction across the USA that followed the May 25, 2020, death of George Floyd under the knee of a white police officer in Minneapolis as an irate crowd looked on, many statues and monuments were defaced and/or torn down as a challenge to their portrayal of history. While some of this Nation's history may have been taught with a slant that warrants correcting, ignoring the context in which that history was lived is extremely dangerous. Only with a clear-eyed understanding of the past and how we got here can we fairly determine which historical figures and actions are worth celebrating with statues and holidays. And it is probably worthwhile to occasionally update those assessments as the USA seems to be doing now. However, we need to approach these issues through peaceful public debate as would be appropriate for a democracy like the USA. Civility is to disagree without being disagreeable. It is now in short supply.

Instead, along with some wingnuts on the right, Woke Cancel Culture mobs, like religious zealots, are tearing through the streets, ripping down statues and monuments or whipping through social media cancelling out ideas, books, or people they disagree with. That is totalitarian and reminiscent of Mao's cultural revolution, the Taliban, and the Khmer Rouge. In February 2023, even Bill Mahar spent a whole monologue

384 - Human Progress

comparing the USA's current Cancel Culture to Mao's cultural revolution in China 50 years ago.

We now have rewrites of history that Orwell's Ministry of Truth (in *1984*) would be proud of. The *Southern Policy Law Center* (SPLC) has developed *Teaching Hard History* frameworks for K-12 schools that line up with the 1619 Project and are being widely distributed. In the preface to the framework for grades 6-12, Dr. Hasan Kwame Jeffries, a professor of history at Ohio State University, states:

> *Some say slavery was our country's original sin, but it is much more than that. Slavery is our country's origin.*

As I have looked at the history of the USA, I must vociferously disagree with that statement. The record is clear. Slavery was not even thought of as Jamestown and Plymouth were being founded. Twelve years after its founding, an English ship showed up at Jamestown with about 20 Africans to sell that had been pirated from a Portuguese slave ship bound for Mexico. Even then, those first black arrivals were sold as indentured servants (as were poor English citizens who had not been able to pay for their transport) because the colony's charter had no provisions for slavery. The only two colonies where it could be argued that slavery was a part of their origin are North and South Carolina. Decades later. Georgia's founding included an explicit ban on slavery. And it was the British King who later removed that prohibition. Although slavery was still virtually everywhere in the world in 1776, including the 13 colonies and central Africa, just 12 years later, when the Constitution was ratified in 1788, slavery had already been banned in some states and the Northwest Territory (among the first places in the world to do so).

Both slavery and emancipation from slavery are unquestionably part of this country's origin and history. Any accurate historical discussion of one must include a discussion of the other. Yet, that statement is what a college professor at an excellent university has put out to teach twelve-year-olds. And then there is the view of Ta-Nehisi Coates, who tells black Americans:

Don't drink the Kool-Aid. Don't believe the hype. F*** the American Dream. You must be kidding me, the <u>American Dream?!</u>

That is what he wants to teach black children about the country where they are birthright citizens. That they will forever have their noses pressed against the candy story window but never be allowed to taste the candy. That they are forever marginalized because they are black.

So this view of the nation as Oppressors vs. the Oppressed, with all whites as oppressors and the rest of humanity as oppressed, as articulated by Hannah-Jones, the *1619 Project,* Dr, Jeffries, and the SPLC (and supported by many activists, educators, media outlets, law makers and public figures), sees the USA as a deeply flawed nation where racism is systemic, where laws and law enforcement are means of oppression rather than safeguarding freedoms, where the courts are not fair and blind, but prejudiced, and where white supremacy and white privilege are baked into the nation's systems and values. Therefore, extensive changes are needed to totally transform American society, including current laws, policies, and practices related to education, law enforcement, health care, immigration, family structure, industrial development, and financial and economic structure. In short, this view of the USA and its history accepts Hannah-Jones conclusion that our *"founding ideals were false when they were written"* and that our free enterprise economic structure is unfair and racist. And that view is now part of the curriculum in many K-12 schools.

Many others think this view is not only grossly distorted, but terribly destructive. One Louden County, VA, mother became outraged in 2021 when her six-year-old came home from school and asked, *"Am I evil because I'm white?* Parents naturally want their children to be taught the truth as they understand it, which, along with COVID restrictions and gender issues, has suddenly elevated local schoolboard elections into the national spotlight. Lines have been drawn. What is the *correct* view of history? How should it be taught?

The opposite lens for looking at the USA and its history was best expressed by Dr. Martin Luther King Jr. when he said the following:

We refuse to believe that there are insufficient funds in the great vaults of opportunity in this Nation. When the architects of our republic wrote the magnificent words of the Constitution and the Declaration of Independence, they were signing a promissory note to which every American was to fall heir. This note was a promise that all men – black men as well as white men – would be guaranteed the unalienable rights of life, liberty and the pursuit of happiness.

He also wrote from the Birmingham jail in 1962 (when Jim Crow was still in full effect):

One day the South will know that when these disinherited children of God sat down at lunch counters, they were in reality standing up for what is best in the American dream and for the most sacred of values in our Judeo-Christian heritage, thereby bringing our nation back to those great wells of democracy which were dug deep by the founding fathers in the formulation of the Constitution and Declaration of Independence...We will reach the goal of freedom in Birmingham and all over the nation because the goal of America is freedom... and our destiny is tied up with America's destiny.

In that view, the USA was a new and glorious concept brought forth in a world full of vicious bigotry and inequities, including slavery and apartheid. It goes along with the USA's motto: *E Pluribus Unum* – out of many, one. And, in that view, while great progress has been made, the nation is still in the process (with much still to do) of trying to fulfill that bright promise for all its citizens and create a more perfect union. It is also the view of Thomas Sowell, who wrote:

Ours may become the first civilization destroyed, not by the power of enemies, but by the ignorance of our teachers and the dangerous nonsense they are teaching our children. In an age of artificial intelligence, they are creating artificial stupidity.

Or, as another writer put it: *"The battle for the soul of our country will be won or lost in our classrooms."* A recent study by the Woodrow Wilson Foundation found that only 19% of Americans under age 45 could pass the citizenship exam (a civics test on U.S history and government given to immigrants seeking citizenship), compared to 74% of those over age 65. Further, in 2018, only 15% of all eighth-grade students scored as "proficient" on the National Assessment of Educational Progress assessment related to history. James Madison wrote in Federalist 10 that the three evils to which democracies are prone are ignorance, instability, and injustice. He felt the checks and balances in the Constitution developed in 1887 would solve the last two. And felt education would solve the first. Our schools are currently failing at that.

For Shelby Steele, a black former English professor now at Stanford's Hoover Institute, the problem is not failing to acknowledge discrimination, but giving it too much priority.

Both racism and a lack of development are problems for blacks. We don't have one problem; we have two. Groups don't learn to read well or open businesses; individuals do. Individuals don't get civil rights legislation passed; groups do.

Why do we cling to an adversarial, victim-focused identity that preoccupies us with white racism? I think this identity is a weight on blacks because it is built around our collective insecurity rather than our faith in our human capacity to seize opportunity as individuals. It amounts to a self-protective collectivism that obsesses us with black unity instead of individual initiative. To be "black" in this identity, one needs only manifest the symbols, postures, and rhetoric of black unity. Not only is personal initiative unnecessary for being "black", but the successful exercise of initiative – working one's way into the middle class, becoming well-off, gaining an important position – may in fact jeopardize one's "blackness", make one somehow less black. The poor black is the true black; the successful black is more marginally black unless he (or she) frequently announces his solidarity with the race in the way politicians declare their patriotism. This sort of identity never works, never translates into actual uplift of black people. It confuses racial unity with initiative by relying on unity to do what only individual initiative can do. Uplift can only come when many millions of blacks seize the possibilities inside the sphere of their personal lives and use them to take themselves forward. Collectively, we can resist oppression, but racial development will always be, as Ralph Ellison once put it, "the gift of its individuals."

In February 2020, several black historians, scholars, and public figures founded *1776 Unites*, and later released their own curriculum to counter claims of the *1619 Project*. The group's leader, Robert Woodson, was born in 1937 and is a veteran of the civil rights campaigns of the 1960s. He has dedicated his life to helping black children and said this about *1776 Unites*:

Most school curricula have traditionally been short on inspiring stories of black achievement. The narrative of racial grievance has been corrupting the instruction of American history and the humanities for many decades – and has accelerated dangerously over the past year. The most damaging effects of such instruction fall on lower income minority children, who are implicitly told that they are helpless victims with no power of agency to shape their own futures.
Our materials both address the terrible chapters of our history and show what is best in our national character and what our freedom makes possible even in the most difficult circumstances.
Our curriculum offers lessons that empower children from all backgrounds to see what is possible in their own lives. It includes stories of black Americans who seized their own destinies and flourished despite the harsh restriction imposed by true institutional racism in the form of slavery and Jim Crow.
It maintains a special focus on stories that celebrate black excellence, reject victimhood culture, and showcase African-Americans who have prospered by embracing America's founding ideals. It embraces the ideas of family, faith, and entrepreneurship that have enabled all Americans, including black Americans – throughout history to move from persecution to prosperity.

While 1776 Unites has received far less public attention than the 1619 Project, there are indeed positive stories to be told. By the beginning of World War I, just 50 years after emancipation, black Americans had accumulated $700 million in wealth, owned more than 40,000 businesses, 40,000 churches, and almost a million farms. And the literacy rate had climbed from 5% to 70%. In that era of legalized discrimination and systemic abuse, the marriage rate was as high as in the white community despite deprivation and racism. In 1925 in New York City, 85% of black families had a man and a woman raising children. Woodson has noted that, growing up in a segregated Philadelphia neighborhood in the 1940s and early 50s, he never heard a gunshot, and that parents didn't worry about their children's safety outside, even after dark. Thomas Sowell said the same thing about growing up in Harlem in the 1940s.

Despite generations of seriously flawed Americans on the issues of racism and bigotry, the nation's founding ideals have enabled it to flourish and become a magnet for immigrants of all races, while those founding ideals reverberated around the world. In short, despite the failings of many of its citizens, the USA's founding ideals have totally changed the world to the benefit of all mankind. Author, columnist, and biographer of Thomas Sowell, Jason L. Riley, wrote:

What makes America unique is not slavery. It's emancipation. It's how we went from slavery to Martin Luther King to a black president.

In a separate speech about Thomas Sowell in February 2022, Riley included the following:

Sowell has long argued that the problems blacks face today involve far more than what whites have done to them in the past. It's no mystery why black activists want to keep the focus on white racism. It helps them raise money and stay relevant. And it's no mystery why politicians use the same tactics – it helps them win votes. But Sowell argued that it's not at all clear that focusing on white racism is helping the black underclass. You can spend all day, every day, pointing out the moral failings of other people, groups, institutions, and society in general. The question is whether that helps the people who most need help.

Many of today's activists go about their business with the assumption that the only real problem facing the black underclass is white racism. A good example of this is the recent focus on policing in black communities. Do racist cops exist? Absolutely. Do some cops abuse their authority? Of course. But are poor black communities as violent as they are because of bad cops? Will reducing police resources improve the situation? Young black men in Chicago or Baltimore or St. Louis may indeed leave the house each morning worried about getting shot – but not by police. [he notes that of 492 homicides in Chicago in 2019, only 3 involved police.]

*In a Gallup poll released in 2020, 81% of blacks nationwide said they wanted police presence in their neighborhood to remain the same or increase, while 59% of both black and Hispanic respondents said they wanted police to spend **more** time in their communities. Nor is this a new phenomenon. In a 1993 Gallup poll, 82% of black respondents said the criminal justice system doesn't treat criminals harshly enough, 75% of blacks wanted more cops on the streets, and 68% said we ought to build more prisons so that longer sentences can be given.*

Sowell would often be asked how it felt to go against the grain of so many other blacks. He would inevitably correct the premise of the question. "You don't mean I go against the grain of most blacks," he would respond. "You mean I go against the grain of most black intellectuals, most black elites. But black intellectuals don't represent most blacks any more than white intellectuals represent most whites."

Most blacks, for example, support voter ID laws and school choice, while most black elites – academics, the NAACP, Black Lives Matter activists, etc – oppose those things. Sowell's writings on intellectual history have stressed time and again, that intellectuals are a special interest group. They have their own self-serving agenda and their own priorities and ought to be understood as such.

I often tell people that if you think Ta-Nehisi Coates and Nicole Hannah-Jones represent the views of most black people, you need to get to know more black people.

As another writer put it: *"Imperfect? Well certainly. Like people from every culture across history, Americans have committed horrible sins. Even so, the character of America is always trying to be 'more perfect,' and we must continue to do so today. What separates America in human history is not its sins but its virtues. And why do many of us often think what we have here – wealth, freedom and safety – is normal in the course of human history or even in the world today? A little perspective is in order."*

In fact, almost two million black Africans and over a million blacks from the Caribbean have immigrated to the USA in just this century while virtually none have gone the other way.

I will continue to celebrate the Fourth of July and our founding fathers. It was a remarkable accomplishment that enabled life as we know it. Further, while those pushing the *1619 Project* have every right to be heard, to foist that distortion of history on our children through the public education system paid for with tax dollars is evil and destructive. It will harm the most those it is supposedly intended to benefit. If the nation's public schools teach our children that the USA's history is only one of unjust oppression and that its laws and structure are still unjust and unfairly enforced on certain groups, we shouldn't expect our children to be proud of the USA, happy to be an American, obey its laws, or accept responsibility for their own lives because they have been taught, and believe, the system is rigged. Such teaching can only limit their liberty and pursuit of happiness. Instead, it is a recipe for anarchy and the destruction of society.

Historian and documentary filmmaker Ken Burns recently said that the present day is one of the worst times in American History. He then quoted Abraham Lincoln:

From whence shall we expect the approach of danger? Shall some trans-Atlantic military giant step the earth and crush us at a blow? Never. All the armies of Europe, Asia, and Africa could not by force take a drink from the Ohio River or make track on the Blue Ridge in a trial of a thousand years. No, if destruction be our lot we must ourselves be its author and finisher. As a nation of free men, we will live forever or die by suicide.

Burns then went on to say:

We're looking right down the muzzle of that gun.

So, the battle lines are drawn, and the stakes are high, with some very smart and articulate people on each side convinced that their view of the USA, and its history, is *The Truth!*

Any look at history and current conditions on this issue needs to acknowledge the changes that have occurred in the USA since World War II. I lived in North Carolina in 1962 and 1963 and saw Jim Crow firsthand. Besides being unable to vote or enter many commercial establishments, there were even segregated public transportation, waiting areas, restrooms, drinking fountains, and housing projects. For President Biden to call Georgia's 2021 election law, whatever its merits or demerits, *"Jim Crow 2.0"* is a slap in the face to those blacks who actually endured Jim Crow across this nation's South in the first two-thirds of the twentieth century.

Teaching American history in school needs to include slavery, the end of slavery, racial bigotry through Jim Crow, and the Civil Rights Movement, including the contexts in which each occurred. But I firmly believe the key to ending remaining racial discrimination in the USA is to further deemphasize race as significant in human interactions rather than current attempts (CRT, DEI, BLM, etc.) to reemphasize race as an important factor in defining who each of us is as an individual. All children, especially those under 12, should be thought of and treated as raceless innocents. For teachers to separate elementary school children and pit them against each other based on race is simply evil. And incredibly destructive. Again, in the words of Thomas Sowell:

Racism does not have a good track record. It's been tried out for a long time and you'd think that by now we'd want to put an end to it instead of putting it under new management.

White America cannot fix black America or brown America, no matter how guilty it might be or feel, how hard it might try, or how much it might pay. The only lasting fix is to recognize that there is only one America that we are all part of and to ensure that it provides equal opportunity for all. And we all, whether black, brown, white, or mixed; rich or poor; native Americans, new immigrants, or descendants of slaves or the pilgrims; need to remember, again in the words of Sowell:

When people get used to preferential treatment, equal treatment seems like discrimination.

THE SIGNIFICANCE OF CULTURE – As we have looked at human progress, it is apparent that culture has mattered. A Lot. In fact, culture is the only ethnic characteristic that has mattered. Not race. Not which language was spoken. Not religion (except to the extent it has influenced culture and values). Not tribe or nationality. Only culture has mattered.

Culture is a changeable human creation. And cultures are not all created equal. Culture is far more than just what we eat and how we dress. There are vast differences in how various cultures around the world have viewed (and may still view) caste, class, individual freedom, slavery, marriage, family ties, personal responsibility, education, good and evil, innovation and change, property ownership, what is honorable and dishonorable, hereditary rights, risk, the value of each individual human life, the form and role of governments, the rule of law, how to view other ethnic groups, etc. William A. Henry, a Pulitzer Prize-winning journalist, wrote in 1995:

Some cultures, though we dare not say it, are more accomplished than others and therefore more worthy of study. Every corner of the human race may have something to contribute. That does not mean that all contributions are equal...It is scarcely the same thing to put a man on the moon as to put a bone in your nose.

As noted earlier, a unique American culture began to form as English immigrants started interacting with the native Indians at Plymouth and

Jamestown. While the cultural roots of the thirteen colonies reach back to western Protestant Europe, primarily England, as the European Enlightenment was still unfolding, the colonial cultures were modified once they got here by the conditions they found and from interaction with different Indian groups and African slaves. Thus, American culture is a unique and distinct branch of what we now think of as *The West*.

There were also characteristics that distinguished those who chose to come to America from the neighbors they left behind. John Steele Gordon summarizes the impact of those differences:

> *And there can be no doubt that if the United States is famous for its get-up-and-go, that is because Americans are descended from those who got up and came. Those who chose to leave all they had ever known and come to a strange and distant land came to pursue their own ideas of happiness. Here, the great majority found conditions that allowed them to do so with less interference than anywhere else and thus gave them a better chance to find it.*
>
> *The willingness to accept present-day discomfort and risk for the hope of future riches that so characterized these immigrants, and the millions who would follow over the next two centuries, has had a profound effect on the history of the American economy.*
>
> *Like most stories of empire, the story of* [the USA] *is an epic one, full of triumph and disaster, daring and timidity, new ideas and old prejudices, great men and utter fools. But most of all it is an epic powered by uncountable millions pursuing their self-interests within the rule of law, which is the essence of liberty. And as with all epics, it is at its heart a window into what makes us human.*

So, those immigrants who left all they had known behind, for a shot at a different and hopefully better future, were far more willing to adapt, improvise, endure present hardships, try new things, and, in short, change. And these characteristics applied not just to those coming from Western Europe before 1776, but also to those millions more who came from all races all over the world since 1776. Together, they have made the USA the most innovative, creative, and upwardly mobile country the world has ever known.

The Smithsonian Institute's *National Museum of African American History and Culture* got it completely wrong in 2021 when it published on its website for a short time a list of *white values*: *"promoting the scientific method, rational linear thinking, the nuclear family, hard work as a key to success, self-reliance, personal responsibility, children having their own rooms, being polite, intent should count when judging crime, being on time or timely, getting the right answer in math, and valuing written communication over other forms."* To the extent that list is even valid, these are now American cultural values, not *white* values. In fact, some of these, like being on time or timely, are needed to thrive in the modern industrial world and apply wherever industrialization goes irrespective of race. White is used to designate a race, like black or Asian, or Native American. There is a **profound truth** we need to emphasize here. Race relates to what we look like, inherited physical traits, not values. Values are not inherited. They come from culture. And while some cultural traits may have been historically linked to some races more than others, cultural traits, including values and bigotry, are learned. It is not only disingenuous but very destructive to claim various values belong to a particular race. While some of the cultural values listed on that website have roots in white Europe, there are plenty of European countries that don't exhibit many of these traits. And millions of non-white USA citizens do exhibit these cultural traits. They are definitely **not** racial or *white* traits.

Add in being open to change and innovation, the right to chart one's own path, upward mobility, disdain for hereditary titles and class, voluntary compliance with the rule of law, respect for property rights, delayed gratification, and a desire to associate with peers and neighbors to get things done. And those are the American cultural values that have enabled the USA, in just 200 years, to become the most powerful nation on Earth, militarily, economically, technologically, and culturally while also making the USA the most ethnically diverse nation on Earth. But this is no more a white culture than the technical innovations and games it invented (stoves, toilets, light bulbs, airplanes, baseball, basketball, football, etc.) are white inventions and white games. These are American products and games invented by an American culture. It is intellectually and morally bankrupt to disown that culture and those values while claiming and embracing the products and games that culture created. Still, much of American culture is a unique extension of what we now think of as *The West*. Which brings us to a multicultural demonstration at Stanford several years ago where the demonstrators repeatedly chanted:

Hey, Hey, Ho, Ho, Western Civ has got to go!

Really? So, is throwing out the civilization we think of as *The West* a good idea? Whatever faults Western culture may have (and it certainly has some), and however one feels about the benefits versus the costs of the Industrial Revolution (totally a product of the West), the West has made other remarkable contributions to the current human condition. The development of the written form we use for music, along with the invention of the violin, the cello, and the piano, all occurred in Italy. For centuries, the best piano makers and beer brewers were German as they spread themselves around the world. Most of the other instruments found in modern orchestras and bands were also invented in the West. The West's enlightenment included religious reformers, scientists, mathematicians, philosophers, composers, and artists who gave us the opera, ballet, symphony, and art gallery. There are governments around the world that are now divided into three branches, legislative, executive, and judicial. Again, a product of the West. The worldwide end of slavery began in the West, which then imposed it on a reluctant world.

Two stories involving Western values.

Ayaan Hirsi Ali was a refugee from Somalia who had also lived in Saudi Arabia, Ethiopia, and Kenya before arriving in Holland in 1992 (at age 22. While enroute to a marriage arranged by her father against her will, she escaped to Holland and changed her name). She was granted asylum and learned Dutch. She then got a job as a translator working with Somali refugees. She was to only translate exactly what was said without interjecting herself into the exchange.

I was called to a school to help a teacher explain to some parents that their seven-year-old was extremely aggressive. If he beat up one more child he would have to be sent to a special school for aggression treatment. I had trouble even finding the words in Somali to explain what aggression treatment might be.

The child told his side of the story: a kid stuck his tongue out at him and called him a bad name, so he beat him up. Doing this was completely congruent with his upbringing. In Somalia, you attack. You hit first. If you wait to be hit, you'll only be bullied more. I was taught that too.

Having heard the kid's story, the parents said, "See: the other kid started it!" The teacher, who was a young woman, said, "But this other child didn't hit." And the parents exclaimed in chorus, "You don't wait to be hit!"

I had to ask to be released from the rule of strict translation so I could explain things. I told the teacher, "Where we come from, aggression is a survival tactic: we teach our children to hit first. You will have to explain more.

The teacher looked at me as though I was mad. She explained that if all the children were allowed to hit each other, then it would be survival of the fittest: the strongest would bully the weakest. And the parents nodded. This satisfied them, because they wanted their child to be the strongest.

Finally I said to the parents, "Look, in Holland, if you hit people, then they think something is wrong with you. Here, they solve disagreements by talking. If your son continues to hit, he will be taken to a place where the children are mentally unwell, to be treated for illness.

So they listened. They made all sorts of agreements and arrangements to meet again. When the meeting ended, all three of them said how illuminating it had been for them, to see that such an unusual culture could exist.

Hyeonseo Lee is a North Korean refugee who, after surviving for eleven years moving around in China under various assumed names (if discovered, China immediately sends North Koreans back to face harsh punishment), was finally able to make her way into South Korea (when she was 28). There, as a North Korean refugee, she was granted citizenship. Lee then tried to help her mother and younger brother come to South Korea. The plan was to sneak them out of North Korea, across China, and into a country with a South Korean embassy where they would be able to ask for asylum. After getting them out of North Korea, Lee managed to sneak them all the way across China on identification papers she had borrowed for them. At China's southern border, they met a human smuggler who then took her mother and brother across the border into Laos. However, they were arrested at the border by the Laotian police. So, Lee, who had a valid South Korean passport, then went across the border herself to find them, get them out of jail, and go to the South Korean Embassy. After a few weeks, through charm and bribes, Lee was finally able to find them and meet with them in jail. She claimed to be there to help North Korean refugees and gave no hint that the woman was her mother and that her son was her brother. If the jailers knew that, they would demand higher bribes. Her mother then asked Lee to help three other North Koreans who were already in jail when they got there. Every time Lee went to the jail, the man in charge would extract a bribe by taking all the money she had with her and then giving her just half of it back. After several trips and extensive haggling, Lee managed to get the fine she would have to pay to get all five of them out of jail trimmed down to $3,500 American dollars. But the man in charge would go no lower.

Lee had already spent virtually all her money on travel and bribes. She was at a loss. As Lee sat in the coffee house where she was staying, wondering what she could do, a tall white man in his fifties, whom she recognized as having been on the same bus with her when she entered Laos and was staying at the same place she was, came up and spoke to her. It was the first time in her life she had ever talked to a white person. Lee understood very little English, so she opened a Korean-English app on her phone, and they began an awkward conversation. He introduced himself as Dick Stolp from Perth, Australia, and wondered why she had been there so long and seemed so distressed. She told him that she was a South Korean trying to get five North Koreans out of jail and on to the South Korean embassy to seek asylum. Her plight saddened him and, after a few minutes' pause, he left to make a phone call. He then stopped at an ATM and brought back some of the money she needed. He said he would have the rest in the morning. She was shocked at his help and asked why he was doing it. He said that he was not doing it for her but for the North Koreans who were seeking freedom (people he had not even met yet). He then went with her to the jail the next day to make sure they all got out of jail and on their way. Along the way, they were stopped at another check point where more bribes were demanded. After pleading poverty, Lee haggled that bribe down to $900. Stolp paid that too. Then, as they parted ways, Stolp then gave Lee money for her airfare home. Lee described her reaction to his help:

When you've lived your whole life as I had, calculating the cost of even the smallest decision, such generosity wasn't easy to accept. It involved a loss of control. All I could do was say thank you. Not once did he ask for anything in return. I had never before experienced such detached generosity without some connection or debt attached. If we had been two lone Koreans from Hyesan meeting in Laos, or two young people meeting in a crowd of old people, I might have understood the impulse. But Dick's simple kindness took no notice of age, race or language. It crossed my mind that perhaps he was so rich that money meant little to him, but I learned later that he was not a rich man.

He didn't know that the lady in prison was my mother, and that her son was my brother. I wanted to tell Dick the truth about my identity. He deserved to know. But North Koreans wear masks from such long habit that it's difficult to cast them off.

My most basic assumptions about human nature were being overturned. In North Korea I'd learned from my mother that to trust anyone outside family was risky and dangerous. In China I'd lived by cunning since I was a teenager, lying to hide the truth of my identity in order to survive. On the only occasion I'd trusted people I'd got into a world of trouble with the Shenyang police. Not only did I believe that humans were selfish and base, I also knew that plenty of them were actually bad – content to destroy lives for their own gain. I'd seen Korean-Chinese expose North Korean escapees to the police in return for money. I'd known people who'd been trafficked by other humans as if they were livestock. That world was familiar to me. All my life, random acts of kindness had been so rare that they'd stick in my memory, and I'd think: "how strange." What Dick had done changed my life. He showed me that there was another world where strangers helped strangers for no other reason than that it was good to do so, and where callousness was unusual, not the norm. Dick had treated me as if I were his family, or an old friend. Even now, I do not fully grasp his motivation. But from the day I met him the world was a less cynical place. I started feeling warmth for other people. This seemed so natural, and yet I'd never felt it before.

That other world where strangers help strangers in need is a cherished value in the USA and much of the West. And, while it may have lost some ground, it is still often the norm rather than the unusual. Lee would later meet and eventually marry an American expat living in South Korea. Of all the many challenges in her life, one of the most challenging was introducing her white American boyfriend to her mother and brother. They reacted with all the shock, revulsion, and despair she had feared. Yet, her mother eventually came around and even went with them to visit his family in Minnesota. While sometimes found in other cultures, the Western values reflected in helping a neighbor or a stranger, or talking through conflict have their roots in Christianity (the Golden Rule and the Good Samaritan) as expounded in the European Reformation and Enlightenment as the Bible was printed in various European languages and read in homes (often the only book in the home), and are not inherited genetic traits of white people. They are learned. They are also characteristics of the Christian Black Church as practiced across this Nation. I have attended a few weddings and funerals in black churches and have always come away deeply impressed by the acceptance, compassion, and fellowship exhibited there.

Unlike other ethnic characteristics that are all constructs of human societies; race is in our DNA. We are what we are. There is nothing we can do about it. And it shouldn't matter. Whatever our racial makeup, while it is a part of our personal heritage and history that connects us to other people and should be appreciated, it is nothing to gloat about or be ashamed of since we have no control over it. In our globalized world, with people everywhere on the move, the number of mixed-race children will continue to increase, and racial distinctions will blur even more.

Henry Louis Gates, Jr., a black Harvard professor, has a show on PBS called *finding your roots,* where he invites public figures to the show and presents them, after exhaustive research, with the details of their ancestry. In early 2023, he had black activist Angela Davis on the show. She had become a household name for her role in the Black Power Movement beginning in the late 1960s. After presenting her with many surprising details about her ancestry (her DNA is 52% African and 48% European), Gates concluded with the fact that among her ancestors was one of the Pilgrims on the Mayflower. She was shocked to find she was a daughter of the Mayflower.

For the 2020 census, 6% of those who answered the questionnaire gave different racial or ethnic responses than they did in 2010. Prior to 1980, the Census Bureau counted most Hispanics as white. Now they are counted as non-white. So what? Currently, mixed race babies account for 10% of new births in the USA while 20% of new marriages cross racial or other ethnic lines. Hopefully, that will help us all reach the day when we will each only judge one another as individuals based *"on the content of our character rather than the color of our skin."*

Over 97% of the population of the USA are not Native American. Thus, they, or their ancestors, came here from some other continent over the last 400+ years. So, as the most ethnically diverse nation on earth and one that continues to attract immigrants from all around the world (in addition to the tens of thousands who enter the USA legally each year, about three million people from at least 145 countries illegally crossed our southern border in 2022, and even more in 2023), is the USA a melting pot or a mosaic? Does it provide a societal and cultural umbrella that is uniquely American while the boundaries of the many ethnic groups under that umbrella become increasingly fussy and blurred (a melting pot) over time? Or is it a nation wherein each race, religion, language, nationality, or tribe largely isolates itself, does its own thing, and retains its own culture with little sense of a common American community (a mosaic)?

I am a strong advocate of the melting pot under an American cultural umbrella, and I believe that, at least until the last few years, it has been winning. I have no sympathy for the blather and fuss about cultural appropriation. I believe it is destructive. If Yo-Yo Ma can play the cello, why is it unacceptable for white women to wear Asian fashion? For new immigrants, share what you bring that is of value. And check out what is already here. Why else would you come? Please don't try to turn America into whatever you left behind. Remember, instead, why you left. Learn what the things are that have made America the place you wanted to come to.

Yet, everyone has a story, and every story is unique. And that is true of each of those millions coming to the USA each year. Dina Nayeri, a refugee from Iran, came to the USA when she was ten years old with her brother and mother in 1990. Her mother was a doctor and her father was a dentist, so they had a very good life there. Each day at school, Dina would chant with her classmates under the approving eye of her teacher, *"Death to America!"* However, her mother had become a Christian. And was far too vocal about it. As the authorities were closing in, she managed to flee for her life with her two children, leaving her husband behind. They spent two years in refugee camps in Europe before finally making it to Oklahoma, thanks to a sponsor. However, her mother's doctor credentials were not accepted here, so she could only find menial work. So, their living conditions here were far below what they had been in Iran. Dina felt the drive to succeed. She has degrees from Princeton and Harvard. She has described Iran:

Modern Iran is a country of refugees making do with small joys, exiled from the prerevolutionary paradise we knew.
What is a credible danger in a country that hangs apostates and homosexuals and adulterers, and where a hateful finger in your direction is enough to make you one? A country so corrupt that one mullah's whim can send you to the firing squad or the crane, your gallows. A country where record keeping is a farce, where in whispers the land's riches are divided among a few, where young men languish without work, where young women wither with unspent ambition and

desire, where the enchanting whisper of opium is always in your ear,
and despair fills your lungs so thickly that your best chance is to be
your own executioner?

Dina Nayeri has spent much of her adult life in Europe and has traced
refugee stories there. For them, the truth isn't the issue. Instead, it all
depends on how each refugee tells his/her story to asylum bureaucrats who
are inclined to disbelieve and will thus try to poke holes in their stories.
Being an economic refugee isn't enough. Their life must be in danger to
qualify. She has made the following comments:

In conversations about the refugee crises, educated people continue to
make the barbaric argument that open doors will benefit the host
nation. The time for this outdated colonialist argument has run out;
migrants don't derive their value from their benefit to the Western-born.
Maybe the West wants the same for me – I have been an investment. It
would be a shame if I offer no return on that investment. But even if I
were to swim against the tide of Western intention and connect to my
native country somehow, would Iran want anything to do with me? I
sound like a foreigner. I act like one. Home is never the same for
anyone, not just refugees.
By the time I was thirty, I had given that hungry immigrant girl
everything she wanted. Left without goals, I felt hollowed out, without
identity. Slowly I filled the void with Iranian things, all that I had
ignored or put away in the quest to become American. Now, firmly
entrenched in my borrowed Western identity, I could afford a few
Iranian flourishes.
I have spent a lot of imagination on the question of who would I be, had
I stayed. What if I hadn't gotten on that plane?
I don't want to go backward. I don't want to witness the ugliness of
assimilation again. I don't want to see my family ashamed, hiding tics,
posturing gratitude as they carry out the endless search for home and
identity. I don't want to face the truth that everything I hold most sacred
and dear about myself was given to me by the West. I don't want to
believe that I am the generic product of Eurocentric colonialist

thinking, that there is no going back because America has remade me in its image. I don't want to believe that I come from an idle, ordinary people or that I am not an inevitable version of myself. I want to believe in my own agency and power.

Though I can't return, the suffering of today's refugees erodes my sense of home, acceptance, and belonging.

So many doors have opened to us, it's impossible to accept that there is no obligation, that we've arrived in a place we can relax and stretch out, that all the honest work to prove our worth, to assuage the helplessness, to rub out previous identities was for nothing. Is it possible to ever repay this imagined debt? What if we allow ourselves to relax and our children grow comfortable and entitled, demanding gratitude from the next batch knocking at the gates?

While she beautifully expresses the angst of being a refugee, she has come to equate Western culture with being white. Therefore, because she has a light complexion when she behaves like a westerner, she feels like she is an inauthentic chameleon acting white. She even states:

It is a question of racial dominance. If whiteness is to be linked to education, culture, the creation of great cities, the brightest people of color cannot have their attention on home. They must belong to white culture.

Maybe this mistake of equating culture with race has been enhanced because she has spent years in Western Europe where they have done more to accommodate, rather than assimilate, refugees from the rest of the world. Europe is now much more of a mosaic than a melting pot. Nayeri doesn't acknowledge that for centuries, as people from a vast variety of European cultures (Irish, Germans, Scandinavians, Italians, Eastern Europeans, Jews) poured into America, they all felt isolated and tended to concentrate in enclaves for generations as they adapted to, and became a part of, American culture. Nayeri does not need to reject Western culture or the American dream in order to be proud of, grateful for, or connect with her Iranian heritage. Again, Western culture is **not** a genetically inherited trait of white people. Nor does it belong to them.

Despite all the barriers refugees face that Nayeri complains about, the West has been far more welcoming to those of all races and cultures than any other culture on earth. In fact, as it relates to those entering Europe, it is the refugees who are colonists, with many wanting to retain their own culture while rejecting the native Western culture. Europe has no obligation to accept any of these colonizing refugees who fail to recognize that it is Western culture that made Europe the place they wanted to come to. So, adapt or go elsewhere.

The quote on the Statue of Liberty *"Give me your tired, your poor, your huddled masses yearning to be free. The wretched refuse of your teeming shore."* was placed there when Ellis Island was the primary portal for entering immigrants. During the 60+ years it served that function, twelve million immigrants came in through Ellis Island. And those immigrants were expected to become part of America and its culture. For them, there was no government effort to provide the masses with food, shelter, or clothes. The idea of *the Good Samaritan* was individuals, and associations of individuals, not the government. New immigrants were free and able to seek employment, but there was no government social safety net for them. Still, despite its faults and shortcomings, the USA and its citizens, thanks to its unique form of Western culture, provides aid and military protection around the world. It is the most generous nation on earth.

Glenn Loury has told of giving a speech to a conservative audience:

The biggest applause line in my speech was when I said "I am a man of the West. Tolstoy is mine. Dickens is mine. Einstein is mine." In other words, the fact that I descend from African slaves does not preclude me from joining with the great intellectual and cultural traditions of the milieu in which I am imbedded, which is the West... I'm black. I'm not only black. I'm not defined by my blackness. I'm embedded within a cultural tradition which is mine. Even if old dead white guys are responsible for much of it. That's my culture.

For both Loury and his audience, skin color didn't matter. Race didn't matter. Culture mattered. And they were connected together in a common culture of free people that they each valued.

I, like Glenn Loury, am a person of the West and an American. As such, I happily claim him along with Mark Twain, George Washington, Frederick Douglas, and many others, including immigrants of other races like Ayaan Hirsi Ali who came to America with reservations and then embraced it. Though he didn't start out there, Frederick Douglas came to view the USA as his country. Peter C. Myers characterized the Evolution of Frederick Douglas' thinking this way:

*He became America's most prominent representative of the aspiration toward racial integration, reconciliation, and uplift. One must emphasize: he **became** that. It didn't come naturally to him. To become the great apostle of those aspirations, Douglass had to overcome a sentiment about and among black Americans that is recurrently present in U.S. history, powerful in his day and again in ours – the feeling or conviction that to be black is to bear an identity antagonistic to American identity.*

In the long history of African-American political thought, there is no more forceful proponent of the cause of integration, and there is no more insightful analyst of the varieties and dangers of national and racial disintegration.

Douglas wrote late in his life: "No people can prosper unless they have a home, or the hope of a home. To have a home, one must have a country." America, in Douglass' abiding vision was black Americans proper home, their only realistic alternative, and also the locus of their highest ideals. For Douglas, as for Abraham Lincoln, their common country was, through it all, the last best hope on earth.

And that was also the view of Martin Luther King Jr., one of only two Americans whose birthdays we celebrate with a National Holiday. The USA was his country. And he had great hope for a future where skin color would no longer matter in it. And that view is still held by a number of prominent blacks. From a May 2022 article published by Glenn Loury:

We talk incessantly about racial identity. But what about culture and values – aspects of our humanity that transcend race? I am a black American economist in this era of racial discontent in my country; an Ivy League professor and descendent of slaves; a beneficiary of a civil rights revolution, now over two generations in the past, which has made possible for me a life that my ancestors could only have dreamed of. More than all of these things, I am a patriot who loves his country. I am a man of the West, an inheritor of its great traditions. As such, I feel compelled to represent the interests of "my people."

Black influence on American culture is stunning and has worldwide resonance. In fact, when viewed in the global comparative perspective, we black Americans are rich and powerful with, for example, ten times the per capita income of the typical Nigerian.

All this disproves the premise that the American Dream does not apply to us black people. To say that it doesn't apply is to tell a lie to our children about their country – a crippling lie which, when taken as gospel, robs our people of agency and a sense of control over our fate. It's also a patronizing lie that betrays a profound doubt about our ability to face up to the responsibilities and to bear the burdens of our freedom. For that is the existential challenge we black American now face in the twenty-first century: not to throw off the shackles of our supposed oppression but to take up the burdens of our freedom. To whom much has been given, of him much shall be required.

Freedom is one thing: equality quite another. As such, it is both futile and dangerous for us black Americans to rely on others to shoulder our communal responsibilities. If we want to walk with dignity – to enjoy truly equal standing within this diverse, prosperous, and dynamic society – then we must accept the fact that "white America" can never give us what we seek in response to our protests and remonstrations.

Equality of dignity, equality of standing, of honor, of security in one's position within society, an equal ability to command respect of others – such things cannot be simply handed over. Nor will they be the fruit of insurrection, violent uprising, or rebellion. We must make ourselves equal. No one can do it for us.

Loury has also told of his interaction with a Chinese American woman, Wai Wah Chin, an activist in New York City pushing to retain exam criteria for admission to several schools with excellent academic achievement records:

And I said casually that the Chinese Americans are overrepresented amongst the students entering into the Bronx High School of Science and Stuyvesant and whatnot. And she said "How is it that they're representing? They're individual human beings. They're not representing anything. What do you mean 'overrepresented,' 'underrepresented'?"

And I was really stunned by the force of that point. I was not conscious of the extent to which I had imported into my own thinking a moral position that is questionable, wherein I see these individual kids about whom one thing that is true is that they're Chinese. But there are a hundred things that you could say about them. And I put that kid in a box and say "represents" something. That's a very significant move. It's a move that I made without any critical reflection. And it's a move on critical thought that I think is dubious.

Group bigotry and feelings of superiority are not limited to ethnic differences or even class differences within an ethnic group. Tribalism seems to be embedded in our nature. That is obvious around the world and in the USA today as we humans believe in and root for our family, school, neighborhood, city, or country. That is why we have full stadiums everywhere seating up to 100,000 people, with millions more watching on television. Competitive spectator sports are all about my group being best, whether it is my city, my school, or whatever. And that is just the tip of the iceberg. Most of us in the USA today understand that, as an ethnically diverse and highly mobile society, to be civilized, we must recognize that, within the context of good sportsmanship and good neighbors among equals, feelings of superiority based on ethnic distinctions are best left in the dustbin of history. However, our destructive tribal instincts remain alive and well. Now, we increasingly see tribes forming around ideas and politics (rather than ethnicity) that regard those who disagree as evil and even flatly reject their right to be heard, all while claiming to decry bigotry and hate. Free speech, a free press, and the right of dissenting views to be heard are no longer cherished values. That is the road to totalitarianism, which crushes individual freedom and threatens the culture that has built the USA and is needed to maintain our modern way of life.

And so I will close out this section on the importance of culture and defense of the West as the culture that enabled our modern world to develop and be sustained, with two quotes from Ayaan Hirsi Ali in her November 2023 explanation of her journey from being a devout Muslim to an atheist, and from an atheist to a Christian, as she outlines the legacy of the Judeo-Christian ethic:

That legacy consists of an elaborate set of ideas and institutions designed to safeguard human life, freedom and dignity — from the nation state and the rule of law to the institutions of science, health and learning... All sorts of apparently secular freedoms — of the market, of conscience and of the press — find their roots in Christianity.

To me, this freedom of conscience and speech is perhaps the greatest benefit of Western civilization. It does not come naturally to man. It is the product of centuries of debate within Jewish and Christian communities. It was these debates that advanced science and reason, diminished cruelty, suppressed superstitions, and built institutions to order and protect life, while guaranteeing freedom to as many people as possible. Unlike Islam, Christianity outgrew its dogmatic stage. It became increasingly clear that Christ's teaching implied not only a circumscribed role for religion as something separate from politics. It also implied compassion for the sinner and humility for the believer.

INSTITUTIONS AND ECONOMIC SYSTEMS MATTER – El Paso, Texas and Juarez, Mexico, are adjacent cities separated by the Rio Grande River, which also separates the USA from Mexico. There are a few other locations, like Nogales, where a population center is split between the two countries. For these cities, both sides share a common Hispanic heritage and culture, while thousands of relatives live on the other side. Yet, life is drastically different between the two sides. Why the difference? Functioning institutions. While recent events have put enormous strain on many of those institutions on the USA side, they are still the civilizing forces that make one side of the border far more livable than the other side.

Some institutions are also critical to human progress, while others may retard it. Human history makes it clear that our modern world could have never come to be without economic activity – the exchange of goods and services between people that extended across a wide range of geographic areas to access needed materials. And that money was a critical catalyst in magnifying the volume of that activity. The rule of law, property rights, and individual freedom were also important elements. In short, an open, civilized society of relatively free people operating in relatively free markets across continents was needed. The rule of law requires courts, police, or other enforcement mechanisms that are not corrupt and are evenhanded enough to have the confidence of most of the population. Only then can voluntary compliance with the law prevail on a large enough scale to enable a stable society of free citizens.

A free society can then develop associations and institutions, from homeowner associations to churches, volunteer fire departments, and many more, to enhance the public good. While some are public (law enforcement) and some may be private, such institutions can provide public services such as municipal electricity, water, sewer, and communication systems and include healthcare facilities, schools, colleges, and research universities. Such institutions are important to a free society governed by the Rule of Law. And such a society, open to change and innovation, then has endless potential and unlimited possibilities.

There are also economic institutions. The Industrial Revolution started in Britain with factories. That led to increased demand for iron to build those factories, including the steam engines and production machines in them. And that took money. The development of a banking system in Britain in the eighteenth century provided the capital needed to finance those factories and iron works based on the hope for high returns. And in those textile mills, more often than not, it worked out well for the financers. It is something the government never could have done. It was too busy borrowing money to finance its wars. In short, thanks to banks, the Industrial Revolution enabled Britain's economic system to begin evolving from a privileged landed rich gentry and feudal system with merchant, artisan, servant, and working classes, into what we now think of as free enterprise *Capitalism.*

As the Industrial Revolution came to the USA, it found a financial system set up by Alexander Hamilton designed to facilitate private investment in industrial enterprises, but not government financing. Some of the early private capital came from Europe, primarily Britain since there had not been that much wealth accumulated in the USA to that point. Since railroads drove much of the industrial expansion in nineteenth century America, the best government could do to aid that expansion was to offer land (and access to minerals) to aid in that expansion. And those sweetheart land deals are what spurred the private investment necessary to build the transcontinental railroad, as well as many others. Then came the gilded era of the late nineteenth century with steel and then petroleum taking center stage. When John Jacob Astor died in 1848 as the world's richest man, he left a fortune of $25 million. Commodore Vanderbilt left $105 million when he died less than 30 years later. Andrew Carnegie sold out in 1901 for $480 million. By 2016 John D. Rockefeller was worth $2 billion (equivalent to $60 billion in 2024).

Many of those who built vast fortunes in industry in the waning years of the nineteenth century not only built mansions for themselves, but also gave away large portions of their fortunes to found or endow museums, concert halls, orchestras, colleges, hospitals, and libraries in astounding numbers in cities across the country, many of which still bear their names. *"The United States in its early days had been a cultural backwater, and artists and writers routinely went to Europe to study. By the turn of the twentieth century, the United States was as great a cultural and intellectual power as it was an economic one, largely thanks to the often poorly educated men who are remembered today as the robber barons.* Carnegie wrote:

A man who dies rich, dies disgraced.

He then gave away most of his fortune, building more than 5,000 town libraries, among numerous other beneficiaries. Rockefeller ended up giving away over $500 million ($15 billion in 2024) to various charities. Giving away significant portions of their vast new wealth was unique to America's wealthiest industrialists. Europe's wealthiest had no such tradition.

In 1901, J. P. Morgan created the largest company the world had ever known when he purchased Carnegie's steel empire and merged it with several other steel companies to create the United States Steel Corporation. However, new president Theodor Roosevelt began to take on corporate mergers and, for the first time, made the federal government an active referee in managing capitalism. A role it has never relinquished. In 1907, President Roosevelt took on Rockefeller's Standard Oil. And ordered it broken up in more than 30 separate companies. Ironically, in the first two years after the breakup, the stock values of the successor companies doubled in value, making Rockefeller twice as rich as he had been before that government intervention.

As the twentieth century began, the USA had a third of the world's railroad mileage and produced 40% of the world's steel. It was the world's greatest exporter of agricultural products. Per capita income had passed Britain and led the world, while 90% of the population were literate. The nation had over 2,200 newspapers, a thousand colleges, and more high school students than any other country in the world. Then came the First World War. Germany had dominated world chemical markets until then. Now, they were shut out from export markets, while Britain and its allies had to buy much of what was needed to wage war. And they bought it from the USA. *"The country had been in recession in 1914, but thanks to the slaughter in Europe, American industry began to prosper as it had not since the Civil War."* By the end of the war, Du Pont Chemical had annual revenues 26 times what they had been in 2013. General Motors' stock went from $39 to $500 by the end of the war. And, by 2020, the industrial might of the USA was unrivaled anywhere in the world thanks to banking institutions and private capital.

In short, private capital built the modern world thanks to financial institutions that facilitated the flow of capital to those enterprises that showed the greatest potential for high financial returns. And private capital has played a major role as modernization has spread around the world over the last 50 years. Even in totalitarian communist states like China and Vietnam, their industrial expansion has only come as they quietly abandoned some of their state-run collective inclinations and allowed private investment into the mix despite remaining totalitarian states. Others, like Venezuela (despite its vast natural resources) and Cuba, have become economic basket cases as they moved to totalitarian socialism. The vast economic differences between West Germany and East Germany by 1989, or between South Korea and North Korea over the past 50 years, also stand for the power of free enterprise.

In July 1975, in the midst of the Cold War, I spent a week in Leningrad, USSR (St. Petersburg), at an international conference. In addition to organized tours, I took a few trips sightseeing and shopping on my own. It was apparent that the government controlled both production and pricing. Some things were shockingly cheap, but would quickly sell out. Other things we think of as common simply did not exist or were very expensive. There was no blue denim or chewing gum. Nor any soft drinks we would recognize. Attendees who had brought a pair of Levi's to barter with had an unimaginable treasure to offer, while a stick of chewing gum would buy a friend for life. The tap water was contaminated, but the only nonalcoholic liquids for sale were two gag-inducing soft drinks, which, after the first two days, were sold out. The large hotel where I stayed served apple juice with meals on the first day. It was quite good. We were offered apple juice every day. By the fifth day, it was black and tasted like vinegar. A good pair of shoes cost a month's wages. A spinet piano cost two year's wages. In short, what was produced, how much of it was produced, and what it would cost, were divorced from supply and demand and even the cost of production. The audio/visual equipment available at the conference was comparable to what we had in the late 1950s in high school. I was amazed at how comforting it felt to finally see a Coca-Cola sign outside Helsinki, a symbol that I was now back in the West.

Western-based corporations, such as Nike, Walmart, and Apple, have taken manufacturing facilities in developing countries, which has helped the spread of modern life while reducing costs to consumers in the West. While it has also taken jobs out of the West, globalization has helped spread wealth around the world. John Steele Gordon:

In 2000, total world trade was 125 times the level of 1950, equaling an astounding $7.5 trillion, including both manufacturers and services. Free trade has proved the greatest engine of economic growth the world has ever known.

With the help of *Antifa,* the rallying cry of the protests and riots during the summer of 2020 was to tear down the system and start over. That cry was as much about capitalism as racism.

Hawk Newsom, of New York Black Lives Matter, told one news outlet in 2020:

If this country doesn't give us what we want, then we will burn down this system and replace it. All right? And I could be speaking... figuratively. I could be speaking literally. It's a matter of interpretation.

Another protester in San Diego, speaking to a reporter, defended a looter with *"If this young man was robbing, that means his state and his government failed to provide him with the resources he needs."* A protest leader in Chicago defended looting as just collecting reparations owed to blacks. It only takes an hour to loot and then burn down a Target or Walmart. But then, where will the community get its groceries and other inexpensive goods? The last two Walmart stores in Portland, Oregon, closed in March 2023. Various chain outlets are closing stores in Chicago, San Francisco, and other cities that no longer prosecute shoplifting.

Young Americans now seem much more enamored with socialism than previous generations. But then, many are saddled with enormous student debt while still living in their parents' basements because many of those college degrees they were awarded have little value in the job market. They feel entitled to the basic comforts of life and have not heeded Thomas Sowell's advice to any young person of any race who would like to do well in the modern world:

Develop skills people are willing to pay for.

That is a profound statement that too many young Americans simply have no grasp of. In addition to the pencil and gasoline examples already discussed, let's look at another example – home air conditioners. The first window unit air conditioners sold in the 1930s were priced from $10,000 to $50,000. Only the filthy rich could afford them. Just 50 years later, a window unit air conditioner was a symbol of poverty. They can now be found on Amazon for $100. *"The story about the mass production of air conditioners is that what were once status symbols are now common. Crucial here is that people got very rich making air conditioners common. It's how the world works. Or at least how to grow rich in the world.* **The best way to become very well to do very quickly is to produce in abundance, and at low prices, what used to be scarce and nosebleed expensive...When you shout about inequality, you're shouting at the very individuals who are aggressively and intrepidly removing unease from your life. From cars, to computers to smart phones, what was initially a bauble of the rich was rendered commonplace by people who attained great wealth by making them commonplace.** (emphasis added)

And that is something socialism can never do. Innovation, risk, and extra effort are incompatible with socialism. It was true for those pilgrims at Plymouth in 1621 trying to feed themselves. It was true for those Brazilian peasants on communal farms Shellenberger worked with in the 1990s. And it remains true today and into the future. Because self-interest almost always trumps public interest in us humans, only when risk or extra effort or extra thought are routinely rewarded individually will people care enough to take the risk or put in the extra effort or thought needed to innovate. Risk, new ideas, and hard work are the keys to human progress. Socialism is a *status quo* form of government. And if its leaders are picked by who they know or how they look rather than merit, it is retrograde, as repeatedly demonstrated around the world.

In 1776, the goal was to establish a government that would not interfere with individual life, liberty, and the pursuit of happiness. However, we now often hear that the basic human rights due each of us from government include free health care and easy access to housing, food, a college education, childcare, a guaranteed minimum income, and basic equity of outcomes across racial groups and genders. For many in the

USA, these new *rights* seem to have replaced liberty and the pursuit of happiness as valued ideals. For them, I guess it makes sense to no longer celebrate the Fourth of July. Life in a birdcage or a zoo, where all needs are provided for, is always easier than liberty (and zoo animals live longer). So, the goal is to become wards of the state. Animals, and people will always go for the easy meal even if it is detrimental to their long-term interests or even freedom, se we have signs in parks saying, *"don't feed the animals."*

And that brings us to the two overriding problems associated with socialism as expressed by Margaret Thatcher:

The government powerful enough to give its citizens everything they want will never be powerful enough to take any of it back.
Eventually you run out of other peoples' money.

Governments can facilitate getting things done, or they can be a roadblock and an enormous cause of delays. In the early 1930s, it took just 18 months for the federal government to build the massive seven story Department of Interior building that covers an entire city block in Washington, D.C. The atomic bomb went from a completely untested idea on paper to detonation over Japan in just three years. The Pentagon, the World's largest office building with its 6.5 million square feet of space, took just 16 months to build. It was completed in 1945. The U2 spy plane, capable of flying at altitudes of 90,000 feet, went from concept to first flight in 18 months, and remained a closely guarded secret for six years until one was shot down over Russia in 1960. In response to the USSR's Sputnik satellite in 1957, the USA created NASA in 1958, selected the first astronauts in 1959, put its first astronaut in space in 1961, and then put men on the moon and brought them safely home in 1969.

Things have changed. While equipment and materials have vastly improved since those accomplishments, the government could not begin to match achievements like that so quickly today. It has lost the ability to be efficient.

In July 2022, President Biden declared:

Climate Change is literally an existential threat to our nation and the world.

He has also talked about the urgency of addressing the situation. His 2020 platform stated: *"We will launch our country's second great railroad revolution by investing in high-speed rail and passenger and freight rail systems, and commit to public transportation as a public good."*

Then, in November 2022, the administration announced plans to remodel Union Station in Washington, D.C as part of this railroad revolution. It is the main passenger and mass transit hub in the city. This existing building, which took four years to build with rather primitive equipment, opened in 1907. It sits near the center of the city, surrounded by other existing buildings. That 2022 announcement noted that the environmental review for this project started in 2015 and is already three years behind schedule. The project is now scheduled to be completed in 2040, but that date may slip. So, even though plans for just remodeling an existing building had already been on the drawing board for seven years, it will take 18+ more years just to finish the remodeling of that building, which is urgently needed as part of an effort to help combat an existential threat to the nation!? Good Grief! How long would it take to do something that wasn't urgent?

A year after pushing through an enormous funding package in 2009 to help stimulate the economy by funding *shovel-ready projects,* President Obama lamented that:

There's no such thing as "shovel-ready projects."

Whatever the merits of promoting railways, the government of the USA is now far more effective at delaying things than doing things. Our government has long since lost the ability to do anything on time and within budget. Thus, it is far less productive. I know. I worked in it as a senior executive for 25 years. Yet, increasing productivity remains the key to modern life. Thus, the more government controls or manages the economy, the poorer people will be.

***THE IMPORTANCE OF HOPE AND OPTIMISM ABOUT THE
FUTURE*** – Many Americans are now pessimistic about the future of the
country. In early 2023, David Brooks noted that in the first year of the
COVID pandemic, 51% of the international stories on the pandemic were
negative, while 87% of the American media stories were negative. Bad
news sells. Or catches the viewer's eye. Brooks then noted that when
Gallup recently asked American adults if they were satisfied with their
personal lives, 85% said they were. And that number has remained stable
for the last 40 years. However, when Gallup asked people if they were
satisfied with the direction of the country, only 17% said they were, down
from 86% in 2000. That is a shocking drop. He blamed that drop on the
news media, which shows a huge and growing disparity between how
people view their personal lives and how they view their country's
direction.

However, I believe the news media is a minor factor in that drop. In
2000, both interest rates and inflation were at their lowest levels in 30
years. The stock market was roaring while the government was running
surpluses for the first time in decades. The West had won the Cold War,
and commentators were talking about the end of history. Neither China
nor Russia was viewed as a strong advisory. Illegal immigration was at
manageable levels. The attacks of 9/11 had not yet happened. Gas was
$1.51 a gallon. Crime was dropping sharply in cities across the USA while
New York City was booming. New dot-com businesses were opening right
and left. The idea of a colorblind society where we would each be *"judged
by the content of our character rather than the color of our skin."* was still
viewed as the ideal. There was no public dispute over the difference
between men and women or boys and girls. We all knew which restrooms
to go to and which sports teams to play on. Until November of 2000, we
all had confidence in our elections, with the results being known late that
night or early the next morning. Law enforcement was an honorable
profession, whether local or state police or the FBI. Life and the country
were good.

In the years since then, divisions over politics, race, gender,
immigration, economic systems, elections, and law enforcement have
become so stark and virulent that they are tribal. And those outside our

tribe are not only wrong but evil. We even seem unable to agree on basic facts and argue over what is hate, accurate history, science, disinformation, censorship, and free speech.

Children who start first grade in the fall of 2024, at the age of six, will be my age (82 years old) in the year 2100. So, the rest of this century is within their lifespan. That makes the issue of what life will be like in the USA and the world in 2100 of personal importance and concern to them. What many school kids are now being taught, and what these first graders will be taught in school and by society at large over the next twelve years of their lives (until they become legal adults at the age of 18) is bound to make them unhappy.

They will be taught that humanity's best years are behind it since, in their lifetimes, the world will come to a burning end because of climate change.

They will also be taught that the world is made up of oppressors and the oppressed, with white people being the oppressors who should check their privilege at the door as they let everyone else pass through. White children must understand that, because of the privilege they were born with, they must walk on eggshells and be constantly on guard, or they will be committing microaggressions against non-whites who might be offended. Meanwhile, there is no point in non-white children doing their best or obeying the law since the deck is stacked against them, and the law is structured to keep them down. They should also be constantly looking for offenses committed against them by insensitive whites oblivious to their privileged status. Further, merit-based systems and capitalism are racist evil tools of the oppressors. Socialism is good because it makes us all equal. Equity of outcomes by racial group, not equality of opportunity for individuals, is the ideal and the only measure that matters.

They will also be taught that if they want to know whether they are a boy or girl, they should not look in their underpants. Instead (unlike race, which they will be told defines them to their core irrespective of how they feel or act), gender depends totally on how they feel. And it is not just a binary choice since there are a range of options. Attending drag queen story hours for five to seven-year-olds will help them understand their options better.

Way back at the beginning, I laid out the four critical needs for any group of humans to survive. In addition to water, food, and shelter, the fourth is *developing the next generation*. For virtually all of human history, children and family have been the major focus and the source of happiness and hope. Family connections have dominated within most societies across distance and time. However, the focus on children and family is now in serious decline. Many nations and cultures now have birthrates well below the replacement rate of 2.1 babies per woman. A series of Wall Street Journal surveys found that, in the USA, those who view having children as very important has dropped from 59% in 1998 to 30% in 2023 (only 23% for those under age 30). At the same time, the role of the nuclear family (mother, father, and children living together) in society is denigrated, as is the role of parents in raising children. Most children now are not raised in a home with both parents. Since COVID, many parents are much more interested in what their children are being taught in school. While not all schools, colleges, and teachers are pushing what is just outlined above, many are. Parental concern played a large role in why Glen Youngkin won the governorship in Virginia in the 2021 election. Senator Tim Scott has said:

We are putting parents back in charge of their kids' education.

On the other hand, Congressman Eric Swalwell recently said:

Please tell me what I'm missing here. What are we going to do next? Putting patients in charge of their own surgeries? Clients in charge of their own trials? When did we stop trusting experts? This is so stupid.

In his Woke view (along with many teachers, the teacher unions, most school administrators, most of the media, and many other politicians), the state, irrespective of parents' wishes or interests, should decide what children will be taught and what parents have a right to know about their children. In short, children are becoming increasingly wards of the state, with parents assigned a limited, state-supervised role in their care.

The number of children in the world in 2100 is expected to be less than 60% of today's number. Les Knight, who, in 2022, received an adoring profile in the New York Times that compared him to the late Fred Rogers of the Mr. Rogers TV show, is the founder of the Voluntary Human Extinction Movement, which advocates for the extinction of humanity through the prevention of childbirth. They advocate that, instead of having babies, we humans should focus on taking care of all those already here as humanity fades into the sunset. *"Feed'em, don't breed'em"* is their slogan. Then, the earth can finally heal once human interference is removed. And all of humanity's Accumulated Knowledge, literature, art, and music would evaporate like the morning dew, along with its future. Let's just take care of me and thee for as long as we can last. It simply doesn't get any more pessimistic or less hopeful than that.

At the beginning, we also noted a spiritual need in humans that has been exhibited across virtually all societies throughout history. Religion and spiritual connections have played important civilizing roles in providing humans with a moral compass, sense of purpose, and hope for the future as we pursue happiness. Yet, the role of religion, with its civilizing influence, has dropped sharply in modern societies over the past several decades. In fact, being Woke, with its inherent pessimism, has replaced religion for many young people.

No wonder kids and young adults are so unhappy. We want to blame all the rise in depression and suicide among the young on smart phones and social media, leaving them feeling bullied and isolated. But that is only part of the problem. Where is the hope? Where is the optimism?

So, what does the twenty-first century hold for the USA or for the rest of the world as the undeveloped countries look to develop? What comes next? Will technology continue to expand as humanity sets aside its ethnocentric inclinations and embraces one another in a bright and promising future? Or will it all collapse in a climate and/or racial war-driven apocalypse?

Climate change is not the end of the world. Children need to be taught that there is hope and that this is an exciting time to be alive. They need to learn all they can and then apply that knowledge to develop solutions. This nation has always been about innovation. They can participate in and

422 - Human Progress

contribute to new ways of doing things that will help sustain our way of life, help the poor nations become rich, and help preserve the natural world with all its beauty and diversity.

To teach black children or any children, that the laws and structure of the society in which they live do not offer them an opportunity to succeed because of gender, the color of their skin, or any other factor, can only make them resentful, unhappy, and discourage them from doing their best while encouraging them to ignore society's laws and structures. Such teaching to children can only limit their liberty and opportunities. It is a recipe for anarchy and the destruction of society.

And it can only make children, and the adults they will become, unhappy. Being a career protester and/or lawbreaker are unhappy life choices. Being offended is a personal choice, irrespective of whether or not offence was intended. And it is always an unhappy choice because it means you have put someone else in charge of how you feel. It is impossible to be offended, mad, insulted, distressed, and happy simultaneously.

For kids to be happy, they need to be able to see the possibilities and opportunities in life, and not give in to life's difficulties, no matter how real, unfair, or challenging those difficulties may be. In fact, it is by overcoming difficulties and challenges that we grow. Remember Abigail Adams' advice to her twelve-year-old son, who went on to be Secretary of State and then President of the USA. Then, after suffering defeat when seeking his second term, he again went on to have a long and impactful career in Congress.

These are the times in which genius would wish to live. It is not in the still calm of life, or the repose of a pacific station, that great characters are formed. The habits of a vigorous mind are formed in contending with difficulties. Great necessities call out great virtues. When a mind is raised, and animated by the scenes that engage the heart, then those qualities which would otherwise lay dormant, wake into life and form the character of the hero and the statesman.

And those words are still applicable for children in 2024. All children need to be taught that race, gender, and economic status should not matter and that they can be happy and productive in a kind society while helping to heal the nation's flaws. And that they are in charge of their own happiness, not some insensitive white klutz doing something offensive. Kmele Foster has said:

Be honest about things as basic as privilege and disadvantage. The notion that my daughter and my son, who will grow up in a two-parent household with parents who are incredibly bright, if I do say so myself, who are well-off, and who travel the world and will give them every opportunity...Any lunatic who would suggest that they're disadvantaged or presume as much needs to have their head checked. And that is the kind of default position on account of our obsession with race. We can do better.

British film actor Idris Elba said recently:

If we spent half the time not talking about the differences but the similarities between us, the entire planet would have to shift in the way we deal with each other. As humans, we are obsessed with race. And that obsession can really hinder people's aspirations, hinder peoples' growth.
Racism is very real. But, from my perspective, it's only as powerful as you allow it to be. I stopped describing myself as a Black actor when I realized it put me in a box. We've got to grow. We've got to. Our skin is no more than that. It's just skin.
*As you get up the ladder, you get asked what it's like to be the first Black to do this or that. Well, it's the same as it would be if I were white. It's the first time for **me**. I don't want to be the first Black. I'm the first Idris.*

With all that history has to teach us, and with optimism and hope for a future I will not live to see, I will conclude with a few quotes from Ian V. Rowe on **the importance of seeing what the past can teach us about**

the possibilities of the future rather than just searching the past for fuel to feed our grievances or our shame:

My parents came to the United States in 1968. They were Black immigrants arriving in the tumultuous year in which both Robert F. Kennedy and the Rev. Martin Luther King Jr. were assassinated, and the country suffered through a wave of civil disturbance and race riots. Yet, while they left their homes and families in Jamaica, my parents were not running from a tyrannical regime or impossible economic conditions. Rather, they were running toward a brighter future in the United States. They wanted to live and raise their children in a "land of opportunity" where anything was possible. My parents, like so many before them, saw the United States as a beacon of hope for billions of people around the world. They believed our founding principles – liberty, equality, personal responsibility – were central to the realization of the American Dream. It strikes me that one building block of agency in young people is that they must believe that they live in a good country, if not a great one; a country that is not hostile to their dreams and that, however flawed, is still full of possibilities that will reward you with great works in return for your great works.

Rowe then quotes a few lines from the Broadway musical *Hamilton*. And then says:

The lyrics of "My Shot" make plain the critical linkage between the sense of possibilities in one's country and the possibility in one's own life. You cannot say you are not "throwin' away my shot" if you think your country doesn't give people like you a shot.
Building agency in the next generation will depend partly on teaching our young people to appreciate and embrace America's founding principles rather than teaching them to denigrate and reject those ideas as somehow illegitimate because they have been too often violated in practice. That is why we must oppose distorted histories that paint America as an irredeemably racist or inherently unjust nation. Meta-narratives of permanent American malignancy of oppression such as

those promoted in The New York Times' 1619 Project are not just fraudulent as history, they also hurt kids and turn them into disempowered victims. Again, why worry about not throwing away your shot if the game is rigged anyway.

Increasingly, American institutions – colleges and universities, businesses, government, the media and even our children's schools – are enforcing a cynical and intolerant orthodoxy. This orthodoxy requires us to view each other based on immutable characteristics like skin color, gender, and sexual orientation. It pits us against each other and diminishes what it means to be human.

Rowe quotes Martin Luther King at the centennial celebration of the Emancipation Proclamation in New York on September 12, 1962, early in the Civil Rights movement:

If our nation had done nothing more in its whole history than to create just two documents, its contribution to civilization would be imperishable. The first of these documents is the Declaration of Independence and the other is that which we honor tonight, the Emancipation Proclamation. All tyrants, past, present, and future, are powerless to bury the truths in these declarations, no matter how extensive their legions, how vast their power and how malignant their evil.

Rowe also notes Alexis de Tocqueville's observation that:

What makes America so unique is its ability to repair its faults.

He then quotes Hendrick Hertzberg and Henry Louis Gates, Jr.:

For African-Americans, the country of oppression and the country of liberation are the same country.

Then Rowe concludes:

The question is this: What are we going to lead our young people to believe they can achieve? Are we going to teach them a narrative of oppression, tyranny and victimization? Or are we going to provide them with the character and tools to thrive?

Just as our founding ideals have allowed America to continue to become a better nation, they also help us as individuals to better ourselves. That is what we need to tell our children – that they also have the inner strength and can learn tools of self-betterment and self-repair and renewal. That is the mindset and skills that the mediating institutions of family, religion and education need to celebrate and cultivate.

Of course, as it relates to the United States, and its young people, our future is still to be written. Here again, Miranda captures the linkage between the promise of America and its people in the closing song that marks Alexander Hamilton's death:

> *Legacy. What is a legacy?*
> *It's planting seeds in a garden you will never see.*
> *I wrote some notes at the beginning of a song someone will sing for me.*
> *You sent for me. You let me make a difference.*
> *A place where even orphan immigrants can leave their fingerprints and rise up.*

Our young people have the power to shape their legacy. As adults, it is our responsibility to prepare them to write the next stanza in their own and their country's unfinished symphony. Rather than teaching them to lament what was or might have been, we need to teach them that they can make a difference in what is to come. We need to show them that they themselves have the capacity – the agency – to wise up, rise up and leave their fingerprints on what is to be.

ACKNOWLEDGEMENTS

This is NOT a scholarly work. I am neither a historian nor an anthropologist. Other than looking at a few census and energy reports online, I have done no original research. No historical fact presented here is news or new to those experts and scholars who have dug into such things. I am particularly grateful to the authors and scholars whose books are listed below. They are the sources for much of the history presented here, including many quotes they cite from other sources. My goal is to tie that known history together to lay out how our modern way of life in the USA came to be since few Americans seem to know much about how that happened. Since the authors listed below documented their sources, I have not. Any mistakes are my own.

The order of the books listed below is, more or less, in descending order of how much I drew from them in writing this. This order does not necessarily reflect which books I liked the most, found the most interesting, or that taught me the most about history or human nature. Some were much easier to read than others. But I found them all worth the effort.

SOURCES

Books:

- **1493: Uncovering the New World Columbus Created.** 2011. Charles C. Mann.
- **1491: New Revelations of the Americas Before Columbus.** 2nd ed. 2011. Charles C. Mann.
- **Mayflower: A Story of Courage, Community, and War.** 2007. Nathaniel Philbrick.
- **Coal: A Human History.** 2003. Barbara Freese.
- **What Hath God Wrought: The Transformation of America, 1815-1848.** 2007. Daniel Walker Howe.
- **Undaunted Courage: Meriwether Lewis, Thomas Jefferson, and the Opening of the American West.** 1996. Stephen E. Ambrose.

- **The Rise and Fall of American Growth: The U.S. Standard of Living Since the Civil War.** 2016. Robert J. Gordon.
- **An Empire of Wealth: The Epic History of American Economic Growth.** 2004. John Steele Gordon.
- **Grant.** 2017. Ron Chernow.
- **Frederick Douglass: Prophet of Freedom.** 2018. David W. Blight.
- **Andrew Jackson: His Life and Times.** 2005. H. W. Brands.
- **The Pioneers: The Heroic Story of the Settlers Who Brought the American Ideal West.** 2019. David McCullough.
- **The Field of Blood: Violence in Congress and the Road to the Civil War.** 2018. Joanne B. Freeman.
- **1776.** 2005. David McCullough.
- **Apocalypse Never: Why Environmental Alarmism Hurts Us All.** 2020. Michael Shellenberger.
- **John Adams.** 2001. David McCullough.
- **Alexander Hamilton.** 2005. Ron Chernow.
- **Unsettled: What Climate Science Tells Us, What It Doesn't, and Why It Matters.** 2021. Steven E. Koonin.
- **Black Rednecks and White Liberals.** 2005. Thomas Sowell.
- **History of the Peloponnesian War.** About 400 BC. Thucydides (Translated by Rex Warner).
- **The Peloponnesian War.** 2003. Donald Kagan.
- **SPQR: A History of Ancient Rome.** 2015. Mary Beard.
- **Maverick: A Biography of Thomas Sowell.** 2021. Jason L. Riley.
- **The Girl with Seven Names: Escape from North Korea.** 2015. Hyeonseo Lee.
- **Infidel.** 2007. Ayaan Hirsi Ali.
- **The Ungrateful Refugee: What Immigrants Never Tell You.** 2019. Dina Nayeri.
- **Outliers: The Story of Success.** 2008. Malcolm Gladwell.
- **Destiny of the Republic: A Tale of Madness, Medicine, and the Murder of a President.** 2011. Candace Millard.
- **The Great Deformation: The Corruption of Capitalism in America.** 2013. David A. Stockman.

- **Capitalism and Freedom.** 1962. Milton Friedman.
- **Economic Facts and Fallacies.** 2nd Edition. 2011. Thomas Sowell.
- **Black Lamb and Grey Falcon: A Journey Through Yugoslavia.** 1940. Rebecca West.
- **Truman.** 1992. David McCullough.
- **The Immortal Life of Henrietta Lacks.** 2010. Rebecca Skloot.
- **Cattle Country: The Hidden Story of the Cowboy West.** 2017. Christopher Knowlton.

Internet Sources:
- U.S. Census and Energy Information Administration reports.
- Various online news articles, opinion pieces, and editorials over the past decade.
- Many other topic- or person-specific searches.
- Various documentary films by Ken Burns.

www.ingramcontent.com/pod-product-compliance
Lightning Source LLC
Chambersburg PA
CBHW030633150426
42811CB00048B/91